INFORMIX®-4GL by Example

INFORMIX®-4GL for UNIX, Version 4.1

Published by P T R Prentice Hall and Informix Software, Inc.

P T R Prentice Hall
Prentice-Hall, Inc.
A Paramount Communications Co.
Englewood Cliffs, New Jersey 07632

Informix Press
Informix Software, Inc.
4100 Bohannon Drive
Menlo Park, CA 94025

Production supervision: *Mary P. Rottino*
Cover design: *Karen Marsilio*
Acquisitions editor: *Mark L. Taub*
Editorial assistant: *Marcy Levine*

Manager, Informix Press: *Todd Katz*
Founder, Informix Press: *Suzanne Fuery*

The publisher offers discounts on this book when ordered in bulk quantities. For more information contact: Corporate Sales Department, P T R Prentice Hall, 113 Sylvan Avenue, Englewood Cliffs, NJ 07632. Phone: 201-592-2863, FAX: 201-592-2249

Printed in the United States of America

10 9 8 7 6 5 4 3 2 1

ISBN 0-13-100355-0

Prentice-Hall International (UK) Limited, *London*
Prentice-Hall of Australia Pty. Limited, *Sydney*
Prentice-Hall Canada Inc., *Toronto*
Prentice-Hall Hispanoamericana, S.A., *Mexico*
Prentice-Hall of India Private Limited, *New Delhi*
Prentice-Hall of Japan, Inc., *Tokyo*
Simon & Schuster Asia Pte. Ltd., *Singapore*
Editora Prentice-Hall do Brasil, Ltda., *Rio de Janeiro*

Acknowledgments

The following people contributed to this book:

Dawn Maneval
Kaye Bonney
Patrick Brown
David Cortesi
Ron Hendricks
Erik Hennum
Elizabeth Knittel

Preface

4GL by Example is an annotated tour of the programming facilities available with **INFORMIX-4GL**.

You do not need **4GL** experience to use this manual. However, a knowledge of SQL (Structured Query Language) is assumed. Informix SQL is described in detail in a separate set of manuals called *The Informix Guide to SQL: Tutorial* and *The Informix Guide to SQL: Reference*. You **4GL** manual set also includes SQL information.

If you are new to the language, *4GL by Example* will introduce you to the principle **4GL** programming techniques. If you are an experienced **4GL** programmer, *4GL by Example* will provide models for programming many common projects.

Note that this is not a complete reference to **4GL**. *4GL by Example* is intended to work with the *INFORMIX-4GL User Guide* and the *INFORMIX-4GL Reference Manual*.

Related Reading

If you have had no prior experience with database management, you may want to refer to an introductory text like C. J. Date's *Database: A Primer* (Addison-Wesley Publishing, 1983). If you want more technical information on database management, consider consulting the following texts, also by C. J. Date:

- *An Introduction to Database Systems, Volume I* (Addison-Wesley Publishing, 1990)
- *An Introduction to Database Systems, Volume II* (Addison-Wesley Publishing, 1983)

This guide assumes you are familiar with your computer operating system. If you have limited UNIX system experience, you may want to look at your operating system manual or a good introductory text before starting to learn about **4GL**.

Some suggested texts about UNIX systems follow:

- *A Practical Guide to the UNIX System* by M. Sobell (Benjamin/Cummings Publishing, 1984)
- *A Practical Guide to UNIX System V* by M. Sobell (Benjamin/Cummings Publishing, 1985)
- *UNIX for People* by Birns, Brown, and Muster (Prentice-Hall, 1985)

Table of Contents

Example 2 Displaying a Message Window

Example 3 Populating a Ring Menu with Options

Example 4 Displaying a Row on a Form

Example 5 Programming a Query by Example

Example 6 Querying and Updating

Example 7 Validating and Inserting a Row

Example 8 Displaying a Screen Array in a Pop-Up Window

Example 9 Accessing a Table with a Single Row Form

Example 10 Accessing a Table with a Multi-Row Form

Example 11 Implementing a Master/Detail Relationship

Example 12 Displaying an Unknown Number of Rows

Example 13 Calling a C Function

Example 14 Generating a Report

Example 15 Reporting Group Totals

Example 16 Creating Vertical Menus

Example 17 Using the DATETIME Data Type

Example 18 Using OnLine Data Types

Example 19 Browsing with a Scroll Cursor

Example 20 Combining Criteria from Successive Queries

Example 24 Using a Hold Cursor

Example 25 Logging Application Errors

Example 26 Managing Multiple Windows

Introduction

About the Product

INFORMIX-4GL is a fourth-generation language designed specifically for relational database applications. It allows the developer to move quickly from the conceptual stage to an application program. **4GL** includes statements that allow you to provide your users with all the essential operations for manipulating information. By offering you procedural statements and allowing calls to C functions, **4GL** also offers a finer granularity of control when needed.

For example, within one **4GL** program you can:

- Create windows, menus, and screen forms that facilitate the user's task of entering and retrieving data.
- Extract information and display it in an attractive report format.

About This Book

INFORMIX-4GL by Example contains a series of 30 example programs that range in complexity from simple procedures like creating ring menus through more advanced topics like handling locked rows and using update cursors.

Each chapter begins with a chapter overview, which consists of general description of the program, followed by a discussion of the programming techniques demonstrated in the example. A summary of all functions used in the example appears at the end of the chapter overview. The remaining pages of the chapter consist of the annotated code samples: code appears on the right page with the corresponding descriptive notes on the left page.

The examples appear in generally increasing order of complexity; later examples build on techniques and functions explained in earlier examples.

Summary of Chapters

4GL by Example contains the following chapters:

Example 1, "Writing a Simple 4GL Program". Explains basic **4GL** program structure by describing how to implement an application logo: a screen which displays the name of the application being started.

Example 2, "Displaying a Message Window". Explains how to implement a generic message window.

Example 3, "Populating a Ring Menu with Options". Describes how to program a simple **4GL** ring menu.

Example 4, "Displaying a Row on a Form". Illustrates how to use forms to provide an interface for interacting with the database.

Example 5, "Programming a Query by Example". Demonstrates how to collect search criteria from the user and then to construct and run a query.

Example 6, "Querying and Updating". Explains how to allow the user to update or delete a row qualified through a query by example.

Example 7, "Validating and Inserting a Row". Contains routines to add a row to the database.

Example 8, "Displaying a Screen Array in a Pop-Up Window". Demonstrates how to manage a simple screen array.

Example 9, "Accessing a Table with a Single Row Form". Combines techniques demonstrated in earlier examples to provide a menu and form interface for the standard SQL operations on a table.

Example 10, "Accessing a Table with a Multi-row Form". Demonstrates how to manage a screen array for the standard SQL operations on a table.

Example 11, "Implementing a Master/Detail Relationship". Illustrates how to program a single-row master form with a multi-row detail form.

Example 12, "Displaying an Unknown Number of Rows". Demonstrates how to handle an unknown number of entries in a fixed-sized program array.

Example 13, "Calling a C Function". Describes how to integrate C functions with a **4GL** program.

Example 14, "Generating a Report". Illustrates how to produce a simple report.

Example 15, "Reporting Group Totals". Demonstrates how to create a more complex report that includes group totals.

Example 16, "Creating Vertical Menus". Illustrates two ways of creating vertical menus: using a simple INPUT statement and a form with menu options, and using an INPUT ARRAY statement and a generic menu form.

Example 17, "Using the DATETIME Data Type". Demonstrates how to handle DATATIME data in a **4GL** program.

Example 18, "Using OnLine Data Types". Explains how to display and update VARCHAR and TEXT columns available with the **OnLine** engine.

Example 19, "Browsing with a Scroll Cursor". Demonstrates how to use a scroll cursor to let the user browse through a set of selected rows.

Example 20, "Combining Criteria from Successive Queries". Describes how to revise a query with additional constraints produced by successive query by example operations.

Example 21, "Using an Update Cursor". Demonstrates how to use an update cursor to let the user selectively update database rows.

Example 22, "Determining Database Features". Demonstrates how to interpret the fields in the SQLCA.SQLAWARN array upon opening a database.

Example 23, "Handling Locked Rows". Illustrates how to handle locked rows in your **4GL** programs.

Example 24, "Using a Hold Cursor". Demonstrates how to write batch-oriented programs that take advantage of the hold cursor.

Example 25, "Logging Application Errors". Demonstrates how to use an error log to record application errors.

Example 26, "Managing Multiple Windows". Illustrates how to program a multi-window application.

Example 27, "Displaying Menu Options Dynamically". Describes how to display menu options based on a user's database permissions.

Example 28, "Writing Recursive Functions". Demonstrates how to use recursive algorithms in **4GL**.

Example 29, "Generating Mailing Labels". Illustrates how to produce multi-column mailing labels.

Example 30, "Generating a Schema Listing". Demonstrates how to interpret the information in the system catalogs and produce a listing of a database schema.

Appendix A. Lists the contents of the demonstration database.

The Function Index. Identifies the location of all functions used in the programs in *4GL by Example.*

Other Documentation that You Will Need

You may want to refer to a number of related Informix product documents that complement *4GL by Example.*

- The *INFORMIX-4GL User Guide* and the *INFORMIX-4GL Reference Manual* are the complete set of reference materials for **4GL**.

  You should refer to these books for additional information about statements and built-in functions.
- The *INFORMIX-4GL Quick Reference Card* summarizes statement syntax.
- The *INFORMIX-4GL Release 4.1 Reference Manual Supplement* documents enhancements made to the product.
- *The Informix Guide to SQL: Tutorial* explains concepts of basic database design and implementation.
- A companion volume to the Tutorial, *The Informix Guide to SQL: Reference,* provides a detailed description of all the SQL statements supported by Informix products.
- If you are using **4GL** across a network, you may also want to refer to the appropriate *I-NET/I-STAR User Guide.*
- Depending on the server you are using, you or your system administrator will need either the *INFORMIX-OnLine Administrator's Guide* or the *INFORMIX-SE Administrator's Guide.*
- Information about program errors appears in the *Error Message* section of the *INFORMIX-4GL Reference Manual.*

  If you prefer, you can look up the error messages in the on-line message file described in the section "Useful On-line Files" later in this Introduction.

How to Use This Manual

4GL by Example contains a series of examples that, in general, build on one another. Later examples use techniques and functions introduced in earlier examples.

The manual was written to meet the needs of **4GL** programmers with varying levels of experience:

- If you are new to **4GL**, you will probably want to begin with Example 1 and read through the examples sequentially.

  While this manual provides a detailed introduction to many common programming techniques, it is not a comprehensive review of all **4GL** features. You will want to refer regularly to the *INFORMIX-4GL User Guide*, the *INFORMIX-4GL Reference Manual*, and the *INFORMIX-4GL Release 4.1 Reference Manual Supplement*.
- If you are familiar with **4GL**, you may want to concentrate on the code listings for each example and refer to the annotations when you need clarification. If you find that you don't understand something, you may want to turn to an earlier example.
- If you are an experienced **4GL** programmer, you can review examples that address programming tasks of interest.

It is assumed that readers will have a **4GL** manual set available to provide complete reference information about all statements and built-in functions.

How to Use These Examples

The programs in *4GL by Example* illustrate how to use **4GL** to solve many common programming tasks. They are presented in a style and sequence that should be helpful to all **4GL** programmers, including those who are new to the language.

The examples illustrate how to perform particular programming tasks; they are not the only ways to program with **4GL**. A task may have many possible solutions and the one best suited to your application may depend on a variety of factors, including your hardware platform, programming conventions and needs, and the database engine.

The examples appear in increasing order of complexity. This sequence allows earlier examples to demonstrate specific techniques without overwhelming the reader. Many examples omit important validations that should appear in a finished application. Indeed, they are not industrial strength programs, and should not be used "as is" in your applications. Rather, they provide a model for addressing various **4GL** tasks and should be treated as the beginning point if you are preparing end-user applications.

Whether you are an experienced **4GL** programmer or someone just getting up to speed in the use of the language, you are encouraged to experiment with the programs to make them more complete and more appropriate for your needs. For this reason, on-line versions of all files are provided as part of the 4.1 release. Suggestions for extensions to the programs appear in the annotation. Similarly, alternate coding methods are discussed at several points.

Typographical Conventions

4GL by Example uses a standard set of conventions to introduce new terms, illustrate screen displays, identify **4GL** keywords, and so forth.

When new terms are introduced, they are printed in *italics*. Illustrations that show what you see on the screen as you use **4GL** appear in `computer font`. All keywords are shown in UPPERCASE LETTERS for ease of identification. However, **4GL** is case insensitive and you need not use uppercase when writing your **4GL** programs.

Useful On-line Files

In addition to the Informix set of manuals, the following on-line files, located in the $INFORMIXDIR/release directory, supplement the information in *4GL by Example*:

Documentation Notes
: describes feature and performance topics not covered inthe manual or which have been modified since publication. The file containing the Documentation Notes for **4GL** is called 4GLDOC_4.1.

README
: lists any changes made to the programs between the time that the book was finished and the product shipped.

You can view error messages and their corrective actions on-line using the error message files installed when you install **4GL** release 4.1.

The *INFORMIX-4GL Release 4.1 Reference Manual Supplement* contains complete information about how to access the error message files.

The Demonstration Database and Application Files

Your **4GL** release 4.1 software includes a script to create a demonstration database called stores2. This database contains information about a fictitious wholesale sporting-goods distributor. Also included in the software is a copy of all application files referenced in the *4GL by Example* manual.

The examples in this book are based on the stores2 demonstration database. The database is described in detail in Appendix A.

Two scripts exist to help you make a copy of the database and the demonstration application:

- The script you use to make a copy of the demonstration database is called sqldemo; it is located in the $INFORMIXDIR/bin directory.
- The script you use to make a copy of the demonstration application is called fglexcopy; it also is located in $INFORMIXDIR/bin.

Instructions on how to use these two scripts appear in the next sections.

If you installed your **4GL** software according to the installation instructions, the files that make up the demonstration database and application are protected so that you cannot make changes to them. You can run sqldemo and fglexcopy again whenever you want a fresh demonstration database and application.

Creating the Demo Database on INFORMIX-OnLine

The following steps create and populate the demonstration database in an **OnLine** environment:

1. Set the INFORMIXDIR environment so that it contains the name of the directory in which your Informix products are installed.

   See Chapter 4 of *The Informix Guide to SQL: Reference* for a full description of environment variables. Appendix C of the *INFORMIX-4GL Reference Manual* also describes environment variables.
2. Set the SQLEXEC environment variable to the pathname of the **OnLine** database engine ($INFORMIXDIR/lib/sqlturbo).
3. Create the demonstration database.

   At the time you create the database you can specify the name of the database and whether it supports transactions or enforces ANSI syntax compliance. By default, the database is named stores2 and does not support transactions or enforce ANSI compliance.

The example programs in this book are written to work with a non-ANSI-compliant database that supports transactions. This database is named stores2t. You should create this stores2t database by entering the following command line command:

```
sqldemo stores2t -log
```

The complete syntax for the sqldemo command follows:

```
sqldemo [dbname] [ -log | -l | -ansi | -a ]
```

When you run sqldemo, the data for the database is put into the root dbspace. For more information on the syntax of sqldemo, see the *INFORMIX-4GL Release 4.1 Reference Manual Supplement.*

To give other users the SQL privileges to access the database, use the GRANT and REVOKE statements. These statements are described in Chapter 7 of *The Informix Guide to SQL: Reference* and in Chapter 7 of the *INFORMIX-4GL Reference Manual.*

Creating the Demo Database on INFORMIX-SE

The following steps create and populate the demonstration database in an **INFORMIX-SE** environment.

1. Set the INFORMIXDIR environment so that it contains the name of the directory in which your Informix products are installed.

   See Chapter 4 of *The Informix Guide to SQL: Reference* for a full description of environment variables. Appendix C of the *INFORMIX-4GL Reference Manual* also describes environment variables.

2. Set the SQLEXEC environment variable to the full pathname of the **INFORMIX-SE** database engine ($INFORMIXDIR/lib/sqlexec).

3. Create a new directory for the demo database by entering

   ```
   mkdir dirname
   ```

   You also may want to place the *4GL by Example* application files in this directory.

4. Make the new directory the current directory by entering

   ```
   cd dirname
   ```

5. Create the demonstration database.

   At the time you create the database you can specify the name of the database and whether it supports transactions or enforces ANSI syntax compliance. By default, the database is named stores2 and does not support transactions or enforce ANSI compliance.

The example programs in this book are written to work with a non-ANSI-compliant database that supports transactions. This database is named stores2t. You should create this stores2t database by entering the following command line command:

```
sqldemo -log stores2t
```

The complete syntax for the sqldemo command follows:

```
sqldemo [dbname] [ -log | -l | -ansi | -a ]
```

When you run the sqldemo script, it creates a subdirectory called *dbname*.dbs (by default, stores2.dbs) in your current directory and places the database files there. For more information on the syntax of sqldemo, see the *INFORMIX4GL Release 4.1 Reference Manual Supplement.*

To use the database, you must have UNIX READ and EXECUTE permissions for each directory in the pathname of the directory that contains the database. Check with your system administrator for more information about operating system file and directory permissions. UNIX permissions are discussed in the *INFORMIX-SE Administrator's Guide.*

To give other users the SQL privileges to access the database, use the GRANT and REVOKE statements. These statements are described in Chapter 7 of *The Informix Guide to SQL: Reference* and in Chapter 7 of the *INFORMIX-4GL Reference Manual.*

Copying the Application Files

The following steps copy the *4GL by Example* application files into your current working directory.

1. If you have not already done so, create a new directory for the application files. Enter

   ```
   mkdir dirname
   ```

2. Make the new directory the current directory by entering

   ```
   cd dirname
   ```

3. Copy the application files.

   At the time you copy the application files you can specify the name of the database that appears in all DATABASE statements. By default, all application files reference the stores2 database.

   The example programs in this book are written to work with a version of the database named stores2t that uses transactions.

You should copy the application files and specify the database name stores2t by entering the following command line command:

```
fglexcopy stores2t
```

The complete syntax for the fglexcopy command follows:

```
fglexcopy [dbname]
```

The fglexcopy script copies a complete set of all application source files into your current directory. These files are not executable. To run the examples you must first compile the files. The compilation procedure is described in the next section.

Running an Example

Before you can run an example, you must first compile the **4GL** module along with any form specifications and help message file used in the example. The following paragraphs briefly outline this process. See Chapter 1 of the *INFORMIX-4GL Reference Manual* for information about compiling source files.

The following steps produce an executable example:

1. Compile the form specifications for the example.

   To compile a form specification file at the command line, enter a command of the form:

   ```
   form4gl formfile.per
   ```

   This generates the compiled formfile.frm file.

   Since a compiled form requires little disk space, you may want to compile all forms at one time.

2. Compile the **4GL** source module for the example.

   To compile a **4GL** source file at the command line (C Compiler version), enter a command of the form:

   ```
   c4gl source.4gl -o output.4ge
   ```

   This generates the compiled output.4ge file. You can run the compiled source file at the command line by entering the following command:

   ```
   output.4ge
   ```

   To compile a **4GL** source file at the command line (RDS version), enter a command of the form:

   ```
   fglpc source.4gl
   ```

This generates the compiled source.4go file. You can run the compiled source file at the command line by entering the following command:

```
fglgo source
```

Compiled **4GL** programs are quite large. If your disk space is limited, you may want to wait to compile a program until you are ready to use it.

3. Compile the help message file.

   To compile the help message file at the command line, enter the following command:

```
mkmessage hlpmsgs.src hlpmsgs
```

   This generates the compiled hlpmsgs file. This help file name appears in the OPTIONS statement in those examples that use a help file.

   Example 13 ("Calling a C Function") requires additional compilation steps. The example overview includes detailed information about how to run the example.

Files Used in Each Example

The following table lists all files used in each example.

Example Number	Files Accessed in the Example
ex1	ex1.4gl, f_logo.per
ex2	ex2.4gl
ex3	ex3.4gl, hlpmsgs.src
ex4	ex4.4gl, f_custkey.per, f_custsum.per
ex5	ex5.4gl, f_customer.per
ex6	ex6.4gl, f_customer.per, hlpmsgs.src
ex7	ex7.4gl, f_stock.per
ex8	ex8.4gl, f_stock.per, f_manufsel.per
ex9	ex9.4gl, f_customer.per, f_statesel.per, hlpmsgs.src
ex10	ex10.4gl, f_manuf.per
ex11	ex11.4gl, f_orders.per, f_custsel.per, f_stocksel.per, f_ship.per, hlpmsgs.scr
ex12	ex12.4gl, f_ship.per, f_custsel.per, f_ordersel.per, hlpmsgs.src
ex13	ex13.4gl, ex13a.4gl, f_name.per, fgiusr.c, fglgets.c, ex13r.sh, ex13i.sh
ex14	ex14.4gl
ex15	ex15.4gl, f_orders.per, f_custsel.per, f_stocksel.per, f_ship.per, hlpmsgs.src
ex16	ex16a.4gl, ex16b.4gl, f_menu.per, f_menu2.per, hlpmsgs.src
ex17	ex17.4gl, f_custcall.per, f_customer.per, f_edit.per, f_statesel.per, hlpmsgs.src
ex18	ex18.4gl, f_catalog.per, f_catadv.per, f_catdescr.per
ex19	ex19.4gl, f_customer.per, hlpmsgs.src

ex20	ex20.4gl, f_customer.per, f_answer.per, hlpmsgs.src
ex21	ex21.4gl, f_custkey.per, f_custsel.per, f_date.per, f_payord.per
ex22	ex22.4gl
ex23	ex23.4gl, f_customer.per, f_custkey.per, f_custsel.per, hlpmsgs.src
ex24	ex24.4gl, ex24.unl
ex25	ex25.4gl, f_customer.per, f_statesel.per, hlpmsgs.src
ex26	ex26.4gl, f_logo.per, f_customer.per, f_orders.per, f_stock.per
ex27	ex27.4gl, f_customer.per, f_answer.per, hlpmsgs.src
ex28	ex28.4gl, ex28pa.unl, ex28pt.unl
ex29	ex29.4gl
ex30	ex30.4gl, f_name.per

The names of all files used in an example appear in the comment header at the top of each **4GL** program module.

Naming Conventions

The *4GL by Example* programs follow a standard set of conventions to name various **4GL** identifiers in the application programs. The naming conventions used in these examples are summarized in the following table.

Program Object	Prefix	Example
Global records and arrays:		
global records	gr_	gr_customer
global arrays	ga_	gr_items
global variables	g_	g_custnum
Module records and arrays:		
module records	mr_	mr_currcust
module arrays	ma_	ma_kidstack
module variables	m_	m_nextkid
Local records and arrays:		
local records	pr_	pr_orders
local arrays	pa_	pa_manuf
local variables	no prefix used	stock_cnt

Screen records and arrays:		
screen records	sr_	sr_customer
screen arrays	sa_	sa_items
screen variables	no prefix used	stock_num
Other objects:		
cursors	c_	c_cust
windows	w_	w_warn
forms	f_	f_customer
queries (in CONSTRUCT)	q_	q_cust
prepared statement	st_	st_selstmt
record elements defined with LIKE:		
	same name as the table's column	

The portion of the name that follows a prefix attempts to describe, as fully as possible, the purpose of the variable.

Using the Examples with Releases Prior to 4.1

The application programs in *4GL by Example* were written to run under release 4.1. You can use the manual and the sample programs with earlier versions of the product; however, you will need to edit several examples to remove or replace the code that takes advantage of the release 4.1 features.

Release 4.1 features appear in the following examples:

- Example 3 includes a MENU statement featuring two options that begin with the same letter.
- Examples 6, 9, 17, 19 and 25 include an AFTER CONSTRUCT clause and a CONTINUE CONSTRUCT statement, and use the HELP clause of the CONSTRUCT statement.
- Examples 10, 12 and 16b include calls to the FGL_LASTKEY() and the FGL_KEYVAL() built-in functions.
- Examples 19, 20 and 27 include calls to the FIELD_TOUCHED() built-in function, as well as HIDE OPTION, SHOW OPTION, and CONTINUE CONSTRUCT statements, and BEFORE MENU and AFTER CONSTRUCT clauses.
- Example 23 includes a WHENEVER ANY statement.
- Example 26 includes a variable as the form name in an OPEN FORM statement.

1

Writing a Simple 4GL Program

This example shows how to display a logo banner to identify a program while the program is initializing. You can copy and adapt the **4GL** code to provide a logo banner for your own application.

This example also illustrates the fundamentals of **4GL** in much the same way that the classic *hello, world* program illustrates the C programming language. **4GL** enhances the set of standard SQL database statements with screen interaction statements, flow control statements, and other statements that make it easier to program a database application.

This example demonstrates the following display techniques:

- Displaying a form.
- Displaying information in a field on the form.
- Displaying text at a row and column location.
- Setting display attributes such as reverse video.

Example 1 also demonstrates the following **4GL** programming techniques:

- Defining a main function for the **4GL** program.
- Defining supporting functions.
- Calling functions with parameters.
- Defining variables.
- Assigning values to variables.
- Opening and closing forms.

Later examples will show you how to display database information and how to collect information from the user.

Displaying Information Using a Form

Forms are the most important screen interaction element provided by **4GL**. A form displays static text and fields. The static text in the form never changes, but information in a field can change during the execution of the program.

For example, a field can display the value of a column. The value might be different in each database row. You can also activate a form so that the user can position the cursor in the form's fields and change the values displayed in the fields.

You don't specify the layout of a form in the code of a function. Instead, you specify the layout of the form in a *form specification* file, which is compiled separately. The structure of the form is independent of the use of the form. For example, one function can use a form to display a database row, another to let the user enter a new database row, and still another to let the user enter criteria for selecting database rows. After compiling a satisfactory form, you rarely need to change the form specification.

In Example 1, the f_logo form uses a field to display the current date.

The MAIN Function

The MAIN function is a special function that executes automatically when the user starts the program. The program starts with the first statement in the MAIN function and ends with the last statement.

To use a block of statements in several locations or to organize a series of statements into a well defined unit, you place the statements in a function defined with the FUNCTION statement. You can invoke the function with the CALL statement to execute the statements within the function. The effect is much the same as if the function's statements had been inserted at the location of the CALL statement.

In Example 1, the statements that display the logo appear in the dsply_logo() function to simplify the MAIN function.

The DISPLAY Statements

The dsply_logo() function uses three versions of the DISPLAY statement:

DISPLAY FORM	Displays a form containing the fixed text of the logo.
DISPLAY AT	Displays text at a specific row and column location. The DISPLAY AT statement isn't associated with a form but rather displays information "on top" of the form.
DISPLAY TO	Displays a value in a field of the form.

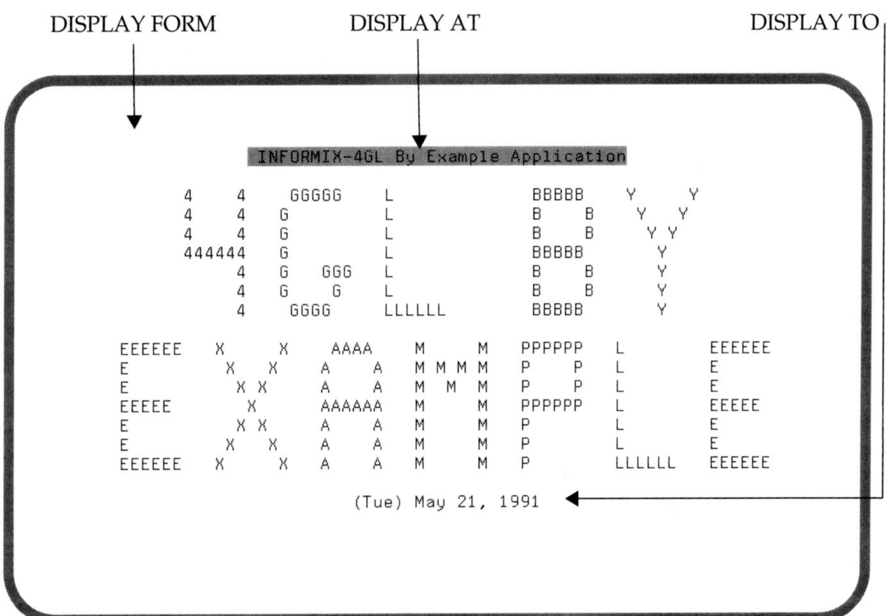

Function Overview

Function Name	Purpose
dsply_logo()	Displays the logo form with the current date.

To locate any function definition see the Function Index on page 728.

The f_logo Form Specification

1➤ When the fields on a form correspond to columns in a database, you can take advantage of some **4GL** shortcuts by identifying the database. The f_logo form doesn't display values from any database column, so the DATABASE section specifies the form as formonly. The DATABASE section is required.

2➤ In the SCREEN section, the lines enclosed by the braces (shaded in gray on the opposite page) are a template for the screen display. All text outside of the brackets is static, displaying as it appears in the file.

3➤ Within the SCREEN section, brackets indicate the beginning and end of a field. Each field must have an identifier tag. In the f_logo form, there is one field with the d1 tag.

4➤ The ATTRIBUTES section maps a field identifier tag to a screen variable name. The screen variable name is what you use in a **4GL** program to address a field. In the f_logo form, the screen variable name is appdate. Because the field tag is distinct from the screen variable name, you can embed a terse tag in a short field and still use a longer, more readable name for the screen variable.

The ATTRIBUTES specification for the screen variable includes the data type. The data type specifies the kind of information handled by a database column or **4GL** variable. Because you specify the data type, **4GL** can manipulate the information efficiently and appropriately. In the f_logo form, the appdate screen variable displays dates.

The ATTRIBUTES specification for a screen variable can also specify formatting for the information displayed in the field. The format controls the insertion of punctuation into the value. The formatting makes the information much more readable without interfering with editing in the field. Special tokens represent the components of the value:

Token	Represents
`ddd`	alphabetic day of the week
`mmm`	alphabetic month
`dd`	two-digit day of the month
`yyyy`	four-digit year

Here is an example: `(Thu) Nov 21, 1991`.

5➤ Ordinarily, the fields of a form have bracket delimiters so the user can clearly distinguish the fields for editing values. If the user can never edit the values, it's a good idea to change the delimiter character to a space so the fields appear to be text within the form. The INSTRUCTIONS section of the f_logo form makes this change.

f_logo form file

```
1➤ DATABASE formonly
   SCREEN
2➤ {

           4    4    GGGGG    L             BBBBB    Y     Y
           4    4   G         L             B    B    Y   Y
           4    4   G         L             B    B     Y Y
           444444   G         L             BBBBB       Y
                4   G   GGG   L             B    B      Y
                4   G    G    L             B    B      Y
                4    GGGG     LLLLLL        BBBBB       Y

     EEEEEE   X     X    AAAA    M     M   PPPPPP   L        EEEEEE
     E         X   X    A    A   M M M M   P    P   L        E
     E          X X     A    A   M  M  M   P    P   L        E
     EEEEE       X      AAAAAA   M     M   PPPPPP   L        EEEEE
     E          X X     A    A   M     M   P        L        E
     E         X   X    A    A   M     M   P        L        E
     EEEEEE   X     X   A    A   M     M   P        LLLLLL   EEEEEE

3➤  [d1                 ]

     }
   ATTRIBUTES
4➤ d1 = formonly.appdate type date, format = "(ddd) mmm dd, yyyy";

   INSTRUCTIONS
5➤   DELIMITERS "  "
```

The MAIN Function

1➤ The statements between the MAIN and END MAIN statements constitute the MAIN function, which is the special function started when the user runs the program.

2➤ The MAIN function uses the CALL statement to execute the dsply_logo() function. When the dsply_logo() function finishes, the line after the CALL statement executes, which in Example 1 is the END MAIN statement. The END MAIN statement terminates the MAIN function and thus the program.

You can execute function calls from within the body of any other function. For example, the dsply_logo() function could call other functions. You can call functions within expressions as well as with the CALL statement.

The CALL statement passes the length of time for displaying the logo as a parameter to the function. In the example, the parameter is three seconds, but in another context, you could call the dsply_logo() function with more or fewer seconds.

The dsply_logo() Function

3➤ The definition for the dsply_logo() function starts with the FUNCTION statement and ends with the END FUNCTION statement.

The FUNCTION statement for dsply_logo() specifies a single parameter named sleep_secs. You must call a function with the specified number of arguments.

4➤ The DEFINE statement defines the thedate and sleep_secs variables. As with the screen variable in the f_logo form specification file, the specification for each variable indicates the type of data stored by the variable. For example, thedate is a variable of type DATE.

Because these variables are defined within the function, they are local to dsply_logo(). That is, the variables exist from the start through the end of dsply_logo() but not outside the function. Also, the variables don't retain their values from one invocation of dsply_logo() to the next.

The sleep_secs variable corresponds to the parameter to the dsply_logo() function. You must define each function parameter as a local variable within the function. **4GL** automatically assigns the value of the parameter to the sleep_secs variable when the dsply_logo() function is called.

4GL source file

```
########################################
1➤ MAIN
########################################

2➤   CALL dsply_logo(3)
   END MAIN

   #######################################
3➤ FUNCTION dsply_logo(sleep_secs)
   #######################################
4➤   DEFINE sleep_secs      SMALLINT,

            thedate         DATE
```

5➤ The OPEN FORM statement loads the f_logo form into memory and assigns the app_logo identifier to the form. After the OPEN FORM statement, you always use the form identifier to manipulate the form rather than the file name.

The OPEN FORM statement does not display the f_logo form. To do that, you use the DISPLAY FORM statement. You can display a form any number of times without having to open it again. You must display a form before you can use it in user interaction statements.

Displaying the form takes much less time if the form is already open. Thus, you may want to open the principal forms in your program when the program is starting up so that the forms can be displayed quickly thereafter.

The f_logo form is available until closed with the CLOSE FORM statement. In Example 1, the form is closed near the end of the dsply_logo() function, but the form could have been closed in the main function or anywhere else in the program. That is, in contrast with a local variable, the form identifier isn't restricted to the function containing the OPEN FORM statement. The form associated with the form identifier is available until you close it explicitly.

6➤ The DISPLAY AT statement places a phrase on the screen starting at the second row and the fifteenth column.

You can think of the terminal screen as a grid composed of each position where you can display a character. On many terminals, the screen grid has 24 rows and 80 columns. The first row is at the top of the screen and the first column at the far left of the screen.

The DISPLAY AT statement doesn't make use of the f_logo form and could have positioned the phrase at any screen location far enough away from the right screen edge to show the entire phrase.

The ATTRIBUTES clause displays the phrase in reverse video and, on color monitors, in green. Many of the **4GL** screen statements let you customize the display with an ATTRIBUTES clause.

The ability to display information at a specific row and column is handy when you need to display status information or other information that changes frequently. As in the dsply_logo() function, you can use the DISPLAY AT statement to give a form a title specific to the context in which the form is being used.

7➤ The LET statement assigns the current date to the variable thedate. To generate the value, Example 1 uses the TODAY function, which is built into **4GL**. In the same way, you can use one of your functions to generate a value for assignment with a LET statement.

5➤
```
OPEN FORM app_logo FROM "f_logo"
DISPLAY FORM app_logo
```

6➤
```
DISPLAY " INFORMIX-4GL By Example Application" AT 2,15
  ATTRIBUTE (REVERSE, GREEN)
```

7➤
```
LET thedate = TODAY
DISPLAY thedate TO formonly.appdate
```

The DISPLAY TO statement displays the value of thedate in the field associated with the screen variable appdate, which was specified in the f_logo form specification file. As in all statements that move data to and from a form, you must supply a corresponding program variable for each screen variable.

A value displayed in a form field must be convertible to the data type of the associated screen variable. Similarly, a value entered in a form field must be convertible to the data type of the program variable that receives it.

For example, **4GL** can convert a character value consisting of numbers for storage in an INTEGER variable. **4GL** can't, however, generate a numeric value for an alphabetic character value.

The safest approach is to use the same data type in both the program variable and the screen variable. In the dsply_logo() function, both appdate and thedate variables are of type DATE.

You can also use closely related data types with confidence as long as the target variable can store a larger value than the source variable. For example, it is safe to display the value of a SMALLINT screen variable in an INTEGER screen variable, but not vice versa.

In the DISPLAY TO statement, the formonly qualification for the appdate variable is optional. You must supply the qualification if the form mixes FORMONLY screen variables with screen variables that correspond to database columns.

8➤ The SLEEP statement suspends execution to give the user time to view the logo. The number of seconds slept was passed by the sleep_secs parameter in the call to the dsply_logo() function.

If you create a logo function, you can omit the SLEEP statement if the program spends enough time opening forms and performing other initialization tasks to let the user view the logo.

9➤ The END FUNCTION statement terminates the dsply_logo() function, returning control to the statement that called dsply_logo().

In this case, control returns to the MAIN function.

```
8➤    SLEEP sleep_secs
      CLOSE FORM app_logo

9➤  END FUNCTION  -- dsply_logo --
```

To locate any function definition see the Function Index on page 728.

2

Displaying a Message Window

One of the most important interface features of **4GL** is its support for windows. You can enclose a form or other information in a window.

This example uses a window to display a message. The message can report an error or convey any other useful information. Because the message appears in a window, you can use it in any context without confusing the user.

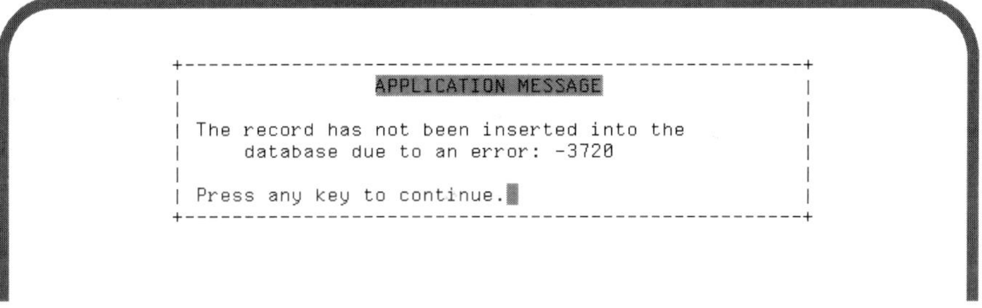

When you display a window on the screen, the window overlays some or all other information on the screen. Some portion of the user's previous activities are behind the window, which can have a border to prevent confusion with the background. When you close the current window, the overlaid information redisplays so the user can resume work.

This example demonstrates the following **4GL** programming techniques:

- Opening and closing a window.
- Testing for conditions before performing actions.
- Performing actions repeatedly in a loop.
- Defining global variables.
- Manipulating a list of values with an array.

- Prompting the user.
- Modifying values with character and arithmetic expressions.

Defining Global Variables

In this program a GLOBALS statement defines an array to store the lines in an error message. An array is a list of variables or records with the same definition. Because Example 2 defines the array globally, the array can be used in any module in a multi-module program.

The MAIN Function

The MAIN function detects an imaginary error condition of which the user should be notified. MAIN assigns each line of the error message to an element of the global array and then calls the message_window() function.

The message_window() function could be called from any other function of the program. That is, this function provides a common subroutine for displaying messages within the application.

Displaying Messages in a Window

The message_window() function performs the following actions:

1. Counts the number of elements of the array that contain text.
2. Opens a message window with enough lines for the text.
3. Displays each element of the array as a separate line of text in the message window.
4. Prompts for confirmation that the user has read the error message.
5. Closes the message window.

Because the program places the text of the message in the global array rather than passing the text as parameters, the call to message_window() does not have to spend time copying the message text to the function variables.

To remove the dependence on a global message array, you could create a message function that accepts the message text as an argument:

```
FUNCTION message_box()
  DEFINE     caution_msg      CHAR(50),
             confirm_msg      CHAR(50),
             dummy            SMALLINT

  LET confirm_msg = "Press any key to continue."
  CALL yesno_box(caution_msg, confirm_msg) RETURNING dummy
END FUNCTION  -- message_box --

FUNCTION yesno_box(caution_msg, confirm_msg)
  DEFINE     caution_msg      CHAR(50),
             confirm_msg      CHAR(50),

             yes_no           CHAR(1)

  OPEN WINDOW w_yesno AT 10, 10
    WITH 4 ROWS, 56 COLUMNS
    ATTRIBUTE (BORDER, MESSAGE LINE FIRST+1,
                PROMPT LINE FIRST+2)

  MESSAGE caution_msg
  PROMPT confirm_msg CLIPPED FOR CHAR yes_no
  CLOSE WINDOW w_yesno

  RETURN (DOWNSHIFT(yes_no) = "y")
END FUNCTION  -- yesno_box --
```

However, to display several lines of text in a message box, you may need to create a function which can separate a single message argument into separate lines.

Example 4 contains a function called prompt_window() that implements a Yes/No box using the global message array.

Function Overview

Function Name	Purpose
message_window()	Opens a window and displays the contents of the ga_dsplymsg global array.
init_msgs()	Initializes the members of the ga_dsplymsg array to null.

To locate any function definition see the Function Index on page 728.

The GLOBALS Statement and MAIN Function

1➤ The GLOBALS statement defines the ga_dsplymsg array as a global array. The array contains five identical character variables that are 48 characters long.

In a program with multiple modules, the global definitions must appear in each module. To reduce maintenance problems, it's usually easier to put the definitions in a file and specify the file with the GLOBALS statement.

Also note that, to make a variable visible in all functions within a module, you can place the definition outside any function.

2➤ The MAIN function uses the INITIALIZE statement to set each element in the ga_dsplymsg array to null. This step is important because the program later tests the value of each element in the array. In general, you must assign a value to a variable at least once before testing the variable. In this example, elements in the array that are null aren't displayed in the message window.

After the ga_dsplymsg array is initialized,the program can use it in any function to display a message to the user. As it happens, the MAIN function immediately uses the array, but many lines could have separated the initialization and the use.

3➤ MAIN sets the first array element to the first line of the message and the second array element to the second line of the message. You supply the number of the array element within brackets after the array name.

The program constructs the second line of the message using a character expression. The first component of the expression is a character constant stated within quotation marks (the phrase *database due to an error:*). The comma, which is the concatenation operator, appends the value of the dbstat variable to the phrase. Finally, the USING keyword introduces a format that controls the punctuation and justification of the value of dbstat. The formatting tokens are the same as those used in the specification of a form field. The format for dbstat justifies the value on the left and prefixes the value with a minus sign if the value is negative.

After assigning the message to the array, MAIN calls the message_window() function to display the message placed in the array. The parameters to message_window() control the row and column at which the top left corner of the window is anchored.

4GL source file

```
GLOBALS
# used by init_msgs(), message_window(), and prompt_window() to allow
#  user to display text in a message or prompt window.
1➤  DEFINE        ga_dsplymsg ARRAY[5] OF CHAR(48)
END GLOBALS

########################################
MAIN
########################################
  DEFINE  i                SMALLINT,
          dbstat           INTEGER

  LET dbstat = -3720
2➤  INITIALIZE ga_dsplymsg TO NULL

3➤  LET ga_dsplymsg[1] = "The record has not been inserted into the"
  LET ga_dsplymsg[2] = "    database due to an error: ",
        dbstat USING "-<<<<<<<<<<<"

  CALL message_window(3,4)
END MAIN
```

The message_window() Function

4➤ The array_sz variable acts as a constant for the size of the ga_dsplymsg global array. The array_sz variable is assigned 5 with first LET statement and keeps the value for the rest of the message_window() function. The benefit of this approach is that, if you change the size of the array, you need only modify the LET statement rather than all of the code that works with the array.

5➤ The message_window() function first determines the height of the message window in lines. It starts by setting the numrows variable to four to reserve space for the border and margin of the window.

The function then counts the number of elements in the ga_dsplymsg array that aren't null, using a FOR statement. The IS NOT NULL operator compares the value of the array element to null.

When an array element has a value, the code block within the IF statement executes. In this case, the block consists of a single LET statement, which adds one to the current value of the numrows variable.

At the end of the FOR loop, the message_window() function has added the number of text lines in the array to the initial value of numrows.

6➤ The OPEN WINDOW statement creates a new window and assigns the w_msg identifier to the window. Like forms, windows remain open until explicitly closed. As it happens, the w_msg window is closed at the end of the message_window() function, but it could be closed in the MAIN function or elsewhere.

The row and column coordinates of the top left corner of the window are obtained from the x and y parameters, which were passed to the message_window() function by the CALL statement in the MAIN function.

To set the number of rows in the height of the window, the OPEN WINDOW statement evaluates the numrows variable. The number of columns in the width of the window is set to 52, which is the maximum length of a text line in the ga_dsplymsg array plus four characters for the margin and border on the left and right sides.

The ATTRIBUTES clause displays the window with a border and sets the location of the prompt. The border takes up an extra character position outside the stated positions for the window.

For example, a window with a stated width of 40 columns actually occupies 42 columns when you add a border. Thus, on a 24 row by 80 column terminal, the maximum size for a bordered window is 22 by 78, and the position for the maximum window would be at row 2 and column 2.

```
   ########################################
   FUNCTION message_window(x,y)
   ########################################
     DEFINE numrows          SMALLINT,
            x,y              SMALLINT,

            rownum,i         SMALLINT,
            answer           CHAR(1),
4➤          array_sz          SMALLINT   -- size of the ga_dsplymsg array

     LET array_sz = 5
5➤   LET numrows = 4                 -- * numrows value:
                                     -- *        1 (for the window header)
                                     -- *        1 (for the window border)
                                     -- *        1 (for the empty line before
                                     -- *            the first line of message)
                                     -- *        1 (for the empty line after
                                     -- *            the last line of message)
     FOR i = 1 TO array_sz
       IF ga_dsplymsg[i] IS NOT NULL THEN
         LET numrows = numrows + 1
       END IF
     END FOR

6➤   OPEN WINDOW w_msg AT x, y
       WITH numrows ROWS, 52 COLUMNS
       ATTRIBUTE (BORDER, PROMPT LINE LAST)
```

Some terminals scroll the screen if you display a character in the bottom right character position. You should also avoid positioning a window border or other display in this location.

7➤ The DISPLAY AT statement displays a generic title for the message.

DISPLAY AT, like FORM and most of the **4GL** screen statements, displays within the current window. When no window is current, the screen is regarded as a window the size of the terminal monitor.

The row and column coordinates apply within the current window. Thus, the title *APPLICATION MESSAGE* appears at the first row and seventeenth column of the w_msg window.

Note that some terminals (such as some Televideo and Wyse models) can't display a character immediately before or after a border or other special attribute (such as reverse video). These terminals have an sg#1 field in their entry in the termcap file. In case someone runs your program on one of these terminals, be sure to leave the first and last column position blank on each line of the window, as well as a blank character before the text that is displayed in reverse video.

8➤ In much the same way that the message_window() function previously used the numrows variable and a FOR statement to calculate the number of lines required for the message, the function uses the rownum variable and a FOR statement to control the display of the message.

The message_window() function sets the rownum variable to three so that the first line of the message displays on the third line of the window.

The FOR statement then iterates through the ga_dsplymsg array. When the IF statement discovers an array element with a value, message_window() uses a DISPLAY AT statement to display the value on the row specified by the rownum variable and at the second column of the current window. The IF statement also increments the rownum variable so that the next value displays on the next lower line of the window.

The CLIPPED operator within the FOR loop removes all trailing spaces before displaying the value. You improve the performance of your program by not displaying the spaces. When concatenating values, clipping trailing spaces can be essential.

7➤
```
DISPLAY " APPLICATION MESSAGE" AT 1, 17
 ATTRIBUTE (REVERSE, BLUE)
```

8➤
```
LET rownum = 3                    -- * start text display at third line
FOR i = 1 TO array_sz
  IF ga_dsplymsg[i] IS NOT NULL THEN
    DISPLAY ga_dsplymsg[i] CLIPPED AT rownum, 2
    LET rownum = rownum + 1
  END IF
END FOR
```

9➤ The PROMPT statement suspends execution until the user enters a single value. In the message_window() function, the purpose of the prompt is to keep the w_msg window on the screen until the user is ready to close it.

The PROMPT statement assigns the value entered by the user to the answer variable. This variable is supplied only because it is required by the PROMPT statement. The value of the answer variable is never used.

10➤ The message_window() function calls the init_msgs() function to initialize the members of the ga_dsplymsg array to null before returning.

You should clear the array to prevent **4GL** from displaying extraneous messages. To see why this step is necessary, consider two messages. The first uses all five elements of the array. The second uses only the first three elements. When the message_window() function is called for the second message, the last two elements of the array still store lines from the first message. To prevent this, the init_msgs() function initializes the array.

The init_msgs() Function

11➤ The init_msgs() function is a separate function rather than part of the message_window() function because the prompt_window() function (see Example 4: Displaying a Row on a Form on page 69) needs the same service.

The init_msgs() function uses LET statements in a loop to initialize the ga_dsplymsg array. You could also use the INITIALIZE statement; however, it is somewhat slower.

```
9     PROMPT " Press RETURN to continue." FOR answer
      CLOSE WINDOW w_msg

10    CALL init_msgs()

    END FUNCTION  -- message_window --



    ########################################
    FUNCTION init_msgs()
    ########################################
      DEFINE  i       SMALLINT

11    FOR i = 1 TO 5
        LET ga_dsplymsg[i] = NULL
      END FOR

    END FUNCTION  -- init_msgs --
```

To locate any function definition see the Function Index on page 728.

3

Populating a Ring Menu with Options

When you need to offer the user a set of possible options, you can create a menu. Each option on the menu executes a separate block of code. You can use menus to prompt the user for an option before continuing with an action. You can also create a hierarchy of menus that structures your program.

This example creates the following menu:

```
DEMO MENU:   First  Second  Third  Fourth  Exit
This is the second option of the menu.
---------------------------------------Press CTRL-W for Help----------
```

This example introduces the following **4GL** programming techniques:

- Populating a menu with options.
- Providing concealed options for experts.
- Running operating system commands.
- Configuring program execution options.
- Placing help in an external file.

Opening a Menu

The MAIN function sets options for execution of the program and then displays a menu with supporting help messages. You place the help messages in a separate file for faster lookup and to make translation easier.

Demonstrating the Choice of a Menu Option

For demonstration purposes, the dsply_option() function reports the option that was chosen. In your programs, options initiate distinct actions or set a flag to distinct values.

Executing a Command Supplied by the User

The bang() function lets the user enter and execute any number of operating system commands. The option that calls this function does not appear on the menu.

Function Overview

Function Name	**Purpose**
dsply_option()	Creates an appropriate message and calls message_window() to report the menu option chosen.
bang()	Prompts the user for a command and executes the command.
message_window()	Opens a window and displays the contents of the ga_dsplymsg global array. *See description in Example 2.*
init_msgs()	Initializes the members of the ga_dsplymsg array to null. *See description in Example 2.*

To locate any function definition see the Function Index on page 728.

The MAIN Function

1➤ The OPTIONS statement configures the execution of Example 3. The HELP FILE clause specifies that the hlpmsgs file stores the help messages. The PROMPT LINE clause specifies that the PROMPT statement should display on the last line of the screen.

Program execution options remain in effect until you change them. Some **4GL** statements let you change an option for a specific entity. For instance, as shown in "Displaying a Message Window" on page 43, the OPEN WINDOW statement can set the prompt line for prompts within the window.

You can use the OPTIONS statement to specify the line location for forms, menus, and most of the other **4GL** screen statements. **4GL** provides the special constants FIRST and LAST for specifying line locations. You can use addition or subtraction to specify a line location relative to FIRST or LAST.

2➤ The DISPLAY AT statement displays a separator line on the third line. As a menu occupies two lines and displays by default on the first two lines, the separator falls immediately below the menu. You would want to position other screen displays on the fourth line or below.

A visual separation between the menu and the information brought up by the menu can improve the quality of the user interface.

3➤ The demonstration menu exists from the MENU statement to the END MENU statement. Unlike a form or window, a menu is a continuous control block residing within a single function.

The MENU statement specifies "DEMO MENU" for the title of the menu. The title provides a fixed point of reference when the menu contains more options than can display at one time.

4➤ The COMMAND statement specifies an option for the demonstration menu. The first character string ("First") is the title of the option within the menu. The second character string ("This is the first option of the menu.") appears on the line below the menu whenever the user highlights the option title.

In Example 3, the option description provides a short explanation. You can also use the option description to provide a preview of the next set of options in a hierarchical menu structure. This technique is used in many popular spreadsheets.

When the user chooses an option, **4GL** executes the code block between the current COMMAND statement and the next COMMAND statement or, for the last option, the END MENU statement. When the code block finishes executing, **4GL** reactivates the menu. You can terminate the block prematurely using the CONTINUE MENU or EXIT MENU statements.

4GL source file

See Example 2.

```
########################################
MAIN
########################################

1➤  OPTIONS
      HELP FILE "hlpmsgs",
      PROMPT LINE LAST

2➤  DISPLAY
      "---------------------------------------Press CTRL-W for Help----------"
      AT 3, 1

3➤  MENU "DEMO MENU"
4➤    COMMAND "First" "This is the first option of the menu." HELP 1
        CALL dsply_option(1)
      COMMAND "Second" "This is the second option of the menu." HELP 2
        CALL dsply_option(2)
      COMMAND "Third" "This is the third option of the menu." HELP 3
        CALL dsply_option(3)
      COMMAND "Fourth" "This is the fourth option of the menu." HELP 4
        CALL dsply_option(4)
```

In Example 3, most of the options call the dsply_option() function, which reports the selected option for demonstration purposes. Your options will initiate distinct, meaningful actions.

The order of the COMMAND statements determines the order in which options appear on a menu. If all of the option titles won't fit within the screen width, **4GL** displays ellipses to indicate the undisplayed options and lets the user scroll to the undisplayed options.

The HELP clause specifies a message that **4GL** displays if the user presses the Help key (usually CONTROL-W) while highlighting the option. The OPTIONS statement specifies the name of the message file.

5➤ The KEY clause of the COMMAND statement specifies the exclamation point as the accelerator key for the menu option. While the menu is active, the user can press an exclamation point to trigger execution of the code block, which calls the bang() function.

An option can have either or both a title and an associated key or set of keys. You can use an option with a key but not title to hide dangerous or confusing options from most users while making the options available to expert users for whom you have provided documentation. In this example, the option is hidden because the bang() function executes operating system commands.

This technique doesn't provide a reliable security mechanism. For that, you can provide restricted application administration functions to maintain a database table of user accounts and their permissions. Examples 25 and 27 demonstrate how to retrieve the user name of the current user.

6➤ The "Exit" option on the demonstration menu executes the EXIT MENU statement. When the user chooses this option, the menu terminates and **4GL** resumes execution with the line following the END MENU statement. As in the example, the option that exits the menu is typically the last option.

If you don't provide an option or other mechanism for executing the EXIT MENU statement, the user can never leave the menu. The menu reactivates after the code block for an option finishes.

You can use a menu also to prompt the user to select one of a set of values, rather than to execute one of a set of actions as here. In such a menu, each command block would consist of a LET statement to store the selected value, followed by EXIT MENU.

7➤ Example 3 executes the CLEAR SCREEN statement at the end of the MAIN function so the screen isn't confused when the command interpreter or other calling program resumes.

```
5➤      COMMAND KEY ("!")
          CALL bang()
6➤      COMMAND "Exit" "Exit the program." HELP 100
          EXIT MENU
        END MENU

7➤    CLEAR SCREEN
      END MAIN
```

The dsply_option() Function

8➤ The CASE statement tests for possible values of the option_num variable and sets the option_name variable to an appropriate name. You could also test the option_num variable with a series of IF statements, but the CASE statement is more readable.

You can also use the CASE statement to list a series of independent tests rather than a series of values. You can use the OTHERWISE clause of the CASE statement as a catch-all for unanticipated cases.

9➤ After setting the option_name variable, dsply_option() uses the message_window() function to report the selected option (see Example 2: "Displaying a Message Window" on page 43). As in Example 2, the text of the message is assigned to the global array ga_dsplymsg before calling message_window(). The GLOBALS statement defining the array appears at the top of the source file but was omitted here for brevity.

```
########################################
FUNCTION dsply_option(option_num)
########################################
  DEFINE  option_num      SMALLINT,

          option_name     CHAR(6)

8➤  CASE option_num
    WHEN 1
      LET option_name = "First"
    WHEN 2
      LET option_name = "Second"
    WHEN 3
      LET option_name = "Third"
    WHEN 4
      LET option_name = "Fourth"
  END CASE

9➤  LET ga_dsplymsg[1] = "You have selected the ", option_name CLIPPED,
                           " option from the"
  LET ga_dsplymsg[2] = "                  DEMO menu."
  CALL message_window(6, 4)

END FUNCTION  -- dsply_option --
```

The bang() Function

10➤ The bang() function uses a WHILE statement to let the user execute any number of operating system commands. Unlike the FOR statement, which loops for a specified number of times, the WHILE statement loops indefinitely until a condition is no longer met.

The WHILE statement in the bang() function requires that the user press the bang (!) key before executing each operating system command. An alternate WHILE statement, which would allow the user to type a series of operating system commands without having to press the bang key, follows.

```
WHILE key_stroke = "!"
    PROMPT "unix! " FOR cmd
    IF LENGTH(cmd) > 0 THEN -- test for empty input
        RUN cmd
    ELSE
        LET key_stroke = ""
    END IF
END WHILE
```

The approach demonstrated in the example works much like the bang facility present in the Unix vi editor; this WHILE statement would be preferable if you expected users to type multiple operating system commands.

11➤ The key_stroke variable controls repetition of the loop. The LET statement immediately before the WHILE statement sets key_stroke so that the loop will execute at least once.

12➤ The first PROMPT statement obtains an operating system command from the user. It displays the following prompt: `UNIX!`

13➤ The RUN statement suspends the **4GL** program and invokes the command. The command has complete control of the screen for the duration of its execution. For example, the RUN statement can start up a command interpreter to execute a batch file or to start an interactive session with the user.

When the operating system command terminates, the **4GL** program resumes. You can use the RETURNING clause to capture the exit status of the command. You can also use the WITHOUT WAITING clause to run a command in the background while the **4GL** program continues to execute.

14➤ The second PROMPT statement preserves the final display of the command until the user is ready to restore the previous **4GL** display. The CHAR clause ends input on any keystroke. This contrasts with the first PROMPT statement, which (to let the user correct errors) requires that the user press the RETURN or Accept key to end input.

```
    #########################################
10➤ FUNCTION bang()
    #########################################
      DEFINE  cmd      CHAR(80),
              key_stroke CHAR(1)

11➤     LET key_stroke = "!"
        WHILE key_stroke = "!"
12➤        PROMPT "unix! " FOR cmd
13➤        RUN cmd
14➤        PROMPT "Type RETURN to continue." FOR CHAR key_stroke
        END WHILE

    END FUNCTION  -- bang --
```

Because the key_stroke variable receives the keystroke, the expert user can type an exclamation point to trigger repetition of the loop. Any other keystroke exits the loop (and the bang() function).

The hlpmsgs Message File

1➤ The help text for this example resides in a message file that is separate from the **4GL** source code files.

Within a message file, each message starts with a message identifier line. The message identifier line consists of a period followed by a unique message number that identifiers the help message. The message number must be a positive small integer (negative numbers are reserved for Informix error messages). The message consists of all lines between the message identifier line and a new message identifier line or the end of the file.

To use the help message file in a program, you must first compile the message file with the mkmessage utility. See Appendix E, "INFORMIX-4GL Utility Programs" in the *INFORMIX-4GL Reference Manual* for information about the mkmessage utility.

Within the program, you use the OPTIONS statement to specify the message file that contains the help messages. You can associate a help message number with an option in the COMMAND clause of the MENU statement. Notes on using the help file with the example appears in the section "The MAIN Function" on page 58.

You can also associate a help message with a form field in the field specification within the ATTRIBUTES section of the form file.

hlpmsgs message file

1➤
```
.1
This is the first option of the sample menu: DEMO MENU. It can be
selected by:
        1. typing the letter "f" followed by the letter "i". The
           second letter is required to distinguish between the "First"
           and the "Fourth" option (also selected with the letter "f").
        2. moving the cursor to the "First" option and pressing RETURN

.2
This is the second option of the sample menu: DEMO MENU. It can be
selected by:
        1. typing the letter "s"
        2. moving the cursor to the "Second" option and pressing RETURN

.3
This is the third option of the sample menu: DEMO MENU. It can be
selected by:
        1. typing the letter "t"
        2. moving the cursor to the "Third" option and pressing RETURN

.4
This is the fourth option of the sample menu: DEMO MENU. It can be
selected by:
        1. typing the letter "f" followed by the letter "o". The
           second letter is required to distinguish between the "Fourth"
           and the "First" option (also selected with the letter "f").
        2. moving the cursor to the "Fourth" option and pressing RETURN
```

```
.100
This option leaves the menu and exits the program. You are returned to
the environment from which you called the program. It can be selected by:
        1. typing the letter "e"
        2. moving the cursor to the "Exit" option and pressing RETURN
```

To locate any function definition see the Function Index on page 728.

4

Displaying a Row on a Form

This example uses forms to collect a customer number from the user and then display a summary of all information about the customer. It illustrates the value of **4GL** forms in giving the user an interface for interacting with the database.

To move information from the database to a form, you first retrieve the information into program variables and then display the information on the form. Similarly, to update a database row, you set program variables based on the values of form fields and then update the database row from the variables.

The following form appears in this example:

```
                        CUSTOMER SUMMARY

CUSTOMER:
  Customer Number:[        117]   Company Name:[Kids Korner         ]

ORDERS:
 Number of unpaid orders:[      2] Total amount due:[      $2953.24]

CALLS:
 Number of open calls:[      0]
        +----------------------------------------------------+
        |                 APPLICATION PROMPT                  |
        |                                                     |
        | Customer summary for customer 117                   |
        |  (Kids Korner) complete.                            |
        |                                                     |
        |Do you want to see another summary? (n/y):[]         |
        +----------------------------------------------------+
```

This example introduces the following **4GL** programming techniques:

- Retrieving information from the database.
- Collecting information from the user with a form.
- Handling data entry, database, and program errors.
- Returning values from functions.
- Manipulating a record composed of values of different types.
- Extracting and addressing a substring within a character value.

Defining Records

This example defines a record to store several kinds of information about customers. Resembling a C *struct* definition or a Pascal *record*, a **4GL** record is a variable that specifies a set of other variables. The advantage of defining a record is that you can manipulate the components of the record as a unit.

A record differs from an array in that an array is a list of values of the same type while a record is a single collection of values that may have many different types. The example defines the record globally so that it is available in all functions.

Returning Values from Functions

A **4GL** function can return values to the calling statement. You list the variables that receive the values in the RETURNING clause of the CALL statement.

If the function returns a single value, you can also call the function in an expression to supply a value for the expression. For example, a function can return a true or false value that is tested by a CASE, IF, or WHILE statement.

Testing a single value may seem strange if you're used to testing Boolean expressions containing an equal sign or other logical operator. You should recognize that a Boolean expression always evaluates to the true or false value. Thus, the conditional statement really determines whether to execute its code block based on a single value.

Entering Information on a Form

Examples 2 and 3 use the PROMPT statement to collect a single value from the user. This example introduces the INPUT statement, which activates a form so that the user can enter multiple values.

To use a form for data entry, you first open and display the form. Then, with the INPUT statement, you associate a list of program variables with the screen variables corresponding to the fields on the form. When the user finishes the data entry session, **4GL** assigns the values of the fields to the program variables.

As demonstrated in this example, an INPUT statement can reference a subset of the fields on the form. The unlisted fields aren't activated. That is, the user can't enter these fields.

This example also gives you a brief introduction to the AFTER FIELD clause of the INPUT statement. The AFTER FIELD clause lets you perform actions such as validation on a field-by-field basis. For more information about using the AFTER FIELD clause, see Example 7.

The form used in this example prompts the user for a customer number. You can also use forms to update existing database rows (see Example 6) or insert new database rows (see Example 7).

Selecting Database Information

To qualify rows in the database and retrieve a single value or row, you use the SQL SELECT statement.

One common use of the SELECT statement is to determine whether a value entered by the user corresponds to a row in the database. This example accomplishes this task by using the built-in COUNT(*) aggregate function to count the number of rows that match the value entered by the user.

The COUNT(*) function is also used to count the number of orders and calls outstanding for a customer, while the SUM() aggregate function totals the charges for those orders.

Other SELECT statements retrieve the company and state for a particular customer.

Recovering from Runtime Errors

By default, **4GL** terminates whenever a statement generates an error. This behavior is desirable in most cases, since you don't want to continue executing with an unknown program state.

However, in some situations you want to recover from the error within the program and continue executing the program. The following technique suppresses termination for the statement that can generate the recoverable error:

- Suppress termination with the WHENEVER ERROR CONTINUE statement.
- Execute the statement.
- Resume termination with the WHENEVER ERROR STOP statement.
- Use an IF statement to execute the recovery code when the built-in status variable has a value less than zero.

4GL automatically sets the status variable to zero when a statement succeeds and to a negative number when a statement fails. After an SQL statement, the status variable shows the same number as the built-in SQLCA.SQLCODE variable. Unlike SQLCODE, however, **4GL** also sets the status variable after a **4GL** screen statement.

The prompt_window() function uses this technique to adjust the positioning of a window, but later examples make extensive use of this technique for SQL statements. SQL statements are particularly appropriate for recovery because an SQL statement can be invalidated at runtime by changes in the database schema or by locks on the desired rows.

You should always use the standard termination behavior for statements for which you aren't providing recovery code. The continuation behavior increases the size of the executable code compiled from the **4GL** code. In addition, terminating the program is the appropriate recovery mechanism for statements for which you haven't provided explicit recovery code.

Note that the WHENEVER statement isn't a run-time statement that applies to statements in the thread of execution. Instead, WHENEVER is an instruction to the compiler that takes effect when the module is compiled. That is, the WHENEVER statement applies to all lower lines within the module until the next WHENEVER statement or the end of the module. The WHENEVER statement doesn't apply to functions called from the covered lines.

Function Overview

Function Name	Purpose
cust_summary()	Loops through the action until the user is done.
get_custnum()	Obtains a customer number from the user.
get_summary()	Uses a series of SELECT statements to fetch from the database and summarize customer information.
dsply_summary()	Displays the customer summary on a form.
tax_rates()	Supplies the appropriate tax schedule for a customer.
init_msgs()	Initializes the members of the ga_dsplymsg array to null. *See description in Example 2.*
prompt_window()	Displays a message and prompts the user for affirmation or negation. This function is a variation on the message_window() function that appears in Example 2.

To locate any function definition see the Function Index on page 728.

The f_custkey and f_custsum Forms

1➤ The SCREEN and ATTRIBUTES sections of the form specification fulfill the same purpose as described in the section "The f_logo Form Specification" in Example 1. In contrast with Example 3, for which the database was FORMONLY, the f_custkey form and f_custsum forms are defined to work with the stores2t demonstration database.

The TABLES section specifies the relevant tables from the database. The ATTRIBUTES section can associate a field tag with a database column to assign the data type of the database column to the corresponding screen variable.

Note that, if the data type of the database column changes, you must recompile the form.

2➤ The f001 field in the f_custkey form is specified as a member of the FORMONLY table. You use this pseudo-table within the specification of a database form for fields that can't or shouldn't correspond to a database column.

The customer_num column of the customer table has a SERIAL data type. To prevent a user from inputting or updating a SERIAL value, **4GL** automatically moves the cursor out of a screen field that is defined like a SERIAL field. Because the user must be able to enter a customer number to select the customer, the f_custkey form specification defines the customer_num screen variable as a member of the FORMONLY table. The customer_num name merely clarifies for any programmer reading the code that the information entered in the field corresponds to the database column. The name doesn't apply any characteristics of the column.

3➤ The f002, f003, and f004 fields in the f_custsum form are also specified as members of the FORMONLY table. These formonly fields display information synthesized from several columns in several tables.

f_custkey form file

1➤
```
DATABASE stores2t

SCREEN
{
 Customer Number:[f001       ]   Company Name:[f002                    ]

}

TABLES
customer

ATTRIBUTES
f001 = formonly.customer_num;
f002 = customer.company;
```
2➤ (at f001 = formonly.customer_num;)

f_custsum form file

```
DATABASE stores2t

SCREEN
{

  CUSTOMER:
    Customer Number:[f000       ]   Company Name:[f001                    ]

  ORDERS:
   Number of unpaid orders:[f002   ] Total amount due:[f003           ]

  CALLS:
   Number of open calls:[f004   ]

}

TABLES
customer

ATTRIBUTES
f000 = customer.customer_num;
f001 = customer.company;
f002 = formonly.unpaid_ords;
f003 = formonly.amount_due;
f004 = formonly.open_calls;
```
3➤ (at f002 = formonly.unpaid_ords;)

The DATABASE and GLOBALS Statements

1➤ The DATABASE statement opens the stores2t demonstration database.

The program uses information in the database to assist with the definition of the program variables. In the same way that the DATABASE section of a form specification file declares a database for field definitions, this program reads information from the database and defines variables based on columns.

If you are developing for an existing database, you may want to make a copy of the database that has the same schema but fewer rows. You can test your program against the copy without affecting the performance or the data in the real database. When your program is ready for use, change the database name from the test database to the real database in the form specifications and all modules and then recompile.

2➤ For convenience, the program groups several variables as a record. For example, the dsply_summary() function displays the gr_customer record in the f_custsum form with a single statement. The gr_custsum record is defined as a global variable so any function can access the record.

Each member of the record is a variable that, like all variables, is defined with a data type. The LIKE clause assigns the data type of a column in the database. Because the data type is determined when the code is compiled, you must recompile the module if the data type of the column changes.

Each member of the gr_custsum record corresponds to a screen variable of the same name in the f_custsum form. Because the names are the same, the program need not specify both the variable and its corresponding field names when exchanging data between the record and the form.

The MAIN Function

3➤ Along with the prompt line, the OPTIONS statement lets you specify the line on which a message appears. The MESSAGE statement displays a line of text that doesn't require a response from the user.

The INPUT ATTRIBUTE clause sets the display attributes for fields in which the user can position. This technique gives the user a visual cue to distinguish input fields from read-only fields.

4GL source file

1 ➤
```
DATABASE stores2t

GLOBALS
  DEFINE        gr_custsum RECORD
                  customer_num  LIKE customer.customer_num,
                  company       LIKE customer.company,
                  unpaid_ords   SMALLINT,
                  amount_due    MONEY(11),
                  open_calls    SMALLINT
                END RECORD
```
2 ➤ (DEFINE)

See Example 2.

```
END GLOBALS

########################################
MAIN
########################################

 OPTIONS
    INPUT ATTRIBUTE (REVERSE, BLUE),
    PROMPT LINE 13,
    MESSAGE LINE LAST

  CALL cust_summary()

END MAIN
```
3 ➤ (OPTIONS)

The cust_summary() Function

4➤ The cust_summary() function executes a loop to let the user see a summary for several different customers.

The search_again variable is the controlling variable for the WHILE loop. The LET statement assigns the value of the built-in TRUE constant. (**4GL** also provides a built-in FALSE constant.)

While the IF and WHILE statements usually test a Boolean expression using a logical operator, these statements can in fact test any expression that yields a single value that is TRUE or FALSE. As demonstrated in cust_summary(), you can evaluate a variable to generate the tested value. You can also generate the tested value using a function call that returns a single value.

5➤ The call to get_custnum() uses the RETURNING clause to fill the gr_custsum.customer_num variable with the value returned by the function. Here only one value is returned, but the RETURNING clause lets you assign a list of values to a list of variables.

If a function returns a single value, you can call it within an expression instead of using the CALL statement. In particular, you can use a function call to generate the value assigned to a variable by the LET statement. For example, you could rewrite the call to get_custnum() as follows:

```
LET gr_custsum.customer_num = get_custnum()
```

If the function call requires a return value and the function doesn't supply it, **4GL** reports a run-time error. Remember that you can return a null value if no other value is appropriate.

Note that the RETURNING clause refers to the gr_custsum.customer_num variable. To address the customer_num member, you qualify it with the gr_custsum record and a separating period.

6➤ The loop calls the dsply_summary() function to generate and display the summary for that customer. The dsply_summary() function sets the search_again variable to TRUE if the user wants to see the summary for another customer and to FALSE if the user is done.

```
   ########################################
   FUNCTION cust_summary()
   ########################################
     DEFINE        search_again    SMALLINT

4➤   LET search_again = TRUE
     WHILE search_again
5➤     CALL get_custnum() RETURNING gr_custsum.customer_num

6➤     CALL dsply_summary() RETURNING search_again
     END WHILE

     CLEAR SCREEN

   END FUNCTION
```

The get_custnum() Function

7➤ The get_custnum() function opens and displays the f_custkey form and uses the DISPLAY AT statement to give the form a title appropriate to the context.

8➤ The INPUT statement suspends execution of the get_custnum() function while the user fills in the input fields of the f_custkey form.

The INPUT statement associates the cust_num local variable with the customer_num screen variable of the form (see Note 2 on74). When the user finishes entering data, **4GL** assigns the value of the customer_num field to the cust_num local variable. Although only one variable appears here, the INPUT statement can associate multiple program variables with screen variables.

Note that although the f_custkey form specification includes the company screen variable, the INPUT statement doesn't refer to this variable. As a result, the user can't move into the company field.

The INPUT statement applies to the currently displayed form. You can open two forms and switch the user between forms by executing a new DISPLAY statement for the appropriate form before executing the INPUT statement.

The user terminates data entry by pressing the Accept key (typically ESCAPE). Data entry also terminates when the user leaves the last activated field on the form, although you can use INPUT WRAP setting of the OPTIONS statement to cycle back to the first field. Because only the customer_num field is activated on the f_custkey form, tabbing exits the form.

The user can terminate the program at any time by pressing the Cancel key. Also referred to as the Interrupt key, the Cancel key is typically CONTROL-C. To stop data entry but continue the program, use the DEFER INTERRUPT statement (see Example 5).

9➤ The AFTER FIELD clause specifies a block of code that **4GL** executes when the user leaves the customer_num field or terminates data entry while in the field. As in get_custnum(), the typical use of the AFTER FIELD clause is to validate the value entered by the user.

The form activation statements also provide a BEFORE FIELD clause, which you can use to initialize a field when the user enters the field (see Example 7).

10➤ **4GL** assigns the value of the customer_num field to the cust_num variable before executing the AFTER FIELD clause. The first IF statement checks the value of the cust_num variable to determine whether the user filled in the customer_num field.

If the user didn't enter a value, the ERROR statement causes the terminal to beep and displays an explanation of the error.

```
########################################
FUNCTION get_custnum()
########################################
  DEFINE  cust_num        INTEGER,
          cust_cnt        SMALLINT

7➤  OPEN FORM f_custkey FROM "f_custkey"
  DISPLAY FORM f_custkey

  DISPLAY "                    "
    AT 2, 30
  DISPLAY "CUSTOMER KEY LOOKUP"
    AT 2, 20
  DISPLAY " Enter customer number and press Accept."
    AT 4, 1 ATTRIBUTE (REVERSE, YELLOW)

8➤  INPUT cust_num FROM customer_num
9➤    AFTER FIELD customer_num
10➤      IF cust_num IS NULL THEN
        ERROR "You must enter a customer number. Please try again."
        NEXT FIELD customer_num
      END IF
```

The NEXT FIELD statement then returns the cursor to the same field. By positioning the cursor in the form, the NEXT FIELD statement implicitly prevents the termination of the form. Thus, this statement is necessary even in a single-field form if you want to stop the user from leaving the form. The NEXT FIELD statement appears within the IF statement's code block so that the user can leave the field if the customer exists.

11➤ The AFTER FIELD clause executes a SELECT statement to try to find a customer that has the customer number entered by the user.

The COUNT(*) aggregate function counts the number of rows qualified by the query. The INTO clause fills the cust_cnt variable with the value generated by the query. The WHERE clause qualifies only the rows in the customer table in which the customer_num column matches the value entered by the user.

12➤ The second IF statement tests the cust_cnt variable to determine whether a customer was found. If not, the ERROR statement reports the problem to the user and the NEXT FIELD statement reactivates the form so that the user can correct the customer number.

13➤ As Example 4 calls the get_custnum() function in a loop, **4GL** opens and closes the f_custkey form on each repetition of the loop. You could make the example more efficient by opening the form once before the loop, displaying the form on each call to get_custnum(), and closing the form after the loop.

Example 4 takes the less efficient approach of opening and closing the form entirely within the get_custnum() function so that the function can be reused in other contexts with nothing more than the function call. In your own programs, you will encounter similar trade-offs between efficiency and reusability that you must evaluate on a case-by-case basis.

14➤ The RETURN statement returns the customer number entered by the user. The RETURNING clause of the call to get_custnum() assigns this value to the gr_custsum.customer_num variable. Because the record is global, the get_custnum() function could have made the assignment instead of returning the value. The return technique was adopted so that get_custnum() could be reused in other programs without requiring the gr_custsum global record.

The RETURN statement terminates the current function immediately. The RETURN statement can return multiple values or, when only termination is required, no values.

```
11➤        SELECT COUNT(*)
           INTO cust_cnt
           FROM customer
           WHERE customer_num = cust_num

12➤        IF (cust_cnt = 0) THEN
             ERROR "Unknown customer number. Please try again."
             LET cust_num = NULL
             NEXT FIELD customer_num
           END IF

       END INPUT

13➤    CLOSE FORM f_custkey

14➤    RETURN (cust_num)

     END FUNCTION  -- get_custnum --
```

The get_summary() Function

15➤ The dsply_summary() function (which is called in the WHILE the loop in the cust_summary() function) calls get_summary() to build the summary of customer information. The get_summary() function executes a series of queries to build the summary.

16➤ The first query retrieves the company and state information from the customer table for the customer supplied by the user in the get_custnum() function. The query places the company name in the company member of the gr_custsum global record for later display in the dsply_summary() function. The query places the state in a local variable for later use within the get_summary() function.

17➤ The second query uses the built-in COUNT(*) aggregate function to count the number of orders for which the customer hasn't paid. The count is stored in the gr_custsum global record for later display. The count is also used to determine whether or not to calculate the amount owed on the outstanding orders.

Only the SELECT statement and reports offer the aggregate functions.

18➤ The third query uses the built-in SUM() aggregate function to total the value of the items belonging to the outstanding orders.

The query includes the orders table because the paid_date column, which indicates whether the order has been paid, resides only in the orders table.

The query includes the items table because the total_price column, which is totaled by the SUM() aggregate function, resides only in the items table.

The WHERE clause requires the order_num column to be the same in both the orders and items tables to join the related rows. The other conditions restrict the query to the appropriate customer and to unpaid orders.

19➤ The fourth query uses the built-in SUM() aggregate function to total the shipping charges for the unpaid orders.

20➤ To calculate the total tax on the unpaid orders, the get_summary() function first calls the tax_rates() function with the customer's state as a parameter. The tax_rates() function returns the applicable tax rate.

The get_summary() function then calculates the sales tax based on the total value of the items established in a previous query.

21➤ The get_summary() function then adds the total value of the items, the sales tax on the items, and the total shipping charge on the orders to obtain the total amount outstanding and saves this figure in the amount_due member variable of the gr_custsum record. For customers without unpaid orders, the ELSE clause sets the total to zero.

```
     ########################################
15➤  FUNCTION get_summary()
     ########################################
       DEFINE  cust_state       LIKE state.code,
               item_total       MONEY(12),
               ship_total       MONEY(7),
               sales_tax        MONEY(9),
               tax_rate         DECIMAL(5,3)

     --* Get customer's company name and state (for later tax evaluation)
16➤    SELECT company, state
       INTO gr_custsum.company, cust_state
       FROM customer
       WHERE customer_num = gr_custsum.customer_num

     --* Calculate number of unpaid orders for customer
17➤    SELECT COUNT(*)
       INTO gr_custsum.unpaid_ords
       FROM orders
       WHERE customer_num = gr_custsum.customer_num
         AND paid_date IS NULL

     --* If customer has unpaid orders, calculate total amount due
       IF (gr_custsum.unpaid_ords > 0) THEN
18➤      SELECT SUM(total_price)
         INTO item_total
         FROM items, orders
         WHERE orders.order_num = items.order_num
           AND customer_num = gr_custsum.customer_num
           AND paid_date IS NULL

19➤      SELECT SUM(ship_charge)
         INTO ship_total
         FROM orders
         WHERE customer_num = gr_custsum.customer_num
           AND paid_date IS NULL

20➤      LET tax_rate = 0.00
         CALL tax_rates(cust_state) RETURNING tax_rate

         LET sales_tax = item_total * (tax_rate / 100)
21➤      LET gr_custsum.amount_due = item_total + sales_tax + ship_total

     --* If customer has no unpaid orders, total amount due = $0.00
       ELSE
         LET gr_custsum.amount_due = 0.00
       END IF
```

22➤ The final query counts the number of customer calls which have not received a response. The query searches the cust_calls table for rows that contain the appropriate customer number and a null value in the res_dtime column. The query saves this value in the open_calls member variable of the gr_custsum global record.

The dsply_summary() Function

23➤ The dsply_summary() function is called by the cust_summary() function. It opens and displays the f_custsum form.The customer summary appears in this form. The DISPLAY AT statement clears the form title from the f_custkey form.

24➤ The CALL statement executes the get_summary() function to generate the summary and place the values in the gr_custsum global record. The call could return the values, but it's faster to place the values in a record accessible in both functions.

25➤ The DISPLAY BY NAME statement uses the asterisk notation to refer to every member of the record, assigning the values of the member variables to the form fields. You can use this mechanism only where each member of the record has a corresponding screen variable with the same name in the form.

The benefit of the asterisk notation is that a change in the record structure doesn't require a change to a statement using the record. However, you may need to change the form specification to accommodate new members.

26➤ The dsply_summary() function then prompts the user to determine whether the user wants to view the summaries for additional customers.

The prompt window operates in much the same way as the message window (see "Displaying a Message Window" on page 43). You assign the text of the prompt to the ga_dsplymsg global array before calling the prompt_window() function.

27➤ The get_more variable stores the user's decision. By default, the decision is TRUE. The IF statement executes a call to the prompt_window() function to obtain the user's decision. If prompt_window() returns FALSE, the get_more variable is also set to FALSE. The value of the get_more variable is then returned to the cust_summary() function to control repetition of the loop.

The IF statement provides an example of a context in which you can call a function to generate a value. The statement calls the prompt_window() function in the same way as the CALL statement calls a function. The only differ-

```
    --* Calculate number of open calls for this customer
22➤   SELECT COUNT(*)
      INTO gr_custsum.open_calls
      FROM cust_calls
      WHERE customer_num = gr_custsum.customer_num
        AND res_dtime IS NULL

    END FUNCTION  -- get_summary --

    ########################################
    FUNCTION dsply_summary()
    ########################################
      DEFINE get_more       SMALLINT

23➤   OPEN FORM f_custsum FROM "f_custsum"
      DISPLAY FORM f_custsum

      DISPLAY "                         "
        AT 2, 20

24➤   CALL get_summary()

25➤   DISPLAY BY NAME gr_custsum.*

26➤   LET ga_dsplymsg[1] = "Customer summary for customer ",
            gr_custsum.customer_num USING "<<<<<<<<<<<"
      LET ga_dsplymsg[2] = " (", gr_custsum.company CLIPPED, ") complete."

27➤   LET get_more = TRUE
      IF NOT prompt_window("Do you want to see another summary?",14,12)
      THEN
        LET get_more = FALSE
      END IF

      RETURN get_more
      CLOSE FORM f_custsum

    END FUNCTION  -- dsply_summary --
```

ence is that, instead of assigning the return value to a variable using the RETURNING clause, the IF statement tests the value to see if it is the same as the TRUE constant.

The tax_rates() Function

28➤ The tax_rates() function executes a large CASE statement on the customer's state, which is passed as a parameter, and returns the appropriate tax rate for the state. (The tax scheme applied here has been simplified for demonstration purposes.)

For the sake of efficiency, the comparison is done at two levels. The outer CASE statement uses the substring operator, which is a set of brackets, to extract the initial letter of the state. The inner CASE statements such as the ones under A and C compare the second letter when several state abbreviations start with the same letter. The OTHERWISE clause sets the tax rate to zero if the rate isn't known.

It would be more efficient and convenient to store the tax rate in a table. As used by Example 4, the tax rate could be a column in the state table. Or, more realistically, the tax rate might appear in a separate table for the county or district which would be joined to the customer table separately.

Sometimes, however, a developer must upgrade a program without modifying the database. The tax_rates() function shows you how to store static information in a function.

The prompt_window() Function

29➤ The prompt_window() function is another generic function that you can incorporate into your own programs without changes.

Before calling the prompt_window() function, the program defines the global ga_dsplymsg array and assigns the text of the prompt to the elements of the global array.

The prompt_window() function is similar to the message_window() function described in Example 2. An important difference is that the prompt_window() checks the success of opening the window. This feature is deliberately omitted from the message_window() function so you can compare the two.

Another difference is that the prompt_window() function requires an additional parameter which is used as the prompt string.

```
#########################################
FUNCTION tax_rates(state_code)
#########################################
 DEFINE   state_code       LIKE state.code,

          tax_rate         DECIMAL(4,2)

28➤  CASE state_code[1]
    WHEN "A"
      CASE state_code
        WHEN "AK"
          LET tax_rate = 0.0
        WHEN "AL"
          LET tax_rate = 0.0
        WHEN "AR"
          LET tax_rate = 0.0
        WHEN "AZ"
          LET tax_rate = 5.5
      END CASE
    WHEN "C"
      CASE state_code
        WHEN "CA"
          LET tax_rate = 6.5
        WHEN "CO"
          LET tax_rate = 3.7
        WHEN "CT"
          LET tax_rate = 8.0
      END CASE
    WHEN "D"
      LET tax_rate = 0.0        -- * tax rate for "DE"
```

See source file.

```
 OTHERWISE
      LET tax_rate = 0.0
  END CASE

  RETURN (tax_rate)

END FUNCTION   -- tax_rates --

########################################
29➤ FUNCTION prompt_window(question, x,y)
########################################
  DEFINE question        CHAR(48),
         x,y             SMALLINT,

         numrows         SMALLINT,
         rownum,i        SMALLINT,
         answer          CHAR(1),
```

30➤ The yes_ans, invalid_resp, and unopen variables are flags set to control execution of IF and WHILE statements within the prompt_window() function. As in the message_window() function, the array_sz variable stores a constant value so that you can later change the value in one location.

31➤ As in the message_window() function, the first FOR loop counts the elements in the array filled with text in the calling function.

32➤ The prompt_window() function uses a WHILE statement to permit a second attempt to open the w_prompt window if there are errors in the first attempt. The unopen variable controls execution of the loop.

33➤ By default, **4GL** terminates if an error occurs. The loop forces continuation after an attempt to open the w_prompt window by preceding the OPEN WINDOW statement with the WHENEVER ERROR CONTINUE statement. The WHENEVER ERROR STOP statement restores the termination behavior.

34➤ To determine whether the w_prompt window was opened successfully, the IF statement tests the built-in status variable. The LET statement assigns the value of status to a local status variable called local_stat. The local variable enables the program to test the success of the OPEN WINDOW statement even if any other **4GL** statements along the way reset status.

35➤ **4GL** sets the status variable to -1138 when a window doesn't fit on the screen and to -1144 when a top left corner of a window is off the screen. You could write code to calculate the window size and positioning, but it's easier to let **4GL** perform these calculations for you.

The loop recovers from these problems by setting the top left corner of the w_prompt window to a coordinate that is guaranteed to fit on the screen. The maximum width of the window is 52 characters and the maximum length of the window is 9 lines (the sum of the five elements of the array and the four lines required for the window margin and borders). The MESSAGE statement notifies the user that the program is recovering from an internal error.

You might consider replacing this message with to a call to the ERRLOG() function to make a permanent entry in the error log. See Example 25 for more information on using error logs.

36➤ The first ELSE statement executes when the attempt to open the w_prompt window failed with a negative error number other than -1138 or -1144. The MESSAGE statement notifies the user that the prompt_window() function can't recover from the error. The EXIT PROGRAM statement terminates the program.

```
30➤        yes_ans         SMALLINT,
           ny_added        SMALLINT,
           invalid_resp    SMALLINT,
           ques_lngth      SMALLINT,
           unopen          SMALLINT,
           array_sz        SMALLINT,
           local_stat      SMALLINT

    LET array_sz = 5
    LET numrows = 4                 -- * numrows value:
                                    -- *        1 (for the window header)
                                    -- *        1 (for the window border)
                                    -- *        1 (for the empty line before
                                    -- *           the first line of message)
                                    -- *        1 (for the empty line after
                                    -- *           the last line of message)
31➤ FOR i = 1 TO array_sz
      IF ga_dsplymsg[i] IS NOT NULL THEN
        LET numrows = numrows + 1
      END IF
    END FOR

32➤ LET unopen = TRUE
    WHILE unopen

33➤ WHENEVER ERROR CONTINUE
      OPEN WINDOW w_prompt AT x, y
        WITH numrows ROWS, 52 COLUMNS
        ATTRIBUTE (BORDER, PROMPT LINE LAST)
    WHENEVER ERROR STOP
34➤   LET local_stat = status
      IF (local_stat < 0) THEN
35➤     IF (local_stat = -1138) OR (local_stat = -1144) THEN
          MESSAGE "prompt_window() error: changing coordinates to 3,3."
          SLEEP 2
          LET x = 3
          LET y = 3
36➤     ELSE
          MESSAGE "prompt_window() error: ", local_stat USING "-<<<<<<<<<<<"
          SLEEP 2
          EXIT PROGRAM
        END IF
```

37➤ The second ELSE statement executes when the w_prompt window opened successfully. The unopen variable is set to FALSE to prevent repetition of the loop.

38➤ As in the message_window() function, the rownum variable controls the vertical placement of text for the prompt. The FOR loop displays the lines in the array that have text and increments the row number.

39➤ If the question string has enough room, the function appends the character string "(n/y):" to this variable. The built-in LENGTH() function determines the length of the question parameter. The IF statement checks to make sure that this length is less than the maximum text line in the window (48 characters) less the appended "(n/y):" string (6 characters) and an additional space. If the question string already exceeds a length of 41, the function does not append the "(n/y):" string.

40➤ The first LET statement uses the substring brackets to refer to the last six character positions in the question variable. The "(n/y):" string is stored in these positions.

41➤ This WHILE loop executes until the user has entered an answer that can be converted to a true or false value. The invalid_resp variable is the controlling variable for the loop.

42➤ The PROMPT statement then displays the modified question.

43➤ The first IF statement following the PROMPT statement uses the MATCHES operator to guarantee that the user enters a character that falls within the set of valid characters: a "y" or "n" in either upper or lower case. The second IF sets the yes_ans variable to TRUE for a positive answer.

As in the message_window() function, the init_msgs() function initializes the global array. The w_prompt window is then closed, and the value of the yes_ans variable returned. The function that called prompt_window() must determine what to do with the user's response.

```
37➤       ELSE
            LET unopen = FALSE
          END IF
        END WHILE

        DISPLAY " APPLICATION PROMPT" AT 1, 17
         ATTRIBUTE (REVERSE, BLUE)

38➤     LET rownum = 3                  -- * start text display at third line
        FOR i = 1 TO array_sz
          IF ga_dsplymsg[i] IS NOT NULL THEN
            DISPLAY ga_dsplymsg[i] CLIPPED AT rownum, 2
            LET rownum = rownum + 1
          END IF
        END FOR

        LET yes_ans = FALSE
39➤     LET ques_lngth = LENGTH(question)
        IF ques_lngth <= 41 THEN   -- * room enough to add "(n/y)" string
40➤       LET question [ques_lngth + 2, ques_lngth + 7] = "(n/y):"
        END IF
        LET invalid_resp = TRUE
41➤     WHILE invalid_resp
42➤       PROMPT question CLIPPED, " " FOR answer
43➤       IF answer MATCHES "[nNyY]" THEN
            LET invalid_resp = FALSE
            IF answer MATCHES "[yY]" THEN
              LET yes_ans = TRUE
            END IF
          END IF
        END WHILE

        CALL init_msgs()
        CLOSE WINDOW w_prompt
        RETURN (yes_ans)

      END FUNCTION  -- prompt_window --
```

To locate any function definition see the Function Index on page 728.

5

Programming a Query by Example

This example executes a query by example using form and dynamic SQL statements. In query by example, the user enters any information known about the target rows, creating an example of what the query should retrieve.

Query-by-example is a user interface technique for querying a database. Because database applications frequently use query-by-example, **4GL** provides several statements to make it easy to collect criteria from a user and construct and run a query.

The following form appears in this example:

```
                         CUSTOMER QUERY-BY-EXAMPLE

Customer Number       :[>113        ] Company Name :[                    ]
 Address: [                   ]
          [                   ]
   City : [                   ]  State:[  ]  Zip Code:[          ]

Contact Name: [               ][               ]
Telephone   : [                   ]



Press Accept to search for customer data, Cancel to exit w/out searching.
```

This example introduces the following **4GL** programming techniques:

- Constructing Boolean criteria from user entry on a form.
- Preparing SQL statements dynamically at run-time.
- Accessing each row within a qualified set of database rows.
- Enabling the Interrupt key as a signal for abandoning entry on a form.

Constructing Criteria from the User's Entry

In this example, the query_cust1() function performs all of the actions necessary to build and run a query by example.

The first step in query by example is to display a form. You then activate the form with the CONSTRUCT statement for entry of the query criteria. The CONSTRUCT statement differs from the INPUT statement as follows:

- The INPUT statement validates the data entered by the user to ensure that the value is appropriate for the data type of the field.

  The CONSTRUCT statement, by contrast, accepts logical operators in any field to indicate ranges, comparisons, sets, and partial matches.
- When the user finishes work with the form, the INPUT statement assigns the value in each field to a corresponding variable.

  The CONSTRUCT statement, on the other hand, fills a single variable with a character string that describes a Boolean expression. The CONSTRUCT statement creates the Boolean expression by generating a logical expression for each field with a value and then applying unions (AND relations) to the field statements.

As demonstrated in this example, you can create a valid SELECT statement by concatenating the constructed Boolean expression to other character values that state the rest of the SELECT statement. You typically use character constants to state the fixed structure of a SELECT statement including the source tables, projected columns, and join conditions. You use the constructed Boolean expression for selection criteria that vary under the control of the user.

You must supply the WHERE keyword to convert the Boolean expression into a complete WHERE clause. This feature gives you the freedom to take advantage of the CONSTRUCT statement anywhere where you can use a Boolean expression stated as a character value. This feature also gives you the ability to combine join conditions or program-supplied selection criteria with the constructed Boolean expression as is most convenient. You must supply the AND operators when combining the constructed Boolean expression with logical expressions in the WHERE clause. One point to watch for is to make sure that you supply the spaces required to separate the constructed Boolean expression from the other parts of the SELECT statement.

Executing an SQL Query Dynamically

To convert the character value that represents the SELECT statement into an executable instruction, you use the PREPARE statement. The PREPARE statement is not limited to the SELECT statement. You can specify most of the SQL statements dynamically at run-time using this statement.

For statements that simply run with no further interaction with your **4GL** function, you can run the prepared statement with the EXECUTE statement.

For query by example, however, one-time execution often isn't sufficient. You need to access one of the rows qualified by the query and perform an action on the row before going on to the next.

Accessing Multiple Rows with Cursors

To access the qualified rows at the discretion of your function, you declare a cursor for the query. Like the screen cursor in an editor that shows you the current line, the query cursor points to the current row within the set of qualified rows.

You create a cursor using the DECLARE CURSOR statement. The DECLARE CURSOR statement can operate on a SELECT statement that is stated explicitly in the code or one that is prepared dynamically at run-time. After declaring the cursor, you have two choices for accessing the qualified rows:

- You can use the FOREACH statement to state a loop that retrieves each row into a set of variables and then executes a block of **4GL** code.
- You can use the OPEN statement to start accessing the qualified rows, the FETCH statement to retrieve rows as needed, and the CLOSE statement to stop accessing the rows.

You can achieve the same effect as the FOREACH statement using the FETCH statement at the top of a WHILE loop. That is, the FETCH gives you greater control than the FOREACH. However, in many cases the FOREACH is more convenient.

The query_cust1() function uses the OPEN and FETCH statements. For each retrieved row, query_cust1() executes the DISPLAY BY NAME statement to show the row on the form. Thus, the sequence of the principal commands in the query is as follows:

- OPEN FORM
- DISPLAY FORM
- CONSTRUCT

- PREPARE
- OPEN
- DECLARE CURSOR
- OPEN (cursor)
- FETCH
- DISPLAY BY NAME
- CLOSE (cursor)
- CLOSE FORM

Handling User Interrupts

When **4GL** receives the Interrupt signal, it immediately stops executing the program. This behavior means that when the user presses the Interrupt key the program exits. However, often you want to provide the user with a means of cancelling an action without exiting the program.

For example, suppose the user performs a query-by-example to select a customer row and begins to update it. The user then realizes that the wrong customer row is being updated. Unless you add interrupt handling code to your program, pressing the Interrupt key will both cancel the update and exit the program. What the user needs is a way to cancel the update and to remain in the program.

To provide such a capability, you can use the DEFER INTERRUPT statement to tell **4GL** to change how it handles the Interrupt signal. Once a program executes a DEFER INTERRUPT statement, **4GL** does the following when it receives the Interrupt signal:

1. Sets a global variable called int_flag to TRUE.
2. Exits the current user interaction statement (INPUT, CONSTRUCT, INPUT ARRAY, DISPLAY ARRAY, PROMPT, MENU).
3. Continues program execution.

To check for when the user presses the Interrupt key, the program needs to:

1. Include the DEFER INTERRUPT statement in the main program.
2. Initialize the int_flag to FALSE before user interaction statements.
3. Check the setting of the int_flag after each user interaction statement exits. If int_flag is TRUE, the program needs to perform whatever action is appropriate for cancelling the current task.

The DEFER statement also supports the QUIT keyword so you can change the way **4GL** responds to the Quit signal. Normally, an application just includes the DEFER INTERRUPT statement so that the Quit key (typically CONTROL-\) still exits the application in an emergency.

Because **4GL** never resets int_flag to FALSE, your program must reset this variable before the next user interaction statement executes. Otherwise, int_flag may have been set to TRUE in some other statement and the program will incorrectly assume that the user pressed Interrupt in the statement just completed.

You should reset int_flag at either of two points in your programs:

- Immediately before each user interaction statement.
- When you check for int_flag after each user interaction statement and find that it is currently TRUE.

This example combines the two methods so that you can see how either might be implemented. However, you only need to use one method to reset int_flag. Whichever method you choose, you should be consistent throughout your application.

If you choose the second approach, you can create a function to automatically reset int_flag when the program checks its value. The following interrupted() function demonstrates this approach:

```
FUNCTION interrupted()

  DEFINE local_intflg     SMALLINT
  LET local_intflg = int_flag -- save current value of
                            --  global int_flag variable
  LET int_flag = FALSE       -- reset global int_flag
  RETURN local_intflg        --* return the original
                             --*  value of int_flag
END FUNCTION  -- Interrupted --
```

To check int_flag, you call the function following each user interaction statement, as demonstrated below:

```
CONSTRUCT BY NAME q_cust ON customer_num
IF interrupted() THEN
   . . .
END IF
```

Utility Functions

This example also introduces some convenient utility functions that display a single line without opening a new window. The msg() function corresponds to the message_window() function from Example 2, and the answer_yes() function to the prompt_window() function from Example 4.

Function Overview

Function Name	Purpose
query_cust1()	Executes a query by example using the f_customer form.
answer_yes()	Gets a yes or no answer for a single-line question.
msg()	Displays a brief, informative message.

To locate any function definition see the Function Index on page 728.

The f_customer Form

1➤ As with the f_custkey and f_custsum forms from Example 4, the f_customer form specifies the database and table in order to base the characteristics of form fields on corresponding database columns. As described in Notes 2 through 4, the fields make use of some special formatting attributes.

2➤ The NOENTRY attribute prevents update of the customer_num field. **4GL** statements can assign a value to the field, but the user can't move into the field to update the value. As with the customer_num field, which is a serial field, the NOENTRY attribute is typically used with fields for which your **4GL** program or the database engine supplies the value.

4GL ignores the NOENTRY attribute when constructing a query because there is no need to validate query criteria. Thus, the NOENTRY attribute is irrelevant in this example. However, you can also use the f_customer form for data entry; in that case **4GL** will apply the NOENTRY attribute.

3➤ The UPSHIFT attribute automatically translates lower-case characters to upper-case characters. This attribute is particularly useful in code fields, such as the state field, to ensure consistent values. If some New York customers have a state code of `NY` and others a state code of `Ny` or `ny`, it is difficult to perform actions such as joins on the state field.

4GL also supplies a DOWNSHIFT attribute.

4➤ The PICTURE attribute states a punctuation format for a character column. Note that the punctuation is actually stored in the value. This result contrasts with the FORMAT clause, which states a punctuation format that isn't stored in the value. The FORMAT clause applies only to date and numeric values.

The f_customer Form

f_customer form file

```
1➤ DATABASE stores2t

   SCREEN
   {

     Customer Number      :[f000        ] Company Name :[f001               ]
      Address: [f002               ]
               [f003               ]
        City : [f004          ]  State:[f5]  Zip Code:[f006           ]

     Contact Name: [f007          ][f008           ]
     Telephone   : [f009              ]

   }

   TABLES
   customer

   ATTRIBUTES
2➤ f000 = customer.customer_num, NOENTRY;
   f001 = customer.company;
   f002 = customer.address1;
   f003 = customer.address2;
   f004 = customer.city;
3➤ f5 = customer.state, UPSHIFT;
   f006 = customer.zipcode;
   f007 = customer.fname;
   f008 = customer.lname;
4➤ f009 = customer.phone, PICTURE = "###-###-#### XXXXX";
```

The GLOBALS Statement and MAIN Function

1➤ The program uses the gr_customer global record to access customer information. In many applications, multiple functions need to access data retrieved from a table. A global record corresponding to the table row is one way to make this data available to many functions.

2➤ The program places prompts and messages on different lines so the two types of displays won't be confused and so that both can appear at the same time. They occupy lines 14 and 15, which places them immediately under the f_customer form.

3➤ The DEFER INTERRUPT statement continues execution of the program after the user presses the Interrupt key (typically CONTROL-C) rather than terminating the program. Because the program takes this approach, the user can signal different intentions with the Interrupt and Accept keys.

Note that the Quit key (typically CONTROL-\) still exits the application in an emergency. You can trap this key as well with the DEFER QUIT statement.

The DEFER statement must appear in the MAIN function and applies to all subsequent statements executed in the course of a program.

4➤ The MAIN function opens and displays the f_customer form and then uses the DISPLAY AT statement to give the form an appropriate title.

The MAIN function then calls the query_cust1() function to perform the actual query. When the query_cust1() function finishes accessing the form, the MAIN function closes the form and clears the screen for the benefit of the environment that invoked the program.

4GL source file

```
   DATABASE stores2t

   GLOBALS
1➤   DEFINE        gr_customer RECORD LIKE customer.*
   END GLOBALS

   ########################################
   MAIN
   ########################################

2➤   OPTIONS
       PROMPT LINE 14,
       MESSAGE LINE 15

3➤   DEFER INTERRUPT

4➤   OPEN FORM f_customer FROM "f_customer"
     DISPLAY FORM f_customer
     DISPLAY "CUSTOMER QUERY-BY-EXAMPLE" AT 2, 25

     CALL query_cust1()

     CLOSE FORM f_customer
     CLEAR SCREEN
   END MAIN
```

The query_cust1() Function

5➤ Most of the query_cust1() function resides within a WHILE loop that lets the user query for and view customers any number of times. Note that this WHILE loop is an infinite loop because the controlling condition is the constant TRUE (it never evaluates to FALSE). The only way to exit this loop is with an EXIT WHILE statement (see Notes 9 and 20).

This type of infinite loop should only be used when the exit conditions are limited and the programming required to set a control flag to FALSE is extensive. If this example used a control variable, both the IF statement in Note 9 and the IF in Note 20 would need ELSE clauses setting the control variable to FALSE and preventing the remaining code from being executed.

6➤ The first act of the loop is to display appropriate instructions to the user for entering query criteria.

7➤ The LET statement sets the built-in int_flag variable to FALSE immediately before the CONSTRUCT so that it can be tested when the CONSTRUCT exits. See the section titled "Handling User Interrupts" in the overview of this example for more information about the int_flag variable.

8➤ The CONSTRUCT statement activates the most recently displayed form (the f_customer form) so the user can enter selection criteria. The q_cust variable is a large variable which receives the character representation of the criteria.

The CONSTRUCT statement must know which database column corresponds to each form field to generate a logical statement for the value entered in the field. The ON clause specifies the database columns. The BY NAME clause is a shortcut that maps a form field to a database column based on the name of the screen variable associated with the field. If the names of the screen variables and database columns differ, you must specify the mapping explicitly using the FROM clause instead of the BY NAME clause.

The size of the constructed query value depends on the number of fields filled in, the size of the values, and the complexity of the criteria. Filling in every field of the f_customer form with its maximum value would supply 140 characters. Because the 10 values must be linked with AND operators, a valid query requires another 45 characters for a total of 185 characters. The user could increase this total by using logical operators in the fields. Unless the user fills out an extraordinarily detailed query, the 200-character defined storage of the q_cust variable will be adequate.

```
########################################
FUNCTION query_cust1()
########################################
  DEFINE        q_cust          CHAR(200),
                selstmt         CHAR(250),
                answer          CHAR(1),
                found_some      SMALLINT,
                invalid_resp    SMALLINT

5➤  WHILE TRUE

6➤    DISPLAY
     " Press Accept to search for customer data, Cancel to exit w/out searching."
       AT 15,1 ATTRIBUTE (REVERSE, YELLOW)

7➤    LET int_flag = FALSE
8➤    CONSTRUCT BY NAME q_cust ON customer.customer_num,
                                customer.company,
                                customer.address1,
                                customer.address2,
                                customer.city,
                                customer.state,
                                customer.zipcode,
                                customer.fname,
                                customer.lname,
                                customer.phone
```

9➤ The test for the int_flag variable checks whether the user pressed the Interrupt key to exit the query by example. If so, the EXIT WHILE statement terminates the loop and executes the first statement after the END WHILE statement. The remainder of the query_cust1() function cleans up before returning.

The LET statement resets the int_flag variable to FALSE. This approach is an alternative to setting int_flag to FALSE before a user interaction statement. This program shows both approaches, but the latter is safer since this approach doesn't depend on good coding practices elsewhere in the program.

10➤ The DISPLAY AT statement removes the direction for entering criteria.

11➤ The test for the q_cust variable determines whether the user has entered any criteria. When the user ends the CONSTRUCT statement without entering criteria, all records are qualified by the query, which might take a long time for a large table. The program gives the user the opportunity to reconsider and enter more specific selection criteria.

When the user enters no criteria, CONSTRUCT must generate a logical statement that is valid as a WHERE clause and yet true for all rows. It produces the string " 1 =1" (with a leading space), which the program tests for here.

The answer_yes() function displays its argument in a prompt and returns a true value if the user enters `y` or a false value if the user enters `n`. Because answer_yes() returns only a single true or false value, the call can be used as the Boolean expression evaluated by the inner IF statement. If the user chooses not to select all rows, the CONTINUE WHILE statement restarts the loop and thus enters the CONSTRUCT statement again.

12➤ The assignment to the selstmt variable includes a character constant that states the basic structure of a SELECT statement that retrieves all columns from the customer table. The comma operator concatenates the user's selection criteria to complete the WHERE clause.

The CLIPPED operator removes trailing spaces from the value of the q_cust variable. When you name a character variable, you always get its full defined length, including trailing spaces. Thus, if the user's selection criteria occupy 150 positions in q_cust, the evaluation includes 50 extra spaces at the end. The CLIPPED function removes any trailing spaces.

13➤ The PREPARE statement converts the character value into an executable SQL statement. The st_selcust identifier stands for the prepared SELECT statement. You can execute the SQL statement in any function within the module that is called after you prepare the statement.

```
9➤        IF int_flag THEN
            LET int_flag = FALSE
            EXIT WHILE
          END IF

      --* User hasn't pressed Cancel, clear out selection instructions
10➤       DISPLAY
         "                                                                              "
            AT 15, 1

      --* Check to see if user has entered search criteria
11➤       IF q_cust = " 1=1" THEN
            IF NOT answer_yes("Do you really want to see all customers? (n/y):")
            THEN
              CONTINUE WHILE
            END IF
          END IF

      --* Create and prepare the SELECT statement
12➤       LET selstmt = "SELECT * FROM customer WHERE ", q_cust CLIPPED
13➤       PREPARE st_selcust FROM selstmt
14➤       DECLARE c_cust CURSOR FOR st_selcust
```

14➤ The cust_query1() function immediately declares the c_cust cursor for the set of rows that the prepared SELECT statement will qualify.

15➤ **4GL** opens the c_cust cursor and executes the prepared SELECT statement. At the time the cursor is opened, **4GL** doesn't know whether the query will yield no rows, one row, or many rows. In part, this is because the set of rows qualified by the query can change even after the cursor is opened.

16➤ The found_some variable is a flag defined by the program to indicate whether the program has a row to display to the user. The assignment assumes that the query has qualified no rows.

The FETCH statement then tests this assumption by trying to retrieve a row into the gr_customer global record. After the FETCH statement, the status variable reflects the success or failure of the statement. For FETCH, status has a value as follows:

- A negative number if an error occurred. Because the program hasn't executed the WHENEVER ERROR CONTINUE statement, an error here will terminate the program.
- The value of the NOTFOUND built-in constant if no qualified rows existed.
- Zero if a row was retrieved. In this case, the gr_customer record contains a row to display, and found_some is set to TRUE.

Besides retrieving the first database row, the FETCH statement also advances the database cursor so that it points to the next database row or, if no following row exists, to the end of the set of selected rows.

17➤ The inner WHILE loop first displays the row that was previously fetched into the gr_customer record and then attempts to fetch another row. After the loop displays the last qualified row, the next fetch fails and the inner loop terminates.

Note that this loop is different from the outer loop, which repeatedly lets the user enter query criteria and see the qualified customer rows.

18➤ The DISPLAY BY NAME statement displays the values of the member variables of the gr_customer record in the corresponding fields of the f_customer form. This statement performs the same action as the DISPLAY TO statement but provides a shortcut by mapping the program variables to the form screen variables using their names.

19➤ The FETCH NEXT statement retrieves the next qualified row and advances the database cursor.

```
     --* Execute the SELECT statement and open the cursor to access the rows
15➤      OPEN c_cust

     --* Fetch first row. If fetch successful, rows found
16➤      LET found_some = 0
         FETCH c_cust INTO gr_customer.*

         IF (status = 0) THEN
           LET found_some = 1
         END IF

17➤      WHILE (found_some = 1)
     --* Display first customer
18➤        DISPLAY BY NAME gr_customer.*

     --* Fetch next customer (fetch ahead)
19➤        FETCH NEXT c_cust INTO gr_customer.*
```

20➤ If the FETCH statement finds no more qualified rows, the status variable has the same value as the built-in NOTFOUND constant. In this case, the test terminates the inner WHILE loop as there are no more rows to display.

21➤ The call to the answer_yes() function answers two needs. First, the query_cust1() function suspends execution during the prompt so the user can view the customer row for as long as the user desires.

Second, the user can skip the remaining qualified rows. The IF statement tests the value returned by answer_yes() and sets the controlling variable for the loop, found_some, to a value that terminates the loop.

22➤ After the inner viewing loop terminates, the CASE statement examines the found_some variable to determine the reason for termination. Each case calls the msg() function to report the cause to the user.

See Note 20 for the assignment of the -1 value, Note 16 for the 0 value, and Note 21 for the -2 value. The actual flag values are arbitrary: for example, query_cust1() could have used 1 instead of -1 to indicate that no more rows existed.

23➤ After finishing working with the rows, the query_cust1() function closes the cursor associated with the query. The next cycle of the outer query loop prompts the user for new selection criteria and opens a new cursor for the new query.

24➤ The outer query loop terminates when the user chooses to stop querying for customers. The query_cust1() function cleans up by removing the query instructions with a DISPLAY AT statement and clearing the values from the form.

```
20➤      IF (status = NOTFOUND) THEN
           LET found_some = -1
           EXIT WHILE
         END IF

    --* Ask user if going to view next row
21➤      IF NOT answer_yes("Display next customer? (n/y):") THEN
           LET found_some = -2
         END IF
       END WHILE
    --* Notify user of various "error" conditions
22➤    CASE found_some
         WHEN -1
           CALL msg("End of selected customers.")
         WHEN 0
           CALL msg("No customers match search criteria.")
         WHEN -2
           CALL msg("Display terminated at your request.")
       END CASE

23➤    CLOSE c_cust
     END WHILE

24➤  DISPLAY
       "
       AT 15,1
     CLEAR FORM

    END FUNCTION  -- query_cust1 --

    ########################################
    FUNCTION answer_yes(question)
    ########################################
      DEFINE  question         CHAR(50),

              invalid_resp     SMALLINT,
              answer           CHAR(1),
              ans_yes          SMALLINT
```

The answer_yes() Function

25➤ The answer_yes() function uses a WHILE loop to prompt until the user responds affirmatively or negatively. The invalid_resp variable controls repetition of the loop.

26➤ The PROMPT statement displays the parameter from the call to answer_yes() as the text of the prompt. By applying the CLIPPED character operator to the value of the parameter, the statement positions the cursor immediately after the last character other than a SPACE or TAB. Otherwise, **4GL** would supply a space for each unused position in the question parameter, forcing the cursor out to the end of the line.

27➤ The first IF statement uses the MATCHES logical operator to compare the user's entry with the valid response characters. The assignment to the invalid_resp controlling variable guarantees that the loop terminates before completing another cycle.

The ans_yes variable stores the return value for the answer_yes() function. The first assignment to the ans_yes variable assumes that the answer is affirmative. The inner IF statement corrects this assumption if the user enters `N` or `n`.

The msg() Function

28➤ The msg() function displays a brief informative message, which the program passes to msg() as a parameter. The first MESSAGE statement displays the text. After three seconds, the second MESSAGE statement clears the text.

By using the msg() function instead of the three statements, you provide somewhat more compact code. More importantly, you make it possible to change the message displaying behavior in the future by modifying the msg() function rather than every location in which the program displays a message.

```
25➤   LET invalid_resp = TRUE
      WHILE invalid_resp
26➤     PROMPT question CLIPPED FOR answer
27➤     IF answer MATCHES "[NnYy]" THEN
          LET invalid_resp = FALSE
          LET ans_yes = TRUE
          IF answer MATCHES "[Nn]" THEN
            LET ans_yes = FALSE
          END IF
        END IF
      END WHILE

      RETURN ans_yes

    END FUNCTION  -- answer_yes --

    ########################################
    FUNCTION msg(str)
    ########################################
      DEFINE  str     CHAR(78)

28➤   MESSAGE str
      SLEEP 3
      MESSAGE ""

    END FUNCTION  -- msg --
```

To locate any function definition see the Function Index on page 728.

6

Querying and Updating

Example 6 lets the user modify or delete rows qualified through a query by example. Over time the data stored in the database may need to be updated or deleted. You can present the information on a form to make it easier for the user to perform these data maintenance tasks. The user can then search for a set of rows that may require modification and the program can present one row at a time to the user for modification.

Example 6 uses one form to collect the query criteria, to display a row, and to collect changes to the values of the columns in the row.

```
CUSTOMER MODIFICATION:  Next  Update  Delete  Exit
View next selected customer.
---------------------------------------Press CTRL-W for Help----------


  Customer Number: [        104] Company Name: [Play Ball!          ]
   Address: [East Shopping Cntr. ]
            [422 Bay Road        ]
      City: [Redwood City   ]   State: [CA]  Zip Code: [94026         ]

   Contact Name: [Anthony        ][Higgins        ]
      Telephone: [415-368-1100      ]
```

Example 6 introduces the following **4GL** programming techniques:

- Using a single form for multiple interactions.
- Using a menu with a form to manage the user's interaction with a table.
- Preserving referential integrity in the database.
- Updating and deleting database rows.

Modifying the Rows Qualified by a Query

Like Example 5, this example uses a form to collect selection criteria from the user, prepares a query from the user's criteria, and (using a database cursor to keep track of the current row) displays each row qualified by the query.

Example 6 goes beyond Example 5 in that the user isn't restricted to passively viewing the retrieved row. After displaying the row, this example activates a menu.

The user can choose menu options to update the displayed row using the form, or to delete the displayed row. When finished with the row, the user can display the next row or stop browsing through the qualified rows.

Checking for Dependent Rows

Before deleting a customer, Example 6 checks the orders and cust_calls tables and refuses to delete any customer who has an order or call. This check ensures referential integrity: each reference to a customer in the orders and cust_calls tables must have a corresponding customer row. You must maintain referential integrity in your database to prevent meaningless data.

When the user deletes a customer, Example 6 displays the row for the previous customer as a mechanism of showing the actual sequence of rows. That is, the user sees the previous row and then the following row without the intervening deleted row.

Function Overview

Function Name	Purpose
query_cust2()	Lets the user create a query by example.
browse_custs()	Retrieves each row qualified by the query.
next_action()	Operates a menu to let the user perform actions on the current row.
change_cust()	Collects changes to current row.
update_cust()	Updates the database row to reflect the changes.
delete_cust()	Deletes the current row if it doesn't have dependent rows in other tables.
verify_delete()	Checks for dependent rows in other tables.
clear_lines()	Clears any number of lines starting at any line.

message_window()	Opens a window and displays the contents of the ga_dsplymsg global array. *See description in Example 2.*
init_msgs()	Initializes the members of the ga_dsplymsg array to null. *See description in Example 2.*
prompt_window()	Displays a message and prompts the user for affirmation or negation. This function is a variation on the message_window() function that appears in Example 2. *See description in Example 4.*
msg()	Displays a brief, informative message. *See description in Example 5.*msg()

To locate any function definition see the Function Index on page 728.

The GLOBALS Statement and MAIN Function

1➤ The GLOBALS statement defines two global records. The program stores the current customer row in the gr_customer record and the previous customer row in the gr_workcust record.

2➤ The OPTIONS statement specifies the help file (not shown) that is used by this example and positions various screen entities at appropriate locations.

3➤ The DEFER INTERRUPT statement lets the program trap the Interrupt key, thus giving the user a graceful mechanism for aborting an action and, if necessary, terminating the program under program control.

4➤ The OPEN FORM statement opens the f_customer form and the DISPLAY FORM statement makes the form visible to the user. Because the program doesn't open any other forms, it can display the f_customer form once at the start of the MAIN function.

5➤ The query_cust2() function manages construction of a query by example. The query_cust2() function returns the query in the form of a character value, which is saved in the st_cust local variable. If the query_cust2() function doesn't succeed in constructing a query, it returns null.

6➤ If the st_cust variable stores a query, the MAIN function calls the browse_custs() function to present each qualified row to the user.

7➤ After the user finishes working with the qualified rows, the MAIN function closes the f_customer form, clears the screen to avoid confusion in other applications, and terminates.

You could integrate the browsing mechanism demonstrated in Example 6 into a larger application. For example, you could execute the query_cust2() and browse_custs() function calls within a WHILE loop to let the user browse through the results of several queries. Or, you could create a menu option on one of the menus in your program that executes all of the statements between the OPEN FORM statement and the CLOSE FORM statement.

The query_cust2() Function

8➤ The clear_lines() function clears any existing text on line four to avoid confusion with any previous displays on this line.

9➤ This DISPLAY AT statement provides a title for the f_customer form to indicate that the form is being activated for query by example.

10➤ These DISPLAY AT statements provides a caption for the form with detailed instructions.

4GL source file

```
   DATABASE stores2t

1  GLOBALS
     DEFINE      gr_customer    RECORD LIKE customer.*,
                 gr_workcust    RECORD LIKE customer.*
```

See Example 2.

```
   END GLOBALS

   ########################################
   MAIN
   ########################################
     DEFINE  st_cust         CHAR(150)

2    OPTIONS
       HELP FILE "hlpmsgs",
       FORM LINE 5,
       COMMENT LINE 5,
       MESSAGE LINE 19

3    DEFER INTERRUPT

4    OPEN FORM f_customer FROM "f_customer"
     DISPLAY FORM f_customer

5    CALL query_cust2() RETURNING st_cust

6    IF st_cust IS NOT NULL THEN
       CALL browse_custs(st_cust)
     END IF

7    CLOSE FORM f_customer
     CLEAR SCREEN
   END MAIN

   ########################################
   FUNCTION query_cust2()
   ########################################
     DEFINE        q_cust          CHAR(100),
                   selstmt         CHAR(150)

8    CALL clear_lines(1,4)
9    DISPLAY "CUSTOMER QUERY-BY-EXAMPLE 2" AT 4, 24
     CALL clear_lines(2,16)
10   DISPLAY " Enter search criteria and press Accept. Press CTRL-W for Help."
          AT 16,1 ATTRIBUTE (REVERSE, YELLOW)
     DISPLAY " Press Cancel to exit w/out searching."
         AT 17,1 ATTRIBUTE (REVERSE, YELLOW)
```

11➤ The LET statement initializes the built-in int_flag variable to FALSE. It is TRUE after the CONSTRUCT statement only if the user presses the Interrupt key.

12➤ The CONSTRUCT statement activates the f_customer form so that the user can create a query by example. The BY NAME clause maps the fields of the form to the listed database columns using the names of the screen variables associated with each field. The CONSTRUCT statement assigns to the q_cust variable the character value stating the criteria. It also includes a HELP clause to specify the help message to display when the user presses CONTROL-W from any field on the form.

13➤ The AFTER CONSTRUCT clause of the CONSTRUCT statement, like the AFTER INPUT clause of the INPUT statement, executes when the user leaves the form by pressing either the Interrupt key or the Accept key. Here the AFTER CONSTRUCT clause checks for an empty query, which qualifies every row in the target table and thus might take more time and return more rows than the user intended.

14➤ The IF statement testing the int_flag variable makes sure the user has terminated construction by pressing the Accept key. If the user presses the Interrupt key, the query validation code block is skipped.

15➤ The FIELD_TOUCHED() built-in function is called with arguments of all of the screen variables on the f_customer form. If the user didn't enter a value in any of the screen variables, the FIELD_TOUCHED() function returns FALSE, and the code block displays a prompt window to let the user indicate whether to continue or revise the query. The CONTINUE CONSTRUCT statement terminates the AFTER CONSTRUCT code block and reactivates the form in the CONSTRUCT statement.

16➤ If the user did press the Interrupt key, the int_flag variable is TRUE and the msg() function confirms the interruption for the user. Finally, the assignment to the selstmt variable sets the return value to prevent execution of the browse_custs() function.

17➤ If the user pressed the Accept key, this assignment appends the user's criteria to the static portion of the SELECT statement.

18➤ The query_cust2() function concludes by clearing the title and instruction spaces and returning the constructed SELECT statement.

19➤ The function returns the character string with the WHERE clause conditions for the user's search criteria. This return string is limited to 150 characters in size. If user queries become extremely complex, you may need to increase the size of the selstmt variable. However, keep in mind that you are limited to returning a maximum of 512 characters

```
11➤   LET int_flag = FALSE
12➤   CONSTRUCT BY NAME q_cust ON customer.customer_num, customer.company,
                                customer.address1, customer.address2,
                                customer.city, customer.state,
                                customer.zipcode, customer.fname,
                                customer.lname, customer.phone
        HELP 30

13➤     AFTER CONSTRUCT
14➤       IF (NOT int_flag) THEN
15➤         IF (NOT FIELD_TOUCHED(customer.*)) THEN
              LET ga_dsplymsg[1] = "You did not enter any search criteria."
              IF NOT prompt_window("Do you really want to see all rows?", 9, 15)
              THEN
                CONTINUE CONSTRUCT
              END IF
            END IF
          END IF
      END CONSTRUCT

16➤   IF int_flag THEN
        LET int_flag = FALSE
        CALL clear_lines(2,16)
        CALL msg("Customer query terminated.")
        LET selstmt = NULL
17➤   ELSE
        LET selstmt = "SELECT * FROM customer WHERE ", q_cust CLIPPED
      END IF
18➤   CALL clear_lines(1,4)
      CALL clear_lines(2,16)

19➤   RETURN (selstmt)

    END FUNCTION  -- query_cust2 --
```

The browse_custs Function

20➤ The MAIN function passes the SELECT statement created by query_cust2() as the selstmt parameter of the browse_custs() function. The PREPARE statement prepares an executable SQL statement from this character value.

The DECLARE statement associates a database cursor with the prepared statement because the statement may qualify more than one row.

21➤ The LET statements initializes two flag variables that are used to determine what to report to the user. The fnd_custs variable identifies whether or not the query has qualified any rows. The end_list variable identifies whether or not the user has reached the end of the list of qualified rows. The initial assignments assume that no rows were found and that the last row has not been displayed.

The gr_workcust global record stores the record previous to the currently displayed record. The INITIALIZE statement sets the members of this variable to a null value because the first record displayed won't have a previous record.

22➤ The FOREACH statement executes the user's query and opens the c_cust database cursor for the qualified rows. FOREACH then loops by fetching a qualified row into the gr_customer global record and executing the code block between the FOREACH and the END FOREACH statements. When the loop terminates in any way, FOREACH closes the database cursor.

Within the code block, the fnd_custs flag is set to TRUE. (If the query doesn't find any rows, the code block never executes and thus the fnd_custs flag retains the initial value of FALSE.)

The DISPLAY BY NAME statement displays the row that was fetched into the gr_customer record on the f_customer form. The BY NAME clause maps the members of gr_customer to the screen variables of the form having the same names.

23➤ The browse_custs() function delegates to the next_action() function the management of the user's interaction with the displayed row. It returns FALSE when the user wants to skip the remaining rows.

24➤ The next_action() function returns a true value when the user wants to view the next row. In this case, the ELSE clause sets the end_list flag to a true value because, if no following row is found, the last row would have been reached. The assignment to the gr_workcust row saves the last row displayed before the FOREACH statement assigns a new row to gr_customer.

```
########################################
FUNCTION browse_custs(selstmt)
########################################
  DEFINE  selstmt          CHAR(150),

          fnd_custs        SMALLINT,
          end_list         SMALLINT

20➤  PREPARE st_selcust FROM selstmt

  DECLARE c_cust CURSOR FOR st_selcust

21➤  LET fnd_custs = FALSE
  LET end_list = FALSE
  INITIALIZE gr_workcust.* TO NULL

22➤  FOREACH c_cust INTO gr_customer.*
    LET fnd_custs = TRUE
    DISPLAY BY NAME gr_customer.*

23➤    IF NOT next_action() THEN

      LET end_list = FALSE
      EXIT FOREACH
24➤    ELSE

      LET end_list = TRUE
    END IF
    LET gr_workcust.* = gr_customer.*
  END FOREACH
```

25➤ After the FOREACH loop finishes, the browse_custs() function displays messages to confirm the cause of the termination:

- If FOREACH didn't find any rows, the loop never executed and the fnd_custs flag remains FALSE. The msg() function reports the failure of the query criteria.
- If FOREACH exited because the last qualified row was displayed, the end_list flag is TRUE. The msg() function reports this condition.

The browse_custs() function doesn't display a message if the user chose to skip the remaining rows.

The next_action() Function

26➤ The nxt_action variable stores the return status, which controls whether or not the browse_custs() function exits or continues the FOREACH loop. The LET statement sets nxt_action to the true value because the default action is to continue the loop.

27➤ The DISPLAY statement notifies the user that help is available for the current menu. It displays this information at the third line of the form so it appears under the active menu.

28➤ The next_action() function opens a menu of user options for responding to the current displayed row. The Next and Exit options both terminate the menu. The code block for the Next option leaves the nxt_action variable with its default value, signaling continuation of the FOREACH loop.

29➤ The code block for the Update option calls the change_cust() function to manage input of the changes. If the change_cust() function returns a true value, the user entered the changes successfully. The IF statement then calls the update_cust() function to apply the changes to the database row.

30➤ The NEXT OPTION statement positions the user on the Next option when the menu reactivates to make this option the default for the user's next action. Otherwise, the Update option would remain the current position.

31➤ The code block for the Delete option calls the delete_cust() function to manage deletion of the current displayed row.

```
25➤    CALL clear_lines(2,16)

       IF NOT fnd_custs THEN
         CALL msg("No customers match search criteria.")
       END IF

       IF end_list THEN
         CALL msg("No more customer rows.")
       END IF

       CLEAR FORM

     END FUNCTION  -- browse_custs --

     ########################################
     FUNCTION next_action()
     ########################################
       DEFINE nxt_action     SMALLINT

       CALL clear_lines(1,16)

26➤    LET nxt_action = TRUE

27➤    DISPLAY
     "---------------------------------------Press CTRL-W for Help----------"
         AT 3, 1
28➤    MENU "CUSTOMER MODIFICATION"
         COMMAND "Next" "View next selected customer." HELP 20
           EXIT MENU

29➤      COMMAND "Update" "Update current customer on screen." HELP 21
           IF change_cust() THEN
             CALL update_cust()
             CALL clear_lines(1,16)
           END IF
30➤        NEXT OPTION "Next"

31➤      COMMAND "Delete" "Delete current customer on screen." HELP 22
           CALL delete_cust()
```

32➤ After the deletion, the IF statement checks if the gr_workcust global record contains values. The test checks the customer_num member variable as this column should have a value in any row. If gr_workcust is not empty, more than one row has been selected and the program tries to display the previously selected row. The gr_workcust record contains the previous displayed row (unless the deleted row was the first selected row). The LET statement assigns the contents of gr_workcust to gr_customer and the DISPLAY BY NAME statement displays the gr_customer.

33➤ If the gr_workcust record is empty, only one row was selected. In this case, the program clears the gr_customer record and sets the nxt_action flag to FALSE. By setting nxt_action to FALSE, the function tells the calling program that there are no more rows to display.

34➤ Before terminating the menu, the code block for the Exit option sets the nxt_action variable to FALSE and thus signals the browse_custs() function to terminate the FOREACH loop.

35➤ The RETURN statement returns the value of the nxt_action variable so the browse_custs() function can act on the user's decision.

The change_cust() Function

36➤ The change_cust() function manages updating of a customer row. The function starts by executing the DISPLAY AT statements to give the user appropriate instructions.

37➤ The INPUT statement activates the f_customer form so the user can modify the values in the fields. The WITHOUT DEFAULTS clause leaves the current values (those displayed by browse_cust()) in the fields rather than filling the form with default values. The HELP clause specifies the help message to display when the user presses CONTROL-W from any field on the form.

38➤ The AFTER FIELD clause makes sure that the company field has a value in the row. Before the user leaves the field, **4GL** assigns the value of the field to the corresponding program variable, which in this case is the company member of the gr_customer record. The IF statement tests the program variable rather than directly testing the field. If the value is null, the ERROR statement notifies the user of the problem and the NEXT FIELD statement positions the user back in the company field rather than letting the user move to a new field.

39➤ When the user presses the Interrupt key, FALSE is returned to signal the next_action() function not to apply the changes. Otherwise, TRUE is returned to affirm the changes.

```
32➤     IF gr_workcust.customer_num IS NOT NULL THEN
          LET gr_customer.* = gr_workcust.*
          DISPLAY BY NAME gr_customer.*
33➤     ELSE
          INITIALIZE gr_customer.* TO NULL
          LET nxt_action = FALSE
          EXIT MENU
        END IF
        NEXT OPTION "Next"

34➤   COMMAND "Exit" "Exit the program." HELP 100
        LET nxt_action = FALSE
        EXIT MENU
    END MENU

35➤ RETURN nxt_action

  END FUNCTION  -- next_action --

  ########################################
  FUNCTION change_cust()
  ########################################

36➤ CALL clear_lines(2,16)
    DISPLAY " Press Accept to save new customer data. Press CTRL-W for Help."
      AT 16, 1 ATTRIBUTE (REVERSE, YELLOW)
    DISPLAY " Press Cancel to exit w/out saving."
      AT 17, 1 ATTRIBUTE (REVERSE, YELLOW)

37➤ INPUT BY NAME gr_customer.company, gr_customer.address1,
                  gr_customer.address2, gr_customer.city,
                  gr_customer.state, gr_customer.zipcode,
                  gr_customer.fname, gr_customer.lname, gr_customer.phone
    WITHOUT DEFAULTS HELP 40

38➤   AFTER FIELD company
        IF gr_customer.company IS NULL THEN
          ERROR "You must enter a company name. Please try again."
          NEXT FIELD company
        END IF
    END INPUT

39➤ IF int_flag THEN
      LET int_flag = FALSE
      CALL clear_lines(2,16)
      RETURN (FALSE)
    END IF

    RETURN (TRUE)

  END FUNCTION  -- change_cust --
```

The update_cust() Function

40➤ The WHENEVER ERROR CONTINUE statement prevents termination of the program if the database engine isn't able to execute the UPDATE statement.

The UPDATE statement sets the values of all columns in the row to the values of the corresponding program variables. The WHERE clause restricts the update to the row that has the same value in the key column. If you don't test the key column in the WHERE clause, the update may apply to multiple rows.

The WHENEVER ERROR STOP statement resumes termination on errors.

41➤ The IF statement tests the value of the built-in status variable. While the WHENEVER CONTINUE statement is in effect, **4GL** sets the status variable to reflect errors after every SQL statement and **4GL** screen statement. Thus, the status variable is negative if the UPDATE statement failed for some reason. The ERROR statement notifies the user of the problem.

Changes in the database schema since compilation and other circumstances can cause SQL statements to fail. For safety, it's a very good idea to adopt the approach demonstrated here as a general rule (see "Recovering from Run-time Errors" on page 72).

42➤ When the update succeeds, the msg() function notifies the user.

The delete_cust() Function

43➤ The program asks the user to confirm that the row is to be discarded. Since a simple slip of the finger could select this menu choice accidentally, an explicit confirmation is essential.

44➤ The verify_delete() function tests whether the current customer row doesn't have dependent rows in other tables.

45➤ As with the UPDATE statement, WHENEVER statements bracket the DELETE statement to prevent termination if there is an SQL error. The WHERE clause matches the row with the same value in the key column. Since SERIAL values are guaranteed to be unique, this WHERE clause matches only one customer row.

46➤ If the DELETE statement generates an error, the status variable contains a negative error number, and the number is reported to the user.

47➤ If the DELETE statement succeeds, the msg() function notifies the user, and the form is cleared, so it no longer displays the nonexistent row.

```
    ########################################
    FUNCTION update_cust()
    ########################################

40➤ WHENEVER ERROR CONTINUE
      UPDATE customer SET customer.* = gr_customer.*
      WHERE customer_num = gr_customer.customer_num
    WHENEVER ERROR STOP

41➤   IF (status < 0) THEN
        ERROR status USING "-<<<<<<<<<<<",
            ": Unable to complete customer update."
        RETURN
      END IF

42➤   CALL msg("Customer has been updated.")

    END FUNCTION  -- update_cust --

    ########################################
    FUNCTION delete_cust()
    ########################################

43➤   IF (prompt_window("Are you sure you want to delete this?", 10, 15)) THEN

44➤     IF verify_delete() THEN

45➤ WHENEVER ERROR CONTINUE
          DELETE FROM customer
          WHERE customer_num = gr_customer.customer_num
    WHENEVER ERROR STOP

46➤       IF (status < 0) THEN
            ERROR status USING "-<<<<<<<<<<<",
              ": Unable to complete customer delete."
47➤       ELSE
            CALL msg("Customer has been deleted.")
            CLEAR FORM
          END IF
```

48➤ When the verify_delete() function finds dependent rows, the message_window() function is used to report the problem.

The verify_delete() Function

49➤ The verify_delete() function first checks for dependent rows in the orders table by selecting all orders that have this customer number as a foreign key. The SQL COUNT(*) aggregate function totals the number of orders, and the INTO clause places the total in the cust_cnt variable.

The SELECT identifies the current customer by checking the value of customer_num in the gr_customer record. Because gr_customer is global, any function within the application can access its members. To remove this dependence on a global variable, you could write the verify_delete() function so that it accepts the customer_num value as a parameter:

```
FUNCTION verify_delete(cust_num)
  DEFINE  cust_num      LIKE customer.customer_num,
          cust_cnt      INTEGER
    ..
  SELECT COUNT(*)
  INTO cust_cnt
  FROM order
  WHERE customer_num = cust_num
    ..
```

The call to this version of the verify_delete() function (see Note 44) would be:

```
IF verify_delete(gr_customer.customer_num) THEN
```

50➤ The function ends, returning FALSE if the SELECT statement found any orders to count. The delete_cust() function uses the return value to determine whether or not to delete the customer row.

51➤ The same validating action is applied to check for dependent rows in the cust_calls table.

52➤ If neither SELECT statement finds dependent rows, the function returns TRUE to authorize the deletion of the customer.

```
48➤     ELSE
          LET ga_dsplymsg[1] = "Customer ",
                    gr_customer.customer_num USING "<<<<<<<<<<<",
                    " has placed orders and cannot be"
          LET ga_dsplymsg[2] = "                  deleted."
          CALL message_window(7, 8)
        END IF
      END IF

    END FUNCTION  -- delete_cust --

    ########################################
    FUNCTION verify_delete()
    ########################################
      DEFINE  cust_cnt        INTEGER

      LET cust_cnt = 0

49➤   SELECT COUNT(*)
      INTO cust_cnt
      FROM orders
      WHERE customer_num = gr_customer.customer_num

50➤   IF (cust_cnt IS NOT NULL) AND (cust_cnt > 0) THEN
        RETURN (FALSE)
      END IF

      LET cust_cnt = 0
51➤   SELECT COUNT(*)
      INTO cust_cnt
      FROM cust_calls
      WHERE customer_num = gr_customer.customer_num

      IF (cust_cnt > 0) THEN
        RETURN (FALSE)
      END IF

52➤   RETURN (TRUE)

    END FUNCTION  -- verify_delete --
```

The clear_lines() Function

53➤ The clear_lines() function uses a FOR loop to clear a block of lines on the screen. On each loop, the DISPLAY AT statement clears the line and the LET statement increments the line number. Thus, when the loop has repeated the requested number of times, the requested block of lines have been cleared.

You can use this utility function in your programs without modification.

```
#########################################
FUNCTION clear_lines(numlines, mrow)
#########################################
  DEFINE  numlines         SMALLINT,
          mrow             SMALLINT,

          i                SMALLINT

53➤  FOR i = 1 TO numlines
    DISPLAY
      "
      AT mrow,1
    LET mrow = mrow + 1
  END FOR

END FUNCTION  -- clear_lines --
```

To locate any function definition see the Function Index on page 728.

7

Validating and Inserting a Row

This example adds a new row to the database, using a form to collect the new information from the user.

```
+-----------------------------------------------------------------------+
| Press Accept to save stock data, Cancel to exit w/out saving.         |
|                           ADD STOCK ITEM                              |
|                                                                       |
|  STOCK INFORMATION                                                    |
|    Stock Number: [        ]            Description: [               ]|
|    Manufacturer Code: [   ]            Name: [               ]        |
|                                                                       |
|  PRICING INFORMATION                                                  |
|    Unit: [     ]                       Unit Price: [          ]       |
|                                                                       |
|                                                                       |
+-----------------------------------------------------------------------+
```

This example introduces the following **4GL** programming techniques:

- Initializing and validating values using field actions.
- Confirming a foreign key by looking up descriptive information from the foreign table.

Validating Data Entry

A database is only as useful as the information it contains is valid. One of the principal tasks of programming a database application is to make sure that only valid data is put in the database.

This example uses the BEFORE FIELD and AFTER FIELD clauses of the INPUT statement to verify the columns of a new stock row as the user is creating the row. The user receives notification of a problem with the value of a field before creating the value for a new column. Validating each column as it is completed is less disruptive than notifying the user of several problems on completing the row.

Retrieving Information from Multiple Tables

The purpose of this example is to insert a row into the stock table of the demonstration database. The stock table contains the manu_code column, which is a foreign key for the manufact table. That is, the purpose of the manu_code column is to make it possible to join manufacturer information with stock information.

As with the manu_code column, keys are usually short codes or numbers. Users often find key values cryptic and difficult to recognize. For that reason, This example displays the manu_name corresponding to the manu_code in the hope that the user will recognize the manufacturer's name and notice the error if the user has entered the wrong manufacturer code.

Function Overview

Function Name	Purpose
input_stock()	Collects a new row from the user.
insert_stock()	Inserts the row into the database.
msg()	Displays a brief, informative message. *See description in Example 5.*
unique_stock()	Determines if combined stock number and manufacturer code is unique.

To locate any function definition see the Function Index on page 728.

The f_stock Form

1➤ This form uses the stock and manufact tables to define screen fields. These tables must exist in the database specified in the DATABASE section of the form file.

2➤ The UPSHIFT attribute ensures that lower case characters entered in the manufacturer code field will be shifted to upper case. To the database, the upper case code is different from the lower case code. This attribute prevents the user from entering both cases of the same code.

3➤ The NOENTRY attribute prevents the cursor from entering the manufacturer name field. The application code displays the name based on the manufacturer code specified by the user.

f_stock form file

```
DATABASE stores2t

SCREEN
{

 STOCK INFORMATION
   Stock Number: [f000  ]           Description: [f001            ]
   Manufacturer Code: [f02]         Name: [f003           ]

 PRICING INFORMATION
   Unit: [f004]                     Unit Price: [f005       ]

}

1➤ TABLES
stock
manufact

ATTRIBUTES
f000 = stock.stock_num;
f001 = stock.description;
2➤ f02 = manufact.manu_code, UPSHIFT;
3➤ f003 = manufact.manu_name, NOENTRY;
f004 = stock.unit, UPSHIFT;
f005 = stock.unit_price;
```

The GLOBALS Statement

1➤ The GLOBALS statement defines the gr_stock record containing a member variable corresponding to each field on the f_stock form. The definition uses the LIKE clause to assign a data type to the variable based on the data type of the stated column at the time of compilation.

The MAIN Function

2➤ The COMMENT clause of the OPTIONS statement sets the display line for descriptions of the form field during an INPUT statement.

The DEFER INTERRUPT statement instructs **4GL** to set the int_flag built-in variable rather than terminate when the user presses the Interrupt key. This uses the Interrupt key as a mechanism for communicating with the program.

3➤ The OPEN WINDOW statement opens the w_stock window, sizes the window to the dimensions of the f_stock form, and displays the form within the window.

This variation of the OPEN WINDOW statement is a shortcut for opening a window and opening the form with separate statements. Use it when this is the only time the form will be displayed in the program.

4➤ The MAIN function calls the input_stock() function to collect a new stock row from the user. If the user fails to create a valid stock row, input_stock() returns FALSE, and nothing further is done.

Otherwise, the insert_stock() function adds the new row to the database. The CLEAR FORM statement removes the row from the form, as it is no longer necessary.

In your own programs, you might turn the IF and END IF statements into WHILE and END WHILE statements to let the user create any number of rows. You might also want to use forms to perform all of the basic SQL operations on a table (see Example 9, which adds the insertion functionality demonstrated in this program to the other functions demonstrated in Example 6.)

5➤ The CLOSE WINDOW statement closes the form as well as the window.

4GL source file

```
   DATABASE stores2t

1➤ GLOBALS
     DEFINE        gr_stock         RECORD
                      stock_num     LIKE stock.stock_num,
                      description   LIKE stock.description,
                      manu_code     LIKE manufact.manu_code,
                      manu_name     LIKE manufact.manu_name,
                      unit          LIKE stock.unit,
                      unit_price    LIKE stock.unit_price
                   END RECORD
   END GLOBALS

   ########################################
   MAIN
   ########################################

2➤   OPTIONS
       COMMENT LINE 7,
       MESSAGE LINE LAST

     DEFER INTERRUPT

3➤   OPEN WINDOW w_stock AT 5, 3
      WITH FORM "f_stock"
      ATTRIBUTE (BORDER)

     DISPLAY "ADD STOCK ITEM" AT 2, 25

4➤   IF input_stock() THEN
       CALL insert_stock()
       CLEAR FORM
     END IF

5➤   CLOSE WINDOW w_stock
     CLEAR SCREEN

   END MAIN
```

The input_stock() Function

6➤ The DISPLAY AT statement displays instructions for filling in the form with a new row. Other functions using the form can display other instructions.

7➤ The INPUT statement activates the form for data entry. The BY NAME clause assigns the values of fields to program variables based on the correspondence between the name of a program variable and the screen variable associated with the field. Because the WITHOUT DEFAULTS clause does not appear, **4GL** fills the fields with default values from the syscolval table and the DEFAULT attribute from the field specification.

The remainder of the INPUT statement consists of BEFORE FIELD clauses to initialize fields and AFTER FIELD clauses to validate the value entered by the user. In part, this strategy works because the sequence of navigation through the fields is fixed. If Example 7 used the INPUT WRAP or FIELD ORDER UNCONSTRAINED settings of the OPTIONS statement, the sequence wouldn't be known.

8➤ The AFTER FIELD clause for the stock_num field tests to make sure the user has entered a stock number. If the user hasn't, the ERROR statement notifies the user of the problem and the NEXT FIELD statement repositions the user in the stock_num field instead of letting the user move to another field.

9➤ The AFTER FIELD clause for the manu_code field first tests to make sure that the user enters a manufacturer code.

10➤ If the user has entered a code, the SELECT statement for manu_name attempts to retrieve the name of the manufacturer that corresponds to the code. If the query fails to find a row, **4GL** sets the status variable to the value of the NOTFOUND built-in constant. The ERROR statement notifies the user that the code doesn't exist in the database. The invalid input is set to NULL for safety's sake.

11➤ If the query did find a manufacturer for the code, the DISPLAY BY NAME statement fills the manu_name field with the name of the manufacturer.

12➤ The unique_stock() function determines if the stock number and manufacturer code just entered define a unique stock item. This function returns TRUE if no stock item currently exists with this combination of stock number and manufacturer code. In this case, the program displays the manufacturer name on the form and moves the cursor to the next field.

If unique_stock() returns FALSE, the program clears out the fields and returns the cursor to the stock_num field so the user can redefine the stock item.

```
########################################
FUNCTION input_stock()
########################################

6➤  DISPLAY
     " Press Accept to save stock data, Cancel to exit w/out saving."
      AT 1, 1 ATTRIBUTE (REVERSE, YELLOW)

7➤  INPUT BY NAME gr_stock.stock_num, gr_stock.description,
                  gr_stock.manu_code, gr_stock.unit,
                  gr_stock.unit_price

8➤    AFTER FIELD stock_num
        IF gr_stock.stock_num IS NULL THEN
          ERROR "You must enter a stock number. Please try again."
          NEXT FIELD stock_num
        END IF

9➤    AFTER FIELD manu_code
        IF gr_stock.manu_code IS NULL THEN
          ERROR "You must enter a manufacturer code. Please try again."
          NEXT FIELD manu_code
        END IF

10➤     IF gr_stock.manu_name IS NULL THEN
          SELECT manu_name
          INTO gr_stock.manu_name
          FROM manufact
          WHERE manu_code = gr_stock.manu_code

          IF (status = NOTFOUND) THEN
            ERROR "Unknown manufacturer's code. Please try again."
            LET gr_stock.manu_code = NULL
            NEXT FIELD manu_code
          END IF
11➤       DISPLAY BY NAME gr_stock.manu_name

12➤       IF unique_stock() THEN
            DISPLAY BY NAME gr_stock.manu_code, gr_stock.manu_name
            NEXT FIELD unit
          ELSE
            DISPLAY BY NAME gr_stock.description, gr_stock.manu_code,
              gr_stock.manu_name
            NEXT FIELD stock_num
          END IF
        END IF
```

13➤ The BEFORE FIELD clause for the unit field displays instructions for filling in the field. By using a BEFORE FIELD clause, you can provide different instructions for the field in different contexts. To provide the same instruction in all contexts, you can use the COMMENTS clause in the field attributes section in the form specification file.

14➤ The AFTER FIELD clause for the unit field sets the gr_stock.unit program variable to a default value if the user hasn't supplied a value. The DISPLAY BY NAME statement displays the default value on the form so the user is aware of the assigned value.

The MESSAGE statement clears the instructions displayed by the BEFORE FIELD clause. As with the DISPLAY AT statement, if the character expression to be displayed contains a null value as the final value, the MESSAGE statement clears the line to the end of the current window or the screen.

15➤ The BEFORE FIELD clause for the unit_price field fills the field with 0.00 as the default price.

16➤ The AFTER FIELD clause for the unit_price field repositions the user in the field if the user didn't enter a value.

17➤ If the user pressed the Interrupt key to cancel insertion of the row, the msg() function confirms that the row wasn't inserted.

The RETURN statements return FALSE if the user interrupted the insertion action and TRUE otherwise.

The unique_stock() Function

18➤ The SELECT statement with the COUNT(*) function searches for an existing stock row with the same values in the stock_num and manu_code columns, as these provide a two-part key for the stock table. That is, type of stock must have a unique combination of stock number and manufacturer code.

19➤ If the query finds a row, the count stored by the stk_cnt variable is greater than zero. In this case, the ERROR statement notifies the user of the problem and the LET statements clear out the fields. The function returns FALSE to indicate that the stock number and manufacturer code are not unique.

```
13➤      BEFORE FIELD unit
           MESSAGE "Enter a unit or press RETURN for 'EACH'"

14➤      AFTER FIELD unit
           IF gr_stock.unit IS NULL THEN
             LET gr_stock.unit = "EACH"
             DISPLAY BY NAME gr_stock.unit
           END IF
           MESSAGE ""

15➤      BEFORE FIELD unit_price
           IF gr_stock.unit_price IS NULL THEN
             LET gr_stock.unit_price = 0.00
           END IF

16➤      AFTER FIELD unit_price
           IF gr_stock.unit_price IS NULL THEN
             ERROR "You must enter a unit price. Please try again."
             NEXT FIELD unit_price
           END IF

       END INPUT

17➤    IF int_flag THEN
         LET int_flag = FALSE
         CALL msg("Stock input terminated.")
         RETURN (FALSE)
       END IF
     RETURN (TRUE)

     END FUNCTION  -- input_stock --

     ########################################
     FUNCTION unique_stock()
     ########################################
       DEFINE  stk_cnt          SMALLINT

18➤    SELECT COUNT(*)
       INTO stk_cnt
       FROM stock
       WHERE stock_num = gr_stock.stock_num
         AND manu_code = gr_stock.manu_code

19➤    IF (stk_cnt > 0) THEN
         ERROR "A stock item with stock number ", gr_stock.stock_num,
                 " and manufacturer code ", gr_stock.manu_code, " exists."
         LET gr_stock.stock_num = NULL
         LET gr_stock.description = NULL
         LET gr_stock.manu_code = NULL
         LET gr_stock.manu_name = NULL
         RETURN (FALSE)
       END IF
```

20➤ If the stock number and manufacturer code are unique, the function returns TRUE.

The insert_stock() Function

21➤ The WHENEVER statements bracketing the INSERT statement prevent termination of the program for the duration of the INSERT statement (for a full discussion of this technique, see Example 4). As database schema changes or table locks can prevent execution of SQL statements, it's a good idea to use this recovery technique.

The INTO clause specifies the columns of the table. The VALUES clause generates the values by evaluating the global variables corresponding to these columns.

22➤ The ERROR statement reports a failed insertion. The call to the msg() function reports a successful insertion.

```
20➤  RETURN (TRUE)

END FUNCTION -- unique_stock --

########################################
FUNCTION insert_stock()
########################################

21➤ WHENEVER ERROR CONTINUE
    INSERT INTO stock (stock_num, description, manu_code, unit,
                       unit_price)
      VALUES (gr_stock.stock_num, gr_stock.description, gr_stock.manu_code,
              gr_stock.unit, gr_stock.unit_price)
WHENEVER ERROR STOP

22➤   IF status < 0 THEN
        ERROR status USING "-<<<<<<<<<<<",
          ": Unable to save stock item in database."
      ELSE
        CALL msg("Stock item added to database.")
      END IF

END FUNCTION  -- insert_stock --
```

To locate any function definition see the Function Index on page 728.

8

Displaying a Screen Array in a Pop-Up Window

This example demonstrates how to pop up a window containing an array form listing the valid values for a field. The user can select a value from the form and the program will display the selected value in the field. A pop-up array form is one way to display the existing values for a foreign key.

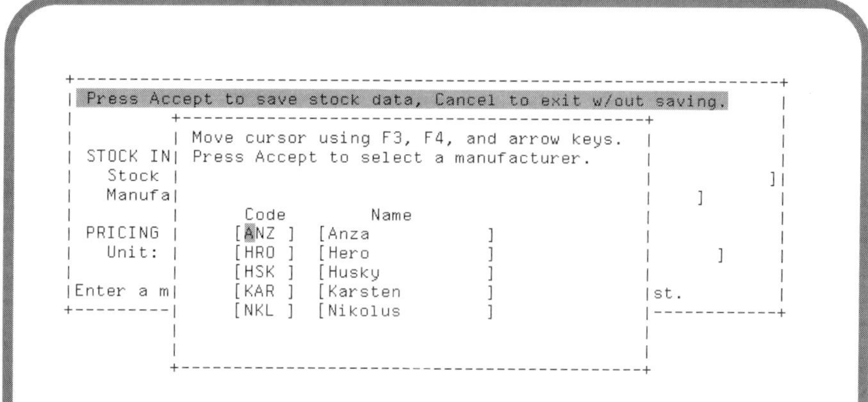

This example builds on Example 7, adding code to support a lookup on the Manufacturer Code field from the manufact table. The annotation section shows differences between the input_stock() function in Example 7 and the input_stock2() function in this example, and describes the manuf_popup() function, which has no correlate in Example 7. Both examples use the same MAIN and insert() functions, so they are omitted from the annotation.

This example introduces the following **4GL** programming techniques:

- Filling an array with rows from the database.
- Displaying an array using an array form.
- Using control or function keys to trigger actions on a form.

Displaying Information in an Array Form

An array form displays multiple rows to the user at one time. The advantage is that the user can view several rows without having to page through the rows individually. As a result, the user has a better sense of the contents of the table and can work with the data more conveniently and more efficiently.

The basic technique for implementing a lookup list using an array form is as follows:

1. Define a program array large enough to store the database rows.

   If you can't anticipate how many rows will be retrieved or if you can't reserve enough memory for all of the rows, you can execute Steps 3 through 5 in a WHILE loop.
2. Open and display the array form in a window.
3. Read the database rows into the program array.

   Although you typically populate an array from the database, you can also populate an array with explicit assignments. For example, you could use this technique to provide a pulldown menu using an array form.

   It's a good idea to read the rows from the database after opening the window so the user has something new to look at in the interim.
4. Call the built-in SET_COUNT() function to tell **4GL** how many rows are stored in the program array.
5. Execute the DISPLAY ARRAY statement to activate the array form for viewing the rows in the program array.
6. Call the built-in ARR_CURR() function to find out the row in the program array that corresponds to the current screen array row at the time the user exits the DISPLAY ARRAY statement.
7. Close the array form and window.
8. Access the values of the row pointed to by the array element.

You can also use an array form to insert, update, and delete the displayed rows (see Example 10).

Triggering Form Actions with Keys

In much the same way that you can provide an AFTER FIELD code block for a form field, you can associate a code block with a CONTROL or FUNCTION key using the ON KEY clause. When the user presses the key while inputting data or constructing a query on the form, the ON KEY clause executes.

The program uses an ON KEY clause in an INPUT statement to display the pop-up window containing the screen array. Unless the ON KEY clause includes an EXIT statement to terminate the user's session with the form, the form reactivates when the ON KEY code block finishes.

Function Overview

Function Name	Purpose
input_stock2()	Collects a new row from the user.
insert_stock()	Inserts the row into the database. *See description in Example 7.*
manuf_popup()	Reads all rows from the manufact table, displays the rows to the user in an array form, and returns the values of the row on which the user positioned before leaving the form.
msg()	Displays a brief, informative message. *See description in Example 5.*
unique_stock()	Determines if combined stock number and manufacturer code is unique. *See description in Example 7.*

To locate any function definition see the Function Index on page 728.

The f_manufsel Form

1➤ The specification for an array form differs from the specification for a single-record form in that the same field tag is applied to multiple fields in the SCREEN section.

The set of distinct field tags constitutes a record, and the duplicate sets of field tags are elements of the form's array. In the f_manufsel form, the f001 and f002 tags make up a single record, and there are five elements in the array.

2➤ The ATTRIBUTES section specifies the characteristics for each unique field tag. Thus, the f_manufsel form specifies the attributes for the f001 and f002 fields once. The fields have the same attributes in each element of the array.

3➤ In the INSTRUCTIONS section you must group the array and the screen variables that make up an element in the array as a SCREEN RECORD. The number 5 appears in brackets after the name of the array because the SCREEN section has five positions for elements of the array.

Although you use the SCREEN RECORD keywords to specify the array, it is typically called a screen array (and not a screen record).

f_manufsel form file

```
DATABASE stores2t

1➤ SCREEN
{

      Code        Name
     [f001]  [f002           ]
     [f001]  [f002           ]
     [f001]  [f002           ]
     [f001]  [f002           ]
     [f001]  [f002           ]
}

TABLES
manufact

2➤ ATTRIBUTES
f001 = manufact.manu_code;
f002 = manufact.manu_name;

INSTRUCTIONS
3➤  SCREEN RECORD sa_manuf[5] (manufact.manu_code THRU manufact.manu_name)
```

The input_stock2() Function

1➤ The input_stock2() function differs from the input_stock() function in Example 7 in the following ways:

- A BEFORE FIELD clause for the manu_code field appears in this function.
- The AFTER FIELD clause associated with the manu_code field differs.
- An ON KEY clause is associated with the manu_code field in this function.

2➤ The BEFORE FIELD clause displays an instruction for filling in the manu_code field.

3➤ The SELECT statement validates the manu_code by verifying that this code is defined in the manufact table.

4➤ The input_stock2() function also revises the error message displayed for an invalid manufacturer code to remind the user about the lookup key.

5➤ The ON KEY clause contains code that is executed when the user presses the F5 function key or CONTROL-F. When choosing control keys, you should be careful to avoid control keys that are reserved for editing in **4GL** forms. Also, you should avoid keys that are used by the operating system. For example, CONTROL-S often stops output to a terminal, and CONTROL-J generates the newline character.

The block of code associated with the key ends with another clause of the INPUT statement or an END INPUT statement.

6➤ The IF statement uses the INFIELD() built-in function to verify that the user pressed the F5 key or CONTROL-F while positioned in the manu_code field. If not, these keys do not perform an action. If so, the ON KEY clause calls the manuf_popup() function to get the code and name for a manufacturer, which are placed in the member variables of the gr_stock record.

To perform different lookup actions in different fields, you can use a series of INFIELD() functions as the WHEN clauses of a CASE statement. Each WHEN clause can execute the appropriate lookup action for the field.

7➤ The IF statement tests the manu_code member of the gr_stock record to find out whether the user selected a manufacturer. If not, the NEXT FIELD statement positions the cursor back in the manu_code field because a manufacturer is still required.

4GL source file

```
   ########################################
1➤ FUNCTION input_stock2()
   ########################################
```

See input_stock() in Example 7.

```
2➤     BEFORE FIELD manu_code
         MESSAGE  "Enter a manufacturer code or press F5 (CTRL-F) for a list."

       AFTER FIELD manu_code
         IF gr_stock.manu_code IS NULL THEN
           ERROR "You must enter a manufacturer code. Please try again."
           NEXT FIELD manu_code
         END IF

3➤       SELECT manu_name
         INTO gr_stock.manu_name
         FROM manufact
         WHERE manu_code = gr_stock.manu_code

         IF (status = NOTFOUND) THEN
4➤         ERROR
     "Unknown manufacturer's code. Use F5 (CTRL-F) to see valid codes."
           LET gr_stock.manu_code = NULL
           NEXT FIELD manu_code
         END IF
         DISPLAY BY NAME gr_stock.manu_name
         MESSAGE ""
       END IF
```

See input_stock() in Example 7.

```
5➤     ON KEY (F5, CONTROL-F)
6➤       IF INFIELD(manu_code) THEN
           CALL manuf_popup() RETURNING gr_stock.manu_code, gr_stock.manu_name
7➤         IF gr_stock.manu_code IS NULL THEN
             NEXT FIELD manu_code
           ELSE
             DISPLAY BY NAME gr_stock.manu_code
           END IF
           MESSAGE ""
```

8➤ The unique_stock() function determines if the stock number and manufacturer code just entered define a unique stock item. This function returns TRUE if no stock item currently exists with this combination of stock number and manufacturer code. In this case, the program displays the manufacturer name on the form and moves the cursor to the next field.

If unique_stock() returns FALSE, the program clears out the fields and returns the cursor to the stock_num field so the user can redefine the stock item.

The manuf_popup() Function

9➤ The DEFINE statement creates the pa_manuf local array to store the rows retrieved from the manufact table. Each element in the array consists of a record with two member variables: manu_code and manu_name.

10➤ The LET statement assigns the size of the pa_manuf array to the local variable array_sz. The function uses the array size to make sure there is enough room in the program array to store the selected manufact rows.

11➤ The manuf_popup() function opens a new window to display the popup list on top of the f_stock form. The manuf_popup() function displays the form with appropriate instructions to the user.

12➤ Example 5 introduced the use of cursors for dynamically prepared queries. As in the manuf_popup() function, you can also state the query in the declaration for the cursor. This technique prepares the query during compilation and thus executes more efficiently.

The query orders the manufacturers by the code sequence so the listing appears in a natural sequence. Otherwise, the manufacturers would appear in their physical sequence in the database table.

```
8➤          IF unique_stock() THEN
              DISPLAY BY NAME gr_stock.manu_name
              NEXT FIELD unit
            ELSE
              DISPLAY BY NAME gr_stock.description, gr_stock.manu_code,
                 gr_stock.manu_name
              NEXT FIELD stock_num
            END IF
          END IF
      END INPUT

      IF int_flag THEN
        LET int_flag = FALSE
        CALL msg("Stock input terminated.")
        RETURN (FALSE)
      END IF
    RETURN (TRUE)

    END FUNCTION  -- input_stock2 --

    ########################################
    FUNCTION manuf_popup()
    ########################################
9➤    DEFINE  pa_manuf ARRAY[200] OF RECORD
                     manu_code LIKE manufact.manu_code,
                     manu_name LIKE manufact.manu_name
                   END RECORD,

            idx              SMALLINT,
            manuf_cnt        SMALLINT,
            array_sz         SMALLINT,
            over_size        SMALLINT

10➤   LET array_sz = 200       --* match size of pa_manuf array

11➤   OPEN WINDOW w_manufpop AT 7, 13
        WITH 12 ROWS, 44 COLUMNS
        ATTRIBUTE(BORDER, FORM LINE 4)

      OPEN FORM f_manufsel FROM "f_manufsel"
      DISPLAY FORM f_manufsel

      DISPLAY "Move cursor using F3, F4, and arrow keys."
        AT 1,2
      DISPLAY "Press Accept to select a manufacturer."
        AT 2,2

12➤   DECLARE c_manufpop CURSOR FOR
        SELECT manu_code, manu_name
        FROM manufact
        ORDER BY manu_code
```

13➤ The FOREACH statement retrieves all of the rows from the manufact table and stores them in the pa_manuf array. The manuf_cnt variable stores the number of the next unoccupied element of the array. Thus, before the FOREACH loop starts executing, the next unoccupied element is the first element. Each iteration of the FOREACH loop increments the manuf_cnt variable before retrieving the next row into the array.

14➤ The array was defined with 200 elements. If the manufact table exceeds 200 rows, the manuf_popup() function cannot store the excess rows in pa_manuf. To prevent the FOREACH loop from failing at run-time, the program compares the current loop index (manuf_cnt) with the size of the array (array_sz). If there is no more room in the pa_manuf array, the function sets the over_size flag to indicate that the program array only contains the first 200 manufacturers.

See Example 12 for a technique for displaying an unknown number of rows in a screen array.

15➤ The IF statement tests whether the query retrieved a row. If no rows are returned, the FOREACH loop is not executed and the manuf_cnt variable keeps its initial value of 1. The call to the msg() function informs the user of this problem and the assignments to the idx variable and manu_code array member insure that the manuf_popup() function returns a null value.

Ordinarily the query should run without a problem and should return all rows in the manufact table; however, an unforeseen database problem could prevent the query from retrieving rows.

16➤ After the FOREACH loop retrieves rows, the ELSE clause displays the rows to the user. If the pa_manuf array is full, the program notifies the user that more manufact rows exist but are not displayed.

17➤ The call to the built-in SET_COUNT() function tells **4GL** how many rows are stored in the array. The call subtracts one from manuf_cnt because, when the FOREACH loop finishes, the variable stores the number of the element after the last element that was filled.

18➤ The DISPLAY ARRAY statement displays the contents of the pa_manuf array in the f_manufsel form. Unlike the DISPLAY BY NAME and DISPLAY TO statements for a single-row form, the DISPLAY ARRAY statement activates the form so the user can scroll rows into the form from the program array and can position on the appropriate manufacturer row.

The syntax requires a list of screen variables in the TO clause. That is, the DISPLAY ARRAY statement requires the asterisk after the name of the screen record.

```
13➤  LET over_size = FALSE
     LET manuf_cnt = 1
     FOREACH c_manufpop INTO pa_manuf[manuf_cnt].*
       LET manuf_cnt = manuf_cnt + 1
14➤    IF manuf_cnt > array_sz THEN
         LET over_size = TRUE
         EXIT FOREACH
       END IF
     END FOREACH

15➤  IF (manuf_cnt = 1) THEN
       CALL msg("No manufacturers exist in the database.")
       LET idx = 1
       LET pa_manuf[idx].manu_code = NULL
     ELSE
16➤    IF over_size THEN
         MESSAGE "Manuf array full: can only display ",
             array_sz USING "<<<<<<"
       END IF

17➤    CALL SET_COUNT(manuf_cnt-1)
       LET int_flag = FALSE
18➤    DISPLAY ARRAY pa_manuf TO sa_manuf.*
```

19➤ The built-in ARR_CURR() function returns the number of the array element on which the user was positioned when the user accepted or interrupted the form session. The idx variable stores this number so the manuf_popup() function can return the values stored in this array element.

Note that the array element is different from the user's current line number on the array form. To obtain this number, you can execute the built-in SCR_LINE() function.

20➤ The IF statement tests the int_flag built-in variable to determine whether the user has canceled the lookup action by pressing the Interrupt key. The msg() function confirms that no row was selected and the assignment to the manu_code member variable ensures that manuf_popup() doesn't return the value of the row the user happened to be on.

21➤ The manuf_popup() function finishes up by closing the popup window and returning the values of the appropriate array element, which are null if the manufact table didn't have any rows or if the user pressed the Interrupt key to leave the form.

```
19➤       LET idx = ARR_CURR()

20➤       IF int_flag THEN
            LET int_flag = FALSE
            CALL msg("No manufacturer code selected.")
            LET pa_manuf[idx].manu_code = NULL
          END IF
        END IF

21➤     CLOSE WINDOW w_manufpop
        RETURN pa_manuf[idx].manu_code, pa_manuf[idx].manu_name

      END FUNCTION  -- manuf_popup --
```

To locate any function definition see the Function Index on page 728.

9

Accessing a Table with a Single Row Form

This example combines the techniques demonstrated in the previous examples to provide a menu and form interface for all of the standard SQL operations on a table. The user can insert, query for, view, update, and delete customer rows. This example also provides a lookup function so the user can select a customer's state from a list displayed in a popup window.

```
+------------------------------------------------------------------------------+
|CUSTOMER:  Add  Query  Exit                                                   |
|Add new customer(s) to the database.                                          |
|---------------------------------------------------Press CTRL-W for Help----------|
|                                                                              |
|                                                                              |
|  Customer Number: [           ] Company Name: [                    ]        |
|   Address: [                    ]                                           |
|            [                    ]                                           |
|      City: [               ]   State: [  ]  Zip Code: [            ]        |
|                                                                              |
|   Contact Name: [               ][               ]                          |
|      Telephone: [                   ]                                       |
|                                                                              |
|                                                                              |
|                                                                              |
|                                                                              |
|                                                                              |
+------------------------------------------------------------------------------+
```

This example also introduces a technique for using a single INPUT statement to collect data for insertion or update. Because much of the field validation is likely to be the same whether the row is inserted or updated, this technique can reduce coding and improve maintainability.

Function Overview

Function Name	Purpose
cust_menu1()	Operates a menu so the user can choose whether to add new customers or query for existing customers.
addupd_cust()	Combines insertion and update functions in a single routine to eliminate duplication of code. This function resembles the input_stock2() function in Example 8.
state_popup()	Displays a lookup list of the states from the state table so the user can choose the appropriate state. This function resembles the manuf_popup() function in Example 8.
insert_cust()	Adds a new row to the customer table. This function resembles the insert_stock() function in Example 7.
browse_custs1()	Retrieves and displays the rows qualified by the query so the user can act on the rows. This function differs from browse_custs() in Example 6 only in that it calls next_action2() rather than next_action().
next_action2()	Operates a menu so the user can choose the appropriate processing for the current row. This function differs from next_action() in Example 6 only in that help isn't provided for the menu options and the Update option calls the addup_cust() function rather than the change_cust() function of Example 6.
message_window()	Opens a window and displays the contents of the ga_dsplymsg global array. *See description in Example 2.*
init_msgs()	Initializes the members of the ga_dsplymsg array to null. *See description in Example 2.*
bang()	Prompts the user for a command and executes the command. *See description in Example 3.*
prompt_window()	Displays a message and prompts the user for affirmation or negation. This function is a variation on the message_window() function that appears in Example 2. *See description in Example 4.*
msg()	Displays a brief, informative message. *See description in Example 5.*
query_cust2()	Lets the user create a query by example. *See description in Example 6.*
update_cust()	Updates the database row to reflect the changes. *See description in Example 6.*
delete_cust()	Deletes the current row if it doesn't have dependent rows in other tables. *See description in Example 6.*

verify_delete()	Checks for dependent rows in other tables. *See description in Example 6.*
clear_lines()	Clears any number of lines starting at any line. *See description in Example 6.*

To locate any function definition see the Function Index on page 728.

The f_statesel Form

1➤ This form is used as a popup window to display valid state codes and names. These state codes are stored in the state table.

2➤ The INSTRUCTIONS section defines the sa_state screen array to hold the state codes and names. To implement this popup window, the program must list this screen array in the TO clause of the DISPLAY ARRAY statement.

f_statesel form file

```
DATABASE stores2t

SCREEN
{

  Code        State
 [f001 ] [f002           ]
 [f001 ] [f002           ]
 [f001 ] [f002           ]
 [f001 ] [f002           ]
 [f001 ] [f002           ]
 [f001 ] [f002           ]
 [f001 ] [f002           ]
 [f001 ] [f002           ]
}

TABLES
state

1➤ ATTRIBUTES
f001 = state.code;
f002 = state.sname;

2➤ INSTRUCTIONS
  SCREEN RECORD sa_state[8] (state.code THRU state.sname)
```

The MAIN Function

1➤ The OPTIONS statement assigns appropriate lines to the top of the form, the comments for fields from the form specification file, and messages. It also specifies that help messages used in this example come from the hlpmsgs file.

2➤ The DEFER INTERRUPT statement traps the Interrupt key.

3➤ The cust_menu1() function executes SQL actions on the customer table. In your own applications, you might have a menu of tables at this point and call the appropriate equivalent to the cust_menu1() function for each table.

4➤ The CLEAR SCREEN statement clears the **4GL** display from the monitor for the benefit of whatever program the user returns to after exiting the program. While Example 9 doesn't close the w_main window or f_customer form explicitly, **4GL** closes all open forms, windows, and cursors when terminating the program.

The cust_menu1() Function

5➤ The Add menu option calls the addupd_cust() function to collect a new customer row from the user. The `A` parameter instructs addupd_cust() to apply insertion validation to the row.

If addupd_cust() succeeds in creating a valid row, the insert_cust() function inserts the row. To restore the form to its default state, the CLEAR FORM statement clears the data from the fields and calls clear_lines() to remove the instructions.

6➤ The Query menu option calls the query_cust2() function to collect query criteria from the user. The query_cust2() function returns the criteria to the st_custs variable. If the st_custs variable is null, query_cust2() failed to construct a query. Otherwise, the Query code block calls the browse_custs1() function to retrieve and process the qualified rows.

7➤ The unnamed menu option provides an expert option for executing an operating system command. The bang() function manages the construction of the command.

4GL source file

see Examples 2 and 6.

```
########################################
MAIN
########################################
1➤  OPTIONS
      HELP FILE "hlpmsgs",
      FORM LINE 5,
      COMMENT LINE 5,
      MESSAGE LINE LAST

2➤  DEFER INTERRUPT

    OPEN WINDOW w_main AT 2,3
      WITH 18 ROWS, 75 COLUMNS
      ATTRIBUTE (BORDER)

    OPEN FORM f_customer FROM "f_customer"
    DISPLAY FORM f_customer
3➤  CALL cust_menu1()
4➤  CLEAR SCREEN
END MAIN

########################################
FUNCTION cust_menu1()
########################################
  DEFINE        st_custs        CHAR(150)

  DISPLAY
"------------------------------------------Press CTRL-W for Help----------"
    AT 3, 1
  MENU "CUSTOMER"
5➤    COMMAND "Add" "Add new customer(s) to the database." HELP 10
        IF addupd_cust("A") THEN
          CALL insert_cust()
        END IF
        CLEAR FORM
        CALL clear_lines(2,16)
        CALL clear_lines(1,4)

6➤    COMMAND "Query" "Look up customer(s) in the database." HELP 11
        CALL query_cust2() RETURNING st_custs
        IF st_custs IS NOT NULL THEN
          CALL browse_custs1(st_custs)
        END IF
        CALL clear_lines(1, 4)

7➤    COMMAND KEY ("!")
        CALL bang()
```

8➤ The Exit menu option lets the user terminate the menu and, thus, the function and program. For the convenience of the user, the KEY clause specifies many accelerator keys for this important command.

The browse_custs1() Function

9➤ The browse_custs1() function prepares the query, declares a cursor, and executes a FOREACH statement to retrieve the qualified rows one at a time.

The browse_custs1() function is almost identical to the browse_custs() function (see page 124 of Example 6). The only difference is that, within the FOREACH statement, the IF statement calls the next_action2() function rather than the next_action() function to let the user act on the current row.

The next_action2() Function

10➤ The next_action2() function opens a menu to let the user update or delete the current row. The next_action2() function returns a false value, exiting the FOREACH loop in the browse_custs1() function, if the user doesn't want to see the rest of the qualified rows. The next_action2() function returns a true value if the user wants to view the next row.

The next_action2() function is almost identical to the next_action() function (see page 126 of Example 6). The only difference is that the Update menu option collects the changes to the row by calling the generic addupd_cust() function rather than the change_cust() function from Example 6. In the call to addupd_cust(), the U parameter triggers validation specific to updating rather than inserting.

The row is updated only if the return value of addupd_cust() indicates that the user accepted the modifications.

```
8➤    COMMAND KEY ("E", "e", "X", "x") "Exit" "Exit the program." HELP 100
        EXIT MENU
    END MENU

  END FUNCTION  -- cust_menu1 --

  ########################################
9➤ FUNCTION browse_custs1(selstmt)
  ########################################
```

see browse_custs() in Example 6.

```
    FOREACH c_cust INTO gr_customer.*
      LET fnd_custs = TRUE
      DISPLAY BY NAME gr_customer.*

      IF NOT next_action2() THEN

        LET end_list = FALSE
        EXIT FOREACH
      ELSE

        LET end_list = TRUE
      END IF
      LET gr_workcust.* = gr_customer.*
    END FOREACH
```

see browse_custs() in Example 6.

```
  END FUNCTION  -- browse_custs1 --

  ########################################
10➤ FUNCTION next_action2()
  ########################################
```

see next_action() in Example 6.

```
    MENU "CUSTOMER MODIFICATION"
      COMMAND "Next" "View next selected customer." HELP 20
        EXIT MENU

      COMMAND "Update" "Update current customer on screen." HELP 21
        IF addupd_cust("U") THEN
          CALL update_cust()
        END IF

        CALL clear_lines(1,16)
        NEXT OPTION "Next"
```

see next_action() in Example 6.

```
    END MENU

    RETURN nxt_action
  END FUNCTION  -- next_action2 --
```

The addupd_cust() Function

11➤ The addupd_cust() function enhances the technique used in the input_stock2() function of Example 9 to handle both inserts and updates.

12➤ The LET statement regularizes the parameter value by calling the UPSHIFT() built-in function to put it in upper case.

13➤ The IF statement makes sure that the calling statement hasn't called addupd_cust() with a flag value that's outside the A and U values that addupd_cust() knows. If so, the ERROR statement notifies the user about this internal problem and the EXIT PROGRAM statement abandons ship.

It would be too dangerous to continue in this unknown state. Defending against such programming mistakes is a good practice.

14➤ If addupd_cust() is called for insertion, the code block for the IF clause displays an insertion title and initializes the program variables to null.

If there were appropriate default values for a new row, you could assign them to the program variables individually.

15➤ If addupd_cust() is called for update, the code block for the ELSE clause displays an update title and places a copy of the current values of the row in the gr_workcust record in case the row must be restored later.

16➤ Before executing the INPUT statement, addupd_cust() sets the int_flag built-in variable to a false value so that int_flag can be tested later to see if the user pressed the Interrupt key.

The INPUT statement uses the WITHOUT DEFAULTS clause so that the values of the program variables are assigned to the fields of the form rather than defaults from the form specification file or the syscolval system table.

The individual program variable names are listed so that the cursor will visit the corresponding screen fields in the specified order. If you did not care about this particular ordering, you could substitute the gr_customer.* notation for the variable name list.

17➤ The BEFORE FIELD clause saves the current company name to avoid validating it in the AFTER FIELD clause if the user doesn't change the name (see Note 19).

18➤ The first IF statement of the company AFTER FIELD clause checks whether the company field has a value and, if not, repositions the user in the field.

```
    #########################################
11➤ FUNCTION addupd_cust(au_flag)
    #########################################
     DEFINE        au_flag         CHAR(1),

                   cust_cnt        INTEGER,
                   state_code      LIKE customer.state,
                   orig_comp       LIKE customer.company

12➤  LET au_flag = UPSHIFT(au_flag)
13➤  IF au_flag <> "A" AND au_flag <> "U" THEN
       ERROR "Incorrect argument to addupd_cust()."
       EXIT PROGRAM
     END IF

     CALL clear_lines(1,4)
14➤  IF au_flag = "A" THEN
       DISPLAY "CUSTOMER ADD" AT 4, 29
       INITIALIZE gr_customer.* TO NULL
15➤  ELSE                          --* au_flag = "U"
       DISPLAY "CUSTOMER UPDATE" AT 4, 29
   --* save current values of customer; if update is terminated, can
   --*    then redisplay original values.
       LET gr_workcust.* = gr_customer.*
     END IF

     CALL clear_lines(2, 16)
     DISPLAY " Press Accept to save new customer data. Press CTRL-W for Help."
       AT 16,1 ATTRIBUTE (REVERSE, YELLOW)
     DISPLAY " Press Cancel to exit w/out saving."
       AT 17,1 ATTRIBUTE (REVERSE, YELLOW)

16➤  LET int_flag = FALSE
     INPUT BY NAME gr_customer.company, gr_customer.address1,
                   gr_customer.address2, gr_customer.city,
                   gr_customer.state, gr_customer.zipcode,
                   gr_customer.fname, gr_customer.lname, gr_customer.phone
       WITHOUT DEFAULTS

17➤    BEFORE FIELD company
         LET orig_comp = gr_customer.company

18➤    AFTER FIELD company
         IF gr_customer.company IS NULL THEN
           ERROR "You must enter a company name. Please re-enter."
           NEXT FIELD company
         END IF

         LET cust_cnt = 0
```

The company field isn't the key for the customer table and thus isn't required for the integrity of the database. The field is, however, the most significant label for the row. That is, the customer data won't be meaningful if there are customers without company names.

19➤ The next IF statement in the company AFTER FIELD clause verifies that the company name is unique in the database. The clause always performs the test when inserting a row but only applies the test if the company has changed when updating the row.

The prompt_window() function notifies the user of a problem and gives the user a chance to correct it. If the user chooses to change the company name, the LET statement restores the original value and the NEXT FIELD statement repositions the user in the field.

Again, duplicate company names are a problem for the meaningfulness of the customer data rather than for the integrity of the database.

20➤ The BEFORE FIELD clause for the state field displays instructions for looking up states. An ON KEY clause implements the lookup action (see Note 22).

21➤ The AFTER FIELD clause for the state field uses a SELECT statement to verify that the state exists in the database. If not, the ERROR statement informs the user and the NEXT FIELD statement repositions the user in the state field.

```
19➤   IF (au_flag = "A")
          OR (au_flag = "U" AND orig_comp <> gr_customer.company)
      THEN
        SELECT COUNT(*)
        INTO cust_cnt
        FROM customer
        WHERE company = gr_customer.company

        IF (cust_cnt > 0) THEN
          LET ga_dsplymsg[1] = "This company name already exists in the "
          LET ga_dsplymsg[2] = "              database."
          IF NOT prompt_window ("Are you sure you want to add another?", 9, 15)
          THEN
            LET gr_customer.company = orig_comp
            NEXT FIELD company
          END IF
        END IF
      END IF

    AFTER FIELD lname
      IF (gr_customer.lname IS NULL) AND (gr_customer.fname IS NOT NULL) THEN
        ERROR "You must enter a last name with a first name."
        NEXT FIELD fname
      END IF

20➤ BEFORE FIELD state
      MESSAGE
        "Enter state code or press F5 (CTRL-F) for a list."

21➤ AFTER FIELD state
      IF gr_customer.state IS NULL THEN
        ERROR "You must enter a state code. Please try again."
        NEXT FIELD state
      END IF

      SELECT COUNT(*)
      INTO cust_cnt
      FROM state
      WHERE code = gr_customer.state

      IF (cust_cnt = 0) THEN
        ERROR
      "Unknown state code. Use F5 (CTRL-F) to see valid codes."
        LET gr_customer.state = NULL
        NEXT FIELD state
      END IF

      MESSAGE ""
```

22➤ The ON KEY clause executes when the user presses the F5 function key or CONTROL-F in any field on the form. The IF statement uses the INFIELD() built-in function to restrict the lookup action to the state field. In other fields, the function key has no effect.

The lookup action calls the state_popup() function to display a list of states. If the user doesn't select a state, state_popup() returns null, and the inner IF statement positions the user in the field. Otherwise, state_popup() returns the selected state, the DISPLAY BY NAME statement displays the value in the field, and the NEXT FIELD statement positions the user in the zipcode field. The explicit NEXT FIELD statement skips the validation in the AFTER FIELD clause for the state field, which is appropriate since the state_popup() can only return a valid state.

You could use similar AFTER FIELD and ON KEY actions in your own programs to provide friendly validation for foreign keys. See Example 8 for a more detailed description of this technique.

23➤ The second ON KEY clause defines field-level help for each of the fields of the f_customer form. Since CONTROL-W is the default help key (and the OPTIONS statement does not redefine the help key), this ON KEY executes when the user requests help. The section uses the built-in INFIELD() function to determine which field the cursor is in and uses the built-in SHOWHELP() function to specify which help message to display. These help messages must exist in the help file specified in the OPTIONS statement (hlpmsgs in this example). An alternative to field-level help is to use the HELP clause of the INPUT statement to specify a help message for all fields in the INPUT (see Example 6). The advantage of defining field-level help is that you can customize the help message that displays for each field.

24➤ The IF statement tests the int_flag built-in variable to check whether the user left the form by pressing the Interrupt key.

In this case, the inner IF statement checks to see if the action is an update and, if so, restores the original version of the row that was saved in the gr_workcust record (see Note 15). The IF statement returns a false value to avoid inserting or updating the row in the calling function.

If the user pressed the Accept key, the addupd_cust() function returns a true value to authorize the insertion or update.

```
22➤      ON KEY (CONTROL-F, F5)
           IF INFIELD(state) THEN
             CALL state_popup() RETURNING state_code

             IF state_code IS NULL THEN
               NEXT FIELD state
             END IF
             LET gr_customer.state = state_code
             DISPLAY BY NAME gr_customer.state

             MESSAGE ""
             NEXT FIELD zipcode
           END IF

23➤      ON KEY (CONTROL-W)
           IF INFIELD(company) THEN
             CALL SHOWHELP(50)
           END IF
           IF INFIELD(address1) OR INFIELD(address2) THEN
             CALL SHOWHELP(51)
           END IF
           IF INFIELD(city) THEN
             CALL SHOWHELP(52)
           END IF
           IF INFIELD(state) THEN
             CALL SHOWHELP(53)
           END IF
           IF INFIELD(zipcode) THEN
             CALL SHOWHELP(54)
           END IF
           IF INFIELD(fname) OR INFIELD(lname) THEN
             CALL SHOWHELP(55)
           END IF
           IF INFIELD(phone) THEN
             CALL SHOWHELP(56)
           END IF

       END INPUT

24➤    IF int_flag THEN
         LET int_flag = FALSE
         CALL clear_lines(2, 16)
         IF au_flag = "U" THEN
           LET gr_customer.* = gr_workcust.*
           DISPLAY BY NAME gr_customer.*
         END IF
         CALL msg("Customer input terminated.")
         RETURN (FALSE)
       END IF

       RETURN (TRUE)

     END FUNCTION  -- addupd_cust --
```

The state_popup() Function

25➤ The state_popup() function uses the same technique as the manuf_popup() function of Example 8 to display a popup list of values to the user.

26➤ The OPEN WINDOW statement displays the w_statepop window on top of any existing open windows. The function then opens and displays the f_statesel array form and displays instructions for using the list.

27➤ The DECLARE statement declares a cursor for retrieving all rows from the state table. The ORDER BY clause of the SELECT statement sorts the retrieved rows alphabetically by state code.

28➤ The FOREACH loop retrieves all of the state rows into the pa_state array. If more than 200 manufacturers exist in the database, the program prevents the pa_state array from overflowing and sets the over_size flag to TRUE so that only the first 200 manufacturers will display.

29➤ The IF statement tests the value of the state_cnt variable. If this variable's value is one, the FOREACH statement didn't find any rows and thus didn't loop. The msg() function notifies the user and the assignments prepare to return null.

30➤ If the FOREACH clause did retrieve rows, the code block for the ELSE statement checks the over_size variable to determine if all retrieved rows can fit into the program array. If not, the program notifies the user that only the first 60 will display.

```
   ########################################
25➤ FUNCTION state_popup()
   ########################################
     DEFINE        pa_state  ARRAY[60] OF RECORD
                           code    LIKE state.code,
                           sname   LIKE state.sname
                   END RECORD,
                   idx             INTEGER,
                   state_cnt       INTEGER,
                   array_sz        SMALLINT,
                   over_size       SMALLINT

     LET array_sz = 60    --* match size of pa_state array

26➤  OPEN WINDOW w_statepop AT 7, 3
       WITH 15 ROWS, 45 COLUMNS
       ATTRIBUTE(BORDER, FORM LINE 4)

     OPEN FORM f_statesel FROM "f_statesel"
     DISPLAY FORM f_statesel

     DISPLAY "Move cursor using F3, F4, and arrow keys."
       AT 1,2
     DISPLAY "Press Accept to select a state."
       AT 2,2

27➤  DECLARE c_statepop CURSOR FOR
       SELECT code, sname
       FROM state
       ORDER BY code

28➤  LET over_size = FALSE
     LET state_cnt = 1
     FOREACH c_statepop INTO pa_state[state_cnt].*
       LET state_cnt = state_cnt + 1
       IF state_cnt > array_sz THEN
         LET over_size = TRUE
         EXIT FOREACH
       END IF
     END FOREACH

29➤  IF state_cnt = 1 THEN
       CALL msg("No states exist in database.")
       LET idx = 1
       LET pa_state[idx].code = NULL
30➤  ELSE
       IF over_size THEN
         MESSAGE "State array full: can only display ",
            array_sz USING "<<<<<<"
       END IF
```

31➤ As with any array form, the program first calls the SET_COUNT() built-in function to specify the number of filled elements in the array. The assignment resets the int_flag variable so state_popup() can trap the Interrupt key after the form session.

The call to the ARR_CURR() built-in function returns the number of the array element corresponding to the user's current position in the form.

Once the size of the program array has been defined, the DISPLAY ARRAY statement then activates the f_statesel form so the user can select a state code.

32➤ The IF statement tests the int_flag to determine whether the user left the form by pressing the Interrupt key. If so, the assignments prepare to return null.

The RETURN statement at the end of state_popup() returns the chosen row or, if there have been errors or the user interrupted the form, null.

The insert_cust() Function

33➤ The insert_cust() function uses the same technique as the insert_stock() function of Example 7 to insert a row into the database.

34➤ The WHENEVER ERROR CONTINUE and WHENEVER ERROR STOP statements bracket the INSERT statement to suppress termination of the **4GL** program if the INSERT encounters a runtime error. The IF statement tests the built-in status variable to see if the insertion succeeded and notifies the user of the problem if the insertion failed.

Use of this technique for SQL statements lets the program recover gracefully from the run-time errors that can arise with dynamic entities such as a database.

35➤ Because the customer_num column is a serial column, the database engine generates a unique customer number when inserting a new customer row. After the insertion, the engine places this number in the second element of the SQLERRD array, which is a member of the built-in SQLCA record. (SQLERRD stands for *SQL error detail* and SQLCA for *SQL communication area.*)

The LET statement assigns this unique number to the customer_num member of the gr_customer record so that the DISPLAY BY NAME statement can show the number to the user.

36➤ The message_window() reports the successful insertion to the user.

```
31➤        CALL SET_COUNT(state_cnt - 1)
           LET int_flag = FALSE
           DISPLAY ARRAY pa_state TO sa_state.*

           LET idx = ARR_CURR()

32➤        IF int_flag THEN
             LET int_flag = FALSE
             CALL msg("No state selected.")
             LET pa_state[idx].code = NULL
           END IF
         END IF

         CLOSE WINDOW w_statepop
         RETURN pa_state[idx].code

       END FUNCTION  -- state_popup --

       ########################################
33➤    FUNCTION insert_cust()
       ########################################

34➤    WHENEVER ERROR CONTINUE
         INSERT INTO CUSTOMER
         VALUES (0, gr_customer.fname, gr_customer.lname,
                 gr_customer.company, gr_customer.address1,
                 gr_customer.address2, gr_customer.city,
                 gr_customer.state, gr_customer.zipcode,
                 gr_customer.phone)
       WHENEVER ERROR STOP

         IF (status < 0) THEN
           ERROR status USING "-<<<<<<<<<<<", ": Unable to complete customer insert."
         ELSE
35➤        LET gr_customer.customer_num = SQLCA.SQLERRD[2]
           DISPLAY BY NAME gr_customer.customer_num

36➤        LET ga_dsplymsg[1] = "Customer has been entered in the database."
           LET ga_dsplymsg[2] = "  Number: ",
                             gr_customer.customer_num USING "<<<<<<<<<<<",
                             "  Name: ", gr_customer.company
           CALL message_window(9, 15)
         END IF

       END FUNCTION  -- insert_cust --
```

To locate any function definition see the Function Index on page 728.

10

Accessing a Table with a Multi-Row Form

This example demonstrates how to use an array form to edit database rows. It uses the INPUT ARRAY WITHOUT DEFAULTS statement to initialize the form with rows fetched from the manufact table. The user can modify or delete these rows, or add new rows on the form.

The following form appears in this program:

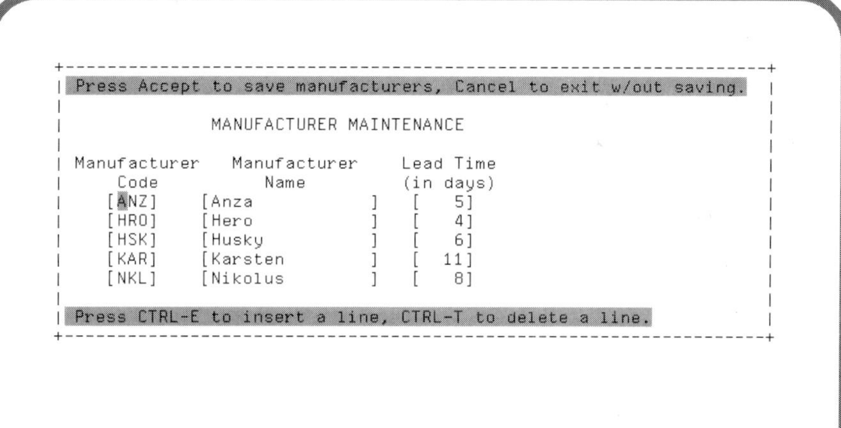

```
+------------------------------------------------------------------+
| Press Accept to save manufacturers, Cancel to exit w/out saving. |
|                                                                  |
|               MANUFACTURER MAINTENANCE                           |
|                                                                  |
| Manufacturer    Manufacturer      Lead Time                      |
|     Code            Name          (in days)                      |
|    [ANZ]      [Anza            ]   [    5]                       |
|    [HRO]      [Hero            ]   [    4]                       |
|    [HSK]      [Husky           ]   [    6]                       |
|    [KAR]      [Karsten         ]   [   11]                       |
|    [NKL]      [Nikolus         ]   [    8]                       |
|                                                                  |
| Press CTRL-E to insert a line, CTRL-T to delete a line.          |
+------------------------------------------------------------------+
```

The program does not perform the database operations while the user is editing. Instead, it keeps track of the operations performed and, after the user presses the Accept key, processes the inserts, updates, and deletes.

Modifying Information in an Array Form

An array form displays multiple rows to the user at one time. This type of form is introduced in Example 8, "Displaying a Screen Array in a Popup Window". Example 8 explains how to display multiple lines on a form using the DISPLAY ARRAY statement.

The INPUT ARRAY statement allows the user to enter multiple lines on an array form. The statement provides an Insert key (F1 by default) and Delete key (F2 by default) to add and delete rows in the array. The INPUT ARRAY statement, like the INPUT statement, supports the WITHOUT DEFAULTS clause to initialize form fields. You can use INPUT ARRAY WITHOUT DEFAULTS to initialize the rows of the array with data fetched from the database. The user can update or delete these rows as well as add new lines to the array (and to the database).

The basic technique for programming an array form is as follows:

1. Create a form specification that includes a screen array.
2. Define a program array large enough to store the database rows.
3. Open and display the array form in a window.
4. Query the database and store the rows into the program array.
5. Call the built-in SET_COUNT() function to tell **4GL** how many rows are stored in the program array. You must call SET_COUNT() before using the WITHOUT DEFAULTS clause of INPUT ARRAY.
6. Execute the INPUT ARRAY WITHOUT DEFAULTS statement to activate the array form for editing the rows in the program array.
7. Call the built-in ARR_CURR(), SCR_CURR(), and ARR_COUNT() functions in a BEFORE ROW clause to identify the current cursor position in the screen and program arrays.
8. Use the other clauses of INPUT ARRAY to perform data validation.

Handling Empty Fields

On any field in a line of the screen array, the user may choose to:

A. Move to another field (with RETURN or TAB)

B. Move to another line (with up or down arrow)

C. Exit the screen array (with Accept or Cancel)

In each of these cases, **4GL** executes the AFTER FIELD clause (if any) associated with the current field. Since a program can validate a field's value in an AFTER FIELD clause, this clause may need to deal with these three possible user actions. For fields that require data, an AFTER FIELD clause can check for a null value. If the field is null, the program can notify the user that a value is required and return the cursor to the field.

If the user tries to move to another field on the line (Action A), and a value is required in the current field, a null value is invalid. The program should prevent the user from continuing to another field.

However, the first field of a line is a special case. When the cursor is on the last line of the array, a null value in the first field is valid if the user is exiting the screen array (Action C) or moving to another line (Action B). For this reason, the AFTER FIELD clause for the first field must perform additional checking when it encounters a null value. This checking requires the following built-in functions:

- The ARR_CURR() and ARR_COUNT() functions determine whether the cursor is on the last line of the array.
- The FGL_LASTKEY() and FGL_KEYVAL() functions determine which key sequence the user pressed.

Extensive field validation should ordinarily appear within a separate function. The AFTER FIELD clause can call the function when it encounters a null value. In this example, the valid_null() function performs these tasks. It returns TRUE or FALSE to indicate whether the null field is valid. If the null is not valid, the AFTER FIELD handles the empty field as it would any other field (it returns the cursor to the field and notifies the user that a value is required). Otherwise, it allows the user to leave the field blank.

Identifying Keystrokes

A program can take different actions depending on which key the user presses. In this example, an empty manufacturer code field is allowed in some cases and not allowed in others. The program can determine whether to allow the user to leave the field empty based on the key the user pressed to leave the field. (For more information about checking empty fields, see the section "Handling Empty Fields" above.)

To identify keystrokes, **4GL** provides two built-in functions:

- FGL_LASTKEY() returns an integer value that identifies the last key pressed by the user.
- FGL_KEYVAL() returns the integer value for a specified key name.

By using the two functions together, the program need not be concerned with the actual integer representations of the keys. Instead, it can compare the return values from the two functions to identify a key.

For example, to see if the user has pressed the Accept key, a program can call these two functions as follows:

```
IF FGL_LASTKEY() = FGL_KEYVAL("accept") THEN
        . . .
END IF
```

The IF statement compares the value that represents the last keystroke with the value that represents the Accept key to see if they are the same. For portable code, it is a good idea to avoid using the actual integer representations.

To check if a keystroke is among a list of keys, assign the return value of FGL_LASTKEY() to a variable and then include the variable in the comparisons:

```
DEFINE last_key SMALLINT
     . . .
LET last_key = FGL_LASTKEY()
IF ( last_key = FGL_KEYVAL("return")
   OR last_key = FGL_KEYVAL("tab")
   OR last_key = FGL_KEYVAL("right") )
THEN
     . . .
END IF
```

By assigning the result of FGL_LASTKEY() to a variable, you only have to call this function once. Since the user's key does not change during the execution of the IF statement, there is no reason to call FGL_LASTKEY() each time you call FGL_KEYVAL().

For more information on using the FGL_LASTKEY() and FGL_KEYVAL() functions, see the *INFORMIX-4GL Release 4.1 Reference Manual Supplement*.

Function Overview

Function Name	Purpose
dsply_manuf()	Displays the f_manuf form and controls the array editing.
valid_null()	Checks to see if the current key stroke is valid when the manu_code field is empty.
reshuffle()	Reshuffles the ga_mrowid array when an item is added to or deleted from the ga_manuf program array.
verify_mdel()	Verifies that the manufacturer to be deleted does not currently have items in the stock table.
choose_op()	Checks the operation flag (op_flag) in the ga_mrowid array for updates and inserts to perform. Checks the ga_drows array for deletes to perform.
insert_manuf()	Adds a manufact row to the database.
update_manuf()	Updates an existing manufact row.
delete_manuf()	Deletes an existing manufact row.
verify_rowid()	Verifies that the ROWID of the row to be updated or deleted has not been deleted by another user.
save_rowid()	Saves the ROWID and the manufacturer code of the row to be deleted in the ga_drows array (before this info is deleted when the ga_mrowid array is reshuffled).
msg()	Displays a brief, informative message. *See description in Example 5.*
init_msgs()	Initializes the members of the ga_dsplymsg array to null. *See description in Example 2.*
message_window()	Opens a window and displays the contents of the ga_dsplymsg global array. *See description in Example 2.*
prompt_window()	Displays a message and prompts the user for affirmation or negation. This function is a variation on the message_window() function that appears in Example 2. *See description in Example 4.*

To locate any function definition see the Function Index on page 728.

The f_manuf Form

1➤ The DATABASE section lists the name of the database the compiler should check for the tables listed in the TABLES section. This form can work with any version of the demonstration database.

2➤ The f00, f01 and f02 fields make up a single record (or line) of the array. Five lines appear in the screen array, so these tags are repeated for each array line.

3➤ The ATTRIBUTES section defines the special features or attributes for each screen field. In the f_manuf form, all three fields are associated with the manufact table. The f00 field uses the UPSHIFT attribute to shift all letters entered in this field to upper case. This attribute ensures that all manufacturer codes will be stored in the database in upper case.

4➤ The INSTRUCTIONS section defines the screen array for the form. This screen array has five elements because five lines appear in the SCREEN section. Each element is a screen record containing the three manufact fields: manu_code, manu_name, and lead_time.

Remember to define a program array in your **4GL** program with elements that match those of this screen array.

f_manuf form file

1➤
```
DATABASE stores2t

SCREEN
{

 Manufacturer    Manufacturer      Lead Time
     Code            Name          (in days)
    [f00]     [f01              ]    [ f02]
    [f00]     [f01              ]    [ f02]
    [f00]     [f01              ]    [ f02]
    [f00]     [f01              ]    [ f02]
    [f00]     [f01              ]    [ f02]
}

TABLES
manufact
```
2➤ (beside the first [f00] row)

3➤
```
ATTRIBUTES
f00 = manufact.manu_code, UPSHIFT;
f01 = manufact.manu_name;
f02 = manufact.lead_time;
```

4➤
```
INSTRUCTIONS
  SCREEN RECORD sa_manuf[5] (manu_code THRU lead_time)
```

The DATABASE and GLOBALS Statements

1➤ The program works with any version of the stores2 database. It uses the manufact table.

2➤ The ga_manuf global array is the program array for the manufacturer rows. It is initialized with the manufacturer code, name, and lead_time of each manufact in the database. It corresponds to the sa_manuf screen array defined in the f_manuf form file.

3➤ The ga_mrowid global array holds the ROWIDs of the manufact rows. Each element of ga_mrowid corresponds to a line in the ga_manuf program array. The ROWIDs are used to quickly access a specified manufact row if the user modifies the row. This array also holds a flag to indicate the operation performed by the user on the associated line of pa_manuf. The possible values for this flag are:

- NULL - no operation has been performed on the row
- "I" - a new line has been inserted (mrowid is null)
- "U" - the line has been updated

4➤ The ga_drows global array holds the ROWIDs of the lines the user has deleted on the f_manuf form. The ROWIDs of deleted rows cannot be stored in the ga_mrowid array because the ga_mrowid array must maintain a one-to-one correspondence with ga_manuf. Once a line is deleted from the screen array on the form, **4GL** automatically deletes the line from the ga_manuf program array and the program deletes the line from ga_mrowid. Thus, the program stores the ROWID of each to-be-deleted row in ga_drows.

5➤ The g_idx global variable is an index into the ga_drows array. It indicates the position of the most recent entry. Before **4GL** deletes the line from the screen array, the program first increments g_idx and then stores the ROWID and op_flag of the line in ga_drows[g_idx].

The MAIN Function

6➤ This program redefines the Insert and Delete keys to CONTROL-E and CONTROL-T respectively. It also displays a message notifying the user of the control sequences which perform these tasks.

7➤ The DEFER INTERRUPT statement prevents the Cancel key from terminating the program. Instead, pressing Cancel sets the global variable int_flag to TRUE (as discussed in Example 5). This flag is tested after the INPUT to see if the user has pressed Cancel to exit the menu.

4GL source file

```
1➤ DATABASE stores2t

   GLOBALS

2➤   DEFINE        ga_manuf        ARRAY[50] OF
                                     RECORD
                                       manu_code LIKE manufact.manu_code,
                                       manu_name LIKE manufact.manu_name,
                                       lead_time LIKE manufact.lead_time
                                     END RECORD,

3➤                 ga_mrowid       ARRAY[50] OF
                                     RECORD
                                       mrowid      INTEGER,
                                       op_flag     CHAR(1)
                                     END RECORD,

4➤                 ga_drows        ARRAY[50] OF
                                     RECORD
                                       mrowid      INTEGER,
                                       manu_code   LIKE manufact.manu_code
                                     END RECORD,
5➤                 g_idx           SMALLINT

     DEFINE        ga_dsplymsg ARRAY[5] OF CHAR(48)

   END GLOBALS

   ########################################
   MAIN
   ########################################

     OPTIONS
         FORM LINE 4,
         MESSAGE LINE LAST,
         COMMENT LINE 2,
6➤       INSERT KEY CONTROL-E,
         DELETE KEY CONTROL-T

7➤  DEFER INTERRUPT
```

8➤ The dsply_manuf() function controls the display and update of the manufact rows on the f_manuf form. It returns TRUE if the user presses the Accept key to save the rows and FALSE if the user presses the Cancel key.

9➤ The choose_op() function cycles through the ga_manuf and ga_drows arrays to determine the operations to perform on the rows. The ga_manuf array contains lines that have been inserted or updated on the form. The ga_drows contains lines that have been deleted.

The dsply_manuf() Function

10➤ The pr_nullman record is a null record for the ga_manuf array. It has the same fields as a line of the ga_manuf array but each field has a null value. To clear a line in ga_manuf, the program assigns pr_nullman to the appropriate line (see Notes 16 and 20). This technique is more efficient than:

- Using the INITIALIZE statement each time the program must clear out a line
- Using a LET statement to assign a null value to each member of the record

INITIALIZE is easier to code than the LET statements because it can set all members of a record to null in a single statement. However, it is slightly more CPU-intensive than setting individual member variables with LET. By using INITIALIZE only once to initialize pr_nullman (see Note 12), and than taking advantage of the record.* syntax available with LET (see Note 20), the program is able to clear a line most efficiently.

11➤ The pr_workman record is a work buffer for the ga_manuf array. It has the same fields as a single line in ga_manuf. This array stores the original values in a line before the user begins editing. It is used to determine whether the user has performed an Insert or an Update (see Note 26) and for restoring the original values to the screen if the user makes a data entry error (see Note 25).

12➤ The program initializes the pr_nullman record to null. When the program needs to clear out a record, it calls the more efficient LET statement (rather than INITIALIZE) to assign the contents of pr_nullman to the record being cleared (see Note 16).

13➤ The manufacturer form f_manuf displays in a bordered window called w_manufs. The DISPLAY statements notify the user of available control keys.

14➤ The c_manufs cursor defines the information to select from manufact. It includes the selection of the ROWID for each manufact row so the program can quickly locate the row when it needs to be updated or deleted.

```
8➤    IF dsply_manuf() THEN
9➤      CALL choose_op()
        CALL msg("Manufacturer maintenance complete.")
      END IF

    END MAIN

    #########################################
    FUNCTION dsply_manuf()
    #########################################
      DEFINE        idx             SMALLINT,
                    curr_pa         SMALLINT,
                    curr_sa         SMALLINT,
                    total_pa        SMALLINT,
                    manuf_cnt       SMALLINT,

10➤                 pr_nullman RECORD
                       manu_code LIKE manufact.manu_code,
                       manu_name LIKE manufact.manu_name,
                       lead_time LIKE manufact.lead_time
                    END RECORD,

11➤                 pr_workman RECORD
                       manu_code LIKE manufact.manu_code,
                       manu_name LIKE manufact.manu_name,
                       lead_time LIKE manufact.lead_time
                    END RECORD

12➤  INITIALIZE pr_nullman.* TO NULL

13➤  OPEN WINDOW w_manufs AT 4,5
        WITH 13 ROWS, 67 COLUMNS
        ATTRIBUTE (BORDER)

      OPEN FORM f_manuf FROM "f_manuf"
      DISPLAY FORM f_manuf

      DISPLAY " Press Accept to save manufacturers, Cancel to exit w/out saving."
        AT 1, 1 ATTRIBUTE (REVERSE, YELLOW)
      DISPLAY " Press CTRL-E to insert a line, CTRL-T to delete a line."
        AT 13, 1 ATTRIBUTE (REVERSE, YELLOW)
      DISPLAY "MANUFACTURER MAINTENANCE"
        AT 3, 15

14➤   DECLARE c_manufs CURSOR FOR
        SELECT ROWID, manu_code, manu_name, lead_time FROM manufact
        ORDER BY manu_code

      LET idx = 1
```

15➤ The FOREACH statement opens the c_manufs cursor and stores the selected data in the ga_manuf and ga_mrowid arrays. The ga_manuf array holds the data to display in the screen array and the ga_mrowid array holds the ROWID for each line of the screen array.

16➤ If idx is one, then no rows exist in the manufact table. The function clears out the first line of ga_manuf.

17➤ The built-in SET_COUNT() function tells the INPUT ARRAY WITHOUT DEFAULTS statement the size of the program array it will display. This statement must know how many lines are in the program array so it can determine how to control the screen array. The SET_COUNT() function initializes the value that is returned by the built-in ARR_COUNT() function.

18➤ The INPUT ARRAY statement controls cursor movement through the sa_manuf screen array. The WITHOUT DEFAULTS clause tells **4GL** to initialize the screen array with the contents of the ga_manuf program array. This program array contains the manufact rows arranged in alphabetical order (see Note 15).

19➤ **4GL** executes the BEFORE ROW clause each time the cursor moves to a new line of the screen array. This clause obtains the current position of the cursor in the screen array (SCR_LINE()), the current position in the program array (ARR_CURR()), and the total number of items in the program array (ARR_COUNT()). By calling these built-in functions in BEFORE ROW, the respective variables are evaluated each time the cursor moves to a new line and are available within other clauses of the INPUT ARRAY.

20➤ **4GL** executes the BEFORE INSERT clause just after the user presses the Insert key (CONTROL-E in this example) and before **4GL** inserts a new line into the screen and program arrays. This clause initializes the work buffer, pr_workman, to NULL so the program can identify the line as an Insert. Lines that are updated will have non-null values in pr_workman (see Note 26).

Notes 21 to 23 The BEFORE DELETE clause performs data validation after the user presses the Delete key (CONTROL-T in this example) and before **4GL** deletes the current line from the screen and program arrays.

21➤ The save_rowid() function saves the ROWID and manufacturer code of the current line in the ga_drows array. This information is used to delete the appropriate manufact row once the user exits the INPUT ARRAY with Accept.

```
15➤  FOREACH c_manufs INTO ga_mrowid[idx].mrowid, ga_manuf[idx].*
       LET idx = idx + 1
     END FOREACH

16➤  IF idx = 1 THEN
       LET ga_manuf[1].* = pr_nullman.*
     END IF

17➤  CALL SET_COUNT(idx - 1)

18➤  INPUT ARRAY ga_manuf WITHOUT DEFAULTS FROM sa_manuf.*
19➤    BEFORE ROW
         LET curr_pa = ARR_CURR()
         LET curr_sa = SCR_LINE()
         LET total_pa = ARR_COUNT()
         LET pr_workman.* = ga_manuf[curr_pa].*

20➤    BEFORE INSERT
         LET pr_workman.* = pr_nullman.*

       BEFORE DELETE
21➤      CALL save_rowid(ga_mrowid[curr_pa].mrowid,
                   ga_manuf[curr_pa].manu_code)
```

22➤ The reshuffle() function deletes the current line from the ga_mrowid array and moves the successive lines up one line. **4GL** has automatically deleted the line and reshuffled the ga_manuf array because ga_manuf is the program array. However, the program must delete the line from ga_mrowid if this array is to remain parallel with the ga_manuf array.

23➤ The program assigns the values of the new current line to the work buffer.

24➤ 4GL executes this BEFORE FIELD clause just before the cursor stops in the manu_code screen field. This LET statement stores the current value of the manu_code field in the work buffer. After the cursor leaves the field, the program can compare the original value (in the work buffer) with the value in the field (in ga_manuf[curr_pa]). If these values are different, the user has updated the field value.

The curr_pa variable serves as the index for the program array. This variable is evaluated in the BEFORE ROW section by ARR_CURR() (see Note 19) and contains the line of the program array which corresponds to the cursor's current position.

Notes 25 to 30 The AFTER FIELD clause performs data validation after the cursor has left the manu_code field.

25➤ This IF statement determines whether a null value is valid in the manu_code field. From this field, the user may choose to:

A. Move to the next field in the current line (with RETURN or TAB)

B. Move to another line of the array (with up or down arrow)

C. Exit the screen array (with Accept or Cancel)

In the first case, a null field value is invalid because it means that the user is defining a manufacturer but has not entered a manufacturer code. However, in either of the other two cases, a null value is valid if the cursor is on the last line of the array. The program calls the valid_null() to check for these three cases. The function returns TRUE if a null value is valid and FALSE otherwise. If the null is invalid, the program notifies the user that a value must be entered, redisplays the field's original value (stored in the work buffer), and then uses the NEXT FIELD statement to move the cursor back to the manu_code field. The NEXT FIELD prevents the user from moving to the next field without first entering a manufacturer code.

For more information on why these three cases must be handled differently, see the section "Handling Empty Fields" in the overview of this example.

```
22➤      CALL reshuffle("D")

23➤      LET pr_workman.* = ga_manuf[curr_pa].*

24➤    BEFORE FIELD manu_code
         LET pr_workman.manu_code = ga_manuf[curr_pa].manu_code

       AFTER FIELD manu_code
25➤      IF (ga_manuf[curr_pa].manu_code IS NULL) THEN
           IF NOT valid_null(curr_pa, total_pa) THEN
             ERROR "You must enter a manufacturer code. Please try again."
             LET ga_manuf[curr_pa].manu_code = pr_workman.manu_code
             NEXT FIELD manu_code
           END IF
         END IF
```

26➤ If execution reaches this point, the manu_code field is not empty. The user has either entered a new manu_code as part of an insert or has modified an existing one as part of an update. To determine which of these operations the user is performing, the program checks the value of manu_code in the work buffer. Before an insert, this field of the work buffer is initialized to null (see Note 20). Before an update, the work buffer is initialized to the existing value of the manufacturer code (see Note 24).

27➤ If the user is performing an insert, the program verifies that the manufacturer code just entered is unique. The SELECT checks the manufact table for the new manufacturer code. If this code already exists, the program notifies the user and returns the cursor to the manu_code field.

28➤ If the new manufacturer code is unique, then the program calls the reshuffle() function to create a new line in the ga_mrowid array. **4GL** has automatically added a line to ga_manuf because ga_manuf is the program array. However, this function must add the line to ga_mrowid if this array is to remain parallel with the ga_manuf array.

Note that the reshuffle() function is called when the cursor is on all but the last line of the screen array (curr_pa <> total_pa). There is no need to create an empty slot in ga_mrowid if the user is simply adding a new line to the end of the array. No existing lines need to be reshuffled to make room for the empty line.

29➤ In the new line of ga_mrowid (see Note 28), the program sets the op_flag field to "I" to indicate that this line is the result of an insert operation. An insert will not have a value in the mrowid field because the ROWID is not assigned until after the new row is added to the manufact table.

30➤ If the condition in Note 26 is FALSE, the user is performing an update on the current line. However, the program does not permit the user to modify the value of the manu_code field because this field is the key of the manufact table. The program tells the user to delete the incorrect line and add a new one with the correct manu_code value. It then restores the manu_code to its original value (contained in the work buffer) and returns the cursor to the manu_code field.

31➤ This BEFORE FIELD clause stores the original value of the manu_name field in the work buffer.

```
26➤       IF (pr_workman.manu_code IS NULL)     --* if doing an Insert
              AND (ga_manuf[curr_pa].manu_code IS NOT NULL)
          THEN
27➤         SELECT COUNT(*)
            INTO manuf_cnt
            FROM manufact
            WHERE manu_code = ga_manuf[curr_pa].manu_code

            IF manuf_cnt > 0 THEN
              ERROR
            "This manufacturer code already exists. Please choose another code."
              LET ga_manuf[curr_pa].manu_code = NULL
              NEXT FIELD manu_code
            ELSE                             --* no manufs exist with new code
28➤           IF curr_pa <> total_pa THEN    --* if not at the last position,
                CALL reshuffle("I")          --*   clear a position in the array
              END IF

29➤            LET ga_mrowid[curr_pa].op_flag = "I"    --* mark the line as new
            END IF

30➤       ELSE                               --* else doing an Update
            IF (ga_manuf[curr_pa].manu_code <> pr_workman.manu_code) THEN
              LET ga_dsplymsg[1] = "You cannot modify the manufacturer code."
              LET ga_dsplymsg[2] = "     "
              LET ga_dsplymsg[3] = "To modify this value, delete the incorrect"
              LET ga_dsplymsg[4] = "  entry and enter a new one with the correct"
              LET ga_dsplymsg[5] = "  manufacturer code."
              CALL message_window(7,7)

              LET ga_manuf[curr_pa].manu_code = pr_workman.manu_code
              NEXT FIELD manu_code
            END IF
          END IF

31➤     BEFORE FIELD manu_name
          LET pr_workman.manu_name = ga_manuf[curr_pa].manu_name
```

Notes 32 to 33 The AFTER FIELD clause performs data validation after the cursor leaves the manu_name field.

32➤ The IF statement ensures that the user enters a manufacturer name. Because manu_name is not the first field of the line, this AFTER FIELD need not check whether a null is valid (See Note 25). It can assume that an empty field is always invalid.

33➤ If the user has modified the field, the program checks the corresponding op_flag field in ga_mrowid. If the user is performing an insert, op_flag is "I" (see Note 29). If op_flag is null, the user is performing an Update and the program sets op_flag to "U".

Notes 34 to 35 The BEFORE FIELD clause performs data validation before the cursor stops on the lead_time field.

34➤ The program sets an empty lead_time field to zero and stores this value in the work buffer.

35➤ The MESSAGE statement tells the user how to enter the lead time value. Since this value is stored in the database in an INTERVAL column, the user must follow a strict format for its data entry. The interval must be entered as a space followed by three digits or **4GL** displays an error.

Notes 36 to 38 The AFTER FIELD clause performs data validation after the cursor leaves the lead_time field.

36➤ If the lead time field is empty, the program displays a zero in the field. This assignment guarantees that the lead_time field will have a non-null value when it is stored in the database.

Note that to display the new lead_time value from within the AFTER FIELD clause, the program must use the DISPLAY statement. To display the new value in the BEFORE FIELD, the DISPLAY is not needed because **4GL** automatically displays the field value after it finished executing the BEFORE FIELD.

37➤ If the user has modified the lead time, the program sets the op_flag field to "U". The op_flag is only set if it does not already contain a value (see Note 33).

38➤ The MESSAGE statement clears the message line (see Note 35). Since the message line is defined as the last line of the window, the text had erased the user message identifying the key sequences for the insert and delete (see Note 13). The DISPLAY statement redisplays this information in the last line.

39➤ If the user presses the Cancel key to terminate the INPUT ARRAY, **4GL** sets the int_flag variable to TRUE. This IF resets the flag and notifies the user that the maintenance has been terminated. The dsply_manuf() function returns FALSE to indicate that the user has pressed Cancel (See Note 8).

```
      AFTER FIELD manu_name
32➤     IF ga_manuf[curr_pa].manu_name IS NULL THEN
          ERROR "You must enter a manufacturer name. Please try again."
          NEXT FIELD manu_name
        END IF

33➤     IF (ga_manuf[curr_pa].manu_name <> pr_workman.manu_name) THEN
          IF ga_mrowid[curr_pa].op_flag IS NULL THEN
            LET ga_mrowid[curr_pa].op_flag = "U"
          END IF
        END IF

      BEFORE FIELD lead_time
34➤     IF ga_manuf[curr_pa].lead_time IS NULL THEN
          LET ga_manuf[curr_pa].lead_time = 0 UNITS DAY
        END IF

        LET pr_workman.lead_time = ga_manuf[curr_pa].lead_time
35➤     MESSAGE "Enter the lead_time in the form ' ###' (e.g. ' 001')."

      AFTER FIELD lead_time
36➤     IF ga_manuf[curr_pa].lead_time IS NULL THEN
          LET ga_manuf[curr_pa].lead_time = 0 UNITS DAY
          DISPLAY ga_manuf[curr_pa].lead_time TO sa_manuf[curr_sa].lead_time
        END IF

37➤     IF (ga_manuf[curr_pa].lead_time <> pr_workman.lead_time) THEN
          IF ga_mrowid[curr_pa].op_flag IS NULL THEN
            LET ga_mrowid[curr_pa].op_flag = "U"
          END IF
        END IF

38➤     MESSAGE ""
        DISPLAY " Press CTRL-E to insert a line, CTRL-T to delete a line."
          AT 13, 1 ATTRIBUTE (REVERSE, YELLOW)

    END INPUT

39➤ IF int_flag THEN
      LET int_flag = FALSE
      CALL msg("Manufacturer maintenance terminated.")
      RETURN (FALSE)
    END IF
```

40➤ If execution reaches this point, the user has pressed Accept to leave the INPUT ARRAY. The program prompts the user to confirm that changes made to the manufact rows should be made in the database. If the user answers "Y", the dsply_manuf() function returns TRUE to indicate that execution should continue. If the user answers "N" to this confirmation, dsply_manuf() returns FALSE to indicate that the maintenance has been cancelled (See Note 8).

The valid_null() Function

41➤ The valid_null() function returns TRUE or FALSE to identify whether the first screen field of a line can be null. Two tests determine the validity of the null:

- Which key did the user press to leave the field?
- Is the cursor on the last line of the screen array?

When the cursor is on the last line, the manu_code field can be null if the user presses the up arrow or the Accept key. However, this field cannot be null if the user presses RETURN, TAB, or right arrow to move to the next field. If the cursor is not on the last line, then the manu_code can never be null. The function displays a message to explain why the null is invalid. If the user pressed up arrow, down arrow, or Accept, then a null manu_code field is not valid because it leaves a gap in the array. If the user pressed RETURN then the null manu_code field is invalid because it would allow input of a null value.

42➤ The FGL_LASTKEY() and FGL_KEYVAL() functions identify the last key pressed by the user. FGL_LASTKEY() returns an integer representation of the user's key. This value is saved in the last_key variable so it can be compared against several key values. For more information on using these two functions, see the section titled "Identifying User Keys" in the orientation of this example.

43➤ The LET statement uses the Boolean OR operator to assign a Boolean value to the next_fld value. If the user pressed a key which moves to the next field (RETURN, TAB, or right arrow), next_fld is set to TRUE. Otherwise, next_fld is set to FALSE.

44➤ The cursor is on the last line of the array if the current cursor position (array_idx) is the size of the screen array (array_size). The array_idx argument is returned by the ARR_CURR() built-in function and the array_size argument is returned by the ARR_COUNT() built-in function.

45➤ If the cursor is on the last line of the array, then the function checks which key the user has pressed. If next_fld is TRUE, the user has tried to move to the next field in the screen array line. The function returns FALSE to indicate that a null field is not valid in this case.

```
40➤   IF prompt_window("Are you sure you want to save these changes?", 8,11)
      THEN
        RETURN (TRUE)
      ELSE
        RETURN (FALSE)
      END IF

    END FUNCTION  -- dsply_manuf --

    ########################################
41➤ FUNCTION valid_null(array_idx, array_size)
    ########################################
      DEFINE        array_idx       SMALLINT,
                    array_size      SMALLINT,

                    next_fld        SMALLINT,
                    last_key        INTEGER

42➤   LET last_key = FGL_LASTKEY()
43➤   LET next_fld = (last_key = FGL_KEYVAL("right"))
                    OR (last_key = FGL_KEYVAL("return"))
                    OR (last_key = FGL_KEYVAL("tab"))

44➤   IF (array_idx >= array_size) THEN     --* cursor is on last, empty line
45➤     IF next_fld THEN        --*  AND user moves to next field
          RETURN (FALSE)
        END IF
```

46➤ If the cursor is not on the last line of the array, then the null field is invalid.

47➤ If next_fld is FALSE, the user has pressed either the Accept key or the up arrow in an attempt to move out of the "empty" line. The function notifies the user that "empty" lines cannot exist in the middle of the array and tells the user to delete the line or fill in the current line. The manu_code field cannot remain null, so the function returns FALSE.

48➤ If execution reaches this point, the cursor is on the last line of the array and the user has pressed either Accept or up arrow. The function returns TRUE to indicate that this condition allows a null manu_code field.

The reshuffle() Function

49➤ The direction variable holds one of two possible values: "I" indicates an insert while "D" indicates a delete. This variable controls the direction that lines are moved within the ga_mrowid array. The clear_it variable contains the array index of the line to clear when the reshuffle is complete.

50➤ The function calls the ARR_CURR() and ARR_COUNT() functions to obtain the current cursor position (pcurr) and the current number of lines in the array (ptotal).

51➤ If the user is performing an insert, the function needs to move all lines from the cursor position to the end of the array down one line to make room for an "empty" line in ga_mrowid.

52➤ The FOR statement starts with the last line in ga_mrowid, moving data down one line at a time until it reaches the current cursor position. The STEP clause defines the increment by which the counter variable (i in this case) is changed each time the FOR loop iterates. With no STEP clause, the FOR loop increments the counter variable by one. The STEP -1 clause tells the FOR to decrement the counting variable, i, by one for each iteration.

53➤ The clear_it variable is set to the current cursor position. This line still contains values and needs to be cleared before the new manufact row can be stored. The line is cleared by the code described in Note 56.

54➤ If the user is performing a delete, the function needs to move all lines from the current cursor position to the end of the array up one line to remove the line associated with the line to be deleted. The FOR statement starts with the line after of the current cursor position, moving the data up by one line until it reaches the last line of ga_mrowid.

The STEP clause is not required because incrementing the counting variable by one is the default behavior of FOR.

```
46➤  ELSE                           --* cursor is on an empty line
                                    --*   within the array

47➤    IF NOT next_fld THEN         --*   user presses key that
                                    --*     does NOT move to next field
        LET ga_dsplymsg[1] = "You cannot leave an empty line in the middle "
        LET ga_dsplymsg[2] = " of the array. To continue, either: "
        LET ga_dsplymsg[3] = "     - enter a manufacturer in the line"
        LET ga_dsplymsg[4] = "     - delete the empty line "
        CALL message_window(7, 12)
      END IF
      RETURN (FALSE)
    END IF

48➤  RETURN (TRUE)

  END FUNCTION  -- valid_null --

  ########################################
  FUNCTION reshuffle(direction)
  ########################################
49➤  DEFINE       direction             CHAR(1),

                  pcurr, ptotal, i      SMALLINT,
                  clear_it              SMALLINT

50➤  LET pcurr = ARR_CURR()
    LET ptotal = ARR_COUNT()

51➤  IF direction = "I" THEN      --* reshuffle to create an open
                                  --*   position in the array
52➤    FOR i = ptotal TO pcurr STEP -1
        LET ga_mrowid[i + 1].* = ga_mrowid[i].*
      END FOR

53➤    LET clear_it = pcurr
    END IF

54➤  IF direction = "D" THEN     --* reshuffle to get rid of the
                                --*   open position in the array

      IF pcurr < ptotal THEN
        FOR i = pcurr TO ptotal
          LET ga_mrowid[i].* = ga_mrowid[i + 1].*
        END FOR
      END IF
```

This FOR loop is only executed if the user is not deleting the last line of the array. To delete the last line, the program need not shuffle the lines of ga_mrowid. The program just removes the deleted line (see Note 56).

55➤ The clear_it variable is set to the last line of the array. After reshuffle() has moved up all lines of ga_mrowid, the program needs to clear only the last line. The line is cleared by the code described in Note 56.

56➤ These LET statements clear the clear_it line of ga_mrowid.

The verify_mdel() Function

57➤ The nested SELECT statement determines if the manufacturer about to be deleted has any stock items currently defined in the database. It performs this verification in three steps:

1. Obtain the ROWID of the row to be deleted from the ga_drows array at the index location specified by array_idx.
2. Use this ROWID as a WHERE condition for the subquery to find the manufacturer code for the row to be deleted.
3. Use the manufacturer code returned by the subquery as a WHERE condition for the outer SELECT to count the number of rows in the stock table which have this manufacturer code.
4. Store the result of the query in the stock_cnt variable.

58➤ If stock items exist, the program notifies the user that the program cannot delete the associated manufacturer. The data in the stock table would be inconsistent if this manufact row was deleted so the verify_mdel() function returns FALSE.

59➤ If no stock items for this manufacturer exist, verify_mdel() returns TRUE to indicate that the manufact row can be deleted without leaving inconsistent data.

```
55➤       LET clear_it = ptotal

        END IF

56➤     LET ga_mrowid[clear_it].mrowid = 0
        LET ga_mrowid[clear_it].op_flag = NULL

      END FUNCTION  -- reshuffle --

      ########################################
      FUNCTION verify_mdel(array_idx)
      ########################################
        DEFINE        array_idx        SMALLINT,

                      stock_cnt        SMALLINT

57➤     SELECT COUNT(*)
        INTO stock_cnt
        FROM stock
        WHERE manu_code = ( SELECT manu_code
                            FROM manufact
                            WHERE ROWID = ga_drows[array_idx].mrowid )

58➤     IF stock_cnt > 0 THEN
          LET ga_dsplymsg[1] = "Inventory currently has stock items made"
          LET ga_dsplymsg[2] = "  by manufacturer ", ga_drows[array_idx].manu_code
          LET ga_dsplymsg[3] = "Cannot delete manufacturer while stock items"
          LET ga_dsplymsg[4] = "  exist."
          CALL message_window(6,9)

          RETURN (FALSE)
        END IF

59➤     RETURN (TRUE)
      END FUNCTION  -- verify_mdel --
```

The choose_op() Function

60➤ The FOR statement moves through the ga_mrowid array, checking the op_flag field in each line. This field indicates what operation to perform on the row identified by the associated mrowid field. If op_flag is null, no operation is performed because the user has neither modified nor added data at this position.

61➤ If the op_flag is "I", the user has added the line. The program calls the insert_manuf() function to insert a new manufact row. The data for this new row is stored at the same index location in the ga_manuf array.

62➤ If the op_flag is "U", the user has updated the line. The program calls update_manuf() to update the row identified by the ROWID in ga_mrowid[idx] with the data in ga_manuf[idx].

63➤ This FOR statement moves through the ga_drows array. Each line of this array contains the ROWID and manufacturer code of a row to be deleted. The program calls the delete_manuf() function to delete the row indicated by ga_drows[idx].

The insert_manuf() Function

64➤ The WHENEVER ERROR statements surround the INSERT to prevent automatic error checking. The function does its own error checking to test the success of the insert (see Note 66).

65➤ The INSERT statement adds a new manufact row to the database. To access the new row's values, it uses the array_idx variable to index into the ga_manuf array.

66➤ If the INSERT is not successful, the function displays an error message containing the error code and the manufacturer code that was not inserted. The error code identifies the cause of the failure and the manufacturer code identifies which manufacturer failed. It is useful to identify which row was not added because all inserts are performed after the user presses the Accept key. If the program cannot add one of the manufacturers, the user needs to know which one failed.

If the INSERT is successful, the function displays a window notifying the user of the row that has been added.

```
      #########################################
      FUNCTION choose_op()
      #########################################
        DEFINE        idx    SMALLINT

60➤     FOR idx = 1 TO ARR_COUNT()
          CASE ga_mrowid[idx].op_flag
61➤         WHEN "I"
              CALL insert_manuf(idx)
62➤         WHEN "U"
              CALL update_manuf(idx)
          END CASE
        END FOR

63➤     FOR idx = 1 TO g_idx
          CALL delete_manuf(idx)
        END FOR

      END FUNCTION  -- choose_op --

      #########################################
      FUNCTION insert_manuf(array_idx)
      #########################################
        DEFINE        array_idx        SMALLINT

64➤   WHENEVER ERROR CONTINUE
65➤     INSERT INTO manufact  (manu_code, manu_name, lead_time)
        VALUES (ga_manuf[array_idx].manu_code,
                ga_manuf[array_idx].manu_name,
                ga_manuf[array_idx].lead_time)
      WHENEVER ERROR STOP

66➤     IF (status < 0) THEN
          ERROR status USING "-<<<<<<<<<<<",
              ": Unable to complete manufact insert of ",
              ga_manuf[array_idx].manu_code
        ELSE
          LET ga_dsplymsg[1] = "Manufacturer ", ga_manuf[array_idx].manu_code,
             " has been inserted."
          CALL message_window(6,6)
        END IF

      END FUNCTION  -- insert_manuf --
```

The update_manuf() Function

67➤ The program obtains the ROWID for the current row from the ga_mrowid array and the current row's manu_code value from the ga_manuf array. These values are needed as arguments to the verify_rowid() function.

68➤ The verify_rowid() function makes sure that the ROWID of the row about to be updated still correctly identifies the row selected for update. Even though a ROWID uniquely identifies a row, the ROWIDs in the ga_drows array were selected from the database at the beginning of the program. In the intervening period, another user may have updated or deleted this row and the database engine may have reassigned this ROWID to a new row.

In any of these cases, this ROWID no longer contains the desired manufacturer information. This check prevents the UPDATE (see Note 69) from updating the wrong manufact row.

69➤ The UPDATE statement updates the row identified by the ROWID in ga_mrowid[array_idx]. This row is updated with the values in ga_manuf[array_idx].

The delete_manuf() Function

70➤ The verify_mdel() function verifies that the row about to be deleted does not have stock items currently defined in the stock table. If stock items exist, verify_mdel() returns FALSE and the delete_manuf() function does not delete the row.

71➤ The verify_rowid() function makes sure that the ROWID of the row about to be deleted still correctly identifies the row selected for deletion. See Note 68 for the ways in which the ROWID can become incorrect. This check prevents the DELETE (see Note 72) from removing a row which the user did not intend to delete.

72➤ If ROWID in ga_drows[del_idx] still identifies the desired manufact row, the DELETE statement deletes this row.

```
########################################
FUNCTION update_manuf(array_idx)
########################################
  DEFINE        array_idx        SMALLINT,

                mrowid           INTEGER,
                mcode            LIKE manufact.manu_code

67➤  LET mrowid = ga_mrowid[array_idx].mrowid
  LET mcode = ga_manuf[array_idx].manu_code
68➤  IF verify_rowid(mrowid, mcode) THEN

WHENEVER ERROR CONTINUE
69➤    UPDATE manufact SET (manu_code, manu_name, lead_time) =
      (ga_manuf[array_idx].manu_code, ga_manuf[array_idx].manu_name,
       ga_manuf[array_idx].lead_time)
    WHERE ROWID = mrowid
WHENEVER ERROR STOP

    IF (status < 0) THEN
      ERROR status USING "-<<<<<<<<<<<",
        ": Unable to complete manufact update of ", mcode
    END IF

    LET ga_dsplymsg[1] = "Manufacturer ", mcode, " has been updated."
    CALL message_window(6,6)
  END IF

END FUNCTION  -- update_manuf --

########################################
FUNCTION delete_manuf(del_idx)
########################################
  DEFINE        del_idx        SMALLINT,

                msg_text       CHAR(40),
                mrowid        INTEGER

70➤  IF verify_mdel(del_idx) THEN
    LET mrowid = ga_drows[del_idx].mrowid
71➤    IF verify_rowid(mrowid, ga_drows[del_idx].manu_code) THEN

WHENEVER ERROR CONTINUE
72➤      DELETE FROM manufact
      WHERE rowid = mrowid
WHENEVER ERROR STOP

      IF (status < 0) THEN
        ERROR status USING "-<<<<<<<<<<<",
          ": Unable to complete manufact delete of ",
          ga_drows[del_idx].manu_code
      END IF
```

The verify_rowid() Function

73➤ The SELECT statement checks for a manufact row with the specified ROWID (mrowid is passed in as an argument).

74➤ If no manufact row has this ROWID, the SELECT returns a status of NOTFOUND. If the manu_code has been updated or the ROWID has been reassigned to another manufact row, then code_on_disk no longer matches the ga_drows[mrowid].manu_code. In any of these cases, the function notifies the user that the row to be deleted has already been deleted. It returns FALSE to indicate that the ROWID is no longer valid.

75➤ If the manu_code of the row identified by mrowid still matches the manu_code of this row on disk, the function returns TRUE.

The save_rowid() Function

76➤ The g_idx variable is a global variable to indicate the last line of the ga_drows array. If this variable is still null, the LET statement initializes it to zero.

77➤ The function increments the g_idx index to move to the next available line of ga_drows. It then stores the ROWID and manu_code of the row to be deleted at this location of ga_drows. This information is now saved so the rows can be deleted at a later time.

```
      LET ga_dsplymsg[1] = "Manufacturer ", ga_drows[del_idx].manu_code,
        " has been deleted."
      CALL message_window(6,6)
    END IF
  END IF

END FUNCTION  -- delete_manuf --

########################################
FUNCTION verify_rowid(mrowid, code_in_mem)
########################################
  DEFINE        mrowid        INTEGER,
                code_in_mem   LIKE manufact.manu_code,

                code_on_disk  LIKE manufact.manu_code

73➤  SELECT manu_code
  INTO code_on_disk
  FROM manufact
  WHERE ROWID = mrowid

74➤  IF (status = NOTFOUND)
      OR (code_on_disk <> code_in_mem)
  THEN
    ERROR "Manufacturer ", code_in_mem,
        " has been deleted by another user."
    RETURN (FALSE)
  END IF

75➤  RETURN (TRUE)

END FUNCTION  -- verify_rowid --

########################################
FUNCTION save_rowid(mrowid, mcode)
########################################
  DEFINE        mrowid        INTEGER,
                mcode         LIKE manufact.manu_code

76➤  IF g_idx IS NULL THEN
    LET g_idx = 0
  END IF

77➤  LET g_idx = g_idx + 1
  LET ga_drows[g_idx].mrowid = mrowid
  LET ga_drows[g_idx].manu_code = mcode

END FUNCTION  -- save_rowid --
```

To locate any function definition see the Function Index on page 728.

11

Implementing a Master/Detail Relationship

This example demonstrates a relatively complicated user interaction, one that involves multiple forms in a master-detail relationship. The INPUT ARRAY statement controls input to the detail form.

A key usability issue in such an interaction is the provision of a reliable escape route for the user, who should have a way of abandoning the interaction at any point without being forced to pass through meaningless input steps (and, needless to say, without risk of entering bad data to the database). This program is designed so that the user can press the Interrupt key to exit cleanly at any point in the interaction.

Program Overview

The program handles the entry of one new sales order for the demonstration database. An order is associated with a set of items, each with a price, quantity and total price. This sort of master-detail relationship is common in business data processing.

The program executes the following sequence of steps:

1. The program collects the information about the order as a whole (the customer and purchase-order numbers).
2. The program collects multiple items as rows in a scrolling array.

   It calculates the total price (line-item extension) automatically and updates the order subtotal as each item is completed.
3. When the user indicates that all items have been entered, the program calculates sales tax.
4. The user enters shipping instructions, if necessary, and confirms the final order, which is then inserted in the database.

Although large and fairly complete, this program would normally be only one phase of an order-entry system. However it illustrates most of the features of this kind of an interaction.

To help you follow the actions of the code, here are sample screens as the program displays them.

Input begins with entry of a customer number in function input_cust().

```
+------------------------------------------------------------------------------+
|                                                                              |
|                                 ORDER ADD                                    |
|Customer Number:[          ] Company Name:[                    ]             |
|Order No:[          ] Order Date:[          ] PO Number:[          ]         |
|------------------------------------------------------------------------------|
|Item No. Stock No Manuf    Description     Quantity    Price        Total     |
|[      ] [      ] [   ] [                ] [      ] [          ] [           ]|
|[      ] [      ] [   ] [                ] [      ] [          ] [           ]|
|[      ] [      ] [   ] [                ] [      ] [          ] [           ]|
|[      ] [      ] [   ] [                ] [      ] [          ] [           ]|
|                                                              ---------------|
|                                                     Sub-Total: [           ]|
|    Tax Rate [      ]% [      ]                      Sales Tax: [           ]|
|------------------------------------------------------------------------------|
|                                                   Order Total: [           ]|
| Enter the customer number and press RETURN. Press CTRL-W for Help.          |
| Press Cancel to exit without saving.                                         |
|Enter a customer number or press F5 (CTRL-F) for a list.                      |
+------------------------------------------------------------------------------+
```

The user can request a list of customer numbers; the cust_popup() function displays a scrolling list in a new window.

```
+------------------------------------------------------------------------------+
|                                                                              |
|                                  ORDER ADD                                   |
|Customer Number:[            ] Company Name:[                     ]           |
|Order No:[              ] Order Date:[            ] PO Number:[          ]    |
|-+------------------------------------------+---------------------------------|
|I| Move cursor using F3, F4, and arrow keys. |ity     Price          Total    |
|[| Press Accept to select a company.         |   ] [           ] [           ]|
|[|                                           |   ] [           ] [           ]|
|[|   Customer No.        Company Name        |   ] [           ] [           ]|
|[|  [          101] [All Sports Supplies ]   |   ] [           ] [           ]|
| |  [          102] [Sports Spot         ]   |              ----------------|
| |  [          103] [Phil's Sports       ]   |     Sub-Total: [            ]|
| |  [          104] [Play Ball!          ]   |     Sales Tax: [            ]|
|-|  [          105] [Los Altos Sports    ]   |------------------------------|
| |                                           |   Order Total: [            ]|
| |                                           |ess CTRL-W for Help.          |
| |                                           |                              |
|E+-------------------------------------------+r a list.                     |
+------------------------------------------------------------------------------+
```

The program automatically supplies the customer name and the current date. After entry of the purchase order (PO) number, the cursor is positioned to enter a stock number for the first line item. Each item must be identified with a stock number and a manufacturer code. The INPUT ARRAY is handled in the input_items() function.

```
+------------------------------------------------------------------------------+
|                                                                              |
|                                ORDER ADD                                     |
|Customer Number:[        104] Company Name:[Play Ball!            ]          |
|Order No:[             ] Order Date:[05/21/1991] PO Number:[ZZ009932   ]     |
|------------------------------------------------------------------------------|
|Item No. Stock No Manuf     Description      Quantity      Price        Total |
|[     1] [       ] [    ] [                ] [        ] [          ] [        ]|
|[      ] [       ] [    ] [                ] [        ] [          ] [        ]|
|[      ] [       ] [    ] [                ] [        ] [          ] [        ]|
|[      ] [       ] [    ] [                ] [        ] [          ] [        ]|
|                                                          -------------------|
|                                                   Sub-Total: [             ]|
|    Tax Rate [        ]%  [      ]                 Sales Tax: [             ]|
|------------------------------------------------------------------------------|
|                                                 Order Total: [             ]|
| Enter the item information and press Accept. Press CTRL-W for Help.          |
| Press Cancel to exit without saving.                                         |
|Enter a stock number or press F5 (CTRL-F) for a list.                         |
+------------------------------------------------------------------------------+
```

If the user requests a list of existing stock numbers, stock_popup() displays a scrolling list of rows joined from the stock and manufact tables.

```
+------------------------------------------------------------------------------+
|                                                                              |
|                                ORDER ADD                                     |
|Customer Number:[        104] Company Name:[Play Ball!            ]          |
|Order No:[             ] Order Date:[05/21/1991] PO Number:[ZZ009932   ]     |
|+--------------------------------------------------------------------------+-|
|| Move cursor using F3, F4, and arrow keys.                                | |
|| Press Accept to select a stock item.                                     |]|
||                                                                          |]|
||  Stock No.   Description      Manufacturer Code/Name     Unit  Unit Price |]|
||  [      1] [baseball gloves] [HRO ][Hero          ] [case] [  $250.00]   |]|
||  [      1] [baseball gloves] [HSK ][Husky         ] [case] [  $800.00]   |-|
||  [      1] [baseball gloves] [SMT ][Smith         ] [case] [  $450.00]   |]|
||  [      2] [baseball       ] [HRO ][Hero          ] [case] [  $126.00]   |]|
||  [      3] [baseball bat   ] [HSK ][Husky         ] [case] [  $240.00]   |-|
||                                                                          |]|
||                                                                          | |
||                                                                          | |
|+--------------------------------------------------------------------------+ |
+------------------------------------------------------------------------------+
```

The item description is supplied from the database, and the total price is recalculated when the cursor leaves the Quantity column. The Subtotal field is updated as each item is completed. The user is allowed to move back to previous rows with the up and down arrow keys, and to edit previous entries of stock number, manufacturer, and quantity. If such corrections were not allowed, the only way to correct a typing error would be to cancel the entire order and start over, which would not be acceptable to most users.

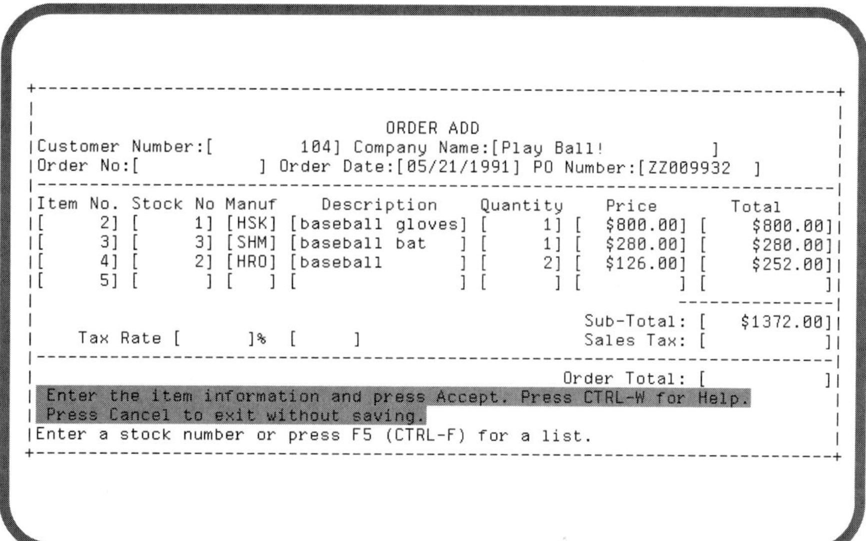

When the user presses Accept the program asks if the order is to be shipped now. If the answer is yes, shipping instructions are taken in another window.

```
+-------------------------------------------------------------------------+
|                                                                         |
|                            ORDER ADD                                   |
|Customer Number:[        104] Company Name:[Play Ball!          ]        |
|Order No:[          ] Order Date:[05/21/1991] PO Number:[ZZ009932  ]     |
|--+------------------------------------------------------------+----|
|It| Press Accept to save shipping information.                 |    |
|[ | Press Cancel to exit w/out saving. Press CTRL-W for Help.  |.00]|
|[ |                                                            |.00]|
|[ |                   SHIPPING INFORMATION                     |.00]|
|[ |  Customer Number:[        104]  Company Name:[Play Ball!      ]|   ]|
|  |  Order No:[          ]          Order Date:[05/21/1991]    |----|
|  |                                                            |.00]|
|  |  Ship Date: [05/21/1991]                                   |.18]|
|--|  Shipping Instructions:[                               ]   |----|
|  |  Shipping Weight (in lbs.): [         ]                    |.18]|
|  |                                                            |    |
|P |           Order Amount (incl. Tax)  :  [    $1461.18]      |    |
|  |           Shipping Charge ($1.50/lb):    [     $0.00]      |    |
+--|          ---------------------------------------           |----+
   |                          Order Total: [    $1461.18]       |
   |                                                            |
   +------------------------------------------------------------+
```

When all input has been gathered, the user is asked to confirm the order before it is finally recorded in the database.

Function Overview

Function Name	Purpose
add_order()	Calls routines needed to add an order.
input_cust()	Accepts user input for the customer number.
cust_popup()	Displays a popup window of customers.
input_order()	Accepts user input for date, PO number.
input_items()	Accepts user input for order line items.
renum_items()	Renumbers the item numbers when an item is added or deleted in the items array.
stock_popup()	Displays a popup window for stock numbers and manufacturer codes.
dsply_taxes()	Displays retail tax rate and sales tax amount based on state in customer's address. Also calculates order's total by adding in sales tax amount.
order_amount()	Calculates the total cost of the order by summing the items entered so far.
tax_rates()	Supplies the appropriate tax schedule for a customer. *See description in Example 4.*

ship_order()	Opens a window and a form for shipping information.
input_ship()	Accepts user input for shipping info. This function resembles the change_cust() function from Example 6.
order_tx()	Performs database operations to insert the order and items in a single transaction.
insert_order()	Adds an order row to the database.
insert_items()	Adds associated items row(s) to the database.
clear_lines()	Clears any number of lines starting at any line. *See description in Example 6.*
init_msgs()	Initializes the members of the ga_dsplymsg array to null. *See description in Example 2.*
msg()	Displays a brief, informative message. *See description in Example 5.*
message_window()	Opens a window and displays the contents of the ga_dsplymsg global array. *See description in Example 2.*
prompt_window()	Displays a message and prompts the user for affirmation or negation. This function is a variation on the message_window() function that appears in Example 2. *See description in Example 4.*

The f_orders Form

1➤ This form is visible at all times, although it is partly covered by popup windows during some phases of the order entry process. Its principal feature is a scrolling array of order items. The INPUT ARRAY statement is used to connect this screen array to the program array of records, ga_items.

2➤ To construct a screen array, you first define a repeating set of fields. All the fields with the same tag (for example, all f005 fields) must be the same size. They do not have to be arranged in regular columns, but any other arrangement would be hard for the user to understand.

The same field tag number must appear in each field. This is only common sense, but the form compiler does check for this.

3➤ Each field in an array row is described once in the ATTRIBUTES section. Here, the f005 fields are associated with the item_num column of the items table. This column of fields is marked NOENTRY; the item numbers are maintained by the program, not input by the user.

4➤ The SCREEN RECORD statement defines the array of records. It specifies a name for the array (sa_items) which is used in the INPUT ARRAY statement. It specifies the number of rows in the array (4). (This is the number on the screen, not the size of the program array that receives the input. In this program, up to 10 item rows can be entered, and the INPUT ARRAY statement lets the user scroll through them using the 4 lines of the screen array.) This statement also specifies which fields are part of a row of the array. It names them by their table and column, not by the screen field tags used earlier.

f_orders form file

1➤
```
DATABASE stores2t

SCREEN
{

Customer Number:[f000       ] Company Name:[f001                ]
Order No:[f002       ] Order Date:[f003      ] PO Number:[f004      ]
----------------------------------------------------------------------------
Item No. Stock No Manuf    Description       Quantity    Price       Total
[f005  ] [f006  ] [f07] [f008              ] [f009  ] [f010     ] [f011       ]
[f005  ] [f006  ] [f07] [f008              ] [f009  ] [f010     ] [f011       ]
[f005  ] [f006  ] [f07] [f008              ] [f009  ] [f010     ] [f011       ]
[f005  ] [f006  ] [f07] [f008              ] [f009  ] [f010     ] [f011       ]
                                                               --------------
                                                   Sub-Total: [f012       ]
    Tax Rate [f013  ]%  [f014 ]                    Sales Tax: [f015       ]
----------------------------------------------------------------------------
                                                 Order Total: [f016       ]
}

TABLES
customer orders items stock state

ATTRIBUTES
f000 = orders.customer_num;
f001 = customer.company;

f002 = orders.order_num;
f003 = orders.order_date, DEFAULT = TODAY;
f004 = orders.po_num;
```
2➤ (marks the first [f005 ...] screen array row above)

3➤
```
f005 = items.item_num, NOENTRY;
f006 = items.stock_num;
f07  = items.manu_code, UPSHIFT;
f008 = stock.description, NOENTRY;
f009 = items.quantity;
f010 = stock.unit_price, NOENTRY;
f011 = items.total_price, NOENTRY;

f012 = formonly.order_amount;
f013 = formonly.tax_rate;
f014 = state.code, NOENTRY;
f015 = formonly.sales_tax TYPE MONEY;
f016 = formonly.order_total;

INSTRUCTIONS
```
4➤
```
SCREEN RECORD sa_items[4](items.item_num, items.stock_num, items.manu_code,
        stock.description, items.quantity, stock.unit_price, items.total_price)
```

The f_custsel Form

1➤ The f_custsel form is s used as a popup window to display valid customer numbers and company names. These customer numbers are stored in the customer table.

2➤ The form defines the sa_cust screen array to use with this popup window.

The f_stocksel Form

1➤ The f_stocksel form is s used as a popup window to display stock items defined in the stock table. The form displays related information from the manufact table as well.

2➤ The screen array for this popup window is sa_stock.

f_custsel form file

```
1➤ DATABASE stores2t

SCREEN
{
    Customer No.      Company Name
   [f001        ]  [f002                  ]
   [f001        ]  [f002                  ]
   [f001        ]  [f002                  ]
   [f001        ]  [f002                  ]
   [f001        ]  [f002                  ]
}

TABLES
customer

ATTRIBUTES
f001 = customer.customer_num, ZEROFILL;
f002 = customer.company;

2➤ INSTRUCTIONS
  SCREEN RECORD sa_cust[5] (customer.customer_num THRU customer.company)
```

f_stocksel form file

```
1➤ DATABASE stores2t

SCREEN
{
  Stock No.   Description       Manufacturer Code/Name    Unit   Unit Price
  [f001  ] [f002              ] [f003][f004             ] [f005] [f006     ]
  [f001  ] [f002              ] [f003][f004             ] [f005] [f006     ]
  [f001  ] [f002              ] [f003][f004             ] [f005] [f006     ]
  [f001  ] [f002              ] [f003][f004             ] [f005] [f006     ]
  [f001  ] [f002              ] [f003][f004             ] [f005] [f006     ]
}

TABLES
stock
manufact

ATTRIBUTES
f001 = stock.stock_num;
f002 = stock.description;
f003 = stock.manu_code;
f004 = manufact.manu_name;
f005 = stock.unit;
f006 = stock.unit_price;

2➤ INSTRUCTIONS
  SCREEN RECORD sa_stock[5] (stock.stock_num THRU stock.unit_price)
```

The f_ship Form

1➤ This form displays the shipping information. In this example, it accepts the shipping information for the order currently being entered. The customer number, company name and order date of the current order display in the fields at the top of the form. The order number field is blank because the order has not yet been saved in the database. Only then is an order assigned an order number.

2➤ The order number field is defined as FORMONLY because it needs to be able to accept user input (see Example 21). Because the order_num column is defined as SERIAL, the database maintains its value. **4GL** prevents the user from modifying SERIAL values by preventing the cursor from entering any field associated with a SERIAL column. If the field was defined as orders.order_num, the user would be unable to enter search criteria in this field.

3➤ The ship_date field uses the DEFAULT attribute and the TODAY function to initialize an empty ship_date field with today's date.

4➤ The order_amount field is defined as NOENTRY because this field does not require user entry. The order amount value is calculated by the application program.

5➤ The form defines the sr_ship screen record so an INPUT statement can access all input fields on the form using the *record*.* notation.

f_ship form file

```
1➤ DATABASE stores2t

   SCREEN
   {

     Customer Number:[f000       ]  Company Name:[f001                  ]
     Order No:[f002       ]         Order Date:[f003       ]

     Ship Date: [f004       ]
     Shipping Instructions:[f005                                      ]
     Shipping Weight (in lbs.): [f006     ]

               Order Amount (incl. Tax)  :  [f007          ]
               Shipping Charge ($1.50/lb):    [f008        ]
              --------------------------------------------
                              Order Total: [f009           ]
   }

   TABLES
   customer orders

   ATTRIBUTES
   f000 = orders.customer_num;
   f001 = customer.company;
2➤ f002 = formonly.order_num;
   f003 = orders.order_date;

3➤ f004 = orders.ship_date, DEFAULT = TODAY;
   f005 = orders.ship_instruct;
   f006 = orders.ship_weight, DEFAULT = 0.00;

4➤ f007 = formonly.order_amount, NOENTRY;
   f008 = orders.ship_charge;
   f009 = formonly.order_total, NOENTRY;


   INSTRUCTIONS
5➤   SCREEN RECORD sr_ship(orders.ship_date, orders.ship_instruct,
                           orders.ship_weight, orders.ship_charge)
```

The DATABASE and GLOBALS Statements

1➤ This program must be used with a version of the demonstration database that supports transactions.

Transaction processing is necessary to ensure that the order row and all of the item rows are inserted successfully, or that none are inserted.

2➤ The gr_customer record holds a row from the customer table.

The gr_orders and ga_items records are used to construct rows for those tables. Note that ga_items is an array of records. Its size determines how many line items may be entered for any order.

3➤ The gr_charges record is used to collect tax and shipping charges.

4➤ The gr_ship record is used to collect shipping information. These fields eventually contribute to the order row.

All these records could, in this program, be module variables. Global variables are only required when the functions that use a record are in different modules.

4GL source file

```
1➤ DATABASE stores2t
   GLOBALS
2➤  DEFINE   gr_customer RECORD LIKE customer.*,
               gr_orders RECORD
                   order_num LIKE orders.order_num,
                   order_date LIKE orders.order_date,
                   po_num  LIKE orders.po_num,
                   order_amount MONEY(8,2),
                   order_total MONEY(10,2)
               END RECORD,

               ga_items ARRAY[10] OF RECORD
                   item_num LIKE items.item_num,
                   stock_num LIKE items.stock_num,
                   manu_code LIKE items.manu_code,
                   description LIKE stock.description,
                   quantity LIKE items.quantity,
                   unit_price LIKE stock.unit_price,
                   total_price LIKE items.total_price
               END RECORD,

3➤             gr_charges RECORD
                   tax_rateDECIMAL(5,3),
                   ship_chargeLIKE orders.ship_charge,
                   sales_taxMONEY(9),
                   order_totalMONEY(11)
               END RECORD,

4➤             gr_ship RECORD
                   ship_dateLIKE orders.ship_date,
                   ship_instructLIKE orders.ship_instruct,
                   ship_weightLIKE orders.ship_weight,
                   ship_chargeLIKE orders.ship_charge
               END RECORD

   # used by init_msgs(), message_window(), and prompt_window() to allow
   # user to display text in a message or prompt window.
     DEFINE        ga_dsplymsg ARRAY[5] OF CHAR(48)

   END GLOBALS
```

The MAIN Function

5➤ As in other examples, the Interrupt key is deferred so that its use will not terminate the program. The use of the key is tested after each input operation, and taken as a signal that the user wants to quit.

6➤ This OPEN WINDOW and the following OPEN FORM and DISPLAY FORM statements could be combined into a single OPEN WINDOW WITH FORM statement.

7➤ All the processing for a single order entry has been delegated to this function.

This example program manages only a single order; in a real application the add_order() function might be called in a loop, or from a vertical menu.

The add_order() Function

8➤ The new order will be constructed in this record. Fields not filled in by the following code will be null.

9➤ This legend reminds the user that the Cancel (or Interrupt) key is available as an escape hatch. It remains on the screen throughout. It could be part of the form definition, but that would commit any program using this form to implement Cancel as an escape in the same way.

10➤ The input process has been divided for simplicity into three phases, each in a separate function. The user might choose to cancel in any of the phases and if he or she does so, the subsequent phase(s) should not be performed.

This set of IF statements shows one way to deal with such a serial dependency among functions. Each function returns TRUE when the user does *not* cancel. If the user does not cancel in input_cust(), input_order() will be called; if the user does not cancel in that function, input_items() is called; if it returns TRUE, the remainder of the entry process begins.

When there are more than 3 sequential dependencies the IF-stack becomes uncomfortably deep. Another method is to accumulate the status using AND as in this hypothetical fragment, which can be replicated as needed.

```
IF ok_so_far THEN
    LET ok_so_far = next_phase()
END IF
```

```
########################################
MAIN
########################################

  OPTIONS
    HELP FILE "hlpmsgs",
    FORM LINE 2,
    COMMENT LINE 1,
    MESSAGE LINE LAST
5➤  DEFER INTERRUPT

6➤  OPEN WINDOW w_main AT 2,3
     WITH 18 ROWS, 76 COLUMNS
     ATTRIBUTE (BORDER)
    OPEN FORM f_orders FROM "f_orders"
    DISPLAY FORM f_orders

7➤  CALL add_order()

    CLOSE FORM f_orders
    CLOSE WINDOW w_main
    CLEAR SCREEN
END MAIN

########################################
FUNCTION add_order()
########################################

8➤  INITIALIZE gr_orders.* TO NULL

    DISPLAY "ORDER ADD" AT 2, 34
    CALL clear_lines(2, 16)
9➤  DISPLAY " Press Cancel to exit without saving."
      AT 17, 1 ATTRIBUTE (REVERSE, YELLOW)

10➤ IF input_cust() THEN
      IF input_order() THEN
        IF input_items() THEN
          CALL dsply_taxes()
          IF prompt_window("Do you want to ship this order now?", 8, 12) THEN
            CALL ship_order()
          ELSE
            LET gr_ship.ship_date = NULL
          END IF

          CALL clear_lines(2, 16)

          LET ga_dsplymsg[1] = "Order entry complete."
```

11➤ A similar technique is used to control the actual insertion process. Prompt_window() returns TRUE when the user replies "Y"; order_tx() inserts the order and returns TRUE when the rows are inserted successfully.

12➤ The order number is a SERIAL value, created only when the order row is inserted. Here it is reported to the user, to be recorded on the entry documents.

The input_cust() Function

13➤ This function assists the user in entering the customer number, and makes certain that a valid one is entered. A valid customer number is essential since the customer number is the key that joins the orders and customer tables.

14➤ By clearing the int_flag just before the start of the INPUT statement, then testing it just afterward, the program can tell whether the INPUT was terminated by the Interrupt key or by the Accept key.

15➤ The INPUT statement begins here and extends onto the next page. Only the single form field named in the INPUT statement is accessible to the cursor.

16➤ Whenever a field is entered by the cursor, its BEFORE FIELD clause is executed. That includes the initial entry to the first (and in this case, only) field.

17➤ Whenever the cursor leaves a field, either due to a cursor-movement key or to the Accept key, its AFTER FIELD clause is executed. This is the normal place to put validation and verification code such as that which follows here.

The AFTER FIELD clause is *not* executed when the Interrupt key is used.

18➤ This test ensures that the user cannot leave this form without entering a customer number of some kind. Even if the Accept key was pressed, the NEXT FIELD statement forces the input process to continue.

If there were truly no escape, of course, users could be very frustrated. However the message "Press Cancel" is visible, and Interrupt will work.

```
11➤        IF prompt_window("Are you ready to save this order?", 8, 12) THEN
             IF order_tx() THEN
               CALL clear_lines(2, 16)

12➤            LET ga_dsplymsg[1] = "Order Number: ",
                           gr_orders.order_num USING "<<<<<<<<<<<"
               LET ga_dsplymsg[2] = " has been placed for Customer: ",
                           gr_customer.customer_num USING "<<<<<<<<<<<"
               LET ga_dsplymsg[3] = "Order Date: ", gr_orders.order_date
               CALL message_window(9, 13)

               CLEAR FORM
             END IF
           ELSE
             CLEAR FORM
             CALL msg("Order has been terminated.")
           END IF
         END IF
       END IF
     END IF

   END FUNCTION  -- add_order --

   ########################################
13➤ FUNCTION input_cust()
   ########################################

     DISPLAY
     " Enter the customer number and press RETURN. Press CTRL-W for Help."
       AT 16, 1 ATTRIBUTE (REVERSE, YELLOW)

14➤  LET int_flag = FALSE
15➤  INPUT BY NAME gr_customer.customer_num HELP 60
16➤    BEFORE FIELD customer_num
         MESSAGE "Enter a customer number or press F5 (CTRL-F) for a list."

17➤    AFTER FIELD customer_num
         IF gr_customer.customer_num IS NULL THEN
           ERROR "You must enter a customer number. Please try again."
18➤        NEXT FIELD customer_num
         END IF
```

19➤ The number entered by the user is validated against the database. Since there is a unique index on the customer.customer_num column, this SELECT can return at most one row, so no cursor is needed.

20➤ If the specified customer number is not in the database, the cursor is returned to the customer_num field and the user is asked to enter another number.

21➤ If the customer number is valid, the program gives visual feedback by filling in the customer name from the database.

22➤ The AFTER FIELD block for the customer number field ends at this point in the code.

23➤ When the user presses either key during the INPUT, the following code block is executed. The cust_popup() function displays a list of customers and returns null only if the user cancels, in which case the NEXT FIELD statement returns the user to input state. If the user does not cancel, the desired data has been selected from the popup list; it is saved and the input is ended.

24➤ Following the input, if Interrupt was entered, this flag will contain TRUE. The cancellation is confirmed with a message and the function returns FALSE, signalling its caller to proceed no further (see Note 10).

Note that the user might press Interrupt while looking at the popup list of customers. The cust_popup() function clears the int_flag before returning, so this IF can be affected only by Interrupt during this INPUT.

```
19➤        SELECT company, state
           INTO gr_customer.company, gr_customer.state
           FROM customer
           WHERE customer_num = gr_customer.customer_num

           IF (status = NOTFOUND) THEN
             ERROR
               "Unknown Customer number. Use F5 (CTRL-F) to see valid customers."
             LET gr_customer.customer_num = NULL
20➤          NEXT FIELD customer_num
           END IF

21➤        DISPLAY BY NAME gr_customer.company
           MESSAGE ""
22➤        EXIT INPUT

23➤      ON KEY (CONTROL-F, F5)
           IF INFIELD(customer_num) THEN
             CALL cust_popup()
               RETURNING gr_customer.customer_num, gr_customer.company

             IF gr_customer.customer_num IS NULL THEN
               NEXT FIELD customer_num
             ELSE
               SELECT state
               INTO gr_customer.state
               FROM customer
               WHERE customer_num = gr_customer.customer_num
               DISPLAY BY NAME gr_customer.customer_num, gr_customer.company
             END IF
           END IF

       END INPUT

24➤    IF int_flag THEN
         LET int_flag = FALSE
         CALL clear_lines(2, 16)
         CLEAR FORM
         CALL msg("Order input terminated.")
         RETURN (FALSE)
       END IF

       RETURN (TRUE)
     END FUNCTION  -- input_cust --
```

The cust_popup() Function

25➤ The cust_popup() function is called from input_cust() when the user requests a display of customer numbers. It displays the list of numbers and names. If the user selects one, it returns both the number and the name. If the user cancels with Interrupt, it returns a null customer number.

26➤ The function loads all of the customer table into the pa_cust array (or as much as will fit).

Since the array is a local variable, it exists only while the function is active and has to be reloaded each time the function is called. In some applications this could cause performance problems, in which case the array could be made global and filled just once, when the program starts up. (While that would fix the performance problem, it would mean that the program would not reflect additions or deletions in the customer table until it was restarted.)

27➤ This window intentionally covers up the legend "Press Cancel to exit without saving" in the main window. If the user presses Cancel in this routine it will not cancel the entire order, but merely the popup display.

28➤ The FOREACH loop loads all customer numbers and names into the pa_cust array for display. The array has a fixed size while the size of the table is unknown. The function counts the rows as they are fetched and if it fills the array, it ends the loop early.

29➤ The IF statement checks for the (remote) possibility that no customers exist in the database. In that case the program sets up to return a null value and does not display the popup list.

30➤ A more likely event is that the array filled before the end of the table is reached. The display can still be performed but the user is told that the list is incomplete.

31➤ The SET_COUNT() library function tells DISPLAY ARRAY how many rows of the array are valid.

32➤ The ARR_CURR() library function returns the row number where the cursor rested when the display ended.

```
    ########################################
25➤ FUNCTION cust_popup()
    ########################################
26➤   DEFINE        pa_cust ARRAY[200] OF RECORD
                           customer_num  LIKE customer.customer_num,
                           company       LIKE customer.company
                    END RECORD,
                    idx          INTEGER,
                    cust_cnt     INTEGER,
                    array_sz     SMALLINT,
                    over_size    SMALLINT

      LET array_sz = 200       --* match size of pa_cust array

27➤   OPEN WINDOW w_custpop AT 7, 5
        WITH 12 ROWS, 44 COLUMNS
        ATTRIBUTE(BORDER, FORM LINE 4)
      OPEN FORM f_custsel FROM "f_custsel"
      DISPLAY FORM f_custsel
      DISPLAY "Move cursor using F3, F4, and arrow keys."
        AT 1,2
      DISPLAY "Press Accept to select a company."
        AT 2,2

      DECLARE c_custpop CURSOR FOR
        SELECT customer_num, company
        FROM customer
        ORDER BY customer_num

      LET over_size = FALSE
      LET cust_cnt = 1
28➤   FOREACH c_custpop INTO pa_cust[cust_cnt].*
        LET cust_cnt = cust_cnt + 1
        IF cust_cnt > array_sz THEN
          LET over_size = TRUE
          EXIT FOREACH
        END IF
      END FOREACH

      IF cust_cnt = 1 THEN
29➤     CALL msg("No customers exist in the database.")
        LET idx = 1
        LET pa_cust[idx].customer_num = NULL
      ELSE
        IF over_size THEN
30➤       MESSAGE "Customer array full: can only display ",
            array_sz USING "<<<<<<"
        END IF
31➤     CALL SET_COUNT(cust_cnt - 1)
        LET int_flag = FALSE
        DISPLAY ARRAY pa_cust TO sa_cust.*

32➤     LET idx = ARR_CURR()
```

33➤ An Interrupt at this stage of the program cancels only this interaction and not the entire order entry. The int_flag is cleared so that it will not affect the calling function. A null value is forced into the current row of the array.

34➤ The customer_num value in this row will be null in two cases: if the customer table was empty, and if the display ended with Interrupt. Otherwise the customer number reflects the user's choice and input_cust() can terminate.

The input_order() Function

35➤ The input_order() function collects the rest of the order header fields: the date and the customer's Purchase Order number. It returns TRUE normally, or FALSE to indicate that the user cancelled.

36➤ The BEFORE FIELD clause is executed when the cursor enters a field. It enters the order_date field as soon as the INPUT statement begins, since it is the first field listed in the BY NAME clause. Thus today's date, the most likely choice, will be displayed initially.

37➤ When the cursor leaves the field, it could only be null if the user had cleared it with control-D. In that case, today's date is again supplied, so as to make sure that a valid date is available.

38➤ Handling of Interrupt is similar to that in the input_cust() function.

```
    IF int_flag THEN
33➤   LET int_flag = FALSE
      CLEAR FORM
      CALL msg("No customer selected.")
      LET pa_cust[idx].customer_num = NULL
    END IF
  END IF

  CLOSE WINDOW w_custpop
34➤ RETURN pa_cust[idx].customer_num, pa_cust[idx].company

END FUNCTION  -- cust_popup --

########################################
35➤ FUNCTION input_order()
########################################

  CALL clear_lines(1, 16)
  DISPLAY
  " Enter the order information and press RETURN. Press CTRL-W for Help."
    AT 16, 1 ATTRIBUTE (REVERSE, YELLOW)

  LET int_flag = FALSE
  INPUT BY NAME gr_orders.order_date, gr_orders.po_num HELP 61
36➤ BEFORE FIELD order_date
      IF gr_orders.order_date IS NULL THEN
        LET gr_orders.order_date = TODAY
      END IF

37➤ AFTER FIELD order_date
      IF gr_orders.order_date IS NULL THEN
        LET gr_orders.order_date = TODAY
      END IF
  END INPUT

38➤ IF int_flag THEN
    LET int_flag = FALSE
    CALL clear_lines(2, 16)
    CLEAR FORM
    CALL msg("Order input terminated.")
    RETURN (FALSE)
  END IF

  RETURN (TRUE)
END FUNCTION  -- input_order --
```

The input_items() Function

39➤ The input_items() function manages the input of the line items. Item rows are entered into the ga_items array of records. The user is allowed to go back and change item rows previously entered.

As with input_cust() and input_order(), if the user cancels the operation the function returns FALSE as a signal.

40➤ The BEFORE ROW block is executed each time the cursor moves to a new row, including the move to the first row when the INPUT ARRAY begins. Two important indexes are captured here: curr_pa gets the row in the program array, ga_items; and curr_sa gets the current screen row.

41➤ The BEFORE INSERT block is executed each time a new row is added to the array. This can happen at the bottom of the array or at another position. The renum_items() function revises the item row numbers and redisplays them.

42➤ The stock number is the primary piece of information in an item row. Nothing else can be determined without a valid stock number. This block executes whenever the cursor leaves the stock number field of a row. This can be caused by several different key signals, processed as follows.

Accept	The user claims to be finished, so a stock number is not required for this row. However at least one item row must be entered for the order to be valid; if none have been, the user is returned to the form to enter one.
Up/Down	The user wants to move to a different row, so it is not essential that the current row have a stock number.
other keys	The user is required to enter a stock number.

The library function FGL_LASTKEY() is used to get the code for the last key pressed, and FGL_KEYVAL() is used to translate from words like "up" to the codes used in this particular implementation.

```
    ########################################
39➤ FUNCTION input_items()
    ########################################
      DEFINE        curr_pa       INTEGER,
                    curr_sa       INTEGER,
                    stock_cnt     INTEGER,
                    stock_item    LIKE stock.stock_num,
                    popup         SMALLINT,
                    keyval        INTEGER,
                    valid_key     SMALLINT

      CALL clear_lines(1, 16)
      DISPLAY
      " Enter the item information and press Accept. Press CTRL-W for Help."
        AT 16, 1 ATTRIBUTE (REVERSE, YELLOW)

      LET int_flag = FALSE
      INPUT ARRAY ga_items FROM sa_items.* HELP 62

40➤     BEFORE ROW
          LET curr_pa = ARR_CURR()
          LET curr_sa = SCR_LINE()

41➤     BEFORE INSERT
          CALL renum_items()

        BEFORE FIELD stock_num
          MESSAGE
       "Enter a stock number or press F5 (CTRL-F) for a list."
          LET popup = FALSE

42➤     AFTER FIELD stock_num
          IF ga_items[curr_pa].stock_num IS NULL THEN

            LET keyval = FGL_LASTKEY()
            IF keyval = FGL_KEYVAL("accept") THEN
              IF curr_pa = 1 THEN --* empty items array
                LET int_flag = TRUE--* code simulates a Cancel
                EXIT INPUT
              END IF
            ELSE    --* FGL_LASTKEY() <> FGL_KEYVAL("accept")
              LET valid_key = (keyval = FGL_KEYVAL("up"))
                  OR (keyval = FGL_KEYVAL("prevpage"))
              IF NOT valid_key THEN
                ERROR "You must enter a stock number. Please try again."
                NEXT FIELD stock_num
              END IF
            END IF
```

43➤ The cursor is leaving the stock number field and the field is not null. The following IF ensures that the user entered a valid number by counting the rows of the stock table that have this number. Multiple rows may appear in the table, since the manufacturer code is needed for uniqueness, but the user's entry is invalid unless the SELECT retrieves at least one row.

The popup variable is set when the stock_popup() function is used to select a stock number and manufacturer code. Since that function returns only good values, validation is not required.

44➤ This statement marks the end of the AFTER FIELD block for the stock number. The cursor will typically enter the manu_code field from stock number.

45➤ Like stock number, a manufacturer code is required to make an item valid. When the cursor leaves the field this code ensures that something has been entered.

46➤ Something was entered to manu_code; this passage validates it in combination with the previously-entered stock number, by selecting other stock information using these values as the key. (As before, if stock_popup() was used to obtain the value, validation is not needed.) If no row is found, something is wrong, and the user is forced to enter another manufacturer code.

It is possible that the user entered an invalid stock number. However, the stock number is known to exist in the table. A corresponding manu_code exists and stock_popup() can be used to find it.

47➤ The stock number and manufacturer have proved valid. Visual feedback is given by filling in the item description and unit price. The cursor is then sent to the quantity field.

```
43➤     ELSE      --* stock number is not null, continue
            IF NOT popup THEN
              LET stock_cnt = 0

              SELECT COUNT(*)
              INTO stock_cnt
              FROM stock
              WHERE stock_num = ga_items[curr_pa].stock_num

              IF (stock_cnt = 0) THEN
                ERROR
                "Unknown stock number. Use F5 (CTRL-F) to see valid stock numbers."
                LET ga_items[curr_pa].stock_num = NULL
                NEXT FIELD stock_num
              END IF
            END IF
        END IF
        MESSAGE ""

44➤   BEFORE FIELD manu_code
        MESSAGE
        "Enter the manufacturer code or press F5 (CTRL-F) for a list."

45➤   AFTER FIELD manu_code
        IF ga_items[curr_pa].manu_code IS NULL THEN
          ERROR
          "You must enter a manufacturer code. Use F5 (CTRL-F) to see valid codes."
          LET ga_items[curr_pa].manu_code = NULL
          NEXT FIELD manu_code

46➤     ELSE
          IF NOT popup THEN
            SELECT description, unit_price
            INTO ga_items[curr_pa].description, ga_items[curr_pa].unit_price
            FROM stock
            WHERE stock_num = ga_items[curr_pa].stock_num
              AND manu_code = ga_items[curr_pa].manu_code

            IF (status = NOTFOUND) THEN
              ERROR
  "Unknown manuf code for this stock number. Use F5 (CTRL-F) to see valid codes."
              LET ga_items[curr_pa].manu_code = NULL
              NEXT FIELD manu_code
             END IF
47➤          DISPLAY ga_items[curr_pa].description, ga_items[curr_pa].unit_price
              TO sa_items[curr_sa].description, sa_items[curr_sa].unit_price
            MESSAGE ""
            NEXT FIELD quantity
          END IF
        END IF
        MESSAGE ""
```

48➤ When the cursor enters the quantity field in this row for the first time, the field is initialized to 1.

49➤ When the cursor leaves the quantity field the program validates that the user has entered a reasonable value. If appropriate, the cursor is returned to the field. Otherwise, the total price (often called the "extension" of the line item) is calculated and displayed.

50➤ Once the total price for a line is known, the program can generate the order subtotal. The order_amount() function performs this operation.

51➤ When a new array row has been completed, this block ensures that the order subtotal is up to date.

This block may be redundant, since it is hard to see how it could be executed without the AFTER FIELD for quantity also having been executed.

52➤ When a row is deleted, the item rows must be renumbered and the order subtotal must be recalculated and displayed.

53➤ The user can request a display of stock numbers and manufacturer codes at any time during input. If the cursor is in the quantity column, the key is ignored. If the cursor is in the stock or manu_code column, the stock_popup() function is called to display a list and return a selected stock item.

54➤ The stock_popup() function can present all stock items, or only the stock with a particular stock number. If the cursor is in the stock number field the program assumes the user does not know a stock number, and sets up to display all. If the cursor is not in the stock number field it must be in the manu_code field; the program assumes the user is interested only in the stock number that was already entered.

55➤ The stock_popup() function returns a null stock_num and manu_code if the user cancels a popup initiated from the stock_num field. It returns a null manu_code if the user cancels a popup initiated from the manu_code field. In any event, the program returns the user to input in the field that was active.

```
48➤     BEFORE FIELD quantity
          IF ga_items[curr_pa].quantity IS NULL THEN
            LET ga_items[curr_pa].quantity = 1
          END IF

49➤     AFTER FIELD quantity
          IF ga_items[curr_pa].quantity IS NULL
              OR ga_items[curr_pa].quantity < 0
          THEN
            ERROR "Quantity must be greater than 0. Please try again."
            NEXT FIELD quantity
          END IF

          LET ga_items[curr_pa].total_price = ga_items[curr_pa].quantity
                    * ga_items[curr_pa].unit_price
          DISPLAY ga_items[curr_pa].total_price TO sa_items[curr_sa].total_price
50➤       CALL order_amount() RETURNING gr_orders.order_amount
          DISPLAY BY NAME gr_orders.order_amount

51➤     AFTER INSERT
          CALL order_amount() RETURNING gr_orders.order_amount
          DISPLAY BY NAME gr_orders.order_amount

52➤     AFTER DELETE
          CALL renum_items()
          CALL order_amount() RETURNING gr_orders.order_amount
          DISPLAY BY NAME gr_orders.order_amount

        AFTER INPUT
          CALL clear_lines(1, 16)
          MESSAGE ""

53➤     ON KEY (CONTROL-F, F5)
          IF INFIELD(stock_num) OR INFIELD(manu_code) THEN
54➤         IF INFIELD(stock_num) THEN
              LET stock_item = NULL
            ELSE
              LET stock_item = ga_items[curr_pa].stock_num
            END IF

            CALL stock_popup(stock_item)
              RETURNING ga_items[curr_pa].stock_num, ga_items[curr_pa].manu_code,
                 ga_items[curr_pa].description, ga_items[curr_pa].unit_price
55➤         IF ga_items[curr_pa].stock_num IS NULL THEN
              NEXT FIELD stock_num
            ELSE
              IF ga_items[curr_pa].manu_code IS NULL THEN
                NEXT FIELD manu_code
              END IF
            END IF
```

56➤ The user made a choice in stock_popup(), and now everything is known about the stock number. The information is displayed on the form and the cursor is sent to the quantity field.

57➤ As with input_cust() and input_order(), this function returns FALSE if the user has cancelled with Interrupt, or TRUE otherwise.

The renum_items() Function

58➤ This function maintains the line numbers in the leftmost column of the line item display. It is called each time a line is inserted or deleted. It resets the line numbers from the current row to the end of the array. There is no need to revise numbers on lines preceding the current line.

59➤ The ARR_CURR() function returns the index into the current array row. The ARR_COUNT() function returns the total number of rows created during the INPUT ARRAY.

60➤ Items can be inserted in the middle of the array, so the last line(s) of the array might be off the screen. The function updates the screen display of lines that are on the screen.

There is no function to return the line number of the last row of the screen array; this limit has to be written into the program.

```
56➤         DISPLAY ga_items[curr_pa].stock_num TO sa_items[curr_sa].stock_num
            DISPLAY ga_items[curr_pa].manu_code TO sa_items[curr_sa].manu_code
            DISPLAY ga_items[curr_pa].description TO
                        sa_items[curr_sa].description
            DISPLAY ga_items[curr_pa].unit_price TO
                        sa_items[curr_sa].unit_price
            NEXT FIELD quantity
          END IF

      END INPUT

57➤   IF int_flag THEN
        LET int_flag = FALSE
        CALL clear_lines(2, 16)
        CLEAR FORM
        CALL msg("Order input terminated.")
        RETURN (FALSE)
      END IF
      RETURN (TRUE)
    END FUNCTION  -- input_items --

    ########################################
58➤ FUNCTION renum_items()
    ########################################
      DEFINE        pcurr         INTEGER,
                    ptotal        INTEGER,
                    scurr         INTEGER,
                    stotal        INTEGER,
                    k             INTEGER

59➤   LET pcurr = ARR_CURR()
      LET ptotal = ARR_COUNT()
      LET scurr = SCR_LINE()
      LET stotal = 4
60➤   FOR k = pcurr TO ptotal
        LET ga_items[k].item_num = k
        IF scurr <= stotal THEN
          DISPLAY k TO sa_items[scurr].item_num
          LET scurr = scurr + 1
        END IF
      END FOR

    END FUNCTION  -- renum_items --
```

The stock_popup() Function

61➤ This function is much like cust_popup() (see "The cust_popup() Function" on page 238). It is called from input_items() to display a list of stock items and to let the user make a selection.

The user may have specified a stock number; if so, only rows with that number are shown. Otherwise, all rows (that will fit the array) are shown. This means that the SELECT statement must use a different WHERE clause, depending on whether the argument, stock_item, is null.

62➤ This window intentionally covers up the legend "Press Cancel to exit without saving." If the user presses Cancel in this routine it will only end the popup display, not the entire order.

63➤ The SELECT statement that will retrieve stock items from the database is initialized here.

64➤ When the function argument is null, all stock numbers are wanted and the WHERE clause contains only a join condition.

65➤ When the function argument is not null, only rows with that number are wanted and the WHERE clause has two conditions.

66➤ The SELECT statement is prepared and associated with a cursor.

```
      ########################################
61➤  FUNCTION stock_popup(stock_item)
      ########################################
        DEFINE        stock_item            INTEGER,

                      pa_stock ARRAY[200] OF RECORD
                        stock_num         LIKE stock.stock_num,
                        description       LIKE stock.description,
                        manu_code         LIKE stock.manu_code,
                        manu_name         LIKE manufact.manu_name,
                        unit              LIKE stock.unit,
                        unit_price        LIKE stock.unit_price
                      END RECORD,

                      idx                   INTEGER,
                      stock_cnt             INTEGER,
                      st_stock              CHAR(300),
                      array_sz              SMALLINT,
                      over_size             SMALLINT

        LET array_sz = 200    --* match size of pa_stock array

62➤    OPEN WINDOW w_stockpop AT 7, 4
          WITH 12 ROWS, 73 COLUMNS
          ATTRIBUTE(BORDER, FORM LINE 4)
        OPEN FORM f_stocksel FROM "f_stocksel"
        DISPLAY FORM f_stocksel
        DISPLAY "Move cursor using F3, F4, and arrow keys."
          AT 1,2
        DISPLAY "Press Accept to select a stock item."
          AT 2,2

63➤    LET st_stock =
          "SELECT stock_num, description, stock.manu_code, manufact.manu_name, ",
          "unit, unit_price FROM stock, manufact"

64➤    IF stock_item IS NOT NULL THEN
          LET st_stock = st_stock CLIPPED, " WHERE stock_num = ", stock_item,
              " AND stock.manu_code = manufact.manu_code",
              " ORDER BY 1, 3"
65➤    ELSE
          LET st_stock = st_stock CLIPPED,
              " WHERE stock.manu_code = manufact.manu_code",
              " ORDER BY 1, 3"
        END IF

66➤    PREPARE slct_run FROM st_stock
        DECLARE c_stockpop CURSOR FOR slct_run

        LET over_size = FALSE
        LET stock_cnt = 1
```

67➤ The FOREACH loop loads stock items into the pa_stock array. The array has a fixed size while the size of the table is unknown. The function counts the rows as it loads them, and if the array fills up, it ends the loop early.

68➤ There is this remote possibility that no rows will be found. Rather than present the user with an empty list, the function displays a message and returns a null stock number to its caller.

69➤ The remainder of the function follows very closely to the pattern of the cust_popup() function.

70➤ If the user chooses to cancel the popup window, the function indicates the Cancel by setting return values to null. If the user initiated the popup from the stock_num field, the function sets both stock_num and manu_code to null. If the user initiated this popup from the manu_code field, the function only sets the manu_code field to null. The stock_num field must retain the value currently displaying on the form.

The dsply_taxes() Function

71➤ The dsply_taxes() function updates the order total to reflect the sales tax rate.

```
67➤   FOREACH c_stockpop INTO pa_stock[stock_cnt].*
        LET stock_cnt = stock_cnt + 1
        IF stock_cnt > array_sz THEN
          LET over_size = TRUE
          EXIT FOREACH
        END IF
      END FOREACH

68➤   IF stock_cnt = 1 THEN
        CALL msg("No stock data in the database.")
        LET idx = 1
        LET pa_stock[idx].stock_num = NULL
      ELSE
69➤     IF over_size THEN
          MESSAGE "Stock array full: can only display ",
                array_sz USING "<<<<<<"
        END IF

        CALL SET_COUNT(stock_cnt - 1)
        LET int_flag = FALSE
        DISPLAY ARRAY pa_stock TO sa_stock.*

        LET idx = ARR_CURR()

70➤     IF int_flag THEN
          LET int_flag = FALSE
          CLEAR FORM
          CALL msg("No stock item selected.")
          LET pa_stock[idx].manu_code = NULL
          IF stock_item IS NULL THEN
            LET pa_stock[idx].stock_num = NULL
          END IF

        END IF
      END IF

      CLOSE WINDOW w_stockpop
      RETURN pa_stock[idx].stock_num, pa_stock[idx].manu_code,
             pa_stock[idx].description, pa_stock[idx].unit_price

    END FUNCTION  -- stock_popup --

    ########################################
71➤ FUNCTION dsply_taxes()
    ########################################

      LET gr_charges.tax_rate = tax_rates(gr_customer.state)
      DISPLAY gr_customer.state TO code
      DISPLAY BY NAME gr_charges.tax_rate

      LET gr_charges.sales_tax = gr_orders.order_amount
                    * (gr_charges.tax_rate / 100)
      DISPLAY BY NAME gr_charges.sales_tax
```

The order_amount() Function

72➤ The function updates the order subtotal to reflect the sum of all items.

It is called from input_items() each time the order subtotal might have changed: when line items are inserted or deleted, and whenever the cursor leaves the quantity field.

The ship_order() Function

73➤ This function is called when the user replies "yes" to the question, "Do you want to ship this order now." It presents a form containing the data fields related to shipping and accepts input for them.

74➤ The w_ship subwindow also covers up the message about Cancel in the main window. Cancelling from this input phase will only cancel the entry of shipping information.

75➤ For clarity, the details of the INPUT statement are located in the input_ship() function. It returns TRUE normally, or FALSE if the user presses the Interrupt key.

```
  LET gr_charges.order_total = gr_orders.order_amount +
        gr_charges.sales_tax
  DISPLAY BY NAME gr_charges.order_total

END FUNCTION  -- dsply_taxes --

########################################
72➤ FUNCTION order_amount()
########################################
  DEFINE        ord_amount      MONEY(8),
                idx             INTEGER

  LET ord_amount = 0.00
  FOR idx = 1 TO ARR_COUNT()
    IF ga_items[idx].total_price IS NOT NULL THEN
      LET ord_amount = ord_amount + ga_items[idx].total_price
    END IF
  END FOR

  RETURN (ord_amount)

END FUNCTION  -- order_amount --

########################################
73➤ FUNCTION ship_order()
########################################

  CALL clear_lines(1, 1)

74➤  OPEN WINDOW w_ship AT 7, 6
    WITH FORM "f_ship"
    ATTRIBUTE (BORDER, COMMENT LINE 3, FORM LINE 4)
  DISPLAY " Press Accept to save shipping information."
    AT 1, 1 ATTRIBUTE (REVERSE, YELLOW)
  DISPLAY " Press Cancel to exit w/out saving. Press CTRL-W for Help."
    AT 2, 1 ATTRIBUTE (REVERSE, YELLOW)

  DISPLAY "SHIPPING INFORMATION"
    AT 4, 20

  DISPLAY BY NAME gr_orders.order_num, gr_orders.order_date,
                  gr_customer.customer_num, gr_customer.company

  INITIALIZE gr_ship.* TO NULL

75➤  IF input_ship() THEN
    CALL msg("Shipping information entered.")
  END IF
  CLOSE WINDOW w_ship

END FUNCTION  -- ship_order --
```

The input_ship() Function

Notes 76 to 83 The input_ship() function displays the financial information generated by the calc_order() function and allows changes on the values stored in the gr_ship global. It encapsulates the details of the INPUT statement so that the logic of function ship_order() can be seen more clearly.

76➤ The DISPLAY TO statement displays the subtotal for the order before the addition of the shipping charges. The DISPLAY BY NAME displays the grand total with the addition of the shipping charges.

77➤ The INPUT statement lets the user change any of the shipping information stored in the orders table. The WITHOUT DEFAULTS clause is necessary to initialize the fields with the values of the variables rather than the default values from the form specification file or the syscolval table.

This INPUT statement doesn't activate the fields displaying the customer number, company, order, order date, order subtotal, and order grand total. The customer and order information shouldn't change when the order is shipped, and the totals can't be updated since they are aggregates.

78➤ As with the date field in input_order(), the date is initialized to TODAY when the cursor first enters it, and any time the user presses CTRL-D to clear the field.

79➤ The BEFORE FIELD clause initializes the null numeric field to zero. This initialization prevents future numeric calculations involving this value from evaluating to null. A null value in a numeric expression makes the entire expression yield a null value. The program could initialize this field (along with the ship_date and ship_charge fields) before the INPUT statement is entered, by setting values in gr_ship and using DISPLAY to show them. However, the program would still need to test for nulls in the AFTER FIELD blocks.

80➤ The AFTER FIELD clause checks for a null value and resets to the default. It then makes sure that the user did not enter a negative value for the ship weight.

81➤ If the ship charge field is $0.00, the program initializes a standard charge (1.5 * shipping weight) based on the value previously entered in the shipping weight field.

In a real application this calculation would involve a table search based on the customer's postal code and/or the shipping weight.

```
########################################
FUNCTION input_ship()
########################################

76➤  DISPLAY gr_charges.order_total TO order_amount

  IF gr_charges.ship_charge IS NULL THEN
    LET gr_charges.ship_charge = 0.00
  END IF
  LET gr_ship.ship_charge = gr_charges.ship_charge

  LET gr_charges.order_total = gr_charges.order_total
              + gr_charges.ship_charge
  DISPLAY BY NAME gr_charges.order_total
77➤  LET int_flag = FALSE
  INPUT BY NAME gr_ship.ship_date, gr_ship.ship_instruct,
        gr_ship.ship_weight, gr_ship.ship_charge
  WITHOUT DEFAULTS HELP 63

78➤    BEFORE FIELD ship_date
      IF gr_ship.ship_date IS NULL THEN
        LET gr_ship.ship_date = TODAY
      END IF

    AFTER FIELD ship_date
      IF gr_ship.ship_date IS NULL THEN
        LET gr_ship.ship_date = TODAY
        DISPLAY BY NAME gr_ship.ship_date
      END IF

79➤    BEFORE FIELD ship_weight
      IF gr_ship.ship_weight IS NULL THEN
        LET gr_ship.ship_weight = 0.00
      END IF

80➤    AFTER FIELD ship_weight
      IF gr_ship.ship_weight IS NULL THEN
        LET gr_ship.ship_weight = 0.00
        DISPLAY BY NAME gr_ship.ship_weight
      END IF

      IF gr_ship.ship_weight < 0.00 THEN
        ERROR
  "Shipping Weight cannot be less than 0.00 lbs. Please try again."
        LET gr_ship.ship_weight = 0.00
        NEXT FIELD ship_weight
      END IF

    BEFORE FIELD ship_charge
      IF gr_ship.ship_charge = 0.00 THEN
81➤        LET gr_ship.ship_charge = 1.5 * gr_ship.ship_weight
      END IF
```

82➤ In the ship_charge field, the AFTER FIELD clause recalculates the grand total based on the new shipping charge and displays this new value.

83➤ The input_ship() function tests to see if the user ended the input session by pressing the Interrupt key.

- If so, input_ship() returns a false value to prevent the calling function from updating the order.
- If not, input_ship() returns a true value to authorize updating the order.

The order_tx() Function

84➤ The name of this function means order *transaction* (not order *tax* as you might suppose). It inserts all the rows that comprise the order into the database.

85➤ This statement starts a database transaction. It is not required (and will produce an error if issued) in an ANSI-compliant database.

86➤ The first step of the transaction must be to insert the row of the orders table. That creates the order number which appears in each row of the items table. If the order row is inserted successfully, the item rows are inserted.

87➤ If either step fails, the ROLLBACK WORK statement ensures that all the inserted items and the orders row are removed. An orders row with no items will not appear in the database, nor will items with no corresponding order.

88➤ Ordinarily all rows are inserted and COMMIT WORK ensures that they are safely written to disk.

```
        AFTER FIELD ship_charge
          IF gr_ship.ship_charge IS NULL THEN
            LET gr_ship.ship_charge = 0.00
            DISPLAY BY NAME gr_ship.ship_charge
          END IF

          IF gr_ship.ship_charge < 0.00 THEN
            ERROR "Shipping Charge cannot be less than $0.00. Please try again."
            LET gr_ship.ship_charge = 0.00
            NEXT FIELD ship_charge
          END IF
82➤       LET gr_charges.order_total = gr_charges.order_total + gr_ship.ship_charge
          DISPLAY BY NAME gr_charges.order_total

      END INPUT

83➤   IF int_flag THEN
        LET int_flag = FALSE
        CALL msg("Shipping input terminated.")
        RETURN (FALSE)
      END IF

      RETURN (TRUE)

    END FUNCTION  -- input_ship --

    ########################################
84➤ FUNCTION order_tx()
    ########################################
      DEFINE        tx_stat         INTEGER,
                    tx_table        CHAR(5)

85➤   BEGIN WORK

        LET tx_table = "order"
86➤     LET tx_stat = insert_order()
        IF (tx_stat = 0) THEN--* insert into "orders" was
                                          --*   successful
          LET tx_table = "items"
          LET tx_stat = insert_items()
        END IF

87➤     IF (tx_stat < 0) THEN             --* insert into "orders" or
                                          --*   "items" failed
          ROLLBACK WORK
          ERROR tx_stat USING "-<<<<<<<<<<<",
            ": Unable to save order: ", tx_table, " insert failed."
          RETURN (FALSE)
        END IF
88➤   COMMIT WORK
      RETURN (TRUE)

    END FUNCTION  -- order_tx --
```

The insert_order() Function

89➤ The insert_order() function inserts the new row into the orders table. When the INSERT succeeds, the function captures the serial value of the new row, which is the order number.

It also displays the order number on the form, an action that might more properly be performed in the order_tx() function.

The insert_items() Function

90➤ The insert_items() function inserts all of the item rows for the order.

It uses the ARR_COUNT() library function to find out how many rows were input during the INPUT ARRAY statement. It is possible for the user to create empty rows in the ga_items array, but any array row that has a non-null stock number contains a valid item.

89➤
```
########################################
FUNCTION insert_order()
########################################
  DEFINE        ins_stat        INTEGER

  LET ins_stat = 0

WHENEVER ERROR CONTINUE
    INSERT INTO orders (order_num, order_date, customer_num, po_num,
        ship_date, ship_instruct, ship_weight, ship_charge)
      VALUES (0, gr_orders.order_date, gr_customer.customer_num,
              gr_orders.po_num, gr_ship.ship_date, gr_ship.ship_instruct,
              gr_ship.ship_weight, gr_ship.ship_charge)
WHENEVER ERROR STOP

    IF status < 0 THEN
      LET ins_stat = status
    ELSE
      LET gr_orders.order_num = SQLCA.SQLERRD[2]
      DISPLAY BY NAME gr_orders.order_num
        ATTRIBUTE (REVERSE, BLUE)
    END IF
    RETURN (ins_stat)
END FUNCTION  -- insert_order --
```

90➤
```
########################################
FUNCTION insert_items()
########################################
  DEFINE        idx             INTEGER,
                ins_stat        INTEGER

  LET ins_stat = 0

  FOR idx = 1 TO ARR_COUNT()
    IF ga_items[idx].stock_num IS NOT NULL THEN
WHENEVER ERROR CONTINUE
      INSERT INTO items
      VALUES (ga_items[idx].item_num, gr_orders.order_num,
              ga_items[idx].stock_num, ga_items[idx].manu_code,
              ga_items[idx].quantity, ga_items[idx].total_price)
WHENEVER ERROR STOP
      IF status < 0 THEN
        LET ins_stat = status
        EXIT FOR
      END IF
    END IF
  END FOR
  RETURN (ins_stat)
END FUNCTION  -- insert_items --
```

To locate any function definition see the Function Index on page 728.

12

Displaying an Unknown Number of Rows

This example implements lookup lists that can handle any number of rows. This technique is essential to provide lookups for tables that may grow indefinitely during the use of the application.

The example also demonstrates an interface for updating a subset of the columns in the row. The particular application is a shipping module, where the shipping data entry staff updates a row created earlier by the order entry staff.

```
+--------------------------------------------------------------------------+
|                                                                          |
|                            ORDER SEARCH                                 |
|                                                                          |
|  Customer Number:[          ]  Company Name:[                    ]      |
|  Order No:[          ]         Order Date:[          ]                   |
|          +------------------------------------------+                   |
|  Ship Da| Move cursor using F3, F4, and arrow keys.  |                   |
|  Shippin| Press Accept to select a customer.         |        ]          |
|  Shippin|                                            |                   |
|         |   Customer No.      Company Name           |                   |
|         |  [         101]  [All Sports Supplies ]    |                   |
|         |  [         102]  [Sports Spot         ]    |                   |
|         |  [         103]  [Phil's Sports       ]    |                   |
|         |  [         104]  [Play Ball!          ]    |                   |
|         |  [         105]  [Los Altos Sports    ]    |                   |
|         |                                            |                   |
| Enter cu|                                            |                   |
| Press Ca|On last row, press F5 (CTRL-B) for more customers |p.           |
|Enter a c+------------------------------------------+                   |
+--------------------------------------------------------------------------+
```

Paging Through Rows Using Array Form

To display an indeterminate number of rows in a single-row form, you retrieve one row at a time and display the row in the form.

To display an indeterminate number of rows in an array form, you adopt a similar approach. Instead of retrieving one row, however, you retrieve and display one group of rows at a time. The number of rows in the group depends on the size of the program array which stores them. The user pages from one group of rows to the next. Here is an overview of the technique:

1. Declare and open a cursor for a query that selects the rows.
2. Repeat the paging action using a WHILE loop.
3. Populate the array with a set of rows using an inner WHILE loop with a FETCH statement.
4. Show the rows in the array form with a DISPLAY ARRAY statement.
5. Provide a key to using an ON KEY clause that leaves the form and sets a flag to trigger repetition of the paging action.
6. Return the current row if the user leaves the form with the Accept key.
7. Return a null value if the user leaves the form with the Interrupt key.

You could enhance this example to permit paging backward as well as forward through the list. You would declare a scroll cursor rather than a standard cursor. You would provide an ON KEY clause for backward paging as well as for forward paging, setting a flag in the ON KEY clauses to indicate the direction of paging. In the inner WHILE loop, you would execute a FETCH NEXT or FETCH PREVIOUS statement based on the value of the paging flag.

This example retrieves more rows than can display in the form. To display the additional rows, the user scrolls the rows using the Arrow keys and can only page forward on the last row. You might size the program array to the array form and let the user page forward or backward from any row.

One final enhancement concerns the SELECT statement, which selects all rows in the table. If the table is large, this action can be time consuming. You might consider letting the user enter partial criteria in the fields for which the popup form lists the values (the customer_num and company fields). You could then pass the value of the field to the popup function as a parameter. Within the popup function, you would state the SELECT clause as a character value, using the MATCHES operator in the WHERE clause to target column. The user could still select all rows from the table by not providing criteria but could also restrict the selection. If the criteria qualified a single row, you would want to return it rather than display it in the array form.

Function Overview

Function Name	Purpose
find_order()	Prompts the user for an order, providing lookup lists to select the customer and order.
cust_popup2()	Retrieves all customers and displays them in an array form so the user can choose the appropriate customer. This function is a variation on the manuf_popup() function from Example 8.
order_popup()	Retrieves all orders for a customer and displays them in an array form so the user can choose the appropriate order. This function is a variation on the cust_popup() function.
calc_order()	Selects information from multiple tables to summarize an order. This function resembles the get_summary() function from Example 4.
input_ship()	Accepts user input for shipping info. This function resembles the change_cust() function from Example 6. *See description in Example 11.*
upd_order()	Applies shipping changes to an order. This function resembles the update_cust() function from Example 6.
message_window()	Opens a window and displays the contents of the ga_dsplymsg global array. *See description in Example 2.*
init_msgs()	Initializes the members of the ga_dsplymsg array to null. *See description in Example 2.*
tax_rates()	Supplies the appropriate tax schedule for a customer. *See description in Example 4.*
msg()	Displays a brief, informative message. *See description in Example 5.*
clear_lines()	Clears any number of lines starting at any line. *See description in Example 6.*

The f_ordersel File

1➤ The f_ordersel form is used as a popup window for order information.

2➤ This form defines the sa_order screen array for use with the DISPLAY ARRAY statement.

f_ordersel form file

```
1➤ DATABASE stores2t

   SCREEN
   {
    Order Number Order Date PO Number Date Shipped Date Paid
    [f001 ] [f002 ] [f003 ] [f004 ] [f005 ]
    [f001 ] [f002 ] [f003 ] [f004 ] [f005 ]
    [f001 ] [f002 ] [f003 ] [f004 ] [f005 ]
    [f001 ] [f002 ] [f003 ] [f004 ] [f005 ]
    [f001 ] [f002 ] [f003 ] [f004 ] [f005 ]
   }

   TABLES
   orders

   ATTRIBUTES
   f001 = orders.order_num;
   f002 = orders.order_date;
   f003 = orders.po_num;
   f004 = orders.ship_date;
   f005 = orders.paid_date;

   INSTRUCTIONS
2➤  SCREEN RECORD sa_order[5] (orders.order_num THRU orders.paid_date)
```

The GLOBALS Statement

1➤ The GLOBALS statement declares three records. Although these records all contain order information, they are defined separately for convenience. For example, the gr_charges record is used by the calc_order() function, which appears in several examples. The gr_ship record is used in a SELECT statement with the asterisk notation.

The GLOBALS statement also defines the ga_dsplymsg array used by the message_window() function.

The MAIN Function

2➤ The MAIN function displays the f_ship form in the w_main window. The program activates different fields of this form at different times to prompt the user for selection criteria or update information.

4GL source file

```
DATABASE stores2t

1➤ GLOBALS
  DEFINE        gr_ordship RECORD
                  customer_num  LIKE customer.customer_num,
                  company       LIKE customer.company,
                  order_num     INTEGER,
                  order_date    LIKE orders.order_date
                END RECORD,

                gr_charges RECORD
                  tax_rate      DECIMAL(5,3),
                  ship_charge   LIKE orders.ship_charge,
                  sales_tax     MONEY(9),
                  order_total   MONEY(11)
                END RECORD,

                gr_ship RECORD
                  ship_date     LIKE orders.ship_date,
                  ship_instruct LIKE orders.ship_instruct,
                  ship_weight   LIKE orders.ship_weight,
                  ship_charge   LIKE orders.ship_charge
                END RECORD

  DEFINE        ga_dsplymsg ARRAY[5] OF CHAR(48)

END GLOBALS

########################################
MAIN
########################################
  DEFINE        upd_stat        INTEGER

  OPTIONS
    HELP FILE "hlpmsgs",
    COMMENT LINE 1,
    MESSAGE LINE LAST

  DEFER INTERRUPT

2➤ OPEN WINDOW w_main AT 2,3
   WITH 19 ROWS, 76 COLUMNS
   ATTRIBUTE (BORDER)

  OPEN FORM f_ship FROM "f_ship"
  DISPLAY FORM f_ship
```

3➤ The find_order() function activates the f_ship form to prompt the user for a customer and order number. These fields identify an order. If the user succeeds in identifying a valid order, find_order() returns a true value and otherwise returns a false value.

4➤ The calc_order() function calculates a financial summary for the order.

5➤ The SELECT statement retrieves the columns of the order row that store shipping information.

6➤ The input_ship() function activates the f_ship form to prompt the user for changes to the shipping information. If the user succeeds in changing the information, input_ship() returns a true value, and the upd_order() function updates the row.

The inner IF statement tests the upd_stat variable to notify the user whether the upd_order() function succeeded in updating the row or failed.

7➤ The MAIN function finishes by closing the form and window and clearing the screen for the benefit of the environment from which the **4GL** program was invoked.

The find_order() Function

8➤ The calls to the clear_lines() function clear existing information before executing the DISPLAY AT statement to display a title and instructions for the input session.

9➤ The LET statement resets the built-in int_flag variable so that, after the input session, the variable will have a true value only if the user pressed the Interrupt key.

The INPUT statement prompts the user for a customer number and order number that uniquely identify the order. Other fields on the f_ship form aren't activated. That is, the user can't position in these fields.

```
3➤   IF find_order() THEN

       DISPLAY
         " Press Accept to save shipping info. Press CTRL-W for Help."
         AT 17, 1 ATTRIBUTE (REVERSE, YELLOW)
       DISPLAY
         " Press Cancel to exit w/out saving."
         AT 18, 1 ATTRIBUTE (REVERSE, YELLOW)

4➤     CALL calc_order(gr_ordship.order_num)

5➤     SELECT ship_date, ship_instruct, ship_weight, ship_charge
       INTO gr_ship.*
       FROM  orders
       WHERE order_num = gr_ordship.order_num

6➤     IF input_ship() THEN
         LET upd_stat = upd_order(gr_ordship.order_num)
         IF (upd_stat < 0) THEN
           ERROR upd_stat USING "-<<<<<<<<<<<",
             ": Unable to update the order."
         ELSE
           CALL msg("Order updated with shipping information.")
         END IF
       END IF
     END IF

7➤   CLOSE FORM f_ship
     CLOSE WINDOW w_main
     CLEAR SCREEN
   END MAIN

   ########################################
   FUNCTION find_order()
   ########################################
     DEFINE       cust_num         LIKE customer.customer_num,
                  last_key         SMALLINT

8➤   CALL clear_lines(1, 3)
     DISPLAY "ORDER SEARCH" AT 2, 34
     CALL clear_lines(2, 17)
     DISPLAY " Enter customer number and order number then press Accept."
       AT 17, 1 ATTRIBUTE (REVERSE, YELLOW)
     DISPLAY " Press Cancel to exit without searching. Press CTRL-W for Help."
       AT 18, 1 ATTRIBUTE (REVERSE, YELLOW)

9➤   LET int_flag = FALSE
     INPUT BY NAME gr_ordship.customer_num, gr_ordship.order_num
           HELP 110
       BEFORE FIELD customer_num
         MESSAGE
           "Enter a customer number or press F5 (CTRL-F) for a list."
```

Notes 10 to 16 The customer_num and order_num fields each have a BEFORE FIELD clause that displays instructions for the field and an AFTER FIELD clause that validates the value entered by the user.

10➤ The AFTER FIELD clause for the customer_num field first verifies that the user supplied a value. If not, the NEXT FIELD statement repositions the user in the customer_num field and resumes the input session.

11➤ The SELECT statement attempts to retrieve the company name for the customer. If the SELECT statement can't locate a row for the customer number, **4GL** sets the status variable to the same value as the NOTFOUND constant. The IF statement notifies the user, resets the customer_num variable, and repositions the user in the customer_num field.

If the SELECT statement locates the row, the DISPLAY BY NAME statement fills the company name into the corresponding field, and the MESSAGE statement clears the message from the BEFORE FIELD clause.

12➤ The first statements of the AFTER FIELD clause for the order_num field check whether the user is returning to the customer_num field. In this case, the user has abandoned the current contents of the order_num field to change the customer number, so validation isn't appropriate.

The FGL_LASTKEY() built-in function returns the internal identifier for the last key pressed by the user. As this value must be compared with two different values, find_order() saves the value in the last_key local variable to avoid the inefficiency of calling the same function twice.

The calls to the FGL_KEYVAL() built-in function return the internal identifiers corresponding to the Left or Up Arrow keys. The Up Arrow key performs the same action as the Left Arrow key because the default field order (CONSTRAINED) applies.

13➤ If the user didn't enter a value, the IF statement repositions the user in the order_num field.

14➤ The SELECT statement attempts to retrieve the order date and customer number from the order's row.

15➤ If the built-in status variable indicates that the SELECT statement couldn't locate a row with the stated order number, the IF statement resets the order number and repositions the user in the order_num field.

```
10➤   AFTER FIELD customer_num
        IF gr_ordship.customer_num IS NULL THEN
          ERROR "You must enter a customer number. Please try again."
          NEXT FIELD customer_num
        END IF

11➤     SELECT company
        INTO gr_ordship.company
        FROM customer
        WHERE customer_num = gr_ordship.customer_num

        IF (status = NOTFOUND) THEN
            ERROR
          "Unknown customer number. Use F5 (CTRL-F) to see valid customers."
            LET gr_ordship.customer_num = NULL
            NEXT FIELD customer_num
        END IF

        DISPLAY BY NAME gr_ordship.company
        MESSAGE ""

      BEFORE FIELD order_num
        MESSAGE
          "Enter an order number or press F5 (CTRL-F) for a list."

12➤   AFTER FIELD order_num
        LET last_key = FGL_LASTKEY()
        IF (last_key <> FGL_KEYVAL("left") )
            AND (last_key <> FGL_KEYVAL("up") )
        THEN
13➤       IF gr_ordship.order_num IS NULL THEN
            ERROR "You must enter an order number. Please try again."
            NEXT FIELD order_num
          END IF

14➤       SELECT order_date, customer_num
          INTO gr_ordship.order_date, cust_num
          FROM orders
          WHERE order_num = gr_ordship.order_num

15➤       IF (status = NOTFOUND) THEN
            ERROR
          "Unknown order number. Use F5 (CTRL-F) to see valid orders."
            LET gr_ordship.order_num = NULL
            NEXT FIELD order_num
          END IF
```

16➤ If the customer number in the order row differs from the customer number entered previously in the customer_num field, the IF statement resets the order number, clears the order_num field, and repositions the user in the order_num field.

17➤ If the order number passes all validations, the DISPLAY BY NAME statement shows the order date to the user.

18➤ If the user is returning to the customer_num field (with the up or left arrow key), the ELSE clause resets the order_num variable and clears the order_num field. By returning to the customer_num field, the user has indicated that any value in the order_num field will have to be validated again.

If the user isn't repositioned in the order_num field with the NEXT FIELD statement, the MESSAGE statement clears the instructions from the BEFORE FIELD clause.

19➤ The ON KEY clause traps the F5 key or CONTROL-F as a lookup signal.

20➤ If the user was positioned in the customer_num field, the IF statement calls the cust_popup2() function for a customer lookup. The cust_popup2() function returns a customer number or, if the user doesn't select a customer, null.

When cust_popup2() returns a null customer_num, a second IF statement tests the company field. If both these variables are null, then the lookup function was unable to locate any customers. If only the customer_num variable is null, the user did not select a customer from the popup window. In either case, the function returns the cursor to the customer_num field.

If the user did select a customer from the popup window, the function displays the selected customer number and company name. It then clears the message line, and positions the cursor in the order_num field.

21➤ If the user was positioned in the order_num field, the IF statement calls the order_popup() function for an order lookup.

Notes 22 to 24 The return value of order_popup() indicates the appropriate action.

22➤ The order_popup() function returns a null order_num and order_date to indicate that the customer specified in the customer_num field doesn't have any orders. The inner IF statement resets the customer_num and company variables, clears the company field, and repositions the user in the customer_num field.

23➤ The order_popup() function returns a null order_num and a non-null order_date to indicate that the user left the popup list without choosing an order. The NEXT FIELD statement repositions the user in the order_num field.

```
16➤       IF (cust_num <> gr_ordship.customer_num) THEN
            ERROR "Order ", gr_ordship.order_num USING "<<<<<<<<<<<",
                  " is not for customer ",
                  gr_ordship.customer_num USING "<<<<<<<<<<<"
            LET gr_ordship.order_num = NULL
            DISPLAY BY NAME gr_ordship.order_num
            NEXT FIELD customer_num
          END IF

17➤       DISPLAY BY NAME gr_ordship.order_date
18➤     ELSE
          LET gr_ordship.order_num = NULL
          DISPLAY BY NAME gr_ordship.order_num
        END IF

        MESSAGE ""

19➤   ON KEY (F5, CONTROL-F)
20➤     IF INFIELD(customer_num) THEN
          CALL cust_popup2()
            RETURNING gr_ordship.customer_num, gr_ordship.company

          IF gr_ordship.customer_num IS NULL THEN
            IF gr_ordship.company IS NULL THEN
              LET ga_dsplymsg[1] = "No customers exist in the database!"
              CALL message_window(11, 12)
            END IF

            NEXT FIELD customer_num
          END IF

          DISPLAY BY NAME gr_ordship.customer_num, gr_ordship.company
          MESSAGE ""
          NEXT FIELD order_num
        END IF

21➤     IF INFIELD(order_num) THEN
          CALL order_popup(gr_ordship.customer_num)
            RETURNING gr_ordship.order_num, gr_ordship.order_date

22➤       IF gr_ordship.order_num IS NULL THEN
            IF gr_ordship.order_date IS NULL THEN
              LET ga_dsplymsg[1]  = "No orders exists for customer ",
                  gr_ordship.customer_num USING "<<<<<<<<<<<", "."
              CALL message_window(11, 12)
              LET gr_ordship.customer_num = NULL
              LET gr_ordship.company = NULL
              DISPLAY BY NAME gr_ordship.company
              NEXT FIELD customer_num
23➤         ELSE
              NEXT FIELD order_num
            END IF
          END IF
```

24➤ If the order_popup() function returns non-null values for both order_num and order_date, the DISPLAY BY NAME statement displays the values. Because the validation has guaranteed a valid customer number and order number, the action finishes by executing the EXIT INPUT statement to skip further validation in the AFTER FIELD and AFTER INPUT clauses.

25➤ The AFTER INPUT clause verifies that the user has filled in both the customer_num and order_num fields.

26➤ If the user pressed the Interrupt key, the int_flag built-in variable evaluates to TRUE and the code block for the IF statement returns a false value. If the user pressed the Accept key, the final RETURN statement returns a true value. The return value notifies the MAIN function whether to continue the shipment entry routine.

The cust_popup2() Function

27➤ The array_size variable stores a constant value representing the number of elements in the array. As the cust_popup2() function makes frequent reference to the array size, this variable makes the code more maintainable. To redefine the size of the program array, you only have to change the size of pa_cust in the DEFINE and the value assigned to the array_size variable.

28➤ The fetch_custs variable is the controlling variable for the WHILE loop that pages through the qualified rows (see Note 34). The LET statement sets fetch_custs to a false value on the assumption that the query will fail to retrieve any rows. The cust_popup2() function resets fetch_custs if the query succeeds (see Note 33).

29➤ The SELECT statement counts the number of rows in the customer table. If no rows exist, the function returns null values for customer_num and company.

```
24➤        DISPLAY BY NAME gr_ordship.order_num, gr_ordship.order_date
           MESSAGE ""
           EXIT INPUT
         END IF

25➤    AFTER INPUT
         IF NOT int_flag THEN
           IF (gr_ordship.customer_num IS NULL)
               OR (gr_ordship.order_num IS NULL) THEN
             ERROR
             "Enter the customer and order numbers or press Cancel to exit."
             NEXT FIELD customer_num
           END IF
         END IF
     END INPUT

26➤  IF int_flag THEN
       LET int_flag = FALSE
       CALL clear_lines(2, 17)
       CALL msg("Order search terminated.")
       RETURN (FALSE)
     END IF

     CALL clear_lines(2, 17)
     RETURN (TRUE)

   END FUNCTION  -- find_order --

   ########################################
   FUNCTION cust_popup2()
   ########################################
     DEFINE  pa_cust ARRAY[10] OF RECORD
                   customer_num    LIKE customer.customer_num,
                   company         LIKE customer.company
             END RECORD,

             idx              SMALLINT,
             i                SMALLINT,
             cust_cnt         SMALLINT,
             fetch_custs      SMALLINT,
             array_size       SMALLINT,
             total_custs      INTEGER,
             number_to_see    INTEGER,
             curr_pa          SMALLINT

27➤  LET array_size = 10
28➤  LET fetch_custs = FALSE

29➤  SELECT COUNT(*)
     INTO total_custs
     FROM customer
```

30➤ The cust_popup2() function opens the w_custpop window and the f_custsel array form to display the customer list.

31➤ While the total_custs variable contains the total number of customers, the number_to_see variable contains the total number of customers left to view. At first, these two values are identical, but as the user pages through the customers, the value of the number_to_see variable decreases.

32➤ The idx variable counts the customer rows as they are fetched into the program array (see Note 35). The LET statement sets idx to zero because no rows have been fetched yet.

33➤ The DECLARE statement declares the c_custpop cursor for a query that selects the customer_num and company columns from every row. The ORDER BY clause sorts the customers by customer number.

If the OPEN statement successfully opened the c_custpop cursor, the LET statement resets the fetch_custs variable to TRUE so the WHILE loop starts paging through the rows. Otherwise, the function displays an error and sets both return values to null. Since fetch_custs remains FALSE, the WHILE loop never executes.

34➤ The WHILE statement that tests the fetch_custs variable loops through the action of filling the pa_cust array with customer rows, activating the f_custsel form so the user can choose a row or press a key to repeat the loop.

35➤ The inner WHILE statement retrieves as many rows as the pa_cust array can hold. The idx index variable reflects the number of rows retrieved.

On each repetition, the LET statement increments idx to indicate the next unoccupied array element. The FETCH statement attempts to assign a row to this unoccupied array element.

If there are no more rows in the table, the FETCH statement sets the status built-in variable to the value of the NOTFOUND constant. The code block for the IF statement resets the fetch_custs variable to prevent further paging by the outer WHILE loop and decrements the idx variable because the array element wasn't filled.

```
     IF total_custs = 0 THEN
       LET pa_cust[1].customer_num = NULL
       LET pa_cust[1].company = NULL
       RETURN pa_cust[1].customer_num, pa_cust[1].company
     END IF

30➤  OPEN WINDOW w_custpop AT 8, 13
       WITH 12 ROWS, 50 COLUMNS
       ATTRIBUTE(BORDER, FORM LINE 4)

     OPEN FORM f_custsel FROM "f_custsel"
     DISPLAY FORM f_custsel

     DISPLAY "Move cursor using F3, F4, and arrow keys."
       AT 1,2
     DISPLAY "Press Accept to select a customer."
       AT 2,2

31➤  LET number_to_see = total_custs
32➤  LET idx = 0

33➤  DECLARE c_custpop CURSOR FOR
       SELECT customer_num, company
       FROM customer
       ORDER BY customer_num

   WHENEVER ERROR CONTINUE
     OPEN c_custpop
   WHENEVER ERROR STOP

     IF (status = 0) THEN
       LET fetch_custs = TRUE
     ELSE
       CALL msg("Unable to open cursor.")
       LET idx = 1
       LET pa_cust[idx].customer_num = NULL
       LET pa_cust[idx].company = NULL
     END IF

34➤  WHILE fetch_custs
35➤    WHILE (idx < array_size)
         LET idx = idx + 1
         FETCH c_custpop INTO pa_cust[idx].*
         IF (status = NOTFOUND) THEN               --* no more orders to see
           LET fetch_custs = FALSE
           LET idx = idx - 1
           EXIT WHILE
         END IF
       END WHILE
```

36➤ If the number_to_see variable exceeds the array_size variable, there are more customer rows to store in the pa_cust array. The MESSAGE statement notifies the user about the key used to trigger the next repetition of the paging loop.

You could enhance this message to display the number of qualified rows (the value of total_custs) and the number of rows remaining (the value of idx subtracted from number-to-see).

37➤ The idx variable is zero only if the inner WHILE loop couldn't retrieve a row on the first execution of the loop. The IF statement sets up cust_popup2() to return null to indicate that the user didn't choose a row.

38➤ If idx is greater than zero, the inner WHILE loop retrieved some rows, and cust_popup2() activates the f_custsel form so the user can view the rows.

The SET_COUNT() built-in function tells **4GL** how many elements of the array were populated. All elements will be filled except on the last execution of the paging WHILE loop.

The LET statement resets the int_flag built-in variable so the cust_popup2() function can trap the Interrupt key (see Note 44).

39➤ The ON KEY clause traps the F5 function key or CONTROL-B to give the user a mechanism for advancing to the next page of customer rows.

40➤ The cust_popup2() function allows paging to the next set of rows only from the last row of the current set. This restriction forces the user to view all rows and thus prevents skipping over a row that might be the desired row.

The ARR_CURR() function returns the number of the array element corresponding to the row on which the cursor is currently positioned. The IF clause executes only when the cursor is on the last element.

41➤ The assignment to number_to_see subtracts the number of rows displayed in this execution of the paging WHILE loop to find the new number remaining.

If there are rows remaining, the IF clause resets the idx variable and ends the display session. Resetting idx to zero indicates that no row has been selected (see Note 43) so the function needs to retrieve the first row of the next set into the first array element (see Note 35). If no rows remain, the ELSE clause notifies the user.

42➤ If the user isn't positioned on the last row in the current set, the ELSE clause notifies the user and then restores the paging instructions.

```
36➤     IF (number_to_see > array_size) THEN
          MESSAGE "On last row, press F5 (CTRL-B) for more customers."
        END IF

37➤     IF (idx = 0) THEN
          CALL msg("No customers exist in the database.")
          LET idx = 1
          LET pa_cust[idx].customer_num = NULL
        ELSE

38➤       CALL SET_COUNT(idx)
          LET int_flag = FALSE
          DISPLAY ARRAY pa_cust TO sa_cust.*
39➤         ON KEY (F5, CONTROL-B)
40➤           LET curr_pa = ARR_CURR()

              IF (curr_pa = idx) THEN
41➤             LET number_to_see = number_to_see - idx
                IF (number_to_see > 0) THEN
                  LET idx = 0
                  EXIT DISPLAY
                ELSE
                  CALL msg("No more customers to see.")
                END IF
42➤           ELSE
                CALL msg("Not on last customer row.")
                MESSAGE
                  "On last row, press F5 (CTRL-B) for more customers."
              END IF
          END DISPLAY
```

43➤ The idx variable is zero only if the ON KEY clause has reset it to prepare for another repetition of the paging WHILE loop (see Note 41). Otherwise, the user ended the form session by pressing the Accept or Interrupt key. In this case, the ARR_CURR() function returns the number of the array element corresponding to the row on which the user was positioned. The program sets fetch_custs to FALSE to exit the outer paging WHILE loop.

44➤ The IF clause executes if the user has pressed the Interrupt key. The msg() function confirms the interrupt for the user and the assignments prepare to return a null value as after the last row (see Note 37).

45➤ The cust_popup2() function finishes by closing the popup form and window and returning the customer and company values. The return values of cust_popup2() have to distinguish a chosen customer, no rows in the customer table, and voluntary exit without choosing a customer.

The order_popup() Function

Notes 46 to 56 The logic of the order_popup() function is essentially similar to the cust_popup2() function. The main difference is, instead of qualifying all order rows, the order_popup() function restricts the query to rows belonging to a customer for whom the customer number is passed by parameter. As the customer table is smaller than the orders table, it is efficient to restrict the selected rows for the larger table. In addition, as customers have a one-to-many relationship with orders, this hierarchical approach is intuitive.

46➤ The SELECT saves the count of the total number of orders for the customer in the total_orders variable. If the customer doesn't have any orders, the test returns all null values to indicate this condition to the calling function.

```
43➤      IF (idx <> 0) THEN
           LET idx = ARR_CURR()
           LET fetch_custs = FALSE
         END IF

44➤      IF int_flag THEN
           LET int_flag = FALSE
           CALL msg("No customer number selected.")
           LET pa_cust[idx].customer_num = NULL
         END IF

       END IF
     END WHILE

45➤  CLOSE FORM f_custsel
     CLOSE WINDOW w_custpop
     RETURN pa_cust[idx].customer_num, pa_cust[idx].company

   END FUNCTION  -- cust_popup2 --


   ########################################
   FUNCTION order_popup(cust_num)
   ########################################
     DEFINE        cust_num        LIKE customer.customer_num,

                   pa_order        ARRAY[10] OF RECORD
                           order_num       LIKE orders.order_num,
                           order_date      LIKE orders.order_date,
                           po_num          LIKE orders.po_num,
                           ship_date       LIKE orders.ship_date,
                           paid_date       LIKE orders.paid_date
                   END RECORD,

                   idx             SMALLINT,
                   i               SMALLINT,
                   order_cnt       SMALLINT,
                   fetch_orders    SMALLINT,
                   array_size      SMALLINT,
                   total_orders    INTEGER,
                   number_to_see   INTEGER,
                   curr_pa         SMALLINT

     LET array_size = 10
     LET fetch_orders = FALSE

46➤  SELECT COUNT(*)
     INTO total_orders
     FROM orders
     WHERE customer_num = cust_num
```

47➤ The order_popup() function opens a window and form in which to display the popup list and instructions to the user.

48➤ The assignments set the variables that keep track of the number of rows remaining to be viewed and the number of rows retrieved in the current execution of the paging WHILE loop.

The function then declares a cursor and query, opens the cursor, and verifies that the engine didn't encounter any problems in attempting to open the cursor. If the OPEN fails, the function returns null values for order_num and order_date.

49➤ The outer WHILE loop shows the user a different set of rows on each repetition.

The inner WHILE loop fetches as many rows as the array will hold, terminating prematurely only after the last row has been retrieved. After the loop finishes, the idx variable stores the number of elements in the array that are populated.

```
    IF total_orders = 0 THEN
      LET pa_order[1].order_num = NULL
      LET pa_order[1].order_date = NULL
      RETURN pa_order[1].order_num, pa_order[1].order_date
    END IF

47➤ OPEN WINDOW w_orderpop AT 9, 5
      WITH 12 ROWS, 71 COLUMNS
      ATTRIBUTE(BORDER, FORM LINE 4)

    OPEN FORM f_ordersel FROM "f_ordersel"
    DISPLAY FORM f_ordersel

    DISPLAY "Move cursor using F3, F4, and arrow keys."
      AT 1,2
    DISPLAY "Press Accept to select an order."
      AT 2,2

48➤ LET number_to_see = total_orders
    LET idx = 0

    DECLARE c_orderpop CURSOR FOR
      SELECT order_num, order_date, po_num, ship_date, paid_date
      FROM orders
      WHERE customer_num = cust_num
      ORDER BY order_num

  WHENEVER ERROR CONTINUE
    OPEN c_orderpop
  WHENEVER ERROR STOP

    IF (status = 0) THEN
      LET fetch_orders = TRUE
    ELSE
      CALL msg("Unable to open cursor.")
      LET idx = 1
      LET pa_order[idx].order_num = NULL
      LET pa_order[idx].order_date = NULL
    END IF

49➤ WHILE fetch_orders
      WHILE (idx < array_size)
        LET idx = idx + 1
        FETCH c_orderpop INTO pa_order[idx].*
        IF (status = NOTFOUND) THEN                --* no more orders to see
          LET fetch_orders = FALSE
          LET idx = idx - 1
          EXIT WHILE
        END IF
      END WHILE
```

50➤ If the outer WHILE loop hasn't reached the last set of rows, a message tells the user how to advance to the next set.

51➤ If no further rows existed for retrieval, the assignment sets up the return values to indicate that the user didn't select a row.

52➤ If rows were retrieved, the ELSE clause displays the populated subset of the array in the f_ordersel form.

53➤ The ON KEY clause traps the paging key:

- If the user was positioned on the last row of the current set before pressing the key and the current set isn't the last set, the idx variable is reset to zero to read a new set of rows starting with the first array element.
- If the current set is the last set, a message notifies the user.
- If the user wasn't on the last row, a message notifies the user.

54➤ If the user didn't press the paging key, the assignment sets idx to the row on which the user positioned and sets fetch_orders to FALSE to prevent repetition of the paging WHILE loop.

55➤ If the user pressed the Interrupt key, the assignment sets the returned order number to null but not the order date, which is used in the calling function to distinguish customers without orders from leaving without selecting an order.

56➤ The order_popup() function finishes by closing the popup form and window and returning the appropriate values.

```
50➤     IF (number_to_see > array_size) THEN
          MESSAGE "On last row, press F5 (CTRL-B) for more orders."
        END IF

51➤     IF (idx = 0) THEN
          CALL msg("No orders exist in the database.")
          LET idx = 1
          LET pa_order[idx].order_num = NULL
52➤     ELSE

          CALL SET_COUNT(idx)
          LET int_flag = FALSE
          DISPLAY ARRAY pa_order TO sa_order.*
53➤         ON KEY (F5, CONTROL-B)
              LET curr_pa = ARR_CURR()

              IF (curr_pa = idx) THEN
                LET number_to_see = number_to_see - idx
                IF (number_to_see > 0) THEN
                  LET idx = 0
                  EXIT DISPLAY
                ELSE
                  CALL msg("No more orders to see.")
                END IF
              ELSE
                CALL msg("Not on last order row.")
                MESSAGE "On last row, press F5 (CTRL-B) for more orders."
              END IF
          END DISPLAY

54➤       IF idx <> 0 THEN
            LET idx = ARR_CURR()
            LET fetch_orders = FALSE
          END IF

55➤       IF int_flag THEN
            LET int_flag = FALSE
            CALL msg("No order number selected.")
            LET pa_order[idx].order_num = NULL
          END IF
        END IF
      END WHILE

56➤   CLOSE FORM f_ordersel
      CLOSE WINDOW w_orderpop
      RETURN pa_order[idx].order_num, pa_order[idx].order_date

    END FUNCTION  -- orders_popup --
```

The calc_order() Function

Notes 57 to 59 The calc_order() function uses a series of SELECT statements to retrieve summary information for an order from several tables in much the same manner as the get_summary() function (see Example 4 for a more complete description of the techniques used in this function).

57➤ The first query uses a join to get the ship_charges column from the orders table and the state code from the customer table. The join is necessary to identify the customer based on the order. If the ship_charges column is empty (null), the function sets the ship_charges variable to zero.

58➤ The second query totals the charges associated with the order from the items table. Again, if the total is null, the default is zero.

59➤ The tax_rates() function returns the percentage of sales tax applied within the state (simplifying the real sales tax structures for demonstration purposes).

The assignment to the sales_tax variable calculates the sales tax on the total item charges. The assignment to the order_total variable subtotals the order charges (the shipping charges are added in the input_ship() function).

The upd_order() Function

60➤ The upd_order() function updates the order row in the database. As in previous examples, upd_order() supports recovery from an SQL error at runtime by

- Suppressing termination on errors with the WHENEVER ERROR CONTINUE statement.
- Executing the SQL statement.

  The UPDATE statement updates only those columns that were accessed by the input_ship() function.
- Resuming termination on errors with the WHENEVER ERROR STOP statement.
- Evaluating the status variable to determine whether an error occurred.

  The upd_order() function returns the status to the MAIN function, which notifies the user of the error or of the success of the update.

```
########################################
FUNCTION calc_order(ord_num)
########################################
  DEFINE        ord_num         LIKE orders.order_num,

                state_code      LIKE customer.state

57➤  SELECT ship_charge, state
  INTO gr_charges.ship_charge, state_code
  FROM orders, customer
  WHERE order_num = ord_num
    AND orders.customer_num = customer.customer_num

  IF gr_charges.ship_charge IS NULL THEN
    LET gr_charges.ship_charge = 0.00
  END IF

58➤  SELECT SUM(total_price)
  INTO gr_charges.order_total
  FROM items
  WHERE order_num = ord_num

  IF gr_charges.order_total IS NULL THEN
    LET gr_charges.order_total = 0.00
  END IF

59➤  CALL tax_rates(state_code) RETURNING gr_charges.tax_rate

  LET gr_charges.sales_tax = gr_charges.order_total *
        (gr_charges.tax_rate / 100)

  LET gr_charges.order_total = gr_charges.order_total +
        gr_charges.sales_tax

END FUNCTION  -- calc_order --


########################################
60➤ FUNCTION upd_order(ord_num)
########################################
    DEFINE        ord_num         LIKE orders.order_num

WHENEVER ERROR CONTINUE
    UPDATE orders SET (ship_date, ship_instruct, ship_weight, ship_charge)
                  = (gr_ship.ship_date, gr_ship.ship_instruct,
                     gr_ship.ship_weight, gr_ship.ship_charge)
    WHERE order_num = ord_num
WHENEVER ERROR STOP

    RETURN (status)
END FUNCTION  -- upd_order --
```

To locate any function definition see the Function Index on page 728.

13

Calling a C Function

When something cannot easily be done in **4GL**, you can code that operation in a C function and call it from the **4GL** program. This example displays a C function of moderate size and shows how it is invoked from a **4GL** program compiled with either **INFORMIX-4GL C Compiler Version** or **INFORMIX-4GL Rapid Development System**.

The fglgets.c module examined here enhances **4GL** with the ability to write command line utility programs in addition to interactive applications more typical of **4GL**. It allows, for example, programs driven by data in text files.

The Interface Between C and 4GL

The interface between **4GL** and C is documented in the *INFORMIX-4GL Reference Manual*, Chapter 2, and in somewhat more detail in the *INFORMIX-4GL Release 4.1 Reference Manual Supplement*. This section provides a brief overview of the concepts.

The Argument Stack

Within a **4GL** program, arguments are passed to functions and results are returned on a pushdown stack of values. When a function is called, its arguments are pushed on the stack. Upon entry to the function the arguments are popped into local variables. When a function executes the RETURN statement, copies of the returned value or values are pushed on the stack. Upon return to the point of call, returned values are popped from the stack.

Each value on the argument stack carries its data type as well as its contents. As a result, values can be type-converted as they are popped. This explains how a function can define its arguments with a different type than its caller may have passed. The types are converted when the arguments are popped.

In the same way, a function can return a value of a type different from what the caller receives. Any conversion supported by the LET statement is allowed.

Passing Arguments to a C Function

A function written in C and linked with a **4GL** program must also receive its arguments from the argument stack. A function receives exactly one formal parameter by the normal C calling conventions. This is an integer that contains a count of the number of arguments that were pushed on the **4GL** argument stack when the function was called. The number of arguments pushed can differ from one call to the next.

The C function acquires the actual values of its arguments by popping them from the argument stack. It does this by calling one of the pop functions built in to **4GL**. There is one pop function for each data type; for example popint() pops the top stack item as an integer. The type popped need not be the same as the type pushed by the caller, so long as type conversion is possible.

Returning Values From a C Function

A C function can return one or more values to the calling **4GL** program. The number of values it returns must agree with the number expected by the caller.

To return a value, the C function uses a return function built into **4GL**. There is one return function for each data type; for example retquote() pushes a character string onto the stack. The return functions make a copy of the value, so that the function can return the contents of local variables that will disappear when it terminates. The type pushed need not be the same as what the caller will pop, so long as type conversion is possible.

The formal value returned from the C function using the RETURN statement must be an integer giving the number of values pushed on the argument stack. Thus a function that returns no values on the stack should exit with the statement return(0). One that pushed a single value before terminating should end with return(1), and so on.

The fglgets.c Module

The C function in this example is named fglgets(). Its purpose is to read lines from text files. It is named after the C library routine fgets(), which it uses.

The fglgets() function adds considerable new power to **4GL**. The usual strengths of **4GL** are in interactive applications, where menus and screen forms make it easy to build an attractive user interface. With fglgets() you can use **4GL** to write command line utility programs; that is, programs that are driven by data in text files or data produced by other command-line utilities. You can write database-access programs that can be used in a command pipeline with other utility programs.

Using fglgets()

The fglgets() function takes one argument, the name of a text file. It reads the next line of input from that file and returns the line as a parameter to the calling function. A return code is available by calling fglgetret(). The following program fragment shows how a **4GL** program can use these two functions.

```
DEFINE fname CHAR(80), fline CHAR(255)
PROMPT "Enter file pathname: " FOR fname

CALL fglgets(fname) RETURNING fline -- read first line
WHILE fglgetret() = 0 -- while not end-of-file nor error
    DISPLAY fline
    CALL fglgets(fname) RETURNING fline
END WHILE
```

Each call to fglgets() returns the next line of text from the specified file. The fglgetret() function returns a nonzero value at end-of-file. The code in the preceding example merely displays the data, but any kind of processing is possible. For example, each input line could have been:

- inserted into a table in a database.
- used as the key to retrieve a row from a database.
- prepared as an SQL statement and executed.

Access to the standard input stream is provided by fglgets() as a special case. When the filename is omitted, or contains a null string or the string "stdin," fglgets() reads from stdin. A **4GL** program that reads from standard input can be used in a command pipeline, processing data that is generated by another program. The DISPLAY statement writes to standard output, so processed data can be passed on to the next program in the pipeline.

As many as eight named files can be open simultaneously, in addition to the standard input.

The Design of fglgets()

The function maintains a list of up to eight standard C file pointers (that is, FILE * values as returned by fopen()). Each one is associated with a character string containing the pathname associated with it.

When it is called, the function checks the number of arguments that were pushed for it. If there were none (that is, if it was called with an empty argument list), or if the argument proves to be an empty string, it uses stdin. Otherwise it looks for that string in its list of filenames. If it does not appear there, fopen() is called to open the file. If it succeeds, the resulting file pointer is saved, along with its name.

After identifying the file, the function reads a line from the file with fgets() and returns it by pushing it on the argument stack.

Returning Both a Value and a Code

The fglgets() function has two pieces of information to return to its caller. One is the line of text from the file; the other is a return code. Six codes are possible:

0	success; a line was read from the file.
100	end-of-file was reached.
-1	error opening file.
-2	too many files open at once.
-3	unable to allocate space to store filename string.
-4	wrong number of arguments passed (more than one).

Three ways of returning such codes were examined during the coding of this example. They are described in the following sections.

Using a Global Variable

The first method is to store the return code in some global variable and let the **4GL** program fetch it from there. Unfortunately, a **4GL** program can refer to C global variables only when it has been compiled by the **C Compiler Version**. When the same program is compiled under the **RDS Version**, it can no longer access C external global variables.

In order to make fglgets() usable from all **4GL** programs, its return code must be returned a different way.

Returning Two Values

When a **4GL** function has two values to return, it may simply return two values. The **4GL** RETURN statement accepts a list of one or more values, separated by commas. Any C function, too, may return two or more values by pushing them on the argument stack. So fglgets() could have been written to return both a string of text and an integer return code.

The only problem with returning two values is that it restricts the form of a CALL statement. If fglgets() returned two values, it could only be called in a statement like the following one.

```
    CALL fglgets(fname) RETURNING text_line, ret_code
```

So long as the function returns a single value, it may also be used in a LET statement or in an expression, as in the following examples.

```
    LET text_line = fglgets()
...or...
    WHILE LENGTH(fglgets(fname)) <> 0
        DISPLAY "flushing..."
    END WHILE
```

Using an Access Function

The third method is to provide a function that will retrieve the return code. This is the method used in this example. A small function, fglgetret(), picks up the most recent return code and stacks it as its return value.

This solution works in all versions of **4GL**, and allows both the input function and the return code to be used in LET statements and expressions.

Handling Arguments

C functions have only incomplete control over the number of arguments that will be passed to them on the **4GL** argument stack. When a function is used with the **RDS Version**, the maximum number of arguments it permits is defined in the fglusr.c file (this is discussed with the next topic). **4GL** functions cannot call it with more arguments. However, the **C Compiler Version** has no information about the interface to an external function. It will permit a **4GL** function to call a C function (or a **4GL** function in a different source module) with any number of arguments. The only restriction is that the same number of arguments must be used in every call within one source module.

As a result the C function must be prepared to handle different numbers of arguments. It can insist on an exact number, or it can define defaults for omitted arguments.

The fglgets() function accepts either zero or one argument. If no argument is passed, it assumes "stdin". One argument is taken to be a filename. If more than one argument is passed, the function sets an error code and returns an empty string.

A function is always supposed to clear the argument stack before pushing return values. When too many arguments are passed it faces a problem: how to pop arguments of unknown type. If it pops an argument using a type that is incompatible with the stacked value, **4GL** will stop with a run-time error. The simplest policy is to pop unknown arguments as character strings. Any data type except BYTE or TEXT can be converted to a character string, and if the string is too long, **4GL** will truncate it without error.

Running the Example

All examples in this manual can run in both the **INFORMIX-4GL Rapid Development System** (**r4gl**) and the **INFORMIX-4GL C Compiler Version** (**i4gl**) environments. However, these two environments differ in the way they call a **4GL** program which uses C functions. To enable Example 13 to run the fglgets() function in either environment, this example is divided into two **4GL** programs:

- ex13.4gl is a front-end menu-driven program that asks:
    - whether to run the example under **i4gl** or **r4gl**.
    - whether to expect the input lines from an ASCII file or from the screen (stdin).
- ex13a.4gl is the program that actually calls the C function fglgets() to read and display the input lines.

The ex13.4gl file displays menus to gather the information it needs to determine how to call the ex13a.4gl program. The actual command to execute ex13a.4gl is stored in a shell script. For **i4gl**, this script is the ex13i.sh file and for **r4gl**, this script is called ex13r.sh. The ex13.4gl program builds a string with the appropriate executable files and then uses the RUN command to the appropriate shell script.

To run this example, you must:

1. Compile the two **4GL** source files. To create the ex13.4go (or ex13.4gi) and ex13a.4go (or ex13a.4gi) files, follow the same procedure you have used to compile the other examples in this manual.
2. Create the executable files that recognize the fglgets() C function. This procedure depends on the environment you are using. It is described in the following section.
3. Run the ex13.4gl program using the same procedure you have used to run the other examples in this manual.

Creating the Executable Files

You must link the binary executable form of the C function with the **4GL** program before you can use it. This procedure depends on the programming environment you are using:

i4gl Add the C source file to the definition of a program, using the Program Modify menu. The C source file will be included when the program is compiled.

c4gl List the C source file along with the **4GL** source files as an argument to the **c4gl** command.

fglpc Compile **4GL** source files as usual. Create a custom program runner to link the C module with **fglgo**.

r4gl Compile **4GL** modules as usual. Create a customer runner program and then use the Program Modify menu to specify this custom runner for the program.

This section outlines the procedure to follow to compile and run Example 13. Refer to Chapter 1 of the *INFORMIX-4GL Reference Manual* for more detailed information.

Note: *To create the executable files, you must have a C compiler installed on your system.*

Using r4gl or fglpc

When you compile the **4GL** modules with **r4gl** (or with **fglpc**), the resulting program is executed by a "runner," or execution module. The standard runner, **fglgo**, supports only the built-in functions that are standard with **4GL**. However, if your program calls a C function, that function must be linked into the runner.

You compile and link the program in two steps:

1. Add lines that describe the C function (or functions) in the fgiusr.c file. This step has been done in the fgiusr.c file that is released with these examples.
2. Use the cfglgo (compile **fglgo**) command to compile and link the fgiusr.c file and the C source file(s) with the base code of the runner. The result is a *custom runner,* that is, a version of **fglgo** that contains your C functions as well as the standard ones.

   To create the customer runner for Example 13, use the command:

   ```
   cfglgo fgiusr.c fglgets.c -o fglgo13
   ```

   This command creates the fglgo13 custom runner to run the ex13a.4go (or ex13a.4gi) file.

   Note: *Because the name of the customer runner (fglgo13) is hardcoded in the ex13.4gl file, you must use this name to execute this example.*

Using i4gl or c4gl

When you compile the **4GL** modules with **i4gl** (or with **c4gl**), the resulting program can be executed directly. To compile and link modules, you just list the module names as arguments to the **c4gl** command. No customer runner is required.

You compile in a single step:

- The **c4gl** command compiles **4GL** and C source files and links them to produce an executable program.

  To create the executable program for Example 13, use the command:

  ```
  c4gl ex13a.4gl fglgets.c -o ex13a.4ge
  ```

  This command creates the ex13a.4ge executable file.

  Note: *Because the name of the executable file (ex13a.4ge) is hardcoded in the ex13.4gl file, you must use this name to execute this example.*

Calling the Executable File

The fglgets() function accepts at most one argument. If it receives no argument, fglgets() reads input lines from standard input (stdin). If it receives an argument, it reads input lines from this file.

The program menu treats it as a filename and asks the user to choose whether input lines are to come from standard input (Stdin) or an ASCII file (Ascii):

- If you select the Stdin option, ex13.4gl calls the appropriate executable file without an argument:
  - **i4gl** and **c4gl**:

    ```
    ex13a.4ge
    ```

  - **r4gl** and **fglgo**:

    ```
    fglgo13 ex13a
    ```

- If you select the Ascii option, ex13.4gl provides a form for the entry of the file name. It then calls the appropriate executable file with the file name as an argument:
  - **i4gl** and **c4gl**:

    ```
    ex13a.4ge filename
    ```

  - **r4gl** and **fglgo**:

    ```
    fglgo13 ex13a filename
    ```

C Module Overview

C Module	Purpose
fgiusr.c	Used to make a custom runner including fglgets.c
fglgets.c	Defines a C function for reading stream input using the fgets() function from the standard C library.

The f_name Form

1➤ This form does not need to specify a specific database because it does not contain fields defined like database columns.

2➤ The form contains a single 50-character field. The TYPE CHAR keywords define the type of data accepted in this field.

f_name form file

1➤
```
DATABASE formonly

SCREEN
{


  Name:[f000                                              ]

}

ATTRIBUTES
f000 = formonly.a_char TYPE CHAR;
```
2➤ (marks the line `f000 = formonly.a_char TYPE CHAR;`)

The MAIN Function

1➤ NUM_ARGS() is a **4GL** built-in function that returns a count of the command-line arguments to the program. When the program was given no command-line arguments, it passes an empty filename, which fglgets() will interpret as meaning stdin.

2➤ Each command-line argument is fetched by culling the built-in function ARG_VAL() and is passed in turn to the fdump() subroutine. If that function returns a status other than NOTFOUND the loop ends.

3➤ If the loop ended because error status was returned, the error is displayed to the user. Note the use of \n to get additional line spaces in the output. The PROMPT start lets the user read the error message before the screen is cleared by the end of the program.

4GL source file

```
#######################################
MAIN
#######################################
    DEFINE        arg          SMALLINT,
                  fstat        SMALLINT,
                  anarg        CHAR(80)

    IF NUM_ARGS() = 0 THEN
1➤      LET anarg = " "
        CALL fdump(anarg) RETURNING fstat
    ELSE
2➤      FOR arg = 1 TO NUM_ARGS()
           LET anarg = ARG_VAL(arg)
           CALL fdump(anarg) RETURNING fstat
           IF fstat <> NOTFOUND THEN
                EXIT FOR
           END IF
        END FOR
    END IF
3➤  IF fstat <> NOTFOUND THEN -- quit due to a problem, diagnose
       CASE fstat
          WHEN -1
            DISPLAY "\nUnable to open file ", anarg CLIPPED, ".\n"
          WHEN -2
            DISPLAY "\nToo many files open in fglgets().\n"
          WHEN -3
            DISPLAY "\nCall to malloc() failed. Couldn't open the file.\n"
          WHEN -4
           DISPLAY "\nToo many parameters to fglgets().\n"
        OTHERWISE
            DISPLAY "\nUnknown return ",fstat," from fglgets().\n"
        END CASE
        PROMPT "Press RETURN to continue." FOR anarg
    END IF

END MAIN
```

The fdump() Function

4➤ Errors are diagnosed when fglgets() is first called with a new filename. If fglgets() cannot save the pathname, or can't open it, a call to fglgetret() will return a negative number. Also, if the file is empty, the end-of-file code of 100 is returned after this first use.

The fgiusr.c source file

```
   /***************************************************************************
    *
    *                        INFORMIX SOFTWARE, INC.
    *
    *                           PROPRIETARY DATA
    *
1➤  *      THIS DOCUMENT CONTAINS TRADE SECRET DATA WHICH IS THE PROPERTY OF
    *      INFORMIX SOFTWARE, INC.  THIS DOCUMENT IS SUBMITTED TO RECIPIENT IN
    *      CONFIDENCE.  INFORMATION CONTAINED HEREIN MAY NOT BE USED, COPIED OR
    *      DISCLOSED IN WHOLE OR IN PART EXCEPT AS PERMITTED BY WRITTEN AGREEMENT
    *      SIGNED BY AN OFFICER OF INFORMIX SOFTWARE, INC.
    *
    *      THIS MATERIAL IS ALSO COPYRIGHTED AS AN UNPUBLISHED WORK UNDER
    *      SECTIONS 104 AND 408 OF TITLE 17 OF THE UNITED STATES CODE.
    *      UNAUTHORIZED USE, COPYING OR OTHER REPRODUCTION IS PROHIBITED BY LAW.
    *
    *  Title:       fgiusr.c
    *  Sccsid:      @(#)fgiusr.c    7.2    7/8/90  13:50:19
    *  Description: definition of user C functions
    *
    *************************************************************************** */

   /***************************************************************************
    * This table is for user-defined C functions.
    * Each initializer has the form:
    *      "name", name, nargs,
    * Variable # of arguments:
    *      set nargs to -(maximum # args)
    *
    * Be sure to declare name before the table and to leave the
    * line of 0's at the end of the table.
    *
    * Example:
    *      You want to call your C function named "mycfunc" and it expects
    *      2 arguments.  You must declare it:
    *              int mycfunc();
    *      and then insert an initializer for it in the table:
    *              "mycfunc", mycfunc, 2,
    *************************************************************************** */
   #include "fgicfunc.h"

2➤ int fglgets();           /* declaring the names of the function */
   int fglgetret();

   cfunc_t usrcfuncs[] =
       {
3➤     "fglgets", fglgets, -1,
       "fglgetret", fglgetret, 0,
       0, 0, 0
       };
```

The fglgets.c Module

1➤ fglgets() never *closes* a file. It does not support rereading of files, nor can it reuse entries in its array of file pointers. It would not be difficult to add these abilities. Possible methods include:

- Close a file whenever end-of-file is seen. This would present the problem that, if the caller does not note the end-of-file status when it appears, the next call would reopen the same file and start reading it from the top again.
- Require two arguments on every call: a filename string and an operation code (perhaps *O*, *R* and *C* for open, read and close).
- Provide a separate function that closes a file, given its name string.

You might want to enhance this module along one of these lines.

2➤ Static variables are used to record the files that fglgets() has opened. nfiles represents the number of files open at any given time. Pointers to their name strings are in fnames[0...nfiles-1]. File pointers returned by fopen() are in files [0...-1].

The fglgets.c source file

```
/* ========================================================================
       This module defines a C function for reading stream input using
       the fgets() function from the standard C library.  The main
       use intended is to read from standard input so that a 4GL program
       can act as a UNIX filter; however any ascii file may be read.
       In 4GL notation the interface to this module is
               DEFINE  input_line, file_pathname CHAR(255)
               CALL fglgets(file_pathname) RETURNING input_line
       fglgets() returns the next input line, to a maximum of 255
       bytes, from the specified file.

       The input file will be standard input in any of three cases:
               * the filename parameter is not specified
               * the filename parameter is a null string (or all-blank)
               * the filename parameter is "stdin"
       Otherwise the specified file is opened mode "r" (if necessary).
       A file is only opened once.  Its name and file pointer are
       saved and used on subsequent calls for that name.  Several files
1➤     may be opened concurrently (see MAXOPEN below).

       The function returns the line of data as a string result.  The
       terminating newline is not returned.  Thus a blank string is
       returned where the file contains a null line.

       This function should not be used for interactive input. The
       reason is that stdout is not flushed prior to input, so a
       prompt string written with DISPLAY may not be seen by the user.
       For interactive applications use PROMPT or INPUT.

       The function has a result code which can have any of the
       following values:
                 0       successful read
               100       end of file
                -1       UNIX would not open the file (fopen returned NULL)
                -2       too many files open (MAXOPEN exceeded)
                -3       malloc failed, we couldn't save the filename
                -4       too many parameters to fglgets()
       When the return code is other than 0, the returned string is
       always null (all-blank).  However, to retrieve the return code
       the 4GL program must call fglgetret(), which returns an integer.
===================================================================== */

#include <stdio.h>
#include <strings.h>
#define MAXOPEN 8
#define MAXSTR 256                  /* includes the null - max data is 255!!! */

2➤ static short nfiles = 0;          /* how many filenames we know about */
static char *fnames[MAXOPEN];     /* ->saved filename strings for compares */
static FILE *files[MAXOPEN];      /* saved fileptrs for open files */
```

The getquote() Function

3➤ The getquote() function gets an argument from the **4GL** argument stack as a character string. The built-in function popquote() does this; however, popquote() always extends the popped value to the size of the receiving buffer. The remaining code strips the trailing blanks so that, if an empty string is passed, it will have zero length.

Note that **4GL** version 4.1 includes the built-in function popvchar() which does precisely this: popping a value as a character string with no trailing spaces. It could be used in place of this function.

The fglgetret() Function

4➤ The fglgetret() function returns the value last stored in the static retcode variable. It does not test the number of arguments passed to it. If it is passed any, they will remain on the stack when it returns and the program will probably terminate with a **4GL** error message.

5➤ The built-in function retshort() pushes a short integer on the argument stack. The formal return value is the count of return values pushed, namely one.

```
static short retcode = 100;      /* return code with initial value */
/* ==========================================================================
        This function performs a 4gl "popquote" or argument fetch.
*/
3➤ void getquote(str,len)
        char *str;        /* place to put the string */
        int len;          /* length of string expected */
{
        register char *p;
        register int n;
        popquote(str,len);
        for( p = str, n = len-1 ;
                        (n >= 0) && (p[n] <= ' ');
                                                        --n )
                ;
        p[n+1] = '\0';
}


/* ==========================================================================
    This function returns the last retcode, using 4GL conventions.
*/
4➤ int fglgetret(numargs)
        int numargs;      /* number of parameters (ignored) */
{
5➤      retshort(retcode);
        return(1);        /* number of values pushed */
}
```

The fglgets() Function

6➤ The C switch statement is very useful for determining the number of arguments. First set up appropriate default values; in this instance, a default null string is placed in astring. Then enter a switch in which the acceptable numbers of arguments are listed as cases in descending order. In each case, pop one argument. Since there is then one fewer argument on the stack, control can fall through into the next case.

7➤ The default is reached when an unknown number of arguments has been passed. Since their types are not known, the safest thing is to pop them as character strings.

8➤ A filename string is looked up in the list of known filenames and opened if necessary. The structure of this passage is described in C commentary on the preceding page.

This code assumes that all elements of the arrays files and fnames from 0 through nfiles-1 are in use. If this module is enhanced to close files (as discussed in Note 1), the close function must maintain this invariant, probably by compacting the arrays.

```
/* ========================================================================
    The steps of the fglgets operation are as follows:
        1. check number of parameters; if >1 return null & -4
        2. get filename string to scratch string space
        3. if we do not have stdin,
            a. if we have never seen this filename before,
                  i. if we have our limit of files, return null & -2
                 ii. if unix will not open it, return null & -1
                iii. if we cannot save the filename string, return null & -3
                 iv. else save filename and matching FILE*
            b. else pick up FILE* matching filename
        4. else pick up FILE* of stdin
        5. apply fgets(astring,MAXSTR,file) and note result
        6. if fgets() returned NULL, return null & 100
        7. check for and zap the trailing newline, return line & 0
*/
int fglgets(numargs)
        int numargs;            /* number of parameters in 4gl call */
{
        register int ret;       /* running success flag --> sqlcode */
        register int j;         /* misc index */
        register char *ptr;     /* misc ptr to string space */
        FILE* afile;            /* selected file */
        char astring[MAXSTR];   /* scratch string space */

        astring[0] = '\0';      /* default parameter is null string */
        ret = 0;                /* default result is whoopee */
        afile = stdin;          /* default file is stdin */

6➤      switch (numargs)
        {
        case 1:                 /* one parameter, pop as string */
                getquote(astring,MAXSTR);
        case 0:                 /* no parameters, ok, astring is null */
                break;
        default:                /* too many parameters, clear stack */
7➤              for( j = numargs; j; --j)
                        popquote(astring,MAXSTR);
                ret = -4;
        }

        if ( (ret == 0)         /* parameters ok and.. */
        &&   (astring[0])/* ..non-blank string passed.. */
        &&   (strcmp(astring,"stdin")) )/* ..but not "stdin".. */
        {                               /* ..look for string in our list */
8➤              for ( j = nfiles-1;
                                (j >= 0) && (strcmp(astring,fnames[j]));
                                        --j )
                        ;
                if (j >= 0)     /* it was there (strcmp returned 0) */
                        afile = files[j];
                else                    /* it was not; try to open it */
                {
```

9➤ If control reaches this point without error, afile contains a valid file handle and a line can be read.

10➤ If control reaches this point without error, a line has been read. If not, this statement prepares an empty string to be returned.

11➤ Since one value, a string, is always pushed on the stack, the function always exits with a formal return value of 1.

```
                if ((j = nfiles) < MAXOPEN)
                {               /* not too many files, try fopen */
                        afile = fopen(astring,"r");
                        if (afile == NULL)
                                ret = -1;
                }
                else ret = -2;
                if (ret == 0)/* fopen worked, get space for name */
                {
                        ptr = (char *)malloc(1+strlen(astring));
                        if (ptr == NULL) ret = -3;
                }
                if (ret == 0)/* have space, copy name & save */
                {
                        files[j] = afile;
                        fnames[j] = ptr;
                        strcpy(ptr,astring);
                        ++nfiles;
                }
        }
}

9➤      if (ret == 0)           /* we have a file to use */
        {
                ptr = fgets(astring,MAXSTR,afile);
                if (ptr != NULL)/* we did read some data */
                {                       /* check for newline, remove */
                        ptr = astring + strlen(astring) -1;
                        if ('\n' == *ptr) *ptr = '\0';
                }
                else ret = 100; /* set eof return code */
        }

10➤     if (ret)                /* not a success */
                astring[0] = '\0';/* .. ensure null string return */

        retcode = ret;          /* save return for fglgetret() */
        retquote(astring);/* set string RETURN value.. */
11➤     return(1);              /* .. and tell 4gl how many pushed */
}
```

To locate any function definition see the Function Index on page 728.

14

Generating a Report

This example demonstrates how to produce a basic report. The **4GL** report tools are among the most important for database application development because they let you view and analyze the data stored in the database.

```
                         MANUFACTURER LISTING
                          Mon. Apr 15, 1991
                          Screen Number:   1



 Manufacturer   Manufacturer      Lead Time
     Code           Name           (in days)
---------------------------------------------------------------------------------

     ANZ       Anza                     5
     HRO       Hero                     4
     HSK       Husky                    6
     KAR       Karsten                 21
     NKL       Nikolus                  8

Press RETURN to display next screen.
```

This example introduces the following **4GL** programming techniques:

- Sending rows to a report.
- Setting page margins.
- Providing headers and footers for the page.
- Formatting database columns as columns in the report.
- Sending the report to the screen.

The Program Model

4GL contains extensive facilities for generating reports based upon a two-part program model:

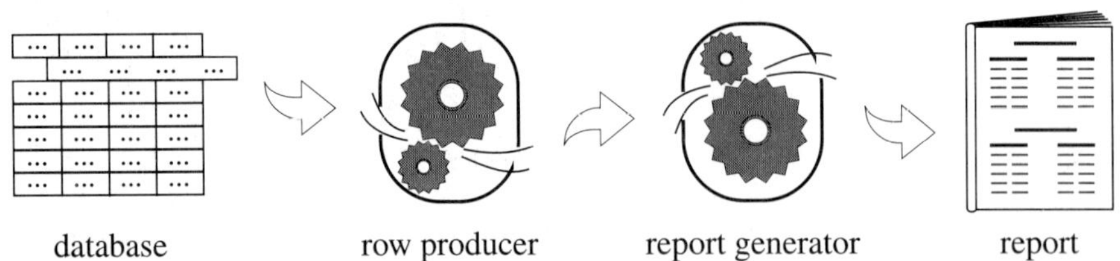

The *row producer* provides a supply of rows of data. The *report generator* (which is a single function) formats those rows into a pleasing report with pagination, group headings, and other features.

This two-part model allows you to structure your report programs in the following ways:

- The row producer (which comprises the MAIN function and most of the functions in the program) is concerned only with the content of the data. It does not format the information.

  This portion of the program essentially fetches rows and passes them, a row at a time, to the report generator.

- The report generator is concerned only with the format of the data. It need not be concerned with the source of the data or with its content, except as it relates to the format.

Steps in Generating a Report

The basic sequence of actions in the row producer portion of the **4GL** program are as follows:

DECLARE CURSOR	You declare a cursor for the query that qualifies the appropriate rows for the report. The column list for the SELECT statement should specify only those columns needed for the report, as the unneeded columns will slow down the report generation. The ORDER BY clause of the SELECT statement is extremely important because it determines the sorting sequence of

rows in the report. The WHERE clause is also important if the report should cover a subset of the rows.

START REPORT — You prepare the report generator to run the report.

FOREACH — You retrieve the rows qualified by the query one at a time into variables of the report driver function. You can also use a WHILE loop that executes a FETCH statement, but the FOREACH statement is more convenient in many cases.

OUPUT TO REPORT — Within the FOREACH loop, you use the OUTPUT TO REPORT statement to pass the data, one row at a time, to the report generator function.

The OUTPUT TO REPORT statement is to a report generator function what the CALL statement is to a standard **4GL** function. As with any function call, the report generator must define a parameter for each value passed by the OUTPUT TO REPORT statement.

FINISH REPORT — You signal the report generator to end the report after passing the last row.

So long as each row sent to the report has the same structure, you can make variations in this basic procedure.

For example, you could declare two different queries on the same table, start the report, send the rows from the first query to the report, send the rows from the second query to the report, and then close the report.

Alternatively, you could retrieve all rows into an array and traverse the array in a special sequence, sending each row to the report as visited.

Basic Parts of a Report

A report generator function cannot execute SQL statements or **4GL** screen interaction statements. Instead, the report generator is dedicated to specifying the format of the report. The following sections control the layout of the report on the page:

OUTPUT — You define the page size and margins. The space available for printing report data is the space within the margins.

The right margin is specified as an offset from the left edge of the page rather than from the right edge of the page, which keeps you from having to specify the page width and right margin separately.

FORMAT You define the blocks that make up the report. A report block consists of the text and data that is output in response to rows passed by the row producer portion of the program.

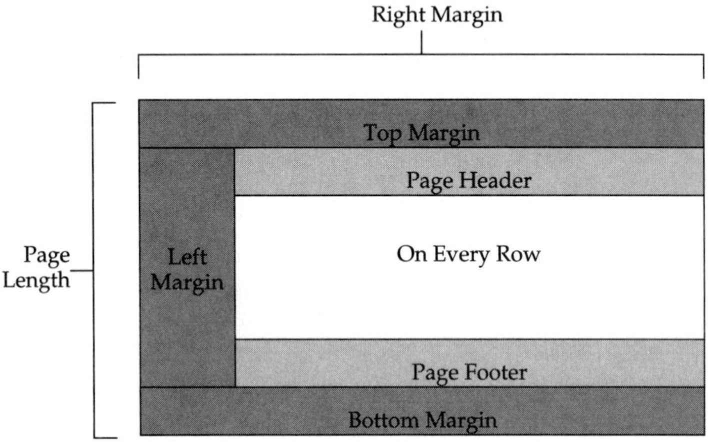

The basic report blocks are as follows:

PAGE HEADER Appears at the top of every page under the top margin. The page header typically contains the page number, the date, and heading text for columns within the report.

ON EVERY ROW Appears for each row passed to the report. This block formats the body of the report. Be sure to leave enough space between the page header and page footer for at least one ON EVERY ROW block.

PAGE FOOTER Appears at the bottom of each page above the bottom margin. The report generator inserts empty lines between the last ON EVERY ROW block and the PAGE FOOTER block so that the PAGE FOOTER block is flush against the bottom margin. The PAGE FOOTER is also a good place to display the page number or date.

Directing a Report to the Screen

By default, reports go to the screen, though you can also use the OUTPUT section of the report generator function to send the report to a printer, file, or operating system command. When sending reports to the screen, you can use the PAUSE function in the PAGE HEADER or PAGE FOOTER block to let the user view the current page before displaying the next.

Function Overview

Function Name	Purpose
manuf_listing()	Retrieves manufacturer information and sends it to the report.
manuf_rpt()	Formats the manufacturer information as a report.
init_msgs()	Initializes the members of the ga_dsplymsg array to null. *See description in Example 2.*
prompt_window()	Displays a message and prompts the user for affirmation or negation. This function is a variation on the message_window() function that appears in Example 2. *See description in Example 4.*

The MAIN Function

1➤ The MAIN function calls the prompt_window() function to confirm that the report should be generated. The reason for this caution is that, if the amount of rows sent to the report is very large, the report might prevent other activities for some time. If the amount of rows is small or the user generates reports frequently, you might want to omit this test.

The manuf_listing() Function

2➤ The DECLARE statement declares a cursor for a query to retrieve manufacturers. NoWHERE clause appears in the SELECT statement because the report covers all manufacturers and no other tables are joined with the manufact table.

The ORDER BY clause ensures the intelligibility of the report by sorting the rows on the manufacturer code. Without the ORDER BY clause, the sequence of rows in the report would be that of the physical order in which the manufacturer rows are stored.

3➤ The START REPORT statement invokes the report generator to prepare the manuf_rpt report.

You can use the START REPORT statement to send a report to a file, printer, or operating system command. If the START REPORT statement doesn't specify the destination, the report generator uses the destination from the OUTPUT section of the report function. If the destination isn't specified explicitly, the report goes to the screen.

4➤ The FOREACH statement opens the cursor at the start of the loop, fetches the next row into the pa_manuf record on each iteration of the loop, and closes the cursor at the end of the loop.

Within the loop, the OUTPUT TO REPORT statement sends the row currently stored in the pa_manuf record to the report generator to be formatted according to the specification in the manuf_rpt() report function and added to the report.

5➤ The FINISH REPORT statement terminates the report generator and ends the report.

4GL source file

```
DATABASE stores2t

   GLOBALS
     DEFINE  ga_dsplymsg  ARRAY[5] OF CHAR(48)
   END GLOBALS

########################################
MAIN
########################################

1➤  LET ga_dsplymsg[1] = "           Manufacturer Listing Report"
  IF prompt_window("Do you want to display this report?", 5, 10)
  THEN
    CALL manuf_listing()
  END IF
END MAIN

########################################
FUNCTION manuf_listing()
########################################
  DEFINE  pa_manuf      RECORD
                          manu_code     LIKE manufact.manu_code,
                          manu_name     LIKE manufact.manu_name,
                          lead_time     LIKE manufact.lead_time
                        END RECORD

2➤  DECLARE c_manuf CURSOR FOR
    SELECT manu_code, manu_name, lead_time
    FROM manufact
    ORDER BY manu_code

3➤  START REPORT manuf_rpt

4➤  FOREACH c_manuf INTO pa_manuf.*
    OUTPUT TO REPORT manuf_rpt(pa_manuf.*)
  END FOREACH

5➤  FINISH REPORT manuf_rpt

END FUNCTION  -- manuf_listing --
```

The manuf_rpt() Report Function

6➤ As with all report functions, the definition of manuf_rpt starts with the REPORT keyword rather than the FUNCTION keyword.

7➤ The OUTPUT section of the manuf_rpt() report function specifies no right and left margins because the destination of the report is the screen. The top and bottom margins are 1 line for readability. The page length is 23 lines so that, on a standard 24-line screen, the paging prompt won't scroll the display.

8➤ The FORMAT section specifies the formatting applied to the rows passed to the manuf_rpt() report function.

9➤ The PAGE HEADER block specifies the layout generated at the top of each page. The specification for the block extends to the start of the next block, which in the manuf_rpt() report function is the ON EVERY ROW block.

The page header block doesn't consume a row but rather appears in addition to the ON EVERY ROW block that appears for the first row on the page.

The SKIP statement inserts empty lines, while the PRINT statement starts a new line containing text or a value. The COLUMN clause specifies the offset of the first character from the first position after the left margin.

The complete page header occupies 13 lines. In your own reports, you may prefer a more terse header to leave more space for the rows.

10➤ The page header uses the built-in TODAY function to generate the current date and the built-in PAGENO function to generate the page number of the current page. The USING clauses format these values. The USING clause employs the same formatting tokens as form fields.

11➤ The PRINT statement can have multiple COLUMN clauses, which all print on the same line.

12➤ The page header uses hyphens to place a separator line between the page header and the rows displayed below the header. Another common character for a separator line is the equal sign. The semicolon at the end of the first PRINT statement suppresses the new line so the two sets of hyphens appear on a single line.

13➤ The ON EVERY ROW block specifies the layout generated for each row. As in the manuf_rpt() report function, you would typically keep this block to one line if at all possible so that data can be read more easily.

14➤ The PAGE TRAILER block specifies the layout generated at the bottom of each page. The SKIP statement puts an empty line under the last row, and the PAUSE statement displays a prompt and suspends output until the user presses a key.

```
   ########################################
6➤ REPORT manuf_rpt(pa_manuf)
   ########################################
     DEFINE  pa_manuf       RECORD
                              manu_code      LIKE manufact.manu_code,
                              manu_name      LIKE manufact.manu_name,
                              lead_time      LIKE manufact.lead_time
                            END RECORD

7➤   OUTPUT
       LEFT MARGIN 0
       RIGHT MARGIN 0
       TOP MARGIN 1
       BOTTOM MARGIN 1
       PAGE LENGTH 23

8➤   FORMAT
9➤     PAGE HEADER
         SKIP 3 LINES
         PRINT COLUMN 30, "MANUFACTURER LISTING"
10➤      PRINT COLUMN 31, TODAY USING "ddd. mmm dd, yyyy"
         PRINT COLUMN 31, "Screen Number: ", PAGENO USING "##&"
         SKIP 5 LINES

11➤      PRINT COLUMN 2, "Manufacturer",
               COLUMN 17, "Manufacturer",
               COLUMN 34, "Lead Time"
         PRINT COLUMN 6, "Code",
               COLUMN 21, "Name",
               COLUMN 36, "(in days)"
12➤      PRINT "----------------------------------------";
         PRINT "----------------------------------------"
         SKIP 1 LINE

13➤    ON EVERY ROW
         PRINT COLUMN 6, pa_manuf.manu_code,
               COLUMN 16, pa_manuf.manu_name,
               COLUMN 36, pa_manuf.lead_time

14➤    PAGE TRAILER
         SKIP 1 LINE
         PAUSE "Press RETURN to display next screen."

   END REPORT  -- manuf_rpt --
```

To locate any function definition see the Function Index on page 728.

15

Reporting Group Totals

This example demonstrates more advanced **4GL** report features. It extends the order-entry program of Example 11 (see "Implementing a Master/Detail Relationship" on page 217) to produce a printed invoice. The invoice is generated as a report.

This example program has the following simple structure:

1. Accept input for a single customer order.
2. Store the order in the database.
3. Generate an invoice report.

In a real application, the program would be designed to accept more than one customer order. Either the order-entry function would be called repeatedly, or else order entry would be one option in a menu. Since the logic for entering one order is isolated in a single function, it can be used in either of these ways.

The invoice report at the heart of this example would also be used differently in a real application. Rather than printing an invoice immediately after an order is entered, a real application might print all new orders, or a range of new orders, in a batch. The invoice logic is isolated to two functions here, so it could be adapted in this way.

Other examples that concentrate on reports include "Generating a Report" on page 317 and "Generating Mailing Labels" on page 655.

Choosing a Report Destination

A report is a series of lines of text. These lines can be directed to one of four destinations:

- The screen (the default destination)
- The default printer
- A disk file
- Another program using a "pipe" (UNIX only)

You can specify the report destination in one of two ways:

- You can code it directly into the report using the REPORT TO statement in the OUTPUT section.

  This is the least flexible method, since no way exists to override the choice at execution time. The only way to change the report destination is to alter the REPORT TO statement and recompile the module.
- You can specify a destination on the START REPORT statement.

  Since this statement is executable (not declarative like REPORT TO), the program can start the report to different destinations under different circumstances.

This example allows the user to specify the report destination. After an order has been inserted in the database, the invoice() function is called to manage the production of the invoice report. It displays a three-item menu in a popup window and prompts the user to choose a report destination.

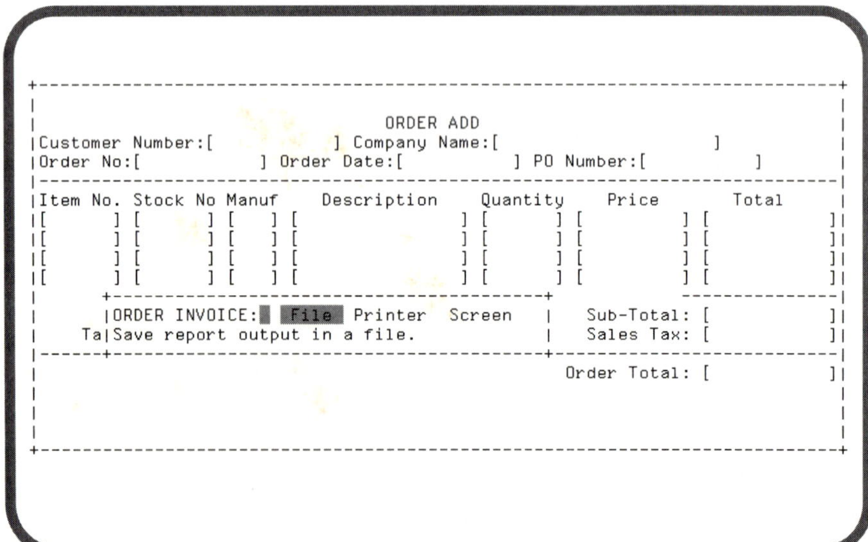

```
+-----------------------------------------------------------------------------+
|                                                                             |
|                               ORDER ADD                                     |
|Customer Number:[          ] Company Name:[                    ]             |
|Order No:[          ] Order Date:[          ] PO Number:[          ]         |
|-----------------------------------------------------------------------------|
|Item No. Stock No Manuf    Description    Quantity    Price        Total     |
|[      ] [      ] [   ] [               ] [       ] [         ] [          ]|
|[      ] [      ] [   ] [               ] [       ] [         ] [          ]|
|[      ] [      ] [   ] [               ] [       ] [         ] [          ]|
|[      ] [      ] [   ] [               ] [       ] [         ] [          ]|
|      +-----------------------------------------+  ----------------------- |
|      |ORDER INVOICE:  File  Printer  Screen   |    Sub-Total: [          ]|
|    Ta|Save report output in a file.           |    Sales Tax: [          ]|
|------+-----------------------------------------+---------------------------|
|                                                 Order Total: [          ]|
|                                                                             |
|                                                                             |
|                                                                             |
+-----------------------------------------------------------------------------+
```

Based on the user's response, the program executes one of three START REPORT statements. When file output is chosen, the program generates a file name from the order number.

The use of the MENU statement is discussed in the annotation of the report_output() function.

The Report Contents

The following is a sample of an invoice report.

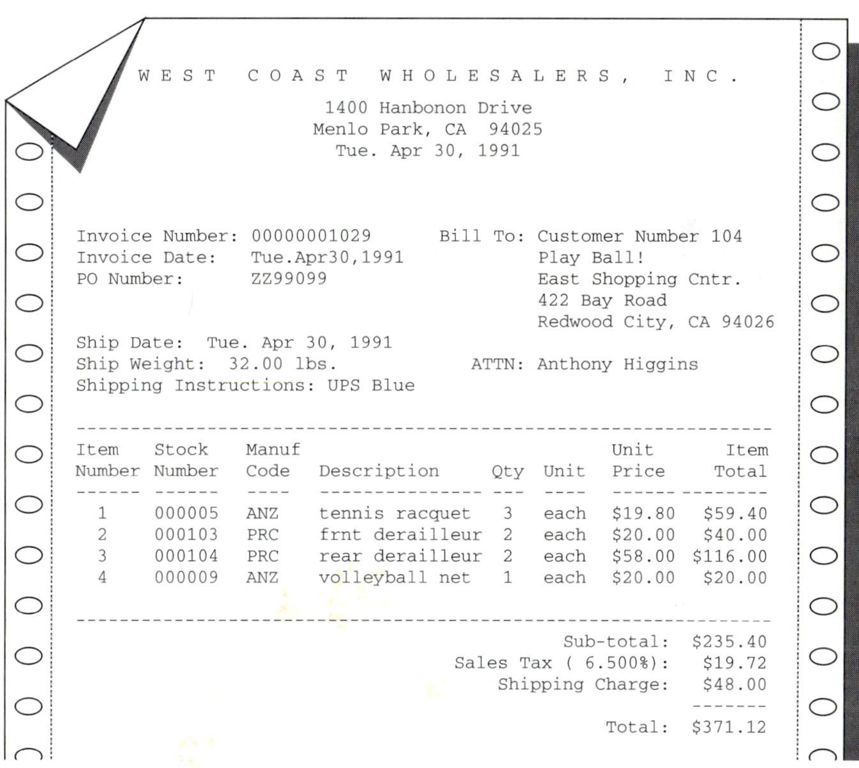

```
W E S T   C O A S T   W H O L E S A L E R S ,   I N C .
              1400 Hanbonon Drive
             Menlo Park, CA  94025
               Tue. Apr 30, 1991


Invoice Number: 00000001029      Bill To: Customer Number 104
Invoice Date:   Tue.Apr30,1991            Play Ball!
PO Number:      ZZ99099                   East Shopping Cntr.
                                          422 Bay Road
                                          Redwood City, CA 94026
Ship Date:  Tue. Apr 30, 1991
Ship Weight:  32.00 lbs.            ATTN: Anthony Higgins
Shipping Instructions: UPS Blue

----------------------------------------------------------------
Item   Stock  Manuf                                Unit     Item
Number Number Code  Description      Qty  Unit   Price    Total
------ ------ ----  ---------------  ---  ----   ------ --------
  1    000005 ANZ   tennis racquet    3   each   $19.80   $59.40
  2    000103 PRC   frnt derailleur   2   each   $20.00   $40.00
  3    000104 PRC   rear derailleur   2   each   $58.00  $116.00
  4    000009 ANZ   volleyball net    1   each   $20.00   $20.00

----------------------------------------------------------------
                                        Sub-total:  $235.40
                              Sales Tax ( 6.500%):   $19.72
                                  Shipping Charge:   $48.00
                                                    -------
                                            Total:  $371.12
```

The heading (name and address of "West Coast Wholesalers") is constant data generated in the report function. In a real application it might not be necessary, since pre-printed forms would normally be used.

The "Bill To" and "Attn" information is selected from the customer table. The invoice number, date, PO number, and shipping information are selected from the orders table. The item information is selected from the items, stock, and manufact tables.

Function Overview

Function Name	Purpose
add_order2()	Allows the user to add an order to the database. It is similar to add_order() in Example 11 except it also calls the invoice() routine to print an invoice after order is inserted.
invoice()	Manages the process of generating the invoice report: selects data from the database; starts the report; calls the report function; finishes the report.
report_output()	Displays the Report Destination menu and returns a flag indicating the user's choice.
invoice_rpt()	The report function, called once for each detail row, generates the report output.
input_cust()	Accepts user input for the customer number. *See description in Example 11.*
cust_popup()	Displays a popup window of customers. *See description in Example 11.*
input_order()	Accepts user input for date, PO number. *See description in Example 11.*
input_items()	Accepts user input for order line items. *See description in Example 11.*
renum_items()	Renumbers the item numbers when an item is added or deleted in the items array. *See description in Example 11.*
stock_popup()	Displays a popup window for stock numbers and manufacturer codes. *See description in Example 11.*
order_amount()	Calculates the total cost of the order by summing the items entered so far. *See description in Example 11.*
ship_order()	Opens a window and a form for shipping information. *See description in Example 11.*
input_ship()	Accepts user input for shipping info. This function resembles the change_cust() function from Example 6. *See description in Example 11.*
order_tx()	Performs database operations to insert the order and items in a single transaction. *See description in Example 11.*
insert_order()	Adds an order row to the database. *See description in Example 11.*
insert_items()	Adds associated items row(s) to the database. *See description in Example 11.*
tax_rates()	Supplies the appropriate tax schedule for a customer. *See description in Example 4.*
clear_lines()	Clears any number of lines starting at any line. *See description in Example 6.*

init_msgs()	Initializes the members of the ga_dsplymsg array to null. *See description in Example 2.*
msg()	Displays a brief, informative message. *See description in Example 5.*
message_window()	Opens a window and displays the contents of the ga_dsplymsg global array. *See description in Example 2.*
prompt_window()	Displays a message and prompts the user for affirmation or negation. This function is a variation on the message_window() function that appears in Example 2. *See description in Example 4.*

The DATABASE and GLOBALS Statements

1➤ This program must be used with a version of the demonstration database that supports transactions.

2➤ For a discussion of the uses of these global records and arrays, see "The DATABASE and GLOBALS Statements" on page 230.

The MAIN Function

3➤ This MAIN program section is identical to that in Example 11, except that it calls the add_order2() function. See "The MAIN Function" on page 230.

4GL source file

```
1➤ DATABASE stores2t

   GLOBALS
2➤   DEFINE     gr_customer RECORD LIKE customer.*,

                gr_orders RECORD
                      order_num      LIKE orders.order_num,
                      order_date     LIKE orders.order_date,
                      po_num         LIKE orders.po_num,
                      order_amount   MONEY(8,2),
                      order_total    MONEY(10,2)
                END RECORD,

                ga_items ARRAY[10] OF RECORD
                      item_num       LIKE items.item_num,
                      stock_num      LIKE items.stock_num,
                      manu_code      LIKE items.manu_code,
                      description    LIKE stock.description,
                      quantity       LIKE items.quantity,
                      unit_price     LIKE stock.unit_price,
                      total_price    LIKE items.total_price
                END RECORD,

                gr_charges RECORD
                      tax_rate       DECIMAL(5,3),
                      ship_charge    LIKE orders.ship_charge,
                      sales_tax      MONEY(9),
                      order_total    MONEY(11)
                END RECORD,

                gr_ship RECORD
                      ship_date      LIKE orders.ship_date,
                      ship_instruct  LIKE orders.ship_instruct,
                      ship_weight    LIKE orders.ship_weight,
                      ship_charge    LIKE orders.ship_charge
                END RECORD


    DEFINE      ga_dsplymsg ARRAY[5] OF CHAR(48)

   END GLOBALS

   ########################################
3➤ MAIN
   ########################################
     OPTIONS
       HELP FILE "hlpmsgs",
       FORM LINE 2,
       COMMENT LINE 1,
       MESSAGE LINE LAST
```

The add_order2() Function

4➤ The add_order2() function is the same as the version in Example 11 (see the "The add_order() Function" on page 232) with one addition. When an order has been completely entered and inserted in the database, add_order2() calls the invoice() function to generate the invoice.

```
 DEFER INTERRUPT

  OPEN WINDOW w_main AT 2,3
   WITH 18 ROWS, 76 COLUMNS
   ATTRIBUTE (BORDER)

  OPEN FORM f_orders FROM “f_orders"
  DISPLAY FORM f_orders
  CALL add_order2()
  CLEAR SCREEN

END MAIN

########################################
4➤ FUNCTION add_order2()
########################################

  INITIALIZE gr_orders.* TO NULL

  DISPLAY "ORDER ADD" AT 2, 34
  CALL clear_lines(2, 16)
  DISPLAY " Press Cancel to exit without saving."
    AT 17, 1 ATTRIBUTE (REVERSE, YELLOW)

  IF input_cust() THEN
    IF input_order() THEN
      IF input_items() THEN
        CALL dsply_taxes()
        IF prompt_window("Do you want to ship this order now?", 8, 12) THEN
          CALL ship_order()
        ELSE
          LET gr_ship.ship_date = NULL
        END IF

        CALL clear_lines(2, 16)

        LET ga_dsplymsg[1] = "Order entry complete."
        IF prompt_window("Are you ready to save this order?", 8, 12) THEN
          IF order_tx() THEN
            CALL clear_lines(2, 16)

            LET ga_dsplymsg[1] = "Order Number: ",
                          gr_orders.order_num USING "<<<<<<<<<<<"
            LET ga_dsplymsg[2] = " has been placed for Customer: ",
                          gr_customer.customer_num USING "<<<<<<<<<<<"
            LET ga_dsplymsg[3] = "Order Date: ", gr_orders.order_date
            CALL message_window(9, 13)

            CLEAR FORM
            CALL invoice()
          END IF
```

The invoice() Function

5➤ The invoice() function manages the production of the invoice for an order.

The function is almost completely independent of the other functions in this program. It depends on a small number of values prepared by add_orders() and its subroutines: gr_customer.customer_num (for the customer key) and gr_orders.order_num (for the order number). It reads all other data out of the database. (It also depends on gr_charges.sales_tax, but this dependency only exists because there is no column for sales tax in the orders table in the demonstration database.)

When few dependencies exist between functions, they can easily be moved to other programs.

6➤ All information about one line of one order is collected in the pr_invoice record. The fields of the record must agree one-for-one with the columns that are listed in a SELECT that follows (see Note 13). The record is also passed as an argument to the invoice_rpt() report function, which must define it identically.

7➤ The report_output() function queries the user for a report destination and returns a flag indicating the choice.

8➤ An "F" indicates that the user specified file output. A file name is constructed from the order number, and the report is started to that destination. No pathname is used, so the file will be in the current working directory.

You could redesign this portion of the program to specify a different directory.

9➤ A "P" indicates that the user specified printer output. In this and the previous case, nothing will be visible on the screen while the report is being written, so a message is displayed.

10➤ An "S" indicates that the user specified screen output. A message is displayed because the report may take a few moments to appear on the screen.

```
        ELSE
          CLEAR FORM
          CALL msg("Order has been terminated.")
        END IF
      END IF
    END IF
  END IF

END FUNCTION  -- add_order2 --

########################################
5➤ FUNCTION invoice()
########################################
6➤  DEFINE     pr_invoice  RECORD
                             order_num      LIKE orders.order_num,
                             order_date     LIKE orders.order_date,
                             ship_instruct  LIKE orders.ship_instruct,
                             po_num         LIKE orders.po_num,
                             ship_date      LIKE orders.ship_date,
                             ship_weight    LIKE orders.ship_weight,
                             ship_charge    LIKE orders.ship_charge,
                             item_num       LIKE items.item_num,
                             stock_num      LIKE items.stock_num,
                             description    LIKE stock.description,
                             manu_code      LIKE items.manu_code,
                             manu_name      LIKE manufact.manu_name,
                             quantity       LIKE items.quantity,
                             total_price    LIKE items.total_price,
                             unit           LIKE stock.unit,
                             unit_price     LIKE stock.unit_price
              END RECORD,

              file_name      CHAR(20),
              inv_msg        CHAR(40),
              print_option   CHAR(1),
              scr_flag       SMALLINT

7➤  LET print_option = report_output("ORDER INVOICE", 13, 10)

    CASE (print_option)
8➤    WHEN "F"
        LET file_name = "inv", gr_orders.order_num USING "<<<<&",".out"
        START REPORT invoice_rpt TO file_name
        MESSAGE "Writing invoice to ", file_name CLIPPED," -- please wait."
9➤    WHEN "P"
        START REPORT invoice_rpt TO PRINTER
        MESSAGE "Sending invoice to printer -- please wait."
10➤   WHEN "S"
        START REPORT invoice_rpt
        MESSAGE "Preparing invoice for screen -- please wait."
    END CASE
```

11➤ Since this SELECT retrieves a single customer row, no cursor is needed.

12➤ The scr_flag variable is passed as an argument to the report function. (For its use, see Note 29.)

13➤ This cursor produces the rows that will be passed to the report function. Each row represents one line item of the order. Each row contains the data unique to that line item (stock number, quantity, and so on) as well as data common to the entire order (order number, date, and so on).

The SELECT joins four tables: orders, items, stock (for unit of measure and description) and manufact (for manufacturer name). The order number in gr_orders.order_num determines which order is retrieved. The stock number and manu_code in each item select appropriate rows from stock and manufact.

The ORDER BY 8 clause causes the rows to be returned in ascending order based on the value in the eighth selected column, the item number. Since the item number corresponds to the order in which the items were inserted into the database, they would probably be retrieved in that sequence even without the ORDER BY clause, but it would be unwise to depend on it. The database engine is not required to return rows in their physical sequence, and in fact in a multi-table join like this one, it might produce them in an order other than the insertion order.

14➤ After fetching the row, all the information for one item of the order is available. It is passed to the report function for output.

15➤ 4GL "finishes" a report by writing any final output, including output generated by an AFTER GROUP OF block, and closing the output file.

16➤ A confirmation message is prepared and displayed before the function ends.

The report_output() Function

17➤ The report_output() function prompts the user for a choice of report destinations and returns the "S", "F", or "P" for screen, file or printer respectively. The choices are presented using a MENU statement in a pop-up window that is just large enough to contain the menu title, options, and option descriptions. (This is a good general technique for prompting the user to make a choice. For another method, see the answer() function used in Example 20 and 27.)

```
11➤  SELECT *
     INTO gr_customer.*
     FROM customer
     WHERE customer_num = gr_customer.customer_num

     LET gr_charges.ship_charge = gr_ship.ship_charge
12➤  IF print_option = "S" THEN
       LET scr_flag = TRUE
     ELSE
       LET scr_flag = FALSE
     END IF

13➤  DECLARE c_invoice CURSOR FOR
       SELECT o.order_num, o.order_date, o.ship_instruct, o.po_num,
              o.ship_date, o.ship_weight, o.ship_charge, i.item_num,
              i.stock_num, s.description, i.manu_code, m.manu_name,
              i.quantity, i.total_price, s.unit, s.unit_price
       FROM orders o, items i, stock s, manufact m
       WHERE ( (o.order_num = gr_orders.order_num) AND
               (i.order_num = o.order_num) AND
               (i.stock_num = s.stock_num AND i.manu_code = s.manu_code) AND
               (i.manu_code = m.manu_code) )
       ORDER BY 8

     FOREACH c_invoice INTO pr_invoice.*
14➤    OUTPUT TO REPORT
         invoice_rpt (gr_customer.*, pr_invoice.*, gr_charges.*, scr_flag)
     END FOREACH

15➤  FINISH REPORT invoice_rpt

16➤  CASE (print_option)
       WHEN "F"
         LET inv_msg = "Invoice written to file ", file_name CLIPPED
       WHEN "P"
         LET inv_msg = "Invoice sent to the printer."
       WHEN "S"
         LET inv_msg = "Invoice sent to the screen."
     END CASE
     CALL msg(inv_msg)

   END FUNCTION  -- invoice --

   ########################################
17➤ FUNCTION report_output(menu_title, x,y)
   ########################################
     DEFINE    menu_title   CHAR(15),
               x            SMALLINT,
               y            SMALLINT,

               rpt_out      CHAR(1)
```

18➤ The coordinates of the upper left corner of the window are passed as arguments to the function.

19➤ The menu title is also passed as an argument to the function. This approach gives the calling function control over the title of the menu (but not the choices in it).

20➤ Because choices are displayed in a menu, you can include an explanation (option description) along with the choice.

21➤ If the user chooses Screen output, the function requests confirmation.

Two LET statements calculate the location of the prompt window relative to the screen coordinates of the menu window. If the user has second thoughts, the menu continues with the File option highlighted. If the user is sure of the choice of Screen, the menu ends.

The invoice_rpt() Report Function

22➤ A report function is similar to other **4GL** functions, except that it contains sections such as OUTPUT and AFTER GROUP. A report function is never called directly using the CALL statement. Its sections are invoked automatically when **4GL** executes the OUTPUT TO REPORT statement.

This function receives three records and a character flag as function arguments.

With a normal function you often have to make a design choice: should you pass all data to the function as arguments, or should you put the data in global variables for the function to access. With a report function, the use of global variables is not always an option. When the BEFORE GROUP and AFTER GROUP clauses are used, as they are in this report, all data must pass into the report as arguments. Otherwise the grouping logic will not work correctly.

```
18➤   OPEN WINDOW w_rpt AT x, y
        WITH 2 ROWS, 41 COLUMNS
        ATTRIBUTE (BORDER)

19➤   MENU menu_title
        COMMAND "File" "Save report output in a file.          "
          LET rpt_out = "F"
          EXIT MENU

20➤     COMMAND "Printer" "Send report output to the printer.     "
          LET rpt_out = "P"
          EXIT MENU

21➤     COMMAND "Screen" "Send report output to the screen.      "
          LET ga_dsplymsg[1] = "Output is not saved after it is sent to "
          LET ga_dsplymsg[2] = "            the screen."
          LET x = x - 1
          LET y = y + 2
          IF prompt_window("Are you sure you want to use the screen?", x, y)
          THEN
            LET rpt_out = "S"
            EXIT MENU
          ELSE
            NEXT OPTION "File"
          END IF
      END MENU
      CLOSE WINDOW w_rpt
      RETURN rpt_out

    END FUNCTION  -- report_output --

    ###############################################################
22➤ REPORT invoice_rpt(pr_cust, pr_invoice, pr_charges, scr_flag)
    ###############################################################
      DEFINE    pr_cust    RECORD LIKE customer.*,
                pr_invoice RECORD
                             order_num        LIKE orders.order_num,
                             order_date       LIKE orders.order_date,
                             ship_instruct    LIKE orders.ship_instruct,
                             po_num           LIKE orders.po_num,
                             ship_date        LIKE orders.ship_date,
                             ship_weight      LIKE orders.ship_weight,
                             ship_charge      LIKE orders.ship_charge,
                             item_num         LIKE items.item_num,
                             stock_num        LIKE items.stock_num,
                             description      LIKE stock.description,
                             manu_code        LIKE items.manu_code,
                             manu_name        LIKE manufact.manu_name,
                             quantity         LIKE items.quantity,
                             total_price      LIKE items.total_price,
                             unit             LIKE stock.unit,
                             unit_price       LIKE stock.unit_price
                         END RECORD,
```

23➤ The OUTPUT section of a report function is static and declarative; these choices cannot be changed at execution time.

24➤ The FORMAT section of a report specifies actions to be performed at certain times during the report. These actions are in blocks of code headed by such clauses as ON EVERY ROW, BEFORE GROUP OF, and the like.

25➤ The BEFORE GROUP OF clause is invoked each time the value of the order number group changes from one row to the next. In this program only one order is printed, so this code will be called just once, on the first row of output. However, if the report function were moved to another program, it could be used for a series of orders, and this code would be executed each time the order number changed (that is, at the beginning of each order).

To help you follow the actions of the code, the lines of a sample report heading produced by this code follow:

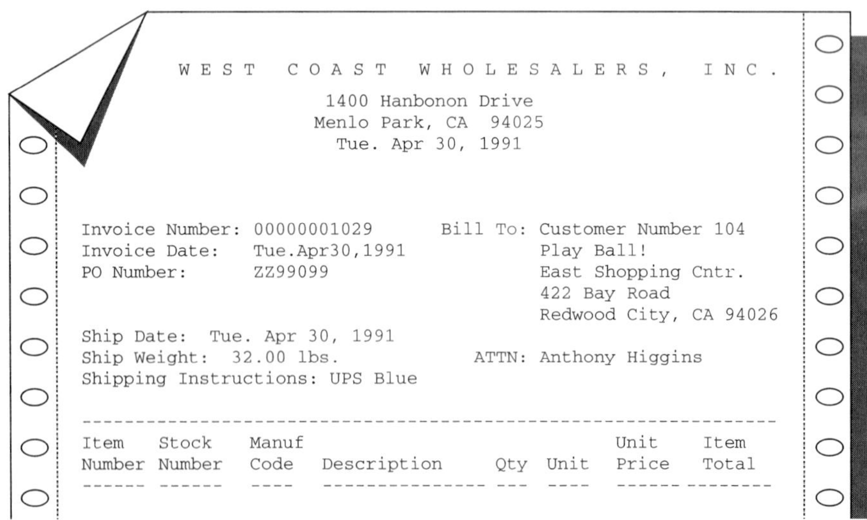

```
               W E S T   C O A S T   W H O L E S A L E R S ,   I N C .
                          1400 Hanbonon Drive
                         Menlo Park, CA  94025
                           Tue. Apr 30, 1991


Invoice Number: 00000001029      Bill To: Customer Number 104
Invoice Date:   Tue.Apr30,1991            Play Ball!
PO Number:      ZZ99099                   East Shopping Cntr.
                                          422 Bay Road
                                          Redwood City, CA 94026
Ship Date:  Tue. Apr 30, 1991
Ship Weight:  32.00 lbs.            ATTN: Anthony Higgins
Shipping Instructions: UPS Blue

------------------------------------------------------------------
Item   Stock  Manuf                                 Unit   Item
Number Number Code   Description     Qty  Unit  Price  Total
------ ------ ----   --------------- ---  ----  ------ --------
```

```
      pr_charges RECORD
                    tax_rate          DECIMAL(5,3),
                    ship_charge       LIKE orders.ship_charge,
                    sales_tax         MONEY(9),
                    order_total       MONEY(11)
                  END RECORD,
     scr_flag         SMALLINT,
     name_str         CHAR(37),
     sub_total        MONEY(10,2)

23➤ OUTPUT
      LEFT MARGIN 0
      RIGHT MARGIN 0
      TOP MARGIN 1
      BOTTOM MARGIN 1
      PAGE LENGTH 48

24➤ FORMAT
25➤   BEFORE GROUP OF pr_invoice.order_num
        LET sub_total = 0.00
        SKIP TO TOP OF PAGE
        SKIP 1 LINE
        PRINT 10 SPACES,
          "   W E S T   C O A S T   W H O L E S A L E R S ,   I N C ."
        PRINT 30 SPACES, " 1400 Hanbonon Drive"
        PRINT 30 SPACES, "Menlo Park, CA  94025"
        PRINT 32 SPACES, TODAY USING "ddd. mmm dd, yyyy"
        SKIP 4 LINES

        PRINT COLUMN 2, "Invoice Number: ",
          pr_invoice.order_num USING "&&&&&&&&&&&",
          COLUMN 46, "Bill To: Customer Number ", pr_cust.customer_num
          USING "<<<<<<<<<<&"
        PRINT COLUMN 2, "Invoice Date:",
          COLUMN 18, pr_invoice.order_date USING "ddd. mmm dd, yyyy",
          COLUMN 55, pr_cust.company
        PRINT COLUMN 2, "PO Number:",
          COLUMN 18, pr_invoice.po_num,
          COLUMN 55, pr_cust.address1
        IF (pr_cust.address2 IS NOT NULL) THEN
          PRINT COLUMN 55, pr_cust.address2
        ELSE
          PRINT COLUMN 55, pr_cust.city CLIPPED, ", ",
            pr_cust.state CLIPPED, "    ", pr_cust.zipcode CLIPPED
        END IF
        IF (pr_cust.address2 IS NOT NULL) THEN
          PRINT COLUMN 55, pr_cust.city CLIPPED, ", ",
            pr_cust.state CLIPPED, "    ", pr_cust.zipcode CLIPPED
        ELSE
          PRINT COLUMN 55, "       "
        END IF
```

```
IF (pr_cust.lname IS NOT NULL) THEN
  LET name_str = "ATTN: ", pr_cust.fname CLIPPED, " ",
      pr_cust.lname CLIPPED
ELSE
  LET name_str = "      "
END IF

PRINT COLUMN 2, "Ship Date:";
IF (pr_invoice.ship_date IS NULL) THEN
  PRINT COLUMN 15, "Not Shipped";
ELSE
  PRINT COLUMN 15, pr_invoice.ship_date USING "ddd. mmm dd, yyyy";
END IF
IF (pr_cust.address2 IS NOT NULL) THEN
  PRINT COLUMN 55, "      "
ELSE
  PRINT COLUMN 49, name_str CLIPPED
END IF

PRINT COLUMN 2, "Ship Weight: ";
IF (pr_invoice.ship_weight IS NULL) THEN
  PRINT "N/A";
ELSE
  PRINT pr_invoice.ship_weight USING "<<<<<<<&.&&", " lbs.";
END IF
IF (pr_cust.address2 IS NOT NULL) THEN
  PRINT COLUMN 49, name_str CLIPPED
ELSE
  PRINT COLUMN 55, "      "
END IF
PRINT COLUMN 2, "Shipping Instructions:";
IF (pr_invoice.ship_instruct IS NULL) THEN
  PRINT COLUMN 25, "None"
ELSE
  PRINT COLUMN 25, pr_invoice.ship_instruct
END IF
SKIP 1 LINE

PRINT "----------------------------------------";
PRINT "---------------------------------------"
PRINT COLUMN 2, "Item",
  COLUMN 10, "Stock",
  COLUMN 18, "Manuf",
  COLUMN 56, "Unit"
PRINT COLUMN 2, "Number",
  COLUMN 10, "Number",
  COLUMN 18, "Code",
  COLUMN 24, "Description",
  COLUMN 41, "Qty",
  COLUMN 49, "Unit",
  COLUMN 56, "Price",
  COLUMN 68, "Item Total"
PRINT " ------  ------  ----- --------------  ------  ----   --------";
```

26➤ This comment appears in the program as a convenient reference while coding the PRINT statement that appears in the following ON EVERY ROW block.

27➤ The ON EVERY ROW block is invoked as a result of any OUTPUT TO REPORT statement.

28➤ The AFTER GROUP OF block is invoked following the last row of each order group. It is entered prior to the BEFORE GROUP block if more than one order is printed.

In this program it only is entered as a result of the FINISH REPORT statement, since the report consists of a single order. A sample of its output follows.

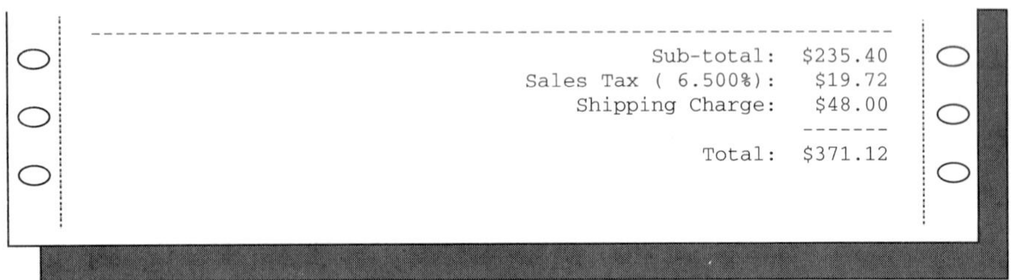

29➤ The scr_flag variable contains the user's choice of report destination. It is passed on every call, but is only tested in the AFTER GROUP OF block. If output is to the screen, the program pauses before the end of the report, at which time the screen is cleared.

```
        PRINT "     ----------"

26➤ {
     Item     Stock    Manuf                                          Unit
     Number   Number   Code   Description       Qty      Unit     Price          Item Total
     ------   ------   -----  ---------------   ------   ----     --------       -----------
     XXXXXX   XXXXXX   XXX    XXXXXXXXXXXXXXX   XXXXXX   XXXX     $X,XXX.XX      $XXX,XXX.XX
    }

27➤   ON EVERY ROW
        PRINT COLUMN 2, pr_invoice.item_num USING "#####&",
          COLUMN 10, pr_invoice.stock_num USING "&&&&&&",
          COLUMN 18, pr_invoice.manu_code,
          COLUMN 24, pr_invoice.description,
          COLUMN 41, pr_invoice.quantity USING "#####&",
          COLUMN 49, pr_invoice.unit,
          COLUMN 56, pr_invoice.unit_price USING "$,$$&.&&",
          COLUMN 68, pr_invoice.total_price USING "$$$,$$&.&&"

        LET sub_total = sub_total + pr_invoice.total_price

28➤   AFTER GROUP OF pr_invoice.order_num
        SKIP 1 LINE

        PRINT "----------------------------------------";
        PRINT "---------------------------------------"

        PRINT COLUMN 53, "Sub-total: ",
          COLUMN 65, sub_total USING "$$,$$$,$$&.&&"

        PRINT COLUMN 43, "Sales Tax (",
            pr_charges.tax_rate USING "#&.&&&", "%): ",
          COLUMN 66, pr_charges.sales_tax USING "$,$$$,$$&.&&"

        IF (pr_invoice.ship_charge IS NULL) THEN
          LET pr_invoice.ship_charge = 0.00
        END IF
        PRINT COLUMN 47, "Shipping Charge: ",
          COLUMN 70, pr_invoice.ship_charge USING "$,$$&.&&"

        PRINT COLUMN 64, "--------------"
        PRINT COLUMN 57, "Total: ",
            pr_charges.order_total USING "$$$,$$$,$$&.&&"

29➤     IF scr_flag THEN
          PAUSE "Press RETURN to continue."
        END IF

    END REPORT  {invoice_rpt}
```

To locate any function definition see the Function Index on page 728.

16

Creating Vertical Menus

This example demonstrates two ways to create vertical menus using **4GL**. A vertical menu is one in which the menu options are presented vertically (one under the other) on the screen. For example, the form file used in Example 16a displays the following vertical menu:

```
+--------------------------------------------------------------------------+
|                         4GL Test MAIN MENU 1                             |
|                                                                          |
|                  1) Customer Maintenance                                 |
|                                                                          |
|                  2) Order Maintenance                                    |
|                                                                          |
|                  3) Stock Maintenance                                    |
|                                                                          |
|                  4) Manufacturer Maintenance                             |
|                                                                          |
|                  5) Customer Calls Maintenance                           |
|                                                                          |
|                  6) State Maintenance                                    |
|                                                                          |
|                  7) Exit MAIN MENU                                       |
|                                                                          |
| Menu Selection:                                                          |
| Enter a menu option number and press Accept or RETURN.                   |
| Choose option 7 to exit the menu. Press CTRL-W for Help.                 |
+--------------------------------------------------------------------------+
```

You can automatically create a horizontal ring menu with the **4GL** MENU statement. Example 3 demonstrates the MENU statement.

This example consists of two parts:

- Example 16a contains a vertical menu implemented with a form file and a simple INPUT statement.
- Example 16b contains a generic vertical menu implemented with an INPUT ARRAY statement.

Both programs accept the option number entered by the user and, using a CASE statement, execute the appropriate function.

A Hardcoded Vertical Menu - Example 16a

Example 16a implements a vertical menu whose menu options are hardcoded in the f_menu form specification file. That is, each menu option is entered as text on the form file.

The form has a single input field for the menu option number. To select a menu option, the user enters the number of the option to execute in this field. The example performs input validation on this option number to ensure that it is a valid menu option.

The advantage of this method is that it is very straightforward to code: it is just a simple INPUT statement on a single numeric field.

The following functions appear in the Example 16a program:

Function Name	Purpose
main_menu()	Displays the f_menu form that contains the vertical menu.
cust_maint()	Displays a message indicating that the routine called was under the Customer Maintenance menu option.
stock_maint()	Displays a message indicating that the routine called was under the Stock Maintenance menu option.
order_maint()	Displays a message indicating that the routine called was under the Order Maintenance menu option.
manuf_maint()	Displays a message indicating that the routine called was under the Manufacturer Maintenance menu option.
ccall_maint()	Displays a message indicating that the routine called was under the Customer Call Maintenance menu option.
state_maint()	Displays a message indicating that the routine called was under the State Maintenance menu option.
init_msgs()	Initializes the members of the ga_dsplymsg array to null. *See description in Example 2.*
message_window()	Opens a window and displays the contents of the ga_dsplymsg global array. *See description in Example 2.*

A Generic Vertical Menu - Example 16b

Example 16b uses the f_menu2 form specification file to implement a generic vertical menu. This menu is generic because the same form file can be used to display any vertical menu in an application.

The form file defines a screen array with fields for the option number and option name. The example fills a corresponding program array with the desired option names and displays them in this screen array using INPUT ARRAY WITHOUT DEFAULTS. To select a menu option, the user moves the cursor to the desired option and presses the Accept key.

Because the menu options are not hardcoded on the f_menu2 form, the form can be used to implement all menus in the application. The developer would just need to write the necessary initialization routine for each vertical menu.

While coding for this menu is more complex than Example 16a, this version provides the following additional features:

- Since the example uses a screen array, the user can scroll through the menu options. This feature allows the menu to contain more options than can be displayed at one time on the screen.
- Each menu option is highlighted when the cursor is on it.

This example uses an INPUT ARRAY WITHOUT DEFAULTS to simulate the behavior of a DISPLAY ARRAY and to highlight the current line. To simulate DISPLAY ARRAY, the INPUT ARRAY has the following features "turned off":

- Inserting and deleting lines of the array
- Scrolling past the end of the items in the array
- Moving to each field in one line of the screen array
- Modifying field input

The following functions appear in the Example 16b program:

Function Name	Purpose
dsply_menu()	Displays the f_menu2 form that contains the generic vertical menu form.
init_menu()	Initializes the global menu structure with the names of the menu options to be displayed.
init_opnum()	Initializes the global menu structure with the option numbers of the menu options to be displayed.
choose_option()	Implements the INPUT ARRAY statement that simulates the DISPLAY ARRAY and the vertical menu selection.

cust_maint()	Displays a message indicating that the routine called was under the Customer Maintenance menu option. *See description in Example 16a.*
stock_maint()	Displays a message indicating that the routine called was under the Stock Maintenance menu option. *See description in Example 16a.*
order_maint()	Displays a message indicating that the routine called was under the Order Maintenance menu option. *See description in Example 16a.*
manuf_maint()	Displays a message indicating that the routine called was under the Manufacturer Maintenance menu option. *See description in Example 16a.*
ccall_maint()	Displays a message indicating that the routine called was under the Customer Call Maintenance menu option. *See description in Example 16a.*
state_maint()	Displays a message indicating that the routine called was under the State Maintenance menu option. *See description in Example 16a.*
init_msgs()	Initializes the members of the ga_dsplymsg array to null. *See description in Example 2.*
message_window()	Opens a window and displays the contents of the ga_dsplymsg global array. *See description in Example 2.*

Example 16a: The f_menu Form

1➤ The f_menu form is not designed to work with a particular database. The single form field is defined as formonly, as is the database in the DATABASE statement.

2➤ The items on the vertical menu are text strings that appear in the form specification. This compares with the use of a screen record in the f_menu2 form in Example 16b.

3➤ The f1 field accepts the menu choice.

Example 16a: The f_menu Form

f_menu form file

```
1➤ DATABASE formonly

2➤ SCREEN
   {
                         4GL Test MAIN MENU 1

                  1) Customer Maintenance

                  2) Order Maintenance

                  3) Stock Maintenance

                  4) Manufacturer Maintenance

                  5) Customer Calls Maintenance

                  6) State Maintenance

                  7) Exit MAIN MENU

    Menu Selection: [f1]
   }
   ATTRIBUTES
3➤ f1 = formonly.option_num;

   INSTRUCTIONS
     DELIMITERS "  "
```

The DATABASE and GLOBALS Statements

1➤ Any version of the stores2 database can be used here.

2➤ The ga_dsplymsg array is used as input to the message_window() function as described in Example 2.

The MAIN Function

3➤ The OPTIONS statement establishes the hlpmsgs file as the help file for the program. It also establishes screen lines for the menu: FORM LINE sets the first line of the form to line 1 of the window and COMMENT LINE sets the comment line to be the blank line after the menu title. This COMMENT LINE setting prevents form text from being erased when the Comment Line is cleared after the cursor leaves the input field.

4➤ The DEFER INTERRUPT statement prevents use of the Interrupt key from terminating the program. Instead, it sets the global variable int_flag (as discussed in Example 5). int_flag is tested following the INPUT in the main_menu() function to see if the user has chosen to exit the menu.

5➤ The main_menu() function displays the vertical menu and accepts user input.

The main_menu() Function

6➤ The LET statement set the Boolean flag dsply to TRUE. This flag is used to determine whether to reprompt the user for a menu option. The program redisplays the menu selection prompt in the following cases:

- If the user enters an invalid menu option number.
- If the user enters no option number.
- After the completion of a menu task.

7➤ The OPEN WINDOW statement opens a window and displays the vertical menu contained in the f_menu for specification file. Usage instructions are then displayed.

4GL source file

```
1➤ DATABASE stores2t

   GLOBALS
2➤   DEFINE    ga_dsplymsg ARRAY[5] OF CHAR(48)
   END GLOBALS

   ########################################
   MAIN
   ########################################

3➤   OPTIONS
       HELP FILE "hlpmsgs",
       FORM LINE FIRST,
       COMMENT LINE 2

4➤     DEFER INTERRUPT

5➤     CALL main_menu()

   END MAIN

   ########################################
   FUNCTION main_menu()
   ########################################
     DEFINE        dsply             SMALLINT,
                   option_num        SMALLINT

6➤   LET dsply = TRUE

7➤   OPEN WINDOW w_menu AT 2, 3
       WITH 19 ROWS, 70 COLUMNS
       ATTRIBUTE (BORDER, MESSAGE LINE LAST)

     OPEN FORM f_menu FROM "f_menu"
     DISPLAY FORM f_menu

     DISPLAY
     " Enter a menu option number and press Accept or RETURN."
       AT 18, 1 ATTRIBUTE (REVERSE, YELLOW)
     DISPLAY
     " Choose option 7 to exit the menu. Press CTRL-W for Help."
       AT 19, 1 ATTRIBUTE (REVERSE, YELLOW)
```

8➤ The WHILE loop controls user input of the menu option number. Because dsply is initially set to TRUE, execution initially enters this loop to allow the user to enter a menu choice. If the user either presses Interrupt or chooses the "Exit" option, dsply is set to FALSE and this loop exits.

9➤ The int_flag flag is set to FALSE before the INPUT begins. The INPUT statement accepts the user input from the form's option_num field and stores it in the option_num variable.

10➤ If the user exits the INPUT statement by pressing Interrupt, the program automatically sets int_flag to TRUE. The LET statement then sets dsply to FALSE. This exits the WHILE loop and leaves the menu. Otherwise, the option number entered by the user determines which function is called in a CASE statement.

11➤ When the user selects option 1, "Customer Maintenance", the program calls the cust_main() function. The CASE statement contains a WHEN clause for each of the menu's valid menu options. Each clause invokes the function to perform the associated menu task. When the function completes execution, the program redisplays the f_menu menu and the user can select another item from the menu (since dsply remains TRUE).

12➤ When the user selects option 7, "Exit", the dsply flag is set to FALSE. This exits the WHILE loop and the function.

13➤ If the user enters a number not on the menu, an ERROR statement displays a message. Because dsply remains TRUE, the WHILE statement iterates and the user is allowed to enter another option number.

The cust_maint() Function

14➤ Two LET statements load strings containing a message into the ga_dsplymsg array. The call to the message_window() function displays the message.

This function would ordinarily contain statements to perform customer maintenance.

The Remaining maint() Functions

15➤ The stock_maint(), order_maint(), manuf_maint(), ccall_maint(), and state_maint() functions are nearly identical to the cust_maint() function described above.

The text of the functions appears in the online example code.

```
8➤    WHILE dsply

9➤      LET int_flag = FALSE
        INPUT BY NAME option_num HELP 120

10➤     IF int_flag THEN
          LET dsply = FALSE
        ELSE
          CASE option_num
            WHEN 1
11➤           CALL cust_maint()
            WHEN 2
              CALL order_maint()
            WHEN 3
              CALL stock_maint()
            WHEN 4
              CALL manuf_maint()
            WHEN 5
              CALL ccall_maint()
            WHEN 6
              CALL state_maint()
12➤         WHEN 7
              LET dsply = FALSE
13➤         OTHERWISE
              ERROR "Invalid menu choice. Please try again."
          END CASE
        END IF
      END WHILE

      CLOSE FORM f_menu
      CLOSE WINDOW w_menu

    END FUNCTION -- main_menu --

    ########################################
    FUNCTION cust_maint()
    ########################################

14➤   LET ga_dsplymsg[1] = "This function would contain the statements to"
      LET ga_dsplymsg[2] = " implement the Customer Maintenance option."
      CALL message_window(6,12)

    END FUNCTION -- cust_maint --
```

See the source file for the text of the remaining maint() functions.

15➤

Example 16b: The f_menu2 Form

1➤ The f_menu2 form is not designed to work with a particular database. All form fields are defined as formonly, as is the database in the DATABASE statement.

2➤ All information displayed on the vertical menu will be passed to the form by the calling program. This includes the title, the number of each option, and the name of each option.

This compares with the use of literal text in the f_menu form in Example 16a.

3➤ The f000 field displays the menu title.

4➤ The fields that comprise the menu options are grouped into a screen array.

f_menu2 form file

1➤
```
DATABASE formonly
```
2➤
```
SCREEN
{
                  [f000                        ]

         [x|f1 ]  [f02                                   ]

         [x|f1 ]  [f02                                   ]

         [x|f1 ]  [f02                                   ]

         [x|f1 ]  [f02                                   ]

         [x|f1 ]  [f02                                   ]
}
```
3➤
```
ATTRIBUTES
f000 = formonly.menu_title;

x    = formonly.x;
f1   = formonly.option_num, NOENTRY;
f02  = formonly.option_name, NOENTRY;

INSTRUCTIONS
  DELIMITERS "  "
```
4➤
```
  SCREEN RECORD sa_menu[5](formonly.x THRU formonly.option_name)
```

The DATABASE and GLOBALS Statements

1➤ Any version of the stores2 database can be used here.

2➤ The ga_menu array is used to contain the menu option information: the menu option name and number. This array of records is the program array used with the INPUT ARRAY statement.

3➤ The g_menutitle variable will contain the name of the menu. This variable is initialized in the init_menu() function and displayed in the dsply_menu() function.

4➤ The ga_dsplymsg array is used as input to the message_window() function as described in Example 2.

The MAIN Function

5➤ The OPTIONS statement establishes the screen lines for the menu: FORM LINE sets the first line of the form to line 1 of the window and COMMENT LINE sets the comment line to be the blank line after the menu title. This COMMENT LINE setting prevents form text from being erased when the Comment Line is cleared after the cursor leaves the input field.

6➤ The DEFER INTERRUPT statement prevents the Interrupt key from terminating the program. Instead, it sets the global variable int_flag (as discussed in Example 5). int_flag is tested following the INPUT ARRAY in the choose_option() function to see if the user wants to exit the menu.

7➤ The dsply_menu() function displays the vertical menu and accepts user input.

The dsply_menu() Function

8➤ The OPEN WINDOW statement opens a window and displays the vertical menu contained in the f_menu2 form specification file. Two DISPLAY statements display the menu usage instructions.

4GL source file

```
1➤ DATABASE stores2t

   GLOBALS
2➤   DEFINE      ga_menu  ARRAY[20] OF RECORD
                     x                CHAR(1),
                     option_num       CHAR(3),
                     option_name      CHAR(35)
                 END RECORD,

3➤               g_menutitle    CHAR(25)

4➤    DEFINE      ga_dsplymsg ARRAY[5] OF CHAR(48)
   END GLOBALS

   ########################################
   MAIN
   ########################################

5➤   OPTIONS
       HELP FILE "hlpmsgs",
       COMMENT LINE FIRST,
       MESSAGE LINE LAST,
       FORM LINE 2

6➤   DEFER INTERRUPT

7➤   CALL dsply_menu()

   END MAIN

   ########################################
   FUNCTION dsply_menu()
   ########################################
     DEFINE        dsply              SMALLINT,
                   option_no          SMALLINT,
                   total_options      SMALLINT

8➤   OPEN WINDOW w_menu2 AT 3,3
       WITH 16 ROWS, 75 COLUMNS
       ATTRIBUTE (BORDER)

     OPEN FORM f_menu FROM "f_menu2"
     DISPLAY FORM f_menu

     DISPLAY " Use F3, F4, and arrow keys to move cursor to desired option."
       AT 15, 1 ATTRIBUTE (REVERSE, YELLOW)
     DISPLAY
     " Press Accept to choose option, Cancel to exit menu. Press CTRL-W for Help."
       AT 16, 1 ATTRIBUTE (REVERSE, YELLOW)
```

9➤ The init_menu() function initializes the ga_menu program array with the names and numbers of the menu options, along with the menu title. The function returns total_options, the number of options in the menu.

10➤ The menu title is displayed to the menu_title field on the current form.

11➤ The WHILE loop controls user input of the menu option number. Because dsply is initially set to TRUE, execution initially enters this loop to allow the user to enter a menu choice. If the user either presses Interrupt or chooses the "Exit" option, dsply is set to FALSE and the loop exits.

12➤ The option_no variable is set to the value returned by the choose_option() function. The choose_option() function allows the user to enter the INPUT ARRAY statement. It expects the number of valid menu options (total_options) as an argument and returns the menu number selected by the user. A more detailed explanation of this function begins with Note 21.

13➤ When the user selects option 1, "Customer Maintenance", the program calls the cust_main() function. The CASE statement contains a WHEN clause for each of the menu's valid menu options. Each clause invokes the function to perform the associated menu task. When the function completes execution, the program redisplays the f_menu2 menu and the user can select another item from the menu (since dsply remains TRUE).

14➤ When the user selects option 7, "Exit", the dsply flag is set to FALSE. This exits the WHILE loop and the function.

15➤ If the user presses Cancel from the menu, the choose_option() function returns zero (0) and the program sets the dsply flag to FALSE. This terminates the WHILE loop.

The init_menu() Function

16➤ The LET statement assigns the menu title to the g_menutitle global variable. The title will be displayed at the top of the f_menu2 form.

17➤ The series of LET statements assigns the option names to the option_name field in the ga_menu array. Options must be assigned in the order they are to be displayed on the screen. For example, the name of Option 1 is stored in ga_menu[1].option_name. Option names are restricted in length to the size of the option_name field (35 characters).

```
9➤     CALL init_menu() RETURNING total_options

10➤    DISPLAY g_menutitle TO menu_title

       LET dsply = TRUE
11➤    WHILE dsply
12➤      LET option_no = choose_option(total_options)
         IF (option_no > 0) THEN
           CASE option_no
13➤          WHEN 1
               CALL cust_maint()
             WHEN 2
               CALL order_maint()
             WHEN 3
               CALL stock_maint()
             WHEN 4
               CALL manuf_maint()
             WHEN 5
               CALL ccall_maint()
             WHEN 6
               CALL state_maint()
14➤          WHEN 7         --* Exit option
               LET dsply = FALSE
           END CASE
         ELSE
15➤        LET dsply = FALSE
         END IF
       END WHILE

       CLOSE FORM f_menu
       CLOSE WINDOW w_menu2

     END FUNCTION -- dsply_menu --

     ########################################
     FUNCTION init_menu()
     ########################################

       DEFINE    total_options    SMALLINT

16➤    LET g_menutitle = "4GL Test MAIN MENU 2"

17➤    LET ga_menu[1].option_name = "Customer Maintenance"
       LET ga_menu[2].option_name = "Order Maintenance"
       LET ga_menu[3].option_name = "Stock Maintenance"
       LET ga_menu[4].option_name = "Manufacturer Maintenance"
       LET ga_menu[5].option_name = "Customer Calls Maintenance"
       LET ga_menu[6].option_name = "State Maintenance"
       LET ga_menu[7].option_name = "Exit MAIN MENU"
```

18➤ The call to the init_opnum() function initializes the option_num fields of the ga_menu array with the option numbers.

19➤ The init_opnum() function returns the total number of options initialized in the ga_menu array.

The init_opnum() Function

20➤ The FOR loop initializes the option_num field of the ga_menu array. The IF statement checks the number of digits in the option number to ensure that the numbers display as right-justified. Doing a straight string assignment of the number (`i`) to the field would cause numbers to be left-justified.

The choose_option() Function

21➤ To highlight the current line of the menu, the choose_option() function uses an INPUT ARRAY statement to simulate the DISPLAY ARRAY statement. Because the DISPLAY ARRAY statement does not have the Insert and Delete key functionality, this OPTIONS statement "disables" these keys in the INPUT ARRAY. The OPTIONS statement assigns to each of these keys the control sequence of CONTROL-A. Because CONTROL-A is one of the special editing features of the **4GL** input statements (INPUT, CONSTRUCT, DISPLAY, INPUT ARRAY, DISPLAY ARRAY), **4GL** interprets it as an editing command. The sequence never executes the Insert or Delete function because it is always interpreted as an editing command.

22➤ Before the DISPLAY ARRAY statement can display the program array, you must initialize the ARR_COUNT() function with the number of items to be displayed. The call to the SET_COUNT() function initializes the number of items in the ga_menu array. This number is the number of menu options.

23➤ The INPUT ARRAY statement displays the current menu options on the screen. The WITHOUT DEFAULTS clause simulates the behavior of the DISPLAY ARRAY statement.

24➤ Before the cursor moves to a new line in the array, the BEFORE ROW clause calculates the current position in the program array (curr_pa), the total number of lines in the program array (total_pa), and the current position in the screen array (curr_sa). These values are needed to determine the line to display.

```
      LET total_options = 7
18➤   CALL init_opnum(total_options)

19➤   RETURN total_options

    END FUNCTION -- init_menu --

    #######################################
    FUNCTION init_opnum(total_options)
    #######################################
      DEFINE        total_options  SMALLINT,

                    i              SMALLINT

20➤   FOR i = 1 TO total_options
        IF i < 10 THEN
          LET ga_menu[i].option_num[2] = i
        ELSE
          LET ga_menu[i].option_num[1,2] = i
        END IF
        LET ga_menu[i].option_num[3] = ")"
      END FOR

    END FUNCTION -- init_opnum --

    #######################################
    FUNCTION choose_option(total_options)
    #######################################
      DEFINE        total_options     SMALLINT,

                    curr_pa           SMALLINT,
                    curr_sa           SMALLINT,
                    total_pa          SMALLINT,
                    lastkey           SMALLINT

21➤   OPTIONS
        DELETE KEY CONTROL-A,
        INSERT KEY CONTROL-A

22➤   CALL SET_COUNT(total_options)
      LET int_flag = FALSE

23➤   INPUT ARRAY ga_menu WITHOUT DEFAULTS FROM sa_menu.* HELP 121
        BEFORE ROW
24➤       LET curr_pa = ARR_CURR()
          LET total_pa = ARR_COUNT()
          LET curr_sa = SCR_LINE()
```

25➤ The current line of the program array (ga_menu[curr_pa].*) is displayed to the current line of the screen array (sa_menu[curr_sa].*) in reverse video. This statement causes the current option in the menu to be highlighted.

26➤ The x field appears in both the program array and the screen array. It serves as a "resting point" for the cursor and as a position for the "highlight" character that displays the line in reverse video. If the user enters input in this field, these statements erase the input.

27➤ The IF statement prevents the cursor from scrolling beyond the end of the menu. This scrolling capability is another of the INPUT ARRAY features that must be disabled to adequately simulate the behavior of the DISPLAY ARRAY statement.

The FGL_LASTKEY() function returns the ASCII code of the last key the user entered. The FGL_KEYVAL() function generates the ASCII code associated with the specified character strings:

- Down arrow (down)
- Carriage return (return)
- Tab (tab)
- Right array (right)

If the user has pressed one of these keys, the cursor would normally move to the next, empty line of the array. To prevent this behavior, the code checks for these keys and, if any one of them has been pressed, it notifies the user there are no more menu options available. The NEXT FIELD statement returns the cursor to the x field of the last line.

28➤ Just before the cursor leaves the current line, the AFTER ROW clause recalculates the current positions in the program array (curr_pa) and screen array (curr_sa) and displays the current menu option in normal display (turns off the highlight).

29➤ If the user presses the Cancel key, **4GL** sets the int_flag to TRUE. In this case, the program resets int_flag to FALSE and returns a value of zero (0). A zero return value indicates to the calling function that the user wants to exit the menu.

30➤ The RETURN statement returns the current position of the cursor in the menu. This position corresponds to the option number of the menu option the user has selected (by pressing the Accept key from within the INPUT ARRAY statement).

```
25➤        DISPLAY ga_menu[curr_pa].* TO sa_menu[curr_sa].*
             ATTRIBUTE (REVERSE)

         AFTER FIELD x
26➤        IF ga_menu[curr_pa].x IS NOT NULL THEN
             LET ga_menu[curr_pa].x = NULL
             DISPLAY BY NAME ga_menu[curr_pa].x
           END IF

27➤        IF curr_pa = total_pa THEN
             LET lastkey = FGL_LASTKEY()
             IF ( (lastkey = FGL_KEYVAL("down"))
                 OR (lastkey = FGL_KEYVAL("return"))
                 OR (lastkey = FGL_KEYVAL("tab"))
                 OR (lastkey = FGL_KEYVAL("right")) )
             THEN
               ERROR "No more menu options in this direction."
               NEXT FIELD x
             END IF
           END IF

         AFTER ROW
28➤        LET curr_pa = ARR_CURR()
           LET curr_sa = SCR_LINE()
           DISPLAY ga_menu[curr_pa].* TO sa_menu[curr_sa].*

       END INPUT

29➤    IF int_flag THEN
         LET int_flag = FALSE
         RETURN (0)
       END IF

30➤    RETURN (curr_pa)

     END FUNCTION -- choose_option --
```

To locate any function definition see the Function Index on page 728.

17

Using the DATETIME Data Type

This example demonstrates how to handle DATETIME data in a **4GL** program. It uses the DATETIME data in the call_dtime and res_dtime columns of the cust_calls table. To access the cust_calls table, this example adds a "Calls" feature to the CUSTOMER MODIFICATION menu implemented in Example 9.

Redefining the DATETIME Data Entry

To enter a DATETIME value, the user must follow a very strict format. **4GL** can only accept a DATETIME value in the form:

```
yyyy-mon-ddd hh:mm:ss.fff
```

where "yyyy" is the year, "mon" is the month, "ddd" is the day, "hh" is the hour, "mm" is the minutes, "ss" is the seconds, and "fff" is the fraction of a second. The spaces and the "-", ":", and "." characters must be entered exactly as shown above.

The DATETIME columns in the cust_calls table are defined as YEAR TO MINUTE. Unless the **4GL** program manipulates the input values, the user must enter the time 3:24 PM 2/25/91 as:

```
1991-2-25 15:24
```

Any other format will generate a **4GL** system error notifying the user of an invalid format. Advantages of using this default DATETIME format is that **4GL** can automatically perform the following data verification for the user:

- A month: between 1 and 12
- A day:
  - Between 1 and 28: if the month is February
  - Between 1 and 30 if the month is April, June, September, or November
  - Between 1 and 31 for all other months
- An hour value: between 0 and 23 (24-hour notation)
- A minute: between 0 and 59

The disadvantage is that this form is not very user-friendly for the novice user.

To provide a friendlier data entry format, this program breaks entry of the DATETIME value into three screen fields:

- call_time is a CHAR(5) field that accepts the hours and minutes in the form:

  ```
  hh:mm
  ```

  It uses a PICTURE attribute "##:##" in the screen form file to display the ":" character between the hour and minute values and to limit entry of these values to numeric characters (0-9).
- am_pm is a CHAR(2) field that accepts an AM or PM specification so the user does not have to use 24-hour notation. It also uses a PICTURE attribute "XM" in the screen form file to display the "M" as the second character. This attribute also limits data entry of the first character to a letter (A-Z). The UPSHIFT screen attribute ensures that this first character is always an upper case letter.
- yr_mon is a DATE field that accepts the date in the form:

  ```
  mon/dd/yy OR mon/dd/yyyy
  ```

These screen fields are defined on the f_custcall form and display after the headings "Call Received at" and "Call Resolved on":

```
+------------------------------------------------------------------------------+
|CUSTOMER CALLS:  Receive  View  Exit                                          |
|Add a new customer call to the database.                                      |
|-----------------------------------------Press CTRL-W for Help----------      |
|                            CUSTOMER CALLS                                    |
|                                                                              |
|  Customer Number:          104  Company Name : Play Ball!                    |
|                                                                              |
|  Call Received at:                                                           |
|    Received By:                                                              |
|    Call Code (B/D/I/L/O):                                                    |
|    Call Description:                                                         |
|                                                                              |
|  Call Resolved on:                                                           |
|    Call Resolution:                                                          |
|                                                                              |
|                                                                              |
|                                                                              |
|                                                                              |
+------------------------------------------------------------------------------+
```

This new data entry format necessitates that the program:

- Perform the data verification for the first two screen fields (call_time and am_pm) that **4GL** would automatically have performed for the DATETIME field. **4GL** can perform data verification on the month, day, and year values because the yr_mon field is defined as DATE.
- Convert these screen fields to a DATETIME value before the time can be added to the appropriate column of cust_calls.
- Convert the DATETIME value to these screen field values before the time can be displayed on the f_custcall form.

This first task is performed within the INPUT statement of the input_call() function. The get_timeflds() function and the get_datetime() function perform the conversions from screen fields and from screen fields to DATETIME respectively.

Conserving Screen Space

The program implements an additional data entry feature on the input of the call_descr and res_descr columns of cust_calls. Both these columns are defined as CHAR(240). However, displaying both these columns would require two fields of 240 characters each. So, for each of these columns, the program displays a single-character flag to indicate whether or not a value currently exists for each of these fields:

- If the flag is "Y": the associated CHAR(240) field contains a non-null value.
- If the flag is "N": the associated CHAR(240) field is null.

Using a single character field, the f_custcall form is able to save space for other columns of cust_calls.

To access the actual value for the column, the user presses either the F2 function key or the control sequence CONTROL-E from within the flag field. These sequences initiate the edit_descr() function to display the CHAR(240) value in a special form (f_edit).

Function Overview

Function Name	**Purpose**
cust_menu2()	Displays the CUSTOMER menu and allows the user to choose whether to add a new customer or query for an existing customer. Differs from cust_menu() in Example 9 by calling browse_cust2() instead of browse_custs().
bang()	Prompts the user for a command and executes the command. *See description in Example 3.*
query_cust2()	Lets the user create a query by example. *See description in Example 6.*
browse_custs2()	Displays results of a query on screen, one at a time and calls next_action3() to allow the user to choose next action. Differs from browse_custs() in Example 9 by calling next_action3() instead of next_action2().
next_action3()	Displays a menu that allows user to choose the action to take on the current customer row: see the next row, update the current row, delete the current row, or see customer calls.
addupd_cust()	Combines insertion and update functions in a single routine to eliminate duplication of code. *See description in Example 9.*
state_popup()	Displays a lookup list of the states from the state table so the user can choose the appropriate state. *See description in Example 9.*
insert_cust()	Adds a new row to the customer table. *See description in Example 9.*
update_cust()	Updates the database row to reflect the changes. *See description in Example 6.*

delete_cust()	Deletes the current row if it doesn't have dependent rows in other tables. *See description in Example 6.*
verify_delete()	Checks for dependent rows in other tables. *See description in Example 6.*
open_calls()	Opens the window and displays the form for the customer calls (f_custcall).
call_menu()	Displays the CUSTOMER CALLS menu that allows the user to choose whether to receive a new call or update an existing call.
addupd_call()	Combines the Add and Update operations on the cust_calls table into a single routine. This enables the required field validation to be contained in a single routine.
input_call()	Accepts user input for customer call information.
browse_calls()	Displays customer call information on the screen, one at a time, then calls nxtact_call() to allow user to choose next action.
nxtact_call()	Displays CUSTOMER CALL MODIFICATION menu and allows user to choose whether to view the next call or update the currently displayed call.
get_timeflds()	Breaks a DATETIME value into three fields: time, AM/PM flag, and date.
get_datetime()	Creates a DATETIME value from three fields: time, AM/PM flag, and date.
init_time()	Initializes the time and AM/PM fields to the current system time.
edit_descr()	Displays a form (f_edit) to allow the user to edit a CHAR(240) field.
insert_call()	Adds a new cust_calls row to the database.
update_call()	Performs a database UPDATE on cust_calls.
init_msgs()	Initializes the members of the ga_dsplymsg array to null. *See description in Example 2.*
message_window()	Opens a window and displays the contents of the ga_dsplymsg global array. *See description in Example 2.*
prompt_window()	Displays a message and prompts the user for affirmation or negation. This function is a variation on the message_window() function that appears in Example 2. *See description in Example 4.*
msg()	Displays a brief, informative message. *See description in Example 5.*
clear_lines()	Clears any number of lines starting at any line. *See description in Example 6.*

The f_custcall Form

1➤ Since this form contains fields connected to database columns, it must specify which database to look up the column definition. This form will work with any version of the stores2 database.

2➤ This form uses columns from two tables: customer and cust_calls.

3➤ The f000 and f001 screen fields display the customer number and name of the current customer. The current customer is the one the user has selected from the CUSTOMER menu.

Notes 4 to 6 describe how the three screen fields implement the data entry for the call receipt time. The **4GL** program combines the data in these fields to create the DATETIME value stored in the call_dtime column of cust_calls.

4➤ The call_time field accepts the call receipt time in the form: "hh:mm" where "hh" is the hour and "mm" is the number of minutes. The PICTURE attribute simplifies user entry by specifying that this CHAR field consists of two sets of two digits separated by a semicolon. The AUTONEXT attribute automatically moves the cursor to the next screen field when this field is filled.

Because this screen field is defined as CHARACTER, **4GL** cannot perform much data validation on the hour and minute values. The "##" specification in the PICTURE attribute does limit the character entry to only digit characters (0-9) but it cannot ensure that an hour value is between 0 and 23 or that a minute value is between 0 and 59. These checks must be made by the **4GL** program.

5➤ The am_pm1 field displays either "AM" or "PM" to indicate the time of day for an hour. The PICTURE attribute simplifies user entry by specifying that the first character of this CHAR field must be a letter character (A-Z) and the second character will always be the letter "M". The AUTONEXT attribute automatically moves the cursor to the next screen field when this field is filled.

This screen field does not limit entry of the first character to either "A" or "P". The "X" specification in the PICTURE attribute limits the character entry to a letter character (A-Z) and the UPSHIFT attribute ensures that this character is always in upper case. But no attributes can ensure that this field is either "A" or "P". This check must be made by the **4GL** program.

6➤ The yr_mon1 field accepts the date that the call was received. Because this field is defined as type DATE, the **4GL** program can ensure that the user enters valid date values for the month, day, and year. The DEFAULT attribute initializes an empty field to today's date.

f_custcall form file

```
1➤ DATABASE stores2t

   SCREEN
   {

     Customer Number: [f000       ] Company Name :[f001                    ]

     Call Received at: [f002 ][f3] [f004       ]
     Received By: [f005                ]
     Call Code (B/D/I/L/O): [a]
     Call Description: [b]

     Call Resolved on: [f006 ][f7] [f008       ]
     Call Resolution: [c]

   }

2➤ TABLES
   customer
   cust_calls

   ATTRIBUTES
3➤ f000 = cust_calls.customer_num;
   f001 = customer.company;

4➤ f002 = formonly.call_time TYPE CHAR, AUTONEXT, PICTURE = "##:##";
5➤ f3 = formonly.am_pm1 TYPE CHAR, AUTONEXT, UPSHIFT, PICTURE = "XM";
6➤ f004 = formonly.yr_mon1 TYPE DATE, DEFAULT = TODAY;
```

7➤ The user_id field accepts the name of the person entering the call. This field is initialized by the **4GL** program with the name of the person currently running the program.

8➤ The call_code field accepts a single character code that identifies the reason for the customer call. The INCLUDE attribute limits valid input to only those letters which represent valid codes and the UPSHIFT attribute ensures that these codes are always in upper case. The AUTONEXT attribute automatically moves the cursor to the next screen field after this code is entered.

9➤ The call_flag field indicates whether the current customer call has a non-null value for the call description. The call description is stored in the call_descr column of cust_calls. If this column is not null, then the call_flag field displays a "Y". Otherwise, call_descr is null and the call_flag field displays a "N". The INCLUDE attribute limits field input to either a "Y" or a "N".

Notes 9 to 11 describe the three screen fields which implement the data entry for the call receipt time. The **4GL** program combines the data in these fields to create the DATETIME value stored in the call_dtime column of cust_calls.

10➤ The res_time field accepts the call resolution time. It is defined in the same way as the call_time field. See Note 4 for more information.

11➤ The am_pm2 field displays either "AM" or "PM" to indicate the time of day for an hour. This field is defined in the same way as the am_pm2 field. See Note 5 for more information.

12➤ The yr_mon2 field accepts the date that the call was received. This field is defined in the same way as the yr_mon1 field. See Note 6 for more information.

13➤ The res_flag field indicates whether the current customer call has a non-null value for the call resolution description. This field is defined in the same way as the call_flag field. See Note 9 for more information.

2➤ Setting the DELIMITERS to blanks means that the f_custcall form uses blank spaces to indicate the data entry field. This assignment has the effect of not displaying the width of the input fields.

The f_edit Form

1➤ The f000 field is made up of six lines of 40 characters for a total of 240 characters.

2➤ The TYPE attribute defines the f000 field as CHARACTER. The WORDWRAP attribute (with the COMPRESS option) specifies that data exceeding 40 characters (the size of one line) will "wrap" to the next line of the f000 field.

```
7➤  f005 = cust_calls.user_id;
8➤  a = cust_calls.call_code, INCLUDE = ("B", "D", "I", "L", "O"),
               UPSHIFT, AUTONEXT;
9➤  b = formonly.call_flag TYPE CHAR, INCLUDE = ("Y", "N"), UPSHIFT;

10➤ f006 = formonly.res_time TYPE CHAR, AUTONEXT, PICTURE = "##:##";
11➤ f7 = formonly.am_pm2 TYPE CHAR, AUTONEXT, UPSHIFT, PICTURE = "XM";
12➤ f008 = formonly.yr_mon2 TYPE DATE, DEFAULT = TODAY;

13➤ c = formonly.res_flag TYPE CHAR, INCLUDE = ("Y", "N"), UPSHIFT;

    INSTRUCTIONS
14➤   DELIMITERS " "
```

f_edit form file

```
    DATABASE formonly

    SCREEN
    {
1 ➤   Description :[f000                                       ]
                   [f000                                       ]
                   [f000                                       ]
                   [f000                                       ]
                   [f000                                       ]
                   [f000                                       ]

    }


    ATTRIBUTES
2➤    f000 = formonly.edit_str TYPE CHAR, WORDWRAP COMPRESS;
```

The DATABASE and GLOBALS Statements

1➤ Any version of the stores2 database may be used here. This example uses the customer and cust_calls tables.

2➤ The global record gr_custcalls holds the column values for a row in the cust_calls table. Throughout this example, this record will be referred to as the *table record*.

3➤ The global record gr_viewcall holds the screen field values for information about a single cust_calls row. The screen fields do not match the columns in the table because the screen:

- Breaks each DATETIME column (call_dtime and res_dtime) into three screen fields so the user does not have to use the DATETIME entry format:
  - Time (hours and minutes)
  - An AM/PM flag (for 24-hour notation)
  - A date (month, day, and year)
- Displays each description column (call_descr and res_descr) as a single-character so the entire column of CHAR(240) does not display on the f_custcall screen. A "Y" indicates that the corresponding description column has a non-null value and an "N" indicates that this column is empty (NULL). For more information, see Note 9 for the f_custcall.per file.

Throughout this example, this record will be referred to as the *screen field record*.

4➤ The gr_workcall record is a second copy of the gr_viewcall record. It serves as a work buffer for the screen information. If the user decides to cancel an update after having changed values on the screen, this working copy restores the original field values. If, after input completes, the work buffer is empty, then the user must be performing an Add. See the function addupd_call() for the implementation.

5➤ The ga_dsplymsg array is used as input to the message_window() function as described in Example 1.

4GL source file

```
1➤ DATABASE stores2t

   GLOBALS
    DEFINE        gr_customer     RECORD LIKE customer.*,    -- table record
                  gr_workcust     RECORD LIKE customer.*,    -- screen field record
2➤                gr_custcalls    RECORD LIKE cust_calls.*,
3➤                gr_viewcall     RECORD
                                    customer_num    LIKE customer.customer_num,
                                    company         LIKE customer.company,
                                    call_time       CHAR(5),
                                    am_pm1          CHAR(2),
                                    yr_mon1         DATE,
                                    user_id         LIKE cust_calls.user_id,
                                    call_code       LIKE cust_calls.call_code,
                                    call_flag       CHAR(1),
                                    res_time        CHAR(5),
                                    am_pm2          CHAR(2),
                                    yr_mon2         DATE,
                                    res_flag        CHAR(1)
                                  END RECORD,
4➤                gr_workcall     RECORD
                                    customer_num    LIKE customer.customer_num,
                                    company         LIKE customer.company,
                                    call_time       CHAR(5),
                                    am_pm1          CHAR(2),
                                    yr_mon1         DATE,
                                    user_id         LIKE cust_calls.user_id,
                                    call_code       LIKE cust_calls.call_code,
                                    call_flag       CHAR(1),
                                    res_time        CHAR(5),
                                    am_pm2          CHAR(2),
                                    yr_mon2         DATE,
                                    res_flag        CHAR(1)
                                  END RECORD

5➤   DEFINE       ga_dsplymsg ARRAY[5] OF CHAR(48)

   END GLOBALS
```

The MAIN Function

6➤ The OPTIONS statement establishes the hlpmsgs file as the help file for the program. It also establishes screen lines for the menu: FORM LINE sets the first line of the form to line 5 of the window, COMMENT LINE sets the comment line to be the blank line after the menu title and MESSAGE LINE sets the message line to the last line of the window. This setting prevents message text from overwriting the screen.

7➤ The DEFER INTERRUPT statement prevents use of the Cancel key from terminating the program. Instead, pressing Cancel sets the global variable int_flag to TRUE (as discussed in Example 5). This flag is tested after the INPUT to see if the user has pressed Cancel to exit the menu.

8➤ The customer form f_customer displays in a bordered window called w_main.

9➤ The cust_menu2() function displays the CUSTOMER menu. See Note 11 for more information about this menu.

10➤ When the program exits, you should deallocate the resources used and then clear the screen. The CLOSE FORM deallocates the memory for the f_customer form and the CLOSE WINDOW deallocates the memory for the w_main window (causing it to disappear).

The cust_menu2() Function

11➤ The CUSTOMER menu allows the user to choose the customer maintenance task to perform: add a new customer ("Add"), query for an existing customer ("Query"), or exit the menu ("Exit"). This menu is almost the same CUSTOMER menu as implemented in Example 9 by the cust_menu1() function. This version calls the browse_custs2() function (instead of browse_custs1()) to display the CUSTOMER MODIFICATION menu with the "Calls" option.

12➤ The query_cust2() function implements a query-by-example on the customer table. This function is described in Example 6.

13➤ If the user has entered search criteria, the browse_cust2() function locates the matching customer rows and displays the first matching row on the f_customer form. This function also displays the CUSTOMER MODIFICATION menu to allow the user to choose the next action to take on the customer. See Note 17 for more information about this menu.

4GL source file

```
########################################
MAIN
########################################

6➤   OPTIONS
       HELP FILE "hlpmsgs",
       FORM LINE 5,
       COMMENT LINE 5,
       MESSAGE LINE LAST

7➤   DEFER INTERRUPT

8➤   OPEN WINDOW w_main AT 2,3
       WITH 18 ROWS, 76 COLUMNS
       ATTRIBUTE (BORDER)

     OPEN FORM f_customer FROM "f_customer"
     DISPLAY FORM f_customer
9➤   CALL cust_menu2()

10➤  CLOSE FORM f_customer
     CLOSE WINDOW w_main
     CLEAR SCREEN

END MAIN

########################################
FUNCTION cust_menu2()
########################################
  DEFINE        st_custs        CHAR(150)

11➤  MENU "CUSTOMER"
```

See cust_menu1() in Example 9.

```
       COMMAND "Query" "Look up customer(s) in the database." HELP 11
12➤      CALL query_cust2() RETURNING st_custs
         IF st_custs IS NOT NULL THEN
13➤        CALL browse_custs2(st_custs)
         END IF
         CALL clear_lines(1, 4)
```

See cust_menu1() in Example 9.

```
  END MENU

END FUNCTION -- cust_menu2 --
```

The browse_custs2() Function

14➤ The browse_custs2() function is based on the browse_custs1() function of Example 9. The only difference between the two functions is that browse_custs2() calls the next_action3() function (instead of next_action2()) to display the CUSTOMER MODIFICATION menu. The next_action3() version of this menu has an additional menu option for Customer Calls.

15➤ If next_action3() returns FALSE, then the user has chosen the "Exit" option from the CUSTOMER MODIFICATION menu. The program sets the end_list flag to FALSE and exits the c_cust FOREACH loop. Because the FOREACH loop exits before the last selected row, the end_list variable is set to FALSE to prevent the "No more customer rows" message from displaying.

16➤ If next_action3() returns TRUE, then the user has chosen the "Next" option from the CUSTOMER MODIFICATION menu. The program sets the end_list flag and saves the current row values in the working buffer gr_workcust. In case this is the last row in the FOREACH loop, the end_list variable is set to TRUE so that the "No more customer rows" message displays.

The next_action3() Function

17➤ The next_action3() function is based on the next_action2() function in Example 9. The function was modified to add a "Calls" menu option to the CUSTOMER MODIFICATION menu. This option provides the user with access to calls received from the current customer. These calls are stored in the cust_calls table.

18➤ The "Calls" option calls the open_calls() function to allow the user access to the customer calls for the current customer.

```
########################################
14➤ FUNCTION browse_custs2(selstmt)
########################################
```

See browse_custs() in Example 6.

```
  FOREACH c_cust INTO gr_customer.*
    LET fnd_custs = TRUE
    DISPLAY BY NAME gr_customer.*

15➤    IF NOT next_action3() THEN

      LET end_list = FALSE
      EXIT FOREACH
16➤    ELSE

      LET end_list = TRUE
    END IF
    LET gr_workcust.* = gr_customer.*
  END FOREACH
```

See browse_custs() in Example 6.

```
 IF end_list THEN
    CALL msg("No more customer rows.")
  END IF

  CLEAR FORM

END FUNCTION -- browse_custs2 --

########################################
17➤ FUNCTION next_action3()
########################################
  DEFINE nxt_action     SMALLINT

  LET nxt_action = TRUE

  MENU "CUSTOMER MODIFICATION"
```

See next_action2() in Example 9.

```
18➤    COMMAND "Calls" "View this customer's calls." HELP 23
      IF gr_customer.customer_num IS NULL THEN
        CALL msg("No customer is current. Please use 'Query'.")
      ELSE
        CALL open_calls()
      END IF
```

See next_action2() in Example 9.

```
END FUNCTION -- next_action3 --
```

The open_calls() Function

19➤ The f_custcall displays in a bordered window called w_call.

20➤ The two DISPLAY statements display a form heading and initialize the form with the current customer's number and name.

21➤ The call_menu() function displays the CUSTOMER CALLS menu. See Note 23 for more information about this menu.

22➤ The program closes the f_custcall form and the w_call window so that the customer form (f_customer) is again visible.

The call_menu() Function

23➤ The CUSTOMER CALLS menu allows the user to perform the customer calls maintenance tasks: receive a new call ("Receive"), look at existing calls for this customer ("View"), and exit the menu ("Exit").

24➤ The "Receive" option calls the addupd_call() function to receive a new call for the current customer. Because this function can handle both an Add or an Update on the f_custcall form, the add/update flag is set to "Add" ("A"). This function is modelled after the addupd_cust() function implemented in Example 9.

25➤ The "View" option calls the browse_calls() function to view existing calls for the current customer. To identify the current customer, the function call sends the current customer number as an argument to browse_calls(). This function is modelled after the browse_custs() function in Example 9.

26➤ The bang() function implements the "bang" ("!") escape to the operating system. The "bang" escape is explained in Example 3. The "Exit" option provides the user with a way out of the menu.

```
########################################
FUNCTION open_calls()
########################################

19➤   OPEN WINDOW w_call AT 2,3
        WITH 18 ROWS, 76 COLUMNS
        ATTRIBUTE (BORDER)

      OPEN FORM f_custcall FROM "f_custcall"
      DISPLAY FORM f_custcall
20➤   DISPLAY "CUSTOMER CALLS" AT 4, 29
      DISPLAY BY NAME gr_customer.customer_num, gr_customer.company
21➤   CALL call_menu()

22➤   CLOSE FORM f_custcall
      CLOSE WINDOW w_call

END FUNCTION -- open_calls --

########################################
FUNCTION call_menu()
########################################

      DISPLAY
      "-----------------------------------------Press CTRL-W for Help----------"
        AT 3, 1
23➤   MENU "CUSTOMER CALLS"
24➤     COMMAND "Receive" "Add a new customer call to the database."
              HELP 70
          CALL addupd_call("A")

25➤     COMMAND "View" "Look at calls for this customer." HELP 71
          CALL browse_calls(gr_customer.customer_num)

26➤     COMMAND KEY ("!")
          CALL bang()

        COMMAND KEY ("E","e","X","x") "Exit" HELP 72
            "Return to the CUSTOMER MODIFICATION menu."
          EXIT MENU
      END MENU

END FUNCTION -- call_menu --
```

The addupd_call() Function

27➤ If the user is receiving a new call, then the au_flag is "A". The global customer call records are initialized to NULL and the date field in the screen field record (gr_viewcall) is initialized to today's date.

28➤ If the user is updating an existing call, then the au_flag is "U". The global work buffer record gr_workcall saves the current values on the screen. If the user terminates an update, these values are used to restore the original column values to the screen.

29➤ The input_call() function accepts the user input values for the customer call. It returns TRUE if the user has entered values and FALSE if the user has terminated the input with the Cancel key.

30➤ If input_call() returns TRUE, then the user has entered values (not pressed Cancel) on the f_custcall form. The prompt_window() function then prompts for a confirmation to save the call in the database.

31➤ If the user confirms the save, then the setting of the au_flag determines which database operation to perform. If this call is new, the insert_call() function performs an INSERT. If this call is being updated, the update_call() function performs an UPDATE.

32➤ If the user does not confirm the save, the keep_going flag is set to FALSE to indicate that the original values should be restored to the screen.

33➤ If input_call() returns FALSE, then the user pressed Cancel during the data entry on f_custcall. The keep_going flag is set to FALSE to indicate that the original values should be restored to the screen.

34➤ If keep_going is FALSE, then the data on the f_custcall form has not been saved. If the user was receiving a new call, clear the screen fields. If the user was updating a call, restore the original values to the screen fields. These values were saved in the work buffer gr_workcall before the INPUT statement began.

```
#########################################
FUNCTION addupd_call(au_flag)
#########################################
  DEFINE        au_flag         CHAR(1),

                keep_going      SMALLINT

  DISPLAY
   " Press Accept to save save call. Press CTRL-W for Help."
    AT 16, 1 ATTRIBUTE (REVERSE, YELLOW)
  DISPLAY
   " Press Cancel to exit w/out saving."
    AT 17, 1 ATTRIBUTE (REVERSE, YELLOW)

27➤ IF au_flag = "A" THEN
    INITIALIZE gr_custcalls.* TO NULL
    INITIALIZE gr_viewcall.* TO NULL
    INITIALIZE gr_workcall.* TO NULL
    LET gr_viewcall.yr_mon1 = TODAY
28➤ ELSE               --* au_flag = "U"
    LET gr_workcall.* = gr_viewcall.*
  END IF

  LET gr_viewcall.customer_num = gr_customer.customer_num
  LET keep_going = TRUE
29➤ IF input_call() THEN
    LET ga_dsplymsg[1] = "Customer call entry complete."
30➤   IF prompt_window("Are you ready to save this customer call?",
                14, 14)
    THEN
31➤     IF (au_flag = "A") THEN
        CALL insert_call()
        CLEAR call_time, am_pm1, yr_mon1, user_id, call_code,
              call_flag, res_time, am_pm2, yr_mon2, res_flag

      ELSE             --* au_flag = “U”
        CALL update_call()
      END IF
32➤   ELSE --* user doesn’t want to update
      LET keep_going = FALSE
    END IF
33➤ ELSE --* user pressed Cancel/Interrupt
    LET keep_going = FALSE
  END IF

34➤ IF NOT keep_going THEN
    IF au_flag = "A" THEN
      CLEAR call_time, am_pm1, yr_mon1, user_id, call_code,
            call_flag, res_time, am_pm2, yr_mon2, res_flag

    ELSE             --* au_flag = "U"
      LET gr_viewcall.* = gr_workcall.*
      DISPLAY BY NAME gr_viewcall.*
```

The input_call() Function

35➤ The pr_calltime record holds the call receipt time; the pr_restime record holds the call resolution time. These local records hold the screen field values for the integer representation of the time values.

36➤ The edit_fld variable contains the description of either the call or the call resolution; call_cnt contains the number of calls that exist for this customer and have been received at the same time as the current call; fld_flag indicates whether edit_fld contains the call description (fld_flag = "C") or the call resolution description (fld_flag = "R"); new_flag is the value of the call_flag or res_flag screen field after the user has edited the call description or call resolution description.

37➤ The INPUT statement lets the user enter values in the screen fields on the f_custcall form. The THRU keyword limits data entry to the fields in the gr_viewcall record starting with call_time and ending with res_flag. The customer_num and company fields in this record do not require input values because they have already been initialized with the number and name of the current customer (see Note 20).

38➤ Before the user can enter data in the call_time field, the program checks if the field is empty (NULL). If so, it uses the init_time() function to initialize the field to current system time.

Notes 39 to 44 The AFTER FIELD clause performs data validation after the cursor leaves the call_time field.

39➤ If the user has cleared the field, the program restores the default time (current system time) and returns the user to the field. This test ensures that the user enters a call receipt time.

40➤ This LET statement uses data conversion to assign the character representation of the hours in the call receipt time to the integer variable pr_calltime.hrs. An integer value makes the data validation in the next step easier.

41➤ The hour value must be between 0 and 23 to be valid. This validation is required because the time field is defined as CHAR, not DATETIME. The only validation that **4GL** performs is to verify that the input is numeric characters. This numeric validation is specified by the PICTURE attribute of the call_time field in the form file, f_custcall.per.

```
      END IF
      CALL msg("Customer call input terminated.")
    END IF

    CALL clear_lines(2,16)
  END FUNCTION -- addupd_call --

  ########################################
  FUNCTION input_call()
  ########################################
35➤ DEFINE        pr_calltime RECORD
                    hrs         SMALLINT,
                    mins        SMALLINT
                  END RECORD,

                  pr_restime  RECORD
                    hrs         SMALLINT,
                    mins        SMALLINT
                  END RECORD,

36➤               edit_fld    LIKE cust_calls.call_descr,
                  call_cnt    SMALLINT,
                  fld_flag    CHAR(1),
                  new_flag    CHAR(1)

    INITIALIZE pr_calltime.* TO NULL
    INITIALIZE pr_restime.* TO NULL

    LET int_flag = FALSE
37➤ INPUT BY NAME gr_viewcall.call_time THRU gr_viewcall.res_flag
      WITHOUT DEFAULTS

      BEFORE FIELD call_time
38➤     IF gr_viewcall.call_time IS NULL THEN
          CALL init_time() RETURNING gr_viewcall.call_time,
                                     gr_viewcall.am_pm1
          DISPLAY BY NAME gr_viewcall.am_pm1
        END IF

      AFTER FIELD call_time
39➤     IF gr_viewcall.call_time IS NULL THEN
          CALL init_time() RETURNING gr_viewcall.call_time,
                                     gr_viewcall.am_pm1
          DISPLAY BY NAME gr_viewcall.call_time
        ELSE
40➤       LET pr_calltime.hrs = gr_viewcall.call_time[1,2]
41➤       IF (pr_calltime.hrs < 0) OR (pr_calltime.hrs > 23) THEN
            ERROR "Hour must be between 0 and 23. Please try again."
            LET gr_viewcall.call_time[1,2] = "00"
            NEXT FIELD call_time
          END IF
```

42➤ This LET statement uses data conversion to assign the character representation of the minutes in the call receipt time to an integer variable pr_calltime.mins. An integer value makes the data validation in the next step easier.

43➤ The minute value must be between 0 and 59 to be valid. Once again, this validation is required because the time field is defined as CHAR, not DATETIME (See Note 41).

44➤ If the hour is between 13 and 23, then the user entered a time in 24-hour notation which is between 1:00 PM and 11:59 PM. The am_pm1 field displays "PM" and the cursor skips over this field. If the hour is between 0 and 12, then it could be either "AM" or "PM" so the cursor must continue to the am_pm1 field.

45➤ After the cursor leaves the am_pm1 field, the program verifies that the field is not empty and that the input is valid.

46➤ Before the user can enter data in the yr_mon1 field, the program checks if the field is empty. If so, it initializes the field with today's date.

Notes 47 to 51 The AFTER FIELD clause performs data validation after the cursor leaves the yr_mon1 field.

47➤ If the user has cleared the field, the program reinitializes the field with today's date. This test ensures that the call receipt date field always has a value.

48➤ The cust_calls table stores the call receipt time in a DATETIME column called call_dtime. However, because the data entry format for a DATETIME can be difficult for the user to remember, the f_custcall form accepts the call time in three different fields: call_time (time in hours and minutes), am_pm1 ("AM" or "PM"), and yr_mon1 (month, day and year). The get_datetime() function converts these three screen field values to a single DATETIME value.

```
42➤       LET pr_calltime.mins = gr_viewcall.call_time[4,5]
43➤       IF (pr_calltime.mins < 0) OR (pr_calltime.mins > 59) THEN
            ERROR "Minutes must be between 0 and 59. Please try again."
            LET gr_viewcall.call_time[4,5] = "00"
            NEXT FIELD call_time
          END IF

44➤       IF pr_calltime.hrs > 12 THEN
            LET gr_viewcall.am_pm1 = "PM"
            DISPLAY BY NAME gr_viewcall.am_pm1
            NEXT FIELD yr_mon1
          END IF
        END IF
      AFTER FIELD am_pm1
45➤     IF (gr_viewcall.am_pm1 IS NULL)
            OR (gr_viewcall.am_pm1[1] NOT MATCHES "[AP]")
        THEN
          ERROR "Time must be either AM or PM."
          LET gr_viewcall.am_pm1[1] = "A"
          NEXT FIELD am_pm1
        END IF

      BEFORE FIELD yr_mon1
46➤     IF gr_viewcall.yr_mon1 IS NULL THEN
          LET gr_viewcall.yr_mon1 = TODAY
        END IF

      AFTER FIELD yr_mon1
47➤     IF gr_viewcall.yr_mon1 IS NULL THEN
          LET gr_viewcall.yr_mon1 = TODAY
          DISPLAY BY NAME gr_viewcall.yr_mon1
        END IF

48➤     CALL get_datetime(pr_calltime.*, gr_viewcall.am_pm1,
                          gr_viewcall.yr_mon1)
          RETURNING gr_custcalls.call_dtime
```

49➤ This IF statement tests whether the INPUT is executed as a result of an Add operation (receiving a new call) or an Update operation (changing an existing call). If the customer_num field of the work buffer is NULL, then the gr_custcalls record was empty before the data entry began. An initial empty record indicates that the user is receiving a new call, rather than updating an existing call (See Notes 27 to 28).

50➤ If this is an Add operation, the program verifies whether the cust_calls table already contains a row for the current customer that has the same receipt time as the current call. The stores2 database has a UNIQUE index on the customer_num and call_dtime columns of cust_calls. This index ensures that two calls are not logged at the same time for the same customer (the receipt time must be unique).

If an INSERT statement attempted to insert a cust_calls row with a customer number and receipt time that already existed in the table, the INSERT would fail. To prevent this error, this SELECT statement counts the number of rows in the cust_calls table that have the same customer number and receipt time as the current call.

51➤ If the SELECT statement in Note 50 finds any rows with the same customer number and receipt time as the current call, then this call will not be unique and cannot be inserted into the database. The program notifies the user of the error, reinitializes the time fields to the current time and day, and returns the cursor to the call_time field so the user can reenter the time.

52➤ Before the user can enter data in the user_id field, the program checks if the field is empty. If so, it initializes the field with the current user's id. To obtain the user id, the program uses the USER function of the SELECT statement. This "dummy" SELECT does not actually select data from the database. It just runs the USER function. Since the SELECT statement must specify a table, it uses the systables system catalog and to ensure that it yields only one row, the SELECT includes a WHERE clause to specify the row having the "systables" table name.

53➤ If the user has cleared the field, the program returns the cursor to the user_id field. This test ensures that the user enters a user id value.

54➤ Before the user can enter data in the call_code field, the program notifies the user of the valid call code values.

55➤ The IF statement ensures that the call_code variable has a value.

56➤ This MESSAGE statement clears the message line once the cursor leaves the field. Leaving this message on the screen could confuse the user because the codes it lists apply only to the call_code field.

```
49➤      IF gr_workcall.customer_num IS NULL THEN
50➤        SELECT COUNT(*)
           INTO call_cnt
           FROM cust_calls
           WHERE customer_num = gr_custcalls.customer_num
             AND call_dtime = gr_custcalls.call_dtime

51➤        IF (call_cnt > 0) THEN
             ERROR "This customer already has a call entered for: ",
               gr_custcalls.call_dtime
             CALL init_time() RETURNING gr_viewcall.call_time,
                                        gr_viewcall.am_pm1
             NEXT FIELD call_time
           END IF
         END IF

       BEFORE FIELD user_id
52➤      IF gr_viewcall.user_id IS NULL THEN
           SELECT USER
           INTO gr_viewcall.user_id
           FROM informix.systables
           WHERE tabname = "systables"
         END IF

       AFTER FIELD user_id
53➤      IF gr_viewcall.user_id IS NULL THEN
           ERROR "You must enter the name of the person logging the call."
           NEXT FIELD user_id
         END IF

       BEFORE FIELD call_code
54➤      MESSAGE "Valid call codes: B, D, I, L, O "

       AFTER FIELD call_code
55➤      IF gr_viewcall.call_code IS NULL THEN
           ERROR "You must enter a call code. Please try again."
           NEXT FIELD call_code
         END IF

56➤      MESSAGE ""
```

Notes 57 to 60 The BEFORE FIELD clause performs field initialization before the user can enter data in the call_flag field.

57➤ The program notifies the user how to use the special feature to edit the call description. See Notes 73 to 76 for a description of the ON KEY section that implements this feature.

58➤ This IF statement determines whether the current call is a new call or an existing call. See Note 49 for more information about this test.

59➤ If this is a new customer call, the f_edit form displays automatically so the user can enter the new call's description. Calling the edit_descr() function with the "C" argument tells this function to assign input from f_edit for the call description field, call_descr. With an argument of "R", this function can also assign input to the call resolution description, res_descr (See Note 71).

The edit_descr() function returns the setting for call_flag. If the user has entered input for the call description, then gr_custcalls.call_descr is not NULL and call_flag remains set to "Y". If the user has not entered input for call_descr, then call_flag is set to "N" (NO).

60➤ This DISPLAY statement initializes the call_flag field. It displays the call_flag value in the screen field of the same name.

Notes 61 to 64 The AFTER FIELD clause performs data validation after the cursor leaves the call_flag field.

61➤ If no call description exists for this call but the user has entered "Y", the call description field needs to be corrected by changing the its value to "N".

62➤ If a call description exists for this call but the user has entered "N", the call description field needs to be corrected by changing its value to "Y".

63➤ This MESSAGE statement clears the message line once the cursor leaves the field. Leaving the message on the screen could confuse the user because this editing feature is only valid from within the call_flag field.

64➤ The user is asked whether to continue on to the call resolution fields. If the user wants to continue, the cursor moves to the next field: res_time. If the user does not want to continue, data entry is complete so the INPUT statement exits.

65➤ This BEFORE FIELD section performs the same field initialization on the res_time field as was performed on the call_time field. See Note 38 for more information.

66➤ This AFTER FIELD section performs the same data validation on the res_time field as was performed on the call_time field. See Notes 39 to 44 for more information.

```
        BEFORE FIELD call_flag
57➤       MESSAGE "Press F2 (CTRL-E) to edit call description."

58➤       IF gr_workcall.customer_num IS NULL THEN --* doing an insert
59➤         LET gr_viewcall.call_flag = edit_descr("C")
60➤         DISPLAY BY NAME gr_viewcall.call_flag
          END IF

        AFTER FIELD call_flag
61➤       IF gr_custcalls.call_descr IS NULL
              AND (gr_viewcall.call_flag = "Y")
          THEN
            ERROR "No call description exists: changing flag to 'N'."
            LET gr_viewcall.call_flag = "N"
            DISPLAY BY NAME gr_viewcall.call_flag
          END IF

62➤       IF gr_custcalls.call_descr IS NOT NULL
              AND (gr_viewcall.call_flag = "N")
          THEN
            ERROR "A call description exists: changing flag to 'Y'."
            LET gr_viewcall.call_flag = "Y"
            DISPLAY BY NAME gr_viewcall.call_flag
          END IF

63➤       MESSAGE ""
64➤       LET ga_dsplymsg[1] = "Call receiving information complete."
          IF prompt_window("Enter call resolution now?", 14, 14) THEN
            NEXT FIELD res_time
          ELSE
            EXIT INPUT
          END IF

65➤     BEFORE FIELD res_time
          IF gr_viewcall.res_time IS NULL THEN
            CALL init_time() RETURNING gr_viewcall.res_time,
                                       gr_viewcall.am_pm2
            DISPLAY BY NAME gr_viewcall.am_pm2
          END IF

66➤     AFTER FIELD res_time
          IF gr_viewcall.res_time IS NULL THEN
            CALL init_time() RETURNING gr_viewcall.res_time,
                                       gr_viewcall.am_pm2
          ELSE

            LET pr_restime.hrs = gr_viewcall.res_time[1,2]
            IF (pr_restime.hrs < 0) OR (pr_restime.hrs > 23) THEN
              ERROR "Hour must be between 0 and 23. Please try again."
              LET gr_viewcall.res_time[1,2] = "00"
              NEXT FIELD res_time
            END IF
```

67➤ This AFTER FIELD clause performs the same data validation on the am_pm2 field as was performed on the am_pm1 field. See Note 45 for more information.

68➤ This BEFORE FIELD clause performs the same field initialization on the yr_mon2 field as was performed on the yr_mon1 field. See Note 46 for more information.

Notes 69 to 70 The AFTER FIELD clause performs data validation after the cursor leaves the yr_mon2 field.

69➤ This test ensures that the call resolution date field always has a value.

70➤ This test ensures that the call resolution date is not before the call receipt date.

71➤ This BEFORE FIELD clause performs the same field initialization on the res_flag field as was performed on the call_flag field. See Notes 57 to 60 for more information.

```
        LET pr_restime.mins = gr_viewcall.res_time[4,5]
        IF (pr_restime.mins < 0) OR (pr_restime.mins > 59) THEN
          ERROR "Minutes must be between 0 and 59. Please try again."
          LET gr_viewcall.res_time[4,5] = "00"
          NEXT FIELD res_time
        END IF

        IF pr_restime.hrs > 12 THEN
          LET gr_viewcall.am_pm2 = "PM"
          DISPLAY BY NAME gr_viewcall.am_pm2
          NEXT FIELD yr_mon2
        END IF
      END IF

67➤   AFTER FIELD am_pm2
        IF (gr_viewcall.am_pm2 IS NULL)
            OR (gr_viewcall.am_pm2[1] NOT MATCHES "[AP]")
        THEN
          ERROR "Time must be either AM or PM."
          LET gr_viewcall.am_pm2[1] = "A"
          NEXT FIELD am_pm2
        END IF

68➤   BEFORE FIELD yr_mon2
        IF gr_viewcall.yr_mon2 IS NULL THEN
          LET gr_viewcall.yr_mon2 = TODAY
        END IF

      AFTER FIELD yr_mon2
69➤     IF gr_viewcall.yr_mon2 IS NULL THEN
          LET gr_viewcall.yr_mon2 = TODAY
          DISPLAY BY NAME gr_viewcall.yr_mon2
        END IF

70➤     IF gr_viewcall.yr_mon2 < gr_viewcall.yr_mon1 THEN
          ERROR "Resolution date should not be before call date."
          LET gr_viewcall.yr_mon2 = TODAY
          NEXT FIELD yr_mon2
        END IF

71➤   BEFORE FIELD res_flag
        MESSAGE "Press F2 (CTRL-E) to edit resolution description."

        IF gr_workcall.customer_num IS NULL THEN    --* doing an insert
          LET gr_viewcall.res_flag = edit_descr("R")
          DISPLAY BY NAME gr_viewcall.res_flag
        END IF
```

72➤ The AFTER FIELD clause performs data validation on the res_flag field. It is similar to the AFTER FIELD clause associated with the call_flag field. See Notes 61 to 63 for more information about that clause.

The AFTER FIELD clause does not include a call to the prompt_window() function as was found with the AFTER FIELD clause associated with the call_flag field (see Note 64). This is because the call resolution information has, at this point, already been entered into the form.

Notes 73 to 76 The ON KEY clause is executed when the user presses CONTROL-E or the F2 function key. These keys initiate a feature to display a form in which to edit the CHAR(240) columns: call_descr and res_descr. This features allows the f_custcall form to omit these columns and instead, to only display a single-character "Y" or "N" flag for each of them.

73➤ The built-in function INFIELD() determines the current field. If the cursor is currently in either the call_flag or the res_flag field then the editing feature can be used. If the cursor is in any other field on the form, then these key sequences have no effect and the cursor remains in the current field.

74➤ The fld_flag variable is set to "C" when the cursor is in the call_flag field. This value tells the edit_descr() function to edit the call_descr column for the current row. If the cursor is not in call_descr, it must be in the res_flag field. A setting of "R" tells edit_descr() to edit the res_descr column.

75➤ The edit_descr() function displays the f_edit form with the appropriate column value. If fld_flag is "C", then the f_edit form displays the call_descr column value so the user can edit it. If fld_flag is "R", then the form displays and edits the res_descr column. The result of edit_descr() is the flag value to display ("Y" if call_descr is not null and "N" otherwise).

76➤ The value of fld_flag determines which field to set and display: "C" displays the call_flag field while "R" displays the res_flag field.

77➤ If the user has interrupted the INPUT statement, **4GL** sets int_flag to TRUE. The user has terminated input on the f_custcall form so the input_call() function returns FALSE.

78➤ Three of the fields in the table record (gr_custcalls) have already been assigned values from within the INPUT statement: call_dtime, call_descr, res_descr (See Notes 48, 59, 76, and 119). These LET statements copy the customer_num, user_id, and call_code values from the screen field record (gr_viewcall) to the table record.

```
72➤   AFTER FIELD res_flag
        IF gr_custcalls.res_descr IS NULL
            AND (gr_viewcall.res_flag = "Y")
        THEN
          ERROR "No resolution description exists: changing flag to 'N'."
          LET gr_viewcall.res_flag = "N"
          DISPLAY BY NAME gr_viewcall.res_flag
        END IF

        IF gr_custcalls.res_descr IS NOT NULL
            AND (gr_viewcall.res_flag = "N")
        THEN
          ERROR "A resolution description exists: changing flag to 'Y'."
          LET gr_viewcall.res_flag = "Y"
          DISPLAY BY NAME gr_viewcall.res_flag
        END IF

        MESSAGE ""

      ON KEY (F2, CONTROL-E)
73➤     IF INFIELD(call_flag) OR INFIELD(res_flag) THEN
74➤       IF INFIELD(call_flag) THEN
            LET fld_flag = "C"
          ELSE                    --* user pressed F2 (CTRL-E) from res_flag
            LET fld_flag = "R"
          END IF

75➤       LET new_flag = edit_descr(fld_flag)

76➤       IF fld_flag = "C" THEN
            LET gr_viewcall.call_flag = newflag
            DISPLAY BY NAME gr_viewcall.call_flag
          ELSE                   --* fld_flag = "R", editing Call Resolution
            LET gr_viewcall.res_flag = newflag
            DISPLAY BY NAME gr_viewcall.res_flag
          END IF
        END IF

      ON KEY (CONTROL-W)
```

see addupd_cust() in Example 6.

```
    END INPUT

77➤ IF int_flag THEN
      LET int_flag = FALSE
      RETURN (FALSE)
    END IF

78➤ LET gr_custcalls.customer_num = gr_viewcall.customer_num
    LET gr_custcalls.user_id = gr_viewcall.user_id
    LET gr_custcalls.call_code = gr_viewcall.call_code
```

79➤ The call to get_datetime() converts the screen fields containing the call resolution time (res_time, am_pm2, and yr_mon2) to a DATETIME value. The res_dtime column of cust_calls stores the resolution time as a DATETIME. See Note 48 for more information on this conversion.

80➤ Since the user has not terminated the INPUT statement, the input_call() function returns TRUE.

The browse_calls() Function

81➤ Local error message flags are initialized: fnd_calls indicates whether any calls exist for the current customer and end_list indicates whether the user has reached the last selected cust_calls row. These flags are tested after the FOREACH loop (See Note 92 to determine if an error message is printed).

82➤ The c_calls cursor locates calls for the current customer, ordered by time of receipt. The cursor reads a selected row into the gr_custcalls global record.

83➤ If execution reaches inside the FOREACH loop, then the c_calls cursor has found one or more cust_calls rows for the current customer. The fnd_calls flag is set to TRUE to indicate that rows have been found.

Notes 84 to 88 This series of statements initialize the screen field record (gr_viewcall) for display.

84➤ The values from the table record (gr_custcalls) that don't need conversion are copied into the corresponding fields in gr_viewcall.

85➤ The DATETIME call receipt time (in call_dtime) is converted to the format used by the screen fields call_time, am_pm1, and yr_mon1. The screen field record displays this DATETIME value as "hh:mm AM mo/dd/yr" to simplify data entry. See Note 48 for more information on this conversion.

86➤ The setting of the call_flag field is based on whether the current call has a call description (a non-null value in the call_descr column).

87➤ If the call receipt time has not yet been entered, the time fields are initialized to a blank time and today's date. Otherwise, the DATETIME call resolution time is converted to the format "hh:mm AM mo/dd/yr". This value displays in the res_time, am_pm2, and yr_mon2 fields. See Note 48 for more information on this conversion.

```
79➤  CALL get_datetime(pr_restime.*, gr_viewcall.am_pm2,
                       gr_viewcall.yr_mon2)
       RETURNING gr_custcalls.res_dtime

80➤  RETURN (TRUE)

END FUNCTION -- input_call --

########################################
FUNCTION browse_calls(cust_num)
########################################
  DEFINE   cust_num      LIKE customer.customer_num,

           fnd_calls     SMALLINT,
           end_list      SMALLINT

81➤  LET fnd_calls = FALSE
     LET end_list = FALSE

82➤  DECLARE c_calls CURSOR FOR
       SELECT *
       FROM cust_calls
       WHERE customer_num = cust_num
       ORDER BY call_dtime

     FOREACH c_calls INTO gr_custcalls.*
83➤    LET fnd_calls = TRUE

84➤    LET gr_viewcall.customer_num = gr_customer.customer_num
       LET gr_viewcall.company = gr_customer.company
       LET gr_viewcall.user_id = gr_custcalls.user_id
       LET gr_viewcall.call_code = gr_custcalls.call_code

85➤    CALL get_timeflds(gr_custcalls.call_dtime)
         RETURNING gr_viewcall.call_time, gr_viewcall.am_pm1,
                   gr_viewcall.yr_mon1

86➤    IF gr_custcalls.call_descr IS NULL THEN
         LET gr_viewcall.call_flag = "N"
       ELSE
         LET gr_viewcall.call_flag = "Y"
       END IF

87➤    IF gr_custcalls.res_dtime IS NULL THEN
         LET gr_viewcall.res_time = NULL
         LET gr_viewcall.am_pm2 = "AM"
         LET gr_viewcall.yr_mon2 = TODAY
       ELSE
         CALL get_timeflds(gr_custcalls.res_dtime)
           RETURNING gr_viewcall.res_time, gr_viewcall.am_pm2,
                     gr_viewcall.yr_mon2
       END IF
```

88➤ The setting of the res_flag field is based on whether the current call has a resolution description (a non-null value in the res_descr column).

89➤ Once the screen field record is initialized, it is displayed on the f_custcall form.

90➤ If nxtact_call() returns FALSE, the user has chosen the "Exit" option from the CUSTOMER CALL MODIFICATION menu. Setting the end_list flag to FALSE indicates that the user chose to exit before reaching the last selected row in the loop. The EXIT FOREACH statement closes the c_calls cursor.

91➤ If nxtact_call() returns TRUE, then the user has chosen the "Next" option from the CUSTOMER CALL MODIFICATION menu. The end_list flag is set to TRUE because the current row may be the last one selected by the c_calls cursor. If this is the last row, then FOREACH exits and the program displays "No more customer calls." If the current row is not the last one, the FOREACH fetches the next row and then calls nxtact_call() to display the CUSTOMER CALL MODIFICATION menu. In this case, end_list is reset based on the value returned by nxtact_call().

92➤ Each error flag (fnd_calls and end_list) indicates the status of a particular error condition. If one of these error conditions has occurred, the program displays the appropriate message.

93➤ The f_custcall form fields are cleared.

The nxtact_call() Function

94➤ The CUSTOMER CALL MODIFICATION menu allows the user to display the next customer call ("Next"), update information in the current call ("Update"), or exit the menu ("Exit").

95➤ The "Next" option exits the menu with nxt_action set to TRUE. Program execution returns to the c_calls FOREACH loop (in browse_calls()) to obtain the next selected cust_calls row (See Note 91).

96➤ The "Update" option calls the addupd_call() function to update the current customer call. Because this function can handle both an Add or an Update on the f_custcall form, the add/update flag is set to "Update" ("U"). This function is modelled after the addupd_cust() function implemented in Example 9.

97➤ The bang() function implements the "bang" ("!") escape to the operating system. This feature is described in Example 3.

```
88➤      IF gr_custcalls.res_descr IS NULL THEN
           LET gr_viewcall.res_flag = "N"
         ELSE
           LET gr_viewcall.res_flag = "Y"
         END IF

89➤      DISPLAY BY NAME gr_viewcall.*

90➤      IF NOT nxtact_call() THEN
           LET end_list = FALSE
           EXIT FOREACH
91➤      ELSE
           LET end_list = TRUE
         END IF
       END FOREACH

92➤    IF NOT fnd_calls THEN
         CALL msg("No calls exist for this customer.")
       END IF

       IF end_list THEN
         CALL msg("No more customer calls.")
       END IF

93➤    CLEAR call_time, am_pm1, yr_mon1, user_id, call_code,
             call_flag, res_time, am_pm2, yr_mon2, res_flag

     END FUNCTION -- browse_calls --

     ########################################
     FUNCTION nxtact_call()
     ########################################
       DEFINE    nxt_action    SMALLINT

       LET nxt_action = TRUE

94➤    MENU "CUSTOMER CALL MODIFICATION"
95➤      COMMAND "Next" "View next selected customer call." HELP 90
           EXIT MENU

96➤      COMMAND "Update" "Update current customer call on screen."
             HELP 91
           CALL addupd_call("U")
           NEXT OPTION "Next"

97➤      COMMAND KEY ("!")
           CALL bang()
```

98➤ The "Exit" option exits the menu with nxt_action set to FALSE. Program execution returns to the browse_calls() function where it encounters the EXIT FOREACH statement to exit the c_calls FOREACH loop (See Note 90).

The get_timeflds() Function

99➤ If the_dtime is NULL, all time screen fields are set to NULL.

100➤ If the_dtime is non-null, the program converts it to a time screen field values: time_fld, am_pm, and yr_mon. The LET statement uses data conversion to assign the current date in the DATETIME to the DATE yr_mon field.

101➤ The built-in function EXTEND() extracts the hour and minute values from the_dtime. This system function uses field qualifiers to adjust the precision of a DATETIME value. In this case, it returns the hour (HOUR TO HOUR) and the minutes (MINUTE TO MINUTE) values.

The LET statements convert the hour and minute values to their character representations and then store them in the appropriate position of the character time string, time_fld: the hours value in positions 1 and 2; the minutes value in positions 4 and 5. Position 3 contains the ":" symbol so that the final value has the format "hh:mm".

102➤ The LET statement uses data conversion to convert the hours value to an integer value so that the numeric comparison is simplified. Because the DATETIME format uses 24-hour time notation, all PM hours will have an hour value greater than or equal to twelve (12) and all AM hours will have an hour value less then twelve. Therefore, the size of the hour value determines the setting of the am_pm field.

The program also converts the 24-hour PM time to a time between 12:00 PM and 11:59 PM and a time of 00:00 as 12:00 AM.

103➤ The get_timeflds() function returns the screen field values of the DATETIME value.

```
98➤     COMMAND KEY ("E","e","X","x") "Exit" "Return to CUSTOMER CALLS Menu"
            HELP 92
          LET nxt_action = FALSE
          EXIT MENU
      END MENU

      RETURN nxt_action

    END FUNCTION -- nxtact_call --

    ########################################
    FUNCTION get_timeflds(the_dtime)
    ########################################
      DEFINE        the_dtime        DATETIME YEAR TO MINUTE,

                    am_pm            CHAR(2),
                    yr_mon           DATE,
                    time_fld         CHAR(5),
                    num_hrs          SMALLINT

99➤   IF the_dtime IS NULL THEN
        LET time_fld = NULL
        LET am_pm = NULL
        LET yr_mon = NULL
100➤  ELSE
        LET yr_mon = the_dtime

101➤    LET time_fld = "00:00"
        LET time_fld[1,2] = EXTEND(the_dtime, HOUR TO HOUR)
        LET time_fld[4,5] = EXTEND(the_dtime, MINUTE TO MINUTE)

102➤    LET num_hrs = time_fld[1,2]
        IF num_hrs >= 12 THEN
          LET am_pm = "PM"
          LET num_hrs = num_hrs - 12
          IF num_hrs > 9 THEN
            LET time_fld[1,2] = num_hrs
          ELSE
            LET time_fld[1] = "0"
            LET time_fld[2] = num_hrs
          END IF
        ELSE
          LET am_pm = "AM"
          IF num_hrs = 0 THEN
            LET time_fld[1,2] = "12"
          END IF
        END IF
      END IF

103➤  RETURN time_fld, am_pm, yr_mon

    END FUNCTION -- get_timeflds --
```

The get_datetime() Function

104➤ A null yr_mon screen field indicates that all screen fields are null so the DATETIME value for these screen fields is set to null.

105➤ If the screen fields are not null, then they must be combined into a DATETIME value. The LET statement uses data conversion to assign the current DATE value (in yr_mon) to a DATETIME value.

106➤ In 24-hour notation (used by DATETIME values), times from 12:00 AM to 12:59 AM are written as 00:00 to 00:59. If the time is an AM value (hour value is between 0 and 12) and it is midnight (12:00 AM), then the hours value must be reset to zero (0) for the 24-hour time representation, 00:00.

107➤ In 24-hour notation (used by DATETIME values), times from 1:00 PM to 11:59 PM are written as 13:00 to 23:59. If the time is a PM value, any hour after 12:00 PM must be converted to 24-hour time notation by adding 12 to the value.

108➤ The addition operator combines the year/month, the hours, and the minutes into a single DATETIME value. The built-in function UNITS is necessary to convert to the INTERVAL values to the integer representation of the hour and minute values. You cannot add integers to a DATETIME value but you can add INTERVAL values.

109➤ The get_datetime() function returns the DATETIME representation of the screen field values.

The init_time() Function

110➤ The CURRENT built-in function returns a DATETIME value of the current system time. The qualifiers HOUR TO MINUTE limit this return value to only a time value. The LET statement then uses data conversion to convert the DATETIME value to a CHARACTER value.

111➤ If the current system time is past 12:59, the time value is in 24-hour notation. The IF block converts the 24-hour time to a 12-hour time, setting the AM/PM flag to the appropriate value.

```
##########################################
FUNCTION get_datetime(pr_time, am_pm, yr_mon)
##########################################
  DEFINE         pr_time     RECORD
                     hrs         SMALLINT,
                     mins        SMALLINT
                 END RECORD,
                 am_pm           CHAR(2),
                 yr_mon          DATE,

                 the_dtime    DATETIME YEAR TO MINUTE

104➤  IF yr_mon IS NULL THEN
    LET the_dtime = NULL
  ELSE
105➤    LET the_dtime = yr_mon        --* use 4GL convertion to
                                      --* convert DATE to DATETIME

106➤    IF am_pm[1] = "A" THEN
      IF pr_time.hrs = 12 THEN
        LET pr_time.hrs = 0
      END IF
    ELSE                              --* am_pm = "P"
107➤      IF pr_time.hrs < 12 THEN
        LET pr_time.hrs = pr_time.hrs + 12       --* convert PM to 24-hour time
      END IF
    END IF

108➤    LET the_dtime = the_dtime + pr_time.hrs UNITS HOUR
              + pr_time.mins UNITS MINUTE     --* add in time (hours and minutes)
                                              --*   to DATETIME value
  END IF

109➤  RETURN (the_dtime)

END FUNCTION -- get_datetime --

##########################################
FUNCTION init_time()
##########################################
  DEFINE         new_time         CHAR(5),
                 am_pm            CHAR(2),
                 hrs              SMALLINT

110➤  LET new_time = CURRENT HOUR TO MINUTE
111➤  IF new_time > "12:59" THEN     -- if 24-hour notation, convert to
    LET hrs = new_time[1,2]       --   12-hour and AM/PM flag
    LET hrs = hrs - 12
```

112➤ The function returns the character representation of the current system time and the AM/PM flag.

The edit_descr() Function

113➤ The character editing form, f_edit, displays in a bordered window called w_edit. This window has redefined the FORM LINE and COMMENT LINE options to customize the appearance of f_edit.

114➤ The first line of the window displays instructions for using this form.

115➤ The value of edit_flg determines the appropriate form title and character field initialization.

116➤ This INPUT statement accepts user input in the character edit field. The WITHOUT DEFAULTS clause ensures that the field is initialized with any existing value. The value has been determined by the code described in Note 115.

117➤ The has_value flag indicates whether the edited CHAR(240) value is null (it has a value) or contains a value. If this field is null, then has_value is set to "N". Otherwise, has_value remains set to "Y".

```
      IF hrs > 9 THEN                -- need to put two digits in
        LET new_time[1,2] = hrs
      ELSE                           -- need to put only 1 digit in
        LET new_time[1] = 0
        LET new_time[2] = hrs
      END IF
      LET am_pm = "PM"
    ELSE
      LET am_pm = "AM"
    END IF

112➤ RETURN new_time, am_pm

  END FUNCTION  -- init_time --

  ########################################
  FUNCTION edit_descr(edit_flg)
  ########################################
    DEFINE        edit_flg        CHAR(1),

                  edit_str        LIKE cust_calls.call_descr,
                  edit_ret        SMALLINT,
                  has_value       CHAR(1)

113➤ OPEN WINDOW w_edit AT 3,11
      WITH 12 ROWS, 60 COLUMNS
      ATTRIBUTE (BORDER, FORM LINE 4, COMMENT LINE 2)

    OPEN FORM f_edit FROM "f_edit"
    DISPLAY FORM f_edit

114➤ DISPLAY " Press Accept to save, Cancel to exit w/out saving."
      AT 1, 1 ATTRIBUTE (REVERSE, YELLOW)

115➤ IF edit_flg = "C" THEN
      DISPLAY "CALL DESCRIPTION"
        AT 3, 24
      LET edit_str = gr_custcalls.call_descr
    ELSE                    --* edit_flg = "R"
      DISPLAY "CALL RESOLUTION"
        AT 3, 24
      LET edit_str = gr_custcalls.res_descr
    END IF

    LET int_flag = FALSE
116➤ INPUT BY NAME edit_str
      WITHOUT DEFAULTS

117➤ LET has_value = "Y"
    IF edit_str IS NULL THEN
      LET has_value = "N"
    END IF
```

118➤ If the user presses Cancel, the INPUT statement exits and the changes to the edit_fld are not saved.

119➤ If the user presses Accept, the contents of the character edit field is saved in the appropriate field of the table record, gr_custcalls.

120➤ Neither the w_ edit window nor the f_edit form are used until the user initiates the edit_descr() function again. For this reason, the memory used by the window and form is deallocated.

121➤ The edit_descr() function returns the value of the has_value flag. This flag is "Y" if the edited CHAR(240) field is non-null and "N" otherwise.

The insert_call() Function

122➤ The INSERT statement inserts the current values of the table record, gr_custcalls, as a row in the cust_calls table.

The INSERT is surrounded with the WHENEVER ERROR statements to control how **4GL** responds to errors. The WHENEVER ERROR CONTINUE statement sets a compiler flag so that the program does not include code to check for runtime errors. Execution of all statements after this WHENEVER will not stop if the program encounters a runtime error unless the program explicitly checks for errors. The WHENEVER ERROR STOP statement sets a compiler flag so that the program does include code to check for runtime errors. Execution of all statements after this WHENEVER will stop if the program encounters a runtime error.

123➤ If the INSERT statement was successful, then **4GL** has set the global variable status to zero. If an error has occurred, the status variable has a negative value. In the case of an error, the function notifies the user and exits.

124➤ If execution reaches this point, the INSERT has been successful. The call to msg() notifies the user that the cust_calls row has been added to the database.

```
118➤   IF int_flag THEN
         LET int_flag = FALSE
       ELSE
119➤     IF edit_flg = "C" THEN
           LET gr_custcalls.call_descr = edit_str
         ELSE
           LET gr_custcalls.res_descr = edit_str
         END IF
       END IF

120➤   CLOSE FORM f_edit
       CLOSE WINDOW w_edit

121➤   RETURN has_value

     END FUNCTION -- edit_descr --

     ########################################
     FUNCTION insert_call()
     ########################################

     WHENEVER ERROR CONTINUE
122➤   INSERT INTO cust_calls
       VALUES (gr_custcalls.*)
     WHENEVER ERROR STOP

123➤   IF (status < 0) THEN
         ERROR status USING "-<<<<<<<<<<<", ": Unable to complete customer call ",
             "insert."
       ELSE
         CALL msg("Customer call has been entered in the database.")
       END IF

124➤   CALL msg("Customer call has been entered in the database.")

     END FUNCTION -- insert_call --
```

The update_call() Function

125➤ The WHENEVER ERROR CONTINUE statement sets a compiler flag so that the program does not include code to check for runtime errors. Execution of all statements after this WHENEVER will not stop if the program encounters a runtime error, unless the program explicitly checks for errors. This WHENEVER allows this function to perform its own error checking after the database operation statement.

126➤ The UPDATE statement updates the cust_calls row associated with the current call for the current user with the values of the table record, gr_custcalls.

127➤ The WHENEVER ERROR STOP statement sets a compiler flag so that the program does include code to check for runtime errors. Execution of all statements after this WHENEVER will stop if the program encounters a runtime error. This WHENEVER causes the program to assume that any errors encountered past this point are unexpected and program execution needs to stop.

128➤ If the UPDATE statement was successful, then **4GL** has set the global variable status to zero. If an error has occurred, the status variable has a negative value. In the case of an error, the function notifies the user and exits.

129➤ If execution reaches this point, the UPDATE has been successful. The call to msg() notifies the user that the current cust_calls row has been updated in the database.

```
    ########################################
    FUNCTION update_call()
    ########################################

125➤ WHENEVER ERROR CONTINUE
126➤   UPDATE cust_calls SET cust_calls.* = gr_custcalls.*
       WHERE customer_num = gr_custcalls.customer_num
         AND call_dtime = gr_custcalls.call_dtime
127➤ WHENEVER ERROR STOP

128➤   IF (status < 0) THEN
         ERROR status USING "-<<<<<<<<<<<",
           ": Unable to complete customer call update."
         RETURN
       END IF

129➤   CALL msg("Customer call has been updated.")

     END FUNCTION -- update_call --
```

To locate any function definition see the Function Index on page 728.

18

Using OnLine Data Types

This example demonstrates how to handle VARCHAR and TEXT data types in a **4GL** program. It uses the cat_advert (VARCHAR) and cat_descr (TEXT) columns of the catalog table.

Note: These data types and the catalog table are only available if you are using an **INFORMIX-OnLine** *database. The catalog table does not exist in the* **INFORMIX-SE** *version of the demonstration database.*

Verifying an OnLine Database

Because this program can only work on the catalog table if the application is using an **INFORMIX-OnLine** database, it first checks the type of database. To do this, the program checks the status of the second element of the SQLAWARN array. This array is part of the global **4GL** SQLCA record. After executing the DATABASE statement, **OnLine** sets the SQLCA.SQLAWARN[2] field to "W". This verification is performed by the is_online() function which returns TRUE if the current database is **OnLine** and FALSE if it is **SE**.

Positioning the DATABASE Statement in a Program

The DATABASE statement specifies the name of the current database. This information is needed at compile time and run time:

- At compile time the **4GL** compiler needs to know which database to use when resolving variable definitions containing the LIKE clause.
- At run time the application needs to know which database to use when executing an SQL statement.

The location of the DATABASE statement within your program is determined by these two uses. It must appear in the code so that:

- The compiler encounters it before any DEFINE statements that use LIKE.
- Program execution encounters it before any SQL statements execute (program execution may not occur sequentially in the file).

In this example, if none of the global definitions used the LIKE clause, the DATABASE statement could appear just before the DECLARE statement (see Note 19) because this is the first SQL statement executed. However, placing the DATABASE statement as the first line of the file is the most common usage: this location is an easy, consistent place to find the application's database and it satisfies both the compile time and the run time conditions.

However, you may find a situation where you need to open the database at some later point in program execution. You can place the DATABASE statement anywhere in the program as long as the compiler and runtime conditions mentioned above are met.

When execution begins, the program initializes the ga_catrows, ga_catrids, and ga_catadv arrays with the data from the catalog table in the load_arrays() function. It then waits for the user to indicate which data to view.

From the catalog number field, the user can choose to:

- View the VARCHAR value (cat_adv): CONTROL-V
- View the TEXT value (cat_descr): CONTROL-T
- Exit the form: CONTROL-E

Using Parallel Arrays to Manage Information

This example program uses a screen array form to access the information in the catalog table. Each line of the form displays information about a single catalog item:

```
+----------------------------------------------------------------------------+
| Catalog #   Pic?  Txt?    Stock #   Stock Description       Manufacturer   |
|  [10001]    [N]   [Y]     [     1]  [baseball gloves]    [Hero         ]   |
|  [10002]    [N]   [Y]     [     1]  [baseball gloves]    [Husky        ]   |
|  [10003]    [Y]   [Y]     [     1]  [baseball gloves]    [Smith        ]   |
|  [10004]    [N]   [Y]     [     2]  [baseball       ]    [Hero         ]   |
|  [10005]    [N]   [Y]     [     3]  [baseball bat   ]    [Husky        ]   |
|                                                                            |
|----------------------------------------------------------------------------|
|       ACTIONS                                   KEY SEQUENCES              |
|    To exit                                   Accept twice or CONTROL-E     |
|    To scroll up and down                     Arrow keys                    |
|    To view or update:                                                      |
|       catalog advertising (varchar)          F4 or CONTROL-V               |
|       catalog description (text)             F5 or CONTROL-T               |
+----------------------------------------------------------------------------+
```

The program uses three global arrays to manage the catalog information:

- The ga_catrows array stores the information that appears in the screen array.
- The ga_catrids array contains the ROWID for each selected item from the catalog table. A ROWID is an internal record number associated with a row in a database table. It uniquely identifies a row and provides a very efficient means of accessing the row.
- The ga_catadv array contains the VARCHAR data for each selected catalog item.

The same index value can be used on all three arrays to access all information about a single catalog item.

Handling VARCHAR Data

The VARCHAR value for a given catalog row appears in a form displayed in a separate window. This window overlays the screen array form. The only special coding required for the VARCHAR data is to:

- Define a multi-line screen field large enough to hold the VARCHAR value.
- Include the WORDWRAP attribute on this screen field to allow text to wrap to the next line of the field. The COMPRESS option removes RETURN spaces inserted in the text by the multi-line editor.

Handling TEXT Data

Unlike the VARCHAR data, the TEXT data for catalog rows is not read into a global array. Implementing such a design would necessitate the creation of a global array with each element defined as a TEXT value.

Because a BLOB column can contain a very large amount of data, a **4GL** program does not allocate space for a BLOB variable as it does other variable types. Instead of containing the actual value, a BLOB variable contains a pointer to the location where this data is stored. This location can be in memory, in a temporary file (created by the program), or in a specified file (named by the programmer). The LOCATE statement initializes the BLOB variable with the location of the BLOB value.

This program does not define a global array for the TEXT data because:

- The global array of TEXT variables would require a great deal of memory to store each of the 200 TEXT variable entries.
- The program would need to initialize each TEXT variable with LOCATE.
- The program would need to allocate storage (on disk or in memory) for every row's TEXT value (200 of them).

For these reasons, the program instead reads in a TEXT value for a particular row only when the user chooses to view this data. The disadvantage of this design is that it takes a little longer to display the TEXT value than it does to display the VARCHAR value: the program must obtain the TEXT value from the database while the VARCHAR values are already available within the program array. However, this loss of speed is made up for by the smaller amount of resources needed to store only one TEXT variable and one TEXT value at a time.

This program stores the pointer to the TEXT data in the g_txtblob global variable. To access the TEXT value, the program must:

1. Use the LOCATE statement to assign a storage location for the TEXT data.
2. Use a SELECT statement to assign the TEXT value to this location.
3. Use an INPUT statement to display the TEXT value on a screen.
4. Allow the user to modify the TEXT value by pressing the exclamation point ("!") from the TEXT field of f_catdescr to access a text editor: the "!" is a standard feature of TEXT fields and the text editor is specified as "vi" by the PROGRAM attribute in the f_catdescr form.
5. Use the UPDATE statement to update the TEXT column with the new value if the user modifies the field.
6. Use the FREE statement to deallocate the storage used by the TEXT data.

The location of the LOCATE and FREE statements within the program are not fixed. However, the LOCATE must be executed before the first time the TEXT variable is accessed (assigned a value or displayed). Trying to access a TEXT variable before if has been located yields a runtime error. Similarly, the FREE statement must follow all accesses of the variable. Otherwise, the program will encounter a runtime error when it tries to access a deallocated TEXT variable.

Handling BYTE Data

Although the main form lists whether or not a given catalog item has an associated catalog picture, this example does not demonstrate use of accessing BYTE information. BYTE values can only be effectively displayed on a graphical user interface, and the program must know the specific graphic interface being used.

The steps for defining, locating, and selecting BYTE data are the same as those for TEXT data. However, the step of displaying the value to the user depends on the nature of the data, and will usually involve running a program that is external to the application.

To see an example of the platform-specific calls needed to display BYTE data, look at the BLOB demo included as part of the 4.1 release. See the *INFORMIX-4GL Release 4.1 Reference Manual Supplement* for more information about the demo.

Function Overview

Function Name	Purpose
is_online()	Checks to see if the current database is an OnLine or SE database. OnLine data types are not available with an SE database.
load_arrays()	Loads the contents of the "catalog" table into global arrays: ga_catrows and ga_catrids. Instead of reading the values of the catalog TEXT columns (cat_descr), this program marks a character field as "Y" or "N", indicating the presence of the TEXT value.
open_wins()	Opens all windows used in the program.
close_wins()	Closes all windows used in the program.
dsply_cat()	Displays the contents of the catalog program array (ga_catrows) on the form f_catalog.
show_advert()	Displays the contents of the VARCHAR column (cat_advert) on the form f_catadv.
show_descr()	Displays the contents of the TEXT column (cat_descr) on the form f_catdescr.
upd_err()	Reports an error if one occurs during an UPDATE.
msg()	Displays a brief, informative message. *See description in Example 5.*
init_msgs()	Initializes the members of the ga_dsplymsg array to null. *See description in Example 2.*
message_window()	Opens a window and displays the contents of the ga_dsplymsg global array. *See description in Example 2.*

The f_catalog Form

1➤ This form compiles and runs with an **OnLine** version of the stores2t database. Only the **OnLine** version contains the catalog table.

2➤ The top portion of the f_catalog form contains the screen array which displays the catalog information. The bottom portion displays instructions for using the form.

3➤ This form uses descriptive field names (cnum and snum) as field tags.

4➤ Fields on this form display information about a stock item retrieved from several database tables. The NOENTRY attribute prevents the cursor from entering all fields except cnum.

f_catalog form file

```
1➤ DATABASE stores2t

2➤ SCREEN
   {
   +--------------------------------------------------------------------------+
   | Catalog #   Pic?   Txt?    Stock #   Stock Description      Manufacturer  |
3➤ |   [cnum ]    [p]    [t]    [snum ]  [sdesc            ]  [manu        ]  |
   |   [cnum ]    [p]    [t]    [snum ]  [sdesc            ]  [manu        ]  |
   |   [cnum ]    [p]    [t]    [snum ]  [sdesc            ]  [manu        ]  |
   |   [cnum ]    [p]    [t]    [snum ]  [sdesc            ]  [manu        ]  |
   |   [cnum ]    [p]    [t]    [snum ]  [sdesc            ]  [manu        ]  |
   |                                                                          |
   |--------------------------------------------------------------------------|
   |          ACTIONS                                  KEY SEQUENCES          |
   |    To exit                                  Accept twice or CONTROL-E    |
   |    To scroll up and down                    Arrow keys                   |
   |    To view or update:                                                    |
   |       catalog advertising (varchar)         F4 or CONTROL-V              |
   |       catalog description (text)            F5 or CONTROL-T              |
   +--------------------------------------------------------------------------+
   }
   END

   TABLES
           catalog, stock, manufact
   END

   ATTRIBUTES
4➤   cnum  = catalog.catalog_num;
      p     = FORMONLY.has_pic TYPE CHAR, NOENTRY;
      t     = FORMONLY.has_desc TYPE CHAR, NOENTRY;
      snum  = catalog.stock_num, NOENTRY;
      sdesc = stock.description, NOENTRY;
      manu  = manufact.manu_name, NOENTRY;

   INSTRUCTIONS
     SCREEN RECORD sa_cat[5] (catalog_num, stock_num, manu_name,
                              has_pic, has_desc, description)

   END
```

The f_catadv Form

1➤ This form compiles and runs with an **OnLine** version of the stores2t database. Only the **OnLine** version contains the catalog table.

2➤ Catalog information for the current item displays at the top of the form in the cnum, sdesc, and man fields.

The NOENTRY attribute prevents the cursor from entering these fields in an INPUT statement.

3➤ The copy field displays the VARCHAR value (cat_advert) for the catalog row. This field consists of four lines of 64 characters each. The WORDWRAP attribute enables the multi-line editor so the user can enter text in the field without having to press RETURN at the end of each line. The COMPRESS option prevents blanks produced by the editor from being included as part of the input.

4➤ The xn and xu fields do not actually accept input text. Rather they serve as a resting point for the cursor so that the user can choose the action to take on the VARCHAR value. The program defines CONTROL-E so that:

- If the user presses CONTROL-E from within xn, the program exits this form without saving the VARCHAR data.
- If the user presses CONTROL-E from within xu, the program saves the VARCHAR data in the catalog table and then exits the form.

The COMMENTS attribute defines text displayed in the form's Comment line. This text notifies the user of the CONTROL-E feature.

f_catadv form file

```
1➤ DATABASE stores2t

   SCREEN
   {
    Ad copy for cat# [cnum ], [sdesc          ] from [man             ]

     [copy                                                            ]
     [copy                                                            ]
     [copy                                                            ]
     [copy                                                            ]

           Exit w/o changes [xn]        Update current ad copy [xu]
   }
   END

   TABLES
     catalog, stock, manufact
   END

   ATTRIBUTES
2➤   cnum  = catalog.catalog_num, NOENTRY;
     sdesc = stock.description, NOENTRY;
     man   = manufact.manu_name, NOENTRY;
3➤   copy  = catalog.cat_advert, WORDWRAP COMPRESS
                COMMENTS = "Press RETURN for next field.";
4➤   xn    = FORMONLY.xn TYPE CHAR,
                COMMENTS = "Press CONTROL-E now to exit with no changes." ;
     xu    = FORMONLY.xu TYPE CHAR,
                COMMENTS = "Press CONTROL-E now to update the ad copy.";

   END
```

The f_catdescr Form

1➤ This form compiles and runs with an **OnLine** version of the stores2t database. Only the **OnLine** version contains the catalog table.

2➤ Catalog information for the current item displays at the top of the form in the cnum, sdesc, and man fields.

3➤ The copy field displays the TEXT value (cat_descr) for the catalog row. This field consists of seven lines of 64 characters each. The WORDWRAP attribute allows the form to display the TEXT value over several lines. To edit the TEXT value, the user must type an exclamation point ("!") from the copy field. The PROGRAM attribute specifies that the "vi" text editor is used to edit the field. Since vi is the default text editor, this attribute specification is not actually required. The COMMENTS attribute defines the Comment line text to tell the user how to edit the TEXT field.

4➤ The xn and xu fields serve as a resting point for the cursor so the user can choose whether to save the TEXT value in the catalog table.

f_catdescr form file

```
1➤ DATABASE stores2t

   SCREEN
   {
    Description for cat# [cnum ], [sdesc          ] from [man            ]

    [copy                                                                ]
    [copy                                                                ]
    [copy                                                                ]
    [copy                                                                ]
    [copy                                                                ]
    [copy                                                                ]
    [copy                                                                ]

          Exit w/o changes [xn]        Update current ad copy [xu]
   }
   END

   TABLES
           catalog, stock, manufact
   END

   ATTRIBUTES
2➤   cnum  = catalog.catalog_num, NOENTRY;
     sdesc = stock.description, NOENTRY;
     man   = manufact.manu_name, NOENTRY;
3➤   copy  = catalog.cat_descr, WORDWRAP, PROGRAM="vi",
                COMMENTS = "Press ! to invoke an editor, RETURN for next field";
4➤   xn    = formonly.xn TYPE CHAR,
                COMMENTS = "Press CONTROL-E now to exit with no changes." ;
     xu    = formonly.xu TYPE CHAR,
                COMMENTS = "Press CONTROL-E now to update the catalog description.";
   END
```

The DATABASE and GLOBALS Statements

1➤ This DATABASE statement tells the compiler which database to use when resolving variable definitions that contain the LIKE clause. For example, the ga_catadv array is defined to contain elements LIKE the column catalog.cat_advert. For the compiler to correctly process this definition, it first must encounter the DATABASE statement.

2➤ Three parallel global arrays manage the information about each catalog item:

- The ga_catrows global array holds the data to be displayed on the f_catalog form. This record structure must match the screen record defined in the form.
- The ga_catadv global array holds the VARCHAR column values of the catalog table. It is in a separate array because it is not displayed on the form.
- The ga_catrids global array holds the ROWIDs of the catalog rows. The ROWIDs are used to quickly access the TEXT or VARCHAR data for a specified catalog row on the f_catalog form.

The same index into each array is used to retrieve complete information about a single catalog item.

3➤ The ga_dsplymsg array is used as input to the message_window() function, as described in Example 2, and the prompt_window() function, as described in Example 3.

The MAIN Function

4➤ The OPTIONS statement sets up the screen options for the form.

5➤ The is_online() function checks whether the current database is an **OnLine** database. If it is not, the program exits because the catalog table does not exist in the demonstration database for the **SE** engine.

6➤ The g_arraysz variable contains the size of the global program arrays used in this program. When the code needs to reference the array size (to check index limits), it uses this variable rather than a constant value of 200.

If, in the future, the size of these arrays needs to be changed, you only need to change the actual array definitions (the DEFINE statements) and the value assigned to this variable. You do not need to search through the code for occurrences of the constant value.

4GL source file

```
1➤ DATABASE stores2t

   GLOBALS
     DEFINE        g_txflag    CHAR(1),   -- TRUE if database uses transactions
                   g_arraysz   SMALLINT,  -- size of arrays used in ARRAY stmts
                   g_txtblob   TEXT,      -- cat_descr value, located in memory

2➤                 ga_catrows ARRAY[200] OF RECORD
                       catalog_num    LIKE catalog.catalog_num,
                       stock_num      LIKE stock.stock_num,
                       manu_name      LIKE manufact.manu_name,
                       has_pic        CHAR(1),
                       has_desc       CHAR(1),
                       description    CHAR(15)
                    END RECORD,

                   ga_catadv ARRAY[200] OF LIKE catalog.cat_advert,

                   ga_catrids ARRAY[200] OF INTEGER,

3➤   DEFINE        ga_dsplymsg ARRAY[5] OF CHAR(48)

   END GLOBALS

   ########################################
   MAIN
   ########################################
     DEFINE        cat_cnt     SMALLINT    -- count of rows actually read

     DEFER INTERRUPT               -- ...do not stop cold on error or ^C

4➤   OPTIONS
       MESSAGE LINE LAST,
       PROMPT LINE LAST,
       COMMENT LINE FIRST,
       FORM LINE FIRST+1

5➤   IF NOT is_online() THEN
       EXIT PROGRAM
     END IF
6➤   LET g_arraysz = 200
```

7➤ All the forms are opened at this point in the program, as opposed to opening the forms only when the form is accessed. Although this method requires more time in the beginning of the program and more memory to store all forms at once, it saves time when the individual form is accessed (because the form is already opened).

8➤ The LOCATE statement defines a temporary file to store the value of the cat_-descr TEXT column.

9➤ The load_arrays() function loads the rows of the catalog table into the ga_catrows, ga_catadv, and ga_catrids global arrays. It returns the number of rows stored in these arrays.

10➤ The open_wins() function opens the windows needed to display the catalog information. This is an alternate to opening the windows only when the window is to display. Although this method requires more time in the beginning of the program to open up all windows and more memory to store all windows at once, it saves time when the individual window is to display because the window is already opened.

11➤ The dsply_cat() function displays the contents of the ga_catrows array on the form f_catalog and allows the user to view the data for the catalog rows.

12➤ The close_wins() function closes all windows used by the example.

The is_online() Function

13➤ To check whether the program is working with an **OnLine** database, the function opens the database. The CLOSE DATABASE statement is issued because an attempt to open a database when one is already open produces an error (-917) if the application is using **INFORMIX-STAR** and the database is on a remote machine.

However, if the application is not using a remote database, an attempt to close a database when none is open produces an error (-349) as well. To prevent the program from terminating at this point, the WHENEVER ERROR statements surround the CLOSE DATABASE. Automatic error checking is turned off before the CLOSE DATABASE and turned back on after the CLOSE DATABASE is performed. Because the automatic checking is off when the CLOSE DATABASE is executed, the program must perform its own error checking to determine the success of the statement.

14➤ The IF statement checks the status in SQLCA.SQLCODE to determine the success of the CLOSE DATABASE statement. An SQLCODE value of zero (success) or -349 (database is not open) is expected. Any other SQLCODE value indicates that an error has occurred.

```
7➤    OPEN FORM f_catalog FROM "f_catalog"
      OPEN FORM f_catadv FROM "f_catadv"
      OPEN FORM f_catdescr FROM "f_catdescr"

8➤    LOCATE g_txtblob IN FILE          -- ...locate the blob variable

9➤    CALL load_arrays()RETURNING cat_cnt

10➤   CALL open_wins()
11➤   CALL dsply_cat(cat_cnt)
12➤   CALL close_wins()
      CLEAR SCREEN
    END MAIN

    ########################################
    FUNCTION is_online()
    ########################################

13➤ WHENEVER ERROR CONTINUE
      CLOSE DATABASE
    WHENEVER ERROR STOP

14➤   IF sqlca.sqlcode <> 0 AND sqlca.sqlcode <> -349 THEN
        ERROR "Error ",sqlca.sqlcode," closing current database."
        RETURN (FALSE)
      END IF          -- either 0 or -349 is OK here
```

15➤ This (second) DATABASE statement allows the program to check the values in the SQLCA record. By placing this DATABASE statement within the code (instead of before the MAIN program block at the top of the module), the function can check the values of SQLCA immediately after the statement is executed. The program cannot check for these values after a DATABASE statement located at the top of the file, because **4GL** statements (like IF) can only appear within a program block.

16➤ The SQLCA record contains a field named SQLAWARN. SQLAWARN is an eight-character string in which the individual characters signal various warning conditions. In this example, the second and fourth characters are of interest:

- SQLCA.SQLAWARN[2] is set to "W" if the database just opened uses transactions. It is set to blank (" ") otherwise.
- SQLCA.SQLAWARN[4] is set to "W" if the database just opened is an **OnLine** database. It is set to blank (" ") otherwise.

The value of the g_txflag indicates whether the current database uses transactions. This flag is used throughout the program to determine whether or not to execute the BEGIN WORK, COMMIT WORK, and ROLLBACK WORK statements. If a database uses transactions, these statements are required to delimit transactions. However, if the database does not use transactions, then executing these transaction statements generates a runtime error.

17➤ If SQLCA.SQLAWARN[4] is not "W", then the current database is *not* an **OnLine** database. The function uses the ga_dsplymsg array with the message_window() function to notify the user that this example cannot continue and then returns a value of FALSE.

18➤ If execution reaches this point, the current database is an **OnLine** version of the stores2t database. Because the catalog table exists, the example can continue.

The load_arrays() Function

19➤ The c_cat cursor selects the rows of the catalog table. It does a three-way join between the catalog, manufact, and stock tables to obtain the data for the f_catalog form. This SELECT also selects the ROWID for each row of the catalog table. For more information about ROWID, see Example 10.

20➤ As it is loading the arrays, the program displays a window with a message telling the user to expect a pause in execution. This message lets the user know that this pause is not a slow response time.

```
15➤  DATABASE stores2t

16➤  LET g_txflag = FALSE
     IF SQLCA.SQLAWARN[2] = "W" THEN -- get use of transaction
       LET g_txflag = TRUE
     END IF

17➤  IF SQLCA.SQLAWARN[4] <> "W" THEN
       LET ga_dsplymsg[1] = "This database is not an INFORMIX OnLine"
       LET ga_dsplymsg[2] = " database. You cannot run this example because"
       LET ga_dsplymsg[3] = " it accesses a table containing data types"
       LET ga_dsplymsg[4] = " specific to OnLine (VARCHAR, TEXT, BYTE)."
       CALL message_window(4,4)
       CLEAR SCREEN
       RETURN (FALSE)
     END IF

18➤  RETURN (TRUE)

   END FUNCTION -- is_online --

   ########################################
   FUNCTION load_arrays()
   ########################################
     DEFINE        idx    SMALLINT

19➤  DECLARE c_cat CURSOR FOR
       SELECT catalog.catalog_num, catalog.stock_num,
              manufact.manu_name, stock.description,
              catalog.cat_advert, catalog.ROWID
       FROM catalog,manufact,stock
       WHERE catalog.stock_num = stock.stock_num
         AND catalog.manu_code = manufact.manu_code
         AND stock.manu_code = manufact.manu_code
       ORDER BY 1

20➤  OPEN WINDOW w_msg AT 5,5
       WITH 4 ROWS, 60 COLUMNS
       ATTRIBUTE (BORDER)

     DISPLAY "ACCESSING OnLine DATA TYPES"
       AT 1, 20
     DISPLAY "Loading catalog data into arrays, please wait..."
       AT 3, 2

     LET idx = 1 { invariant: idx-1 rows have been loaded }
```

21➤ The FOREACH opens the c_cat cursor and fetches the data into the associated program variables:

- The ga_catrows array stores information to display on the f_catalog form (catalog number, stock number, manufacturer name, and stock description).
- The ga_catadv array stores the VARCHAR catalog advertising column (cat_advert).
- The ga_catrids array stores the catalog row's ROWID.

The information for a single row of the cursor is stored in each array at the same index location.

22➤ The FOREACH statement loads into global arrays all catalog data except the TEXT value. This value is not loaded now because it would take too much memory and because it is not displayed on the f_catalog form. However, it is useful to tell the user if the current row has values for the TEXT and BYTE columns. The f_catalog form displays an "N" (NO) or "Y" (YES) in two fields: one for the TEXT value and one for the BYTE value.

To set the has_desc field, the function initializes the has_desc array flag for the current row to "N" and then selects a literal value of "Y" over it only if the value of the cat_descr column is not null. Using the row's ROWID for the search makes this access very efficient. The function follows the same procedure to set the has_pic field.

Notice that the user cannot access the BYTE value from this example.

23➤ The idx variable is the index into each global array. It counts the number of elements in these arrays and consequently the number of rows selected. This variable is incremented after the arrays are filled so that the next row fetched can be stored at the next location of the arrays.

Because the global arrays are limited to 200 elements (the value of g_arraysz), the program must check that room is available for the next catalog row. If no room exists, the program exits the FOREACH loop and fetches no more rows.

24➤ Since idx is incremented after the arrays are filled (to prepare for the next iteration of the FOREACH), it contains one more than the actual number of rows loaded when the FOREACH loop exits. The LET statement decrements idx by one to obtain the correct number of rows selected.

25➤ Once the arrays are loaded, the function closes the message window and returns the number of elements in these arrays.

```
21➤  FOREACH c_cat INTO ga_catrows[idx].catalog_num,
                         ga_catrows[idx].stock_num,
                         ga_catrows[idx].manu_name,
                         ga_catrows[idx].description,
                         ga_catadv[idx],
                         ga_catrids[idx]

22➤    LET ga_catrows[idx].has_desc = "N"
       SELECT "Y"
       INTO ga_catrows[idx].has_desc
       FROM catalog
       WHERE rowid = ga_catrids[idx]
         AND cat_descr IS NOT NULL

       LET ga_catrows[idx].has_pic = "N"
       SELECT "Y"
       INTO ga_catrows[idx].has_pic
       FROM catalog
       WHERE ROWID = ga_catrids[idx]
         AND cat_picture IS NOT NULL

23➤    LET idx = idx + 1
       IF idx > g_arraysz THEN -- make sure we don't run overfill arrays
         EXIT FOREACH
       END IF
     END FOREACH

24➤  LET idx = idx - 1 -- actual number of rows loaded

25➤  CLOSE WINDOW w_msg

     RETURN (idx)

   END FUNCTION -- load_arrays --
```

The open_wins() Function

26➤ The open_wins() function opens a window for each form used in this example:

- The f_catadv form appears in the w_advert window.
- The f_catdescr form appears in the w_descr window.
- The f_catalog form appears in the w_cat window.

Windows are opened in the reverse order of their use so that the first window to be used appears "on top" of all others, thereby hiding the others from view until they are needed.

The close_wins() Function

27➤ The close_wins() function closes each of the windows used in the example.

The dsply_cat() Function

28➤ The CURRENT WINDOW statement ensures that the w_cat window is the current window before displaying the f_catalog form. For a more complete example of using the CURRENT WINDOW statement, see Example 26.

29➤ The built-in function SET_COUNT() initializes the built-in function ARR_-COUNT() with the number of catalog rows that have been selected.

30➤ The DISPLAY ARRAY statement displays the first five items of the ga_catrows program array in the sa_cat screen array. DISPLAY ARRAY must be preceded by a call to SET_COUNT() to know how many rows to display.

An ON KEY clause allows the user to press CONTROL-E to exit the DISPLAY ARRAY (and the f_catalog form). The Cancel key also will exit the array.

```
########################################
FUNCTION open_wins()
########################################

26➤  OPEN WINDOW w_advert AT 6, 6
       WITH 11 ROWS, 68 COLUMNS
       ATTRIBUTE(BORDER, COMMENT LINE LAST)

     OPEN WINDOW w_descr AT 4, 4
       WITH 13 ROWS, 72 COLUMNS
       ATTRIBUTE(BORDER, COMMENT LINE LAST)

     OPEN WINDOW w_cat AT 2, 2
       WITH 20 ROWS, 77 COLUMNS

END FUNCTION -- open_wins --

########################################
FUNCTION close_wins()
########################################

27➤  CLOSE WINDOW w_advert
     CLOSE WINDOW w_descr
     CLOSE WINDOW w_cat

END FUNCTION -- close_wins --

########################################
FUNCTION dsply_cat(cat_cnt)
########################################
     DEFINE        cat_cnt    SMALLINT

28➤  CURRENT WINDOW IS w_cat

     DISPLAY FORM f_catalog

29➤  CALL SET_COUNT(cat_cnt)
     LET int_flag = FALSE
     DISPLAY ARRAY ga_catrows TO sa_cat.*
30➤    ON KEY (CONTROL-E)
         EXIT DISPLAY
```

31➤ This ON KEY clause defines a special feature for the CONTROL-V or F4 key sequences. The user can press either key to view the VARCHAR advertising copy for the current catalog row.

The show_advert() function implements this feature. The function accepts as an argument the index position of the cursor (returned by the ARR_CURR() function) so it can tell which catalog item is the current row. Before show_advert() begins execution, **4GL** evaluates ARR_CURR() and passes its result as the argument to show_advert().

32➤ This ON KEY clause defines a special feature for the CONTROL-T or F5 key sequences. The user can press either key to view the TEXT catalog item description for the current catalog row.

The show_descr() function implements this feature. Like the show_advert() function, this function accepts as an argument the current cursor position.

33➤ Once the user has exited the screen array, the FREE statement releases the space used to store the TEXT value.

The show_advert() Function

34➤ The CURRENT WINDOW statement ensures that the w_advert window is the current window before the f_catadv form is displayed. For a more complete example of using the CURRENT WINDOW statement, see Example 26.

35➤ The DISPLAY statement initializes the f_catadv form with the catalog information for the current catalog row.

36➤ The LET statement assigns the VARCHAR value stored in the ga_catadv array to a local variable. It uses the current cursor position as an index into the array.

37➤ The exit_fld and upd_fld variables initialize the screen fields xn and xu, respectively, to an underscore character ("_"). These fields are not used to accept user input but rather to receive the user's exit command. If the user presses CONTROL-E from the exit_fld, execution leaves the f_catadv form without saving the contents of advert (the current catalog item's advertising copy). If the user presses CONTROL-E from the upd_fld field, execution saves the current advert value in the catalog table and then leaves f_catadv.

38➤ The upd_advert flag is tested after the INPUT statement to see whether or not to perform the update of the cat_advert column. It is initialized here to FALSE and set to TRUE in the BEFORE FIELD section for the xu field (see Note 40).

```
31➤      ON KEY (CONTROL-V,F4)
           CALL show_advert(ARR_CURR())

32➤      ON KEY (CONTROL-T,F5)
           CALL show_descr(ARR_CURR())

       END DISPLAY

33➤    FREE g_txtblob       -- free temp file

     END FUNCTION -- dsply_cat --


     ########################################
     FUNCTION show_advert(rownum)
     ########################################
       DEFINE          rownum          INTEGER,

                       upd_advert      SMALLINT,
                       advert          LIKE catalog.cat_advert,
                       exit_fld        CHAR(2),
                       upd_fld         CHAR(2)

34➤    CURRENT WINDOW IS w_advert

       DISPLAY FORM f_catadv
35➤    DISPLAY ga_catrows[rownum].catalog_num, ga_catrows[rownum].description,
               ga_catrows[rownum].manu_name
         TO catalog_num, description, manu_name

36➤    LET advert = ga_catadv[rownum]
37➤    LET exit_fld = "__"
       LET upd_fld = "__"
38➤    LET upd_advert = FALSE

       LET int_flag = FALSE
```

39➤ The INPUT statement displays the initialized input fields and accepts user input from the cat_advert field. The input fields are initialized with the values of the variables advert, exit_fld, and upd_fld respectively because this INPUT statement contains a WITHOUT DEFAULTS clause.

40➤ These BEFORE FIELD sections set the value of the update flag upd_advert. This flag is only set to TRUE when the cursor reaches the xu field. If the user presses CONTROL-E from this field, the catalog row will be updated. If the user presses CONTROL-E from either the cat_advert or the xn fields, upd_advert is set to FALSE.

41➤ The AFTER FIELD section performs a wraparound function. If the user presses RETURN, the cursor loops back to the cat_advert field.

42➤ The ON KEY clause defines a special feature for the CONTROL-E or ESC key sequences. The user can press either key to exit the f_catadv form.

43➤ If the user has exited the INPUT from the xu field, upd_advert is TRUE and the function updates the cat_advert column of the catalog table.

44➤ The setting of the g_txflag variable determines whether or not to execute the BEGIN WORK statement. If the database uses transactions (stores2t does), then BEGIN WORK marks the beginning of a new transaction. If the database doesn't use transactions, the program skips over the BEGIN WORK to avoid generating a runtime error. In such a database, each SQL statement is a singleton transaction. For a description of how g_txflag is set, see Note 16.

45➤ The UPDATE statement updates the cat_advert column of the current catalog row. The WHENEVER ERROR CONTINUE statement prevents the function from terminating if the UPDATE generates an error. The function does its own error checking by testing the value of the global status variable.

46➤ If the status is negative, the UPDATE has failed and the function calls the upd_err() function to notify the user of the cause.

47➤ If the status is zero (0), the UPDATE is successful. The setting of the g_txflag variable determines whether or not to execute the COMMIT WORK statement. If the database uses transactions (stores2t does), then COMMIT WORK saves the database changes and ends the current transaction. If the database does not use transactions, the program skips over the COMMIT WORK to avoid generating a runtime error. For a description of how g_txflag is set, see Note 16.

```
39➤  INPUT advert, exit_fld, upd_fld
       WITHOUT DEFAULTS FROM cat_advert, xn, xu

40➤    BEFORE FIELD cat_advert
         LET upd_advert = FALSE

       BEFORE FIELD xn
         LET upd_advert = FALSE

       BEFORE FIELD xu
         LET upd_advert = TRUE

41➤    AFTER FIELD xu
         NEXT FIELD cat_advert

42➤    ON KEY(CONTROL-E, ESC)
         EXIT INPUT

     END INPUT

43➤  IF upd_advert THEN -- user wants to update field
44➤    IF g_txflag THEN
         BEGIN WORK
       END IF

45➤ WHENEVER ERROR CONTINUE
       UPDATE catalog SET cat_advert = advert
       WHERE rowid = ga_catrids[rownum]
    WHENEVER ERROR STOP

46➤    IF (status < 0) THEN
         CALL upd_err()
       ELSE
47➤      IF g_txflag THEN
           COMMIT WORK
         END IF
```

48➤ If the advert field has been updated, then the value in the global VARCHAR array needs to be updated. This LET statement assigns the new advert value to the appropriate element of the ga_catadv array.

49➤ When this function is done, the w_advert window no longer needs to be current. This CURRENT WINDOW makes the window containing the f_catalog form the current window.

The show_descr() Function

50➤ The show_descr() function is almost identical to the show_advert() function. While show_advert() displays the current row's VARCHAR value on the f_catadv form, show_descr() displays the current row's TEXT value on the f_catdescr form. Only steps that differ significantly from the behavior of show_advert() are described here. Refer to the description of show_advert() if you have questions about unmarked sections of this function.

51➤ The SELECT statement selects the current catalog item's description from the catalog table. This TEXT value is stored in the temporary file pointed to by the g_txtblob variable. This variable must be initialized with the location where to store the TEXT value before it can store the TEXT value (see Note 8).

To optimize the access of the TEXT column, the SELECT uses the row's ROWID. The ROWID for each catalog row has been stored in the ga_catrids array. When show_descr() was called, the program passed in the result of the ARR_CURR() function. This value is the index into the ga_catrids array where the current rows' ROWID is stored.

52➤ The upd_descr flag is tested after the INPUT statement to determine whether to perform the update of the cat_descr column. It is initialized here to FALSE and set to TRUE in the BEFORE FIELD xu program block (see Note 53).

53➤ The INPUT statement displays the initialized input fields and accepts user input from the cat_descr field. The input fields xn and xu are initialized with the values of the variables exit_fld, and upd_fld respectively. The cat_descr field is initialized with the value pointed to by the g_txtblob variable.

Notice that to edit the value in the cat_descr field, the user must escape to a system editor with the exclamation symbol ("!"). The editor brings up the value pointed to by the g_txtblob variable and, if the user saves changes, writes the new value to the location indicated by g_txtblob.

```
48➤        LET ga_catadv[rownum] = advert
         END IF
       END IF

49➤    CURRENT WINDOW IS w_cat

     END FUNCTION -- show_advert --

     ########################################
50➤  FUNCTION show_descr(rownum)
     ########################################
       DEFINE        rownum          INTEGER,

                     upd_descr       SMALLINT,
                     exit_fld        CHAR(2),
                     upd_fld         CHAR(2)

       CURRENT WINDOW IS w_descr

       DISPLAY FORM f_catdescr
       DISPLAY ga_catrows[rownum].catalog_num, ga_catrows[rownum].description,
               ga_catrows[rownum].manu_name
         TO  catalog_num, description, manu_name

51➤    SELECT cat_descr
       INTO g_txtblob
       FROM catalog
       WHERE ROWID = ga_catrids[rownum]

       LET exit_fld = "__"
       LET upd_fld = "__"
52➤    LET upd_descr = FALSE

       LET int_flag = FALSE
53➤    INPUT g_txtblob, exit_fld, upd_fld WITHOUT DEFAULTS FROM cat_descr, xn, xu
         BEFORE FIELD xn
           LET upd_descr = FALSE

         BEFORE FIELD xu
           LET upd_descr = TRUE

         AFTER FIELD xu
           NEXT FIELD cat_descr

         ON KEY(ESC,CONTROL-E)
           EXIT INPUT
       END INPUT

       IF upd_descr THEN -- user wants to update field
         IF g_txflag THEN
           BEGIN WORK
         END IF
```

54➤ The UPDATE statement updates the cat_descr column of the current catalog row. The WHENEVER ERROR CONTINUE statement prevents the function from terminating if the UPDATE generates an error. The function does its own error checking by testing the value of the global status variable.

The upd_err() Function

55➤ The scode variable stores the status of the most recently executed SQL statement. By containing the value of SQLCA. SQLCODE instead of the status variable, this variable is guaranteed to reflect the status of the most recently executed SQL statement. The status variable contains the value of the most recently executed **4GL** statement. The icode variable stores the current **ISAM** error code. **4GL** stores the **ISAM** error code in SQLCA.SQLERRD[2] after an SQL statement.

56➤ The g_txflag variable determines whether or not to execute the ROLLBACK WORK statement. If the database uses transactions (stores2t does), then ROLLBACK WORK cancels the changes made to the database by the current transaction and ends the current transaction. If the database doesn't use transactions, the program skips over the ROLLBACK WORK and avoids generating a runtime error. In such a database, each SQL statement is a singleton transaction. For a description of how g_txflag is set, see Note 16.

57➤ The function notifies the user of the failed database operation with the ga_dsplymsg array and the message_window() function. This message includes both the SQLCA.SQLCODE code and the **ISAM** error code.

```
54➤ WHENEVER ERROR CONTINUE
        UPDATE catalog SET cat_descr = g_txtblob
        WHERE ROWID = ga_catrids[rownum]
    WHENEVER ERROR STOP

        IF (status < 0) THEN
          CALL upd_err()
        ELSE
          IF g_txflag THEN
            COMMIT WORK
          END IF
        END IF
      END IF

      CURRENT WINDOW IS w_cat

    END FUNCTION -- show_descr --

    ########################################
    FUNCTION upd_err()
    ########################################
      DEFINE scode, icode      INTEGER

55➤   LET scode = SQLCA.SQLCODE
      LET icode = SQLCA.SQLERRD[2] -- isam error code
56➤   IF g_txflag THEN
        ROLLBACK WORK
      END IF

57➤   LET ga_dsplymsg[1] = "Update failed, sql code=",scode,", isam code=",icode
      LET ga_dsplymsg[2] = "Database not changed."
      CALL message_window(2,2)

    END FUNCTION -- upd_err --
```

To locate any function definition see the Function Index on page 728.

19

Browsing with a Scroll Cursor

This example demonstrates how to use a scroll cursor to browse through a selection of rows. The response time of the application is minimized by "reading ahead"; that is, by fetching the next row after displaying the current row, while the user is busy viewing the current data.

```
View Customers:   Query  First  Next  Last  Exit
Display next customer in selected set
--------------------------------------------Press CTRL-W for Help----------

  Customer Number: [        101] Company Name: [All Sports Supplies ]
   Address: [213 Erstwild Court  ]
            [                    ]
      City: [Sunnyvale      ]   State: [CA]  Zip Code: [94086         ]

   Contact Name: [Ludwig         ][Pauli          ]
      Telephone: [408-789-8075      ]
```

The Main Function

The main program contains a two-step loop. In the first step, the user is asked to enter selection criteria in a query-by-example form. (This step is the same as that in Example 6.) If the user interrupts this step, the program ends.

In the second step, the user's criteria are assembled into a SELECT statement which is associated with a scroll cursor. The cursor is opened and the browsing function is called. It returns a Boolean flag to indicate whether the user selected the Exit menu choice; if so, the program ends.

The Browsing Function

The purpose of the browsing function is to display a menu across the top of the familiar "customer" form and to execute the choices in that menu. The following choices appear on the menu:

Query	Stop browsing and return to the query-by-example phase to specify new selection criteria.
Exit	Stop browsing and end the program.
First	Display the first row in the selected set.
Next	Display the next row in the set.
Prior	Display the prior row in the set.
Last	Display the last row in the set.

A Simple Approach to Scrolling

The simplest way to implement the scrolling choices would be to translate each into the corresponding FETCH statement. The code would read like the following:

```
COMMAND "First"
    FETCH FIRST cust_row INTO curr_cust.*
    DISPLAY BY NAME curr_cust.*
COMMAND "Next"
    FETCH NEXT cust_row INTO curr_cust.*
    IF SQLCA.SQLCODE = 0 THEN
        DISPLAY BY NAME curr_cust.*
    ELSE
        ERROR "There are no further rows in the selected set."
    END IF
COMMAND "Prior"
    FETCH PRIOR cust_row INTO curr_cust.*
    IF SQLCA.SQLCODE = 0 THEN
        DISPLAY BY NAME curr_cust.*
    ELSE
       ERROR "There are no preceding rows in the selected set."
    END IF
COMMAND "Last"
    FETCH LAST cust_row INTO curr_cust
    DISPLAY BY NAME curr_cust.*
```

This approach works well and takes good advantage of the features of a scroll cursor. (An ordinary cursor supports only FETCH NEXT operations.) However, it has at least two drawbacks:

- It does not warn the user when the end of the list is reached. The user only discovers it by asking for a next or prior record and receiving an error message. This presents a minor usability problem.
- The desired row is fetched at the point the user asks for it. If the fetch takes more than half a second to execute, the user will perceive a delay between choosing the menu option and seeing the display. Some users may experience the delay as dead time.

Fetching Ahead

This example demonstrates methods for resolving each of these potential problems. Both objections can be met if the program can stay one row ahead of the user. When the user chooses Next or Prior, a row that was previously fetched is displayed. While the user is looking at the current row, a FETCH is executed to retrieve the next row in the same direction. In most instances it will complete before the user is ready to enter another menu choice.

Manipulating the Menu

The first objection (that the user is not warned of the end of the list) is handled by hiding all but the usable menu options. The following cases occur:

- When the selection produces no rows at all, only Query and Exit menu options are displayed.
- When no next row exists, the Next option is hidden.
- When no prior row exists, the Prior option is hidden.

In addition to hiding irrelevant options, the default menu option is manipulated to anticipate the user's likely next action:

- When the selection produces no rows or only a single row, Query is the default option. When multiple rows are retrieved, Next is the default.
- When the user reaches the end of the set going forward, First is made the default option. A user can press RETURN and cycle through the list.
- When the user reaches the first record by going backward, Last is made the default option.

Error Handling

This program contains no WHENEVER statement; it does not trap errors. If an SQL statement produces a negative return code the program terminates with a message. In this program, no error conditions are expected. The only likely error is one showing that a row is locked by another user. The simplest way to minimize the risk of a locking conflict is to execute SET LOCK MODE TO WAIT early in the program. You could insert the statement just after the DEFER INTERRUPT in the MAIN section. (An alternative method of handling locked rows is demonstrated in Example 23.)

Function Overview

Function Name	Purpose
scroller_1()	Runs the browsing menu, fetching rows on request
query_cust2()	Lets the user create a query by example. *See description in Example 6.*
clear_lines()	Clears any number of lines starting at any line. *See description in Example 6.*
init_msgs()	Initializes the members of the ga_dsplymsg array to null. *See description in Example 2.*
prompt_window()	Displays a message and prompts the user for affirmation or negation. This function is a variation on the message_window() function that appears in Example 2. *See description in Example 4.*
message_window()	Opens a window and displays the contents of the ga_dsplymsg global array. *See description in Example 2.*
msg()	Displays a brief, informative message. *See description in Example 5.*

The DATABASE and GLOBALS Statements

1➤ This example works with any version of the example database.

2➤ The ga_dsplymsg array is used as input to the message_window() function, as discussed in Example 2.

The MAIN Function

3➤ The more variable controls the main loop. As long as it is TRUE, more work remains.

4➤ The DEFER INTERRUPT statement prevents the Interrupt key from terminating the program. Instead, it sets the global variable int_flag (as discussed in Example 5). It is tested following a CONSTRUCT to see if the user cancelled the statement. Also, the Interrupt key is associated with the Exit option of the browsing menu.

The program would still work if this statement were removed, but pressing Interrupt would terminate the program immediately.

5➤ These OPTIONS are used with the f_customer form, as described in Example 6.

6➤ The query_cust2() function, introduced in Example 6, executes a CONSTRUCT statement using the f_customer form and returns a character string that holds a SELECT statement. If the user cancels the CONSTRUCT, the function returns a null string, which is a signal to end the program.

7➤ The SELECT statement is prepared, associated with a scroll cursor, and opened. Since no WHENEVER statement has been executed, any error in these three statements will terminate the program. An error could only occur on the PREPARE if the SELECT statement were syntactically invalid. An error on a DECLARE at this stage of a program is almost impossible.

An error might occur on the OPEN because the table or a column could not be found; that would usually indicate that the wrong database had been selected or the database schema had been changed. The OPEN would also fail if the table was locked by another user.

4GL source file

```
1➤ DATABASE stores2t

   GLOBALS
2➤     DEFINE ga_dsplymsgs      ARRAY[5] OF CHAR(48)
   END GLOBALS

   ########################################
   MAIN
   ########################################
     DEFINE stmt CHAR(150),    -- select statement from CONSTRUCT
3➤          more SMALLINT      -- continue flag

4➤   DEFER INTERRUPT

5➤   OPTIONS
       HELP FILE "hlpmsgs",
       FORM LINE 5,
       COMMENT LINE 3,
       MESSAGE LINE 19

     OPEN FORM f_customer FROM "f_customer"
     DISPLAY FORM f_customer

     LET more = TRUE
     WHILE more

6➤     CALL query_cust2() RETURNING stmt
       IF stmt IS NOT NULL THEN
7➤         PREPARE prep_stmt FROM stmt
           DECLARE cust_row SCROLL CURSOR FOR prep_stmt
           OPEN cust_row
           LET more = scroller_1()-- Query returns TRUE, Exit returns FALSE
           CLOSE cust_row
       ELSE  -- query was cancelled
           LET more = FALSE
       END IF

     END WHILE

     CLOSE FORM f_customer
     CLEAR SCREEN
   END MAIN
```

The scroller_1() Function

8➤ The scroller_1() function controls the order in which rows are fetched and displayed to the user. It is called by the MAIN function and returns only when the user chooses the Exit or Query menu options.

9➤ Three records will contain cached rows that can be shown to the user. In general, moving forward in the selection set involves:

- copying curr_cust into prior_cust
- copying next_cust into curr_cust
- displaying curr_cust
- fetching the following record into next_cust

Moving backward in the selection set is the same process with the roles of next_cust and prior_cust reversed. This simple picture is complicated by two considerations:

- A following record may not exist in the current direction. This end-of-list condition requires special handling.
- The position of the cursor, relative to the three row records, depends on which menu choice was used most recently. When the Next option is selected, the cursor is used to fetch the row in next_cust. When the Prior is selected, the cursor is used to fetch the row in prior_cust. This introduces complications when the user reverses the direction of travel (for example, selects Next and then Prior, or Prior and then Next).

10➤ fetch_dir contains a flag showing the direction in which the user is displaying records, that is, which menu option was executed most recently (Next or Prior). Its value reveals the relationship between the cursor and the three cached rows, as discussed in the preceding note.

11➤ 4GL currently does not support a means of declaring constant values with names, so read-only flag values like these must be defined as variables and assigned.

12➤ The MENU statement begins here and extends through the END MENU statement on page 461.

13➤ The BEFORE MENU block is executed before the menu options are displayed on the screen. It determines whether the selected set of rows contains zero, one, or many rows and sets the menu options accordingly.

14➤ If NOTFOUND is signalled on the very first FETCH, the menu is reduced to two options: Exit and Query; Query is the default option.

```
8➤ ########################################
   FUNCTION scroller_1()
   ########################################
9➤   DEFINE        curr_cust,    -- the row now being displayed
                   next_cust,    -- the row to display when Next is chosen
                   prior_cust    -- the row to display when Prior is chosen
                           RECORD LIKE customer.*,
                   retval,                 -- value to RETURN from function
10➤                fetch_dir,              -- flag showing direction of travel in list
                   toward_last             -- flag values: going Next-wise,
                   toward_first,           -- ...going Prior-wise, or at
                   at_end     SMALLINT     -- ...(either) end of the list

11➤    LET toward_last = +1
       LET toward_first = -1
       LET at_end = 0

       DISPLAY
     "--------------------------------------------Press CTRL-W for Help----------"
         AT 3, 1
12➤    MENU "View Customers"

13➤        BEFORE MENU -- Set up as for First, but with chance of zero rows
               FETCH FIRST cust_row INTO curr_cust.*
               IF SQLCA.SQLCODE = NOTFOUND THEN
14➤                ERROR "There are no rows that satisfy this query."
                   HIDE OPTION ALL
                   SHOW OPTION "Query"
                   SHOW OPTION "Exit"
                   NEXT OPTION "Query"
```

15➤ The ELSE portion of the IF statement is executed when the fetch returns one row. It is displayed to the user immediately. Since it is the first row, no prior record exists, and the Prior menu option is hidden. While the user views this row, the next row is fetched.

16➤ If the fetch is successful, the second row is read into next_cust and the Next menu option (which will be visible since it has not been hidden) is made the default choice.

17➤ The ELSE is executed only when the query returns a single row. The Next option is hidden (only Query, Exit, First and Last remain visible) and Query is made the default.

18➤ The KEY keyword associates the Escape key with the Query option. Users should be told about such hidden accelerator keys in the program documentation.

19➤ The First and Last choices perform a FETCH while the user waits. In certain rare cases the first or last row may be sitting in the prior_cust or the curr_cust record. The program could be modified to detect these cases and avoid this FETCH operation, but the extra code does not seem to be justified.

20➤ The IF statement checks for a situation very similar to that present in the BEFORE MENU section (see Notes 16 and 17). The difference is that, before the menu was displayed, the choice "Next" was sure to be visible. In this instance, the previous operation might have been Last (which hides the Next choice) so the SHOW OPTION statement is used to make certain that "Next" will be visible.

21➤ The Next option is visible only when a next record exists (it is stored in the next_cust record). The rows are shuffled around in the cache and the new current row is displayed.

22➤ The CASE statement uses the value of fetch_dir to fetch the row that the user will probably want to see next.

23➤ The previous operation used the cursor to fetch the row that is now in curr_cust, so fetching the following row requires only FETCH NEXT.

24➤ The previous operation used the cursor to fetch the row that is now in prior_cust. (It tried to fetch a row prior to that one, but there was none.) The row now in curr_cust is relative +1 to that; the one needed in next_cust is relative +2.

25➤ The previous operation used the cursor to fetch the row that was in prior_cust and has since been discarded. The row now in prior_cust was relative +1 to that; the one needed in next_cust is +3.

```
        ELSE -- found at least one row
15➤         DISPLAY BY NAME curr_cust.*
            HIDE OPTION "Prior"
            LET fetch_dir = toward_last
            FETCH NEXT cust_row INTO next_cust.*
            IF SQLCA.SQLCODE = 0 THEN       -- at least 2 rows
16➤             NEXT OPTION "Next"
            ELSE                            -- only 1 row in set
17➤             HIDE OPTION "Next"
                NEXT OPTION "Query"
            END IF
        END IF

18➤ COMMAND KEY(ESC,Q) "Query"
            "Query for a different set of customers" HELP 130
        LET retval = TRUE
        EXIT MENU

    COMMAND "First" "Display first customer in selected set"
            HELP 133
19➤     FETCH FIRST cust_row INTO curr_cust.* -- this cannot return 100
        DISPLAY BY NAME curr_cust.* -- give user something to look at
        HIDE OPTION "Prior"         -- can't back up from #1
        LET fetch_dir = toward_last
        FETCH NEXT cust_row INTO next_cust.*
20➤     IF SQLCA.SQLCODE = 0 THEN   -- at least 2 rows
            SHOW OPTION "Next"      -- it might be hidden
            NEXT OPTION "Next"
        ELSE                    -- only 1 row in set
            HIDE OPTION "Next"
            NEXT OPTION "Query"
        END IF

    COMMAND "Next" "Display next customer in selected set"
            HELP 134
21➤     LET prior_cust.* = curr_cust.*
        SHOW OPTION "Prior"
        LET curr_cust.* = next_cust.*
        DISPLAY BY NAME curr_cust.*
22➤     CASE (fetch_dir)
          WHEN toward_last
23➤         FETCH NEXT cust_row INTO next_cust.*
          WHEN at_end
24➤         FETCH RELATIVE +2 cust_row INTO next_cust.*
            LET fetch_dir = toward_last
          WHEN toward_first
25➤         FETCH RELATIVE +3 cust_row INTO next_cust.*
            LET fetch_dir = toward_last
        END CASE
```

26➤ No row exists after curr_cust. The Next option is hidden and First is made the default.

27➤ The logic of the Prior option is just like the logic of the Next option, with the roles of the cache records and the relative fetch offsets reversed.

28➤ The logic of Last is just like the logic of First, but with the roles of the cache records reversed and with PRIOR replacing NEXT in both the FETCH and HIDE OPTION statements.

29➤ The Interrupt signal is associated with the Exit menu choice. As a result, if the user interrupts the display function, the program will terminate quietly.

```
          IF SQLCA.SQLCODE = NOTFOUND THEN
              LET fetch_dir = at_end
26➤           HIDE OPTION "Next"
              NEXT OPTION "First"
          END IF

      COMMAND "Prior" "Display previous customer in selected set"
              HELP 135
27➤       LET next_cust.* = curr_cust.*
          SHOW OPTION "Next"
          LET curr_cust.* = prior_cust.*
          DISPLAY BY NAME curr_cust.*
          CASE (fetch_dir)
            WHEN toward_first
              FETCH PRIOR cust_row INTO prior_cust.*
            WHEN at_end
              FETCH RELATIVE -2 cust_row INTO prior_cust.*
              LET fetch_dir = toward_first
            WHEN toward_last
              FETCH RELATIVE -3 cust_row INTO prior_cust.*
              LET fetch_dir = toward_first
          END CASE
          IF SQLCA.SQLCODE = NOTFOUND THEN
              LET fetch_dir = at_end
              HIDE OPTION "Prior"
              NEXT OPTION "Last"
          END IF

      COMMAND "Last" "Display final customer in selected set"
              HELP 136
28➤       FETCH LAST cust_row INTO curr_cust.* -- this cannot return 100
          DISPLAY BY NAME curr_cust.* -- give user something to look at
          HIDE OPTION "Next"-- can't go onward from here
          LET fetch_dir = toward_first
          FETCH PRIOR cust_row INTO prior_cust.*
          IF SQLCA.SQLCODE = 0 THEN-- at least 2 rows
              SHOW OPTION "Prior" -- it might be hidden
              NEXT OPTION "Prior"
          ELSE                -- only 1 row in set
              HIDE OPTION "Prior"
              NEXT OPTION "Query"
          END IF

29➤   COMMAND KEY(INTERRUPT,"E", "X") "Exit" "Exit program." HELP 100
          LET retval = FALSE
          EXIT MENU
    END MENU
    RETURN retval

END FUNCTION - scroller_1 -
```

To locate any function definition see the Function Index on page 728.

20

1. *Writing a Simple 4GL Program*
2. *Displaying a Message Window*
3. *Populating a Ring Menu with Options*
4. *Displaying a Row on a Form*
5. *Programming a Query by Example*
6. *Querying and Updating*
7. *Validating and Inserting a Row*
8. *Displaying a Screen Array in a Pop-Up Window*
9. *Accessing a Table with a Single Row Form*
10. *Accessing a Table with a Multi-Row Form*
11. *Implementing a Master/Detail Relationship*
12. *Displaying an Unknown Number of Rows*
13. *Calling a C Function*
14. *Generating a Report*
15. *Reporting Group Totals*
16. *Creating Vertical Menus*
17. *Using the DATETIME Data Type*
18. *Using OnLine Data Types*
19. *Browsing with a Scroll Cursor*
20. *Combining Criteria from Successive Queries*
21. *Using an Update Cursor*
22. *Determining Database Features*
23. *Handling Locked Rows*
24. *Using a Hold Cursor*
25. *Logging Application Errors*
26. *Managing Multiple Windows*
27. *Displaying Menu Options Dynamically*
28. *Writing Recursive Functions*
29. *Generating Mailing Labels*
30. *Generating a Schema Listing*

Combining Criteria from Successive Queries

This example builds on Example 19. It gives its user the new ability to revise a query, adding constraints to exclude rows from the selected set. This is done by performing a subsequent CONSTRUCT and combining the new conditions with those produced in prior CONSTRUCT operations.

```
View Customers:   Query  Revise  Show-cond  First  Next  Last  Exit
Display the current query conditions.
------------------------------------------Press CTRL-W for Help----------
            CUSTOMER QUERY-BY-EXAMPLE: Additional Conditions

  Customer Number: [           ] Company Name: [                   ]
   Address: [                    ]
            [                    ]
      City: [Sunnyvale      ]   State: [  ]  Zip Code: [              ]

   Contact Name: [               ][               ]
      Telephone: [                  ]


 Enter additional criteria and press Accept. Press CTRL-W for Help.
 Press Cancel to exit w/out changing query.
```

The Main Function

The main program contains a two-step loop. In the first step, the user is asked to enter selection criteria in a query-by-example form. The code is similar to that of Example 6 and 19, but it differs in that it does not assemble a complete

SELECT statement. Instead, it returns only the conditional expression output from the CONSTRUCT. If the user cancels the CONSTRUCT, a null string is returned and the main loop takes this as a signal to end the program.

In the second step, the conditional expression is passed to a browsing function. The function prepares a SELECT statement, associates it with a cursor, and opens it. A browsing menu like the one in Example 19 is displayed. However, the menu includes a Revise option and a Show_cond option.

If the user selects Revise, the program allows entry of additional selection criteria. These new criteria are added to the previous conditional expression, a new SELECT is prepared and opened, and browsing resumes.

The main program ends when the browsing function returns a Boolean value indicating that the user chose the Exit menu option or pressed the Interrupt key.

The Browsing Function

The browsing function, scroller_2(), is based on the scroller_1() function found in Example 19. You should understand the read-ahead logic used in Example 19 before studying scroller_2().

The browsing function supports the following menu choices:

Query	Stop browsing and return to the query phase to choose a new selection of rows.
Revise	Place additional conditions on the current query.
Show_cond	Display the conditional expression for the current query.
First	Display the first row of the selected set.
Next	Display the next row in the set.
Prior	Display the prior row in the set.
Last	Display the last row in the set.
Exit	Stop browsing and end the program.

The Query, Exit, and First through Last options are identical to those in Example 19. The Revise and Show_cond options are new in this example.

Revising a Query

The user completes a query-by-example to specify additional criteria. The **4GL** code that supports the query-by-example is the same as used in the initial query, except for some informational messages (see the section "The Query-By-Example Functions" on page 466). The new criteria are appended to the existing criteria, creating a new conditional expression. A new SELECT statement, incorporating the enhanced conditional expression, is prepared and opened.

Note that the new set of selected rows might have no rows in it, or only one row. The BEFORE MENU section of the browsing function checks for these conditions.

The code to PREPARE, DECLARE and OPEN a cursor already precedes the start of the menu operation. Instead of repeating the same logic as part of the Revise option, the program simply collects the new conditional expression, exits the menu, and starts over again as if the extended condition had been the original one.

This restart could be done in either of two ways:

- Cursor management could appear in the main loop. When Revise was chosen, the browsing function would terminate, returning a flag so that the main loop could tell the difference between the Query, Exit and Revise choices. It would be up to the main loop to close and reopen the cursor and restart the browse.
- Cursor management could appear in the browsing function. When Revise was chosen, it would close and reopen the cursor and resume the menu execution.

This example uses the second design; you might try rewriting the example using the first design.

Displaying the Search Criteria

The menu option Show_cond displays the current search criteria as a text string in a new window.

This feature is primarily a debugging aid while the program is being developed. Whether it should appear in a finished application depends on the audience for the program. It would be very useful to some kinds of users and meaningless to others.

The Query-By-Example Functions

This program contains two functions which execute CONSTRUCT statements and collect query conditions. The first, query_cust3a(), is the same as the query_cust2() function of Example 6, except that it returns only the conditional expression and not a complete SELECT statement. This allows the calling function to store the conditions apart from the SELECT, so they can be used in other statements or modified. (In Example 27, the same conditional expression will be used with two different SELECT statements and with UPDATE and DELETE statements.)

The second query function, query_cust3b(), is almost identical. It differs in the prompting messages it displays on the form ("Enter additional conditions" instead of "Enter query conditions") and, more significantly, in the way it handles a null response.

When query_cust3a() sees a null response to CONSTRUCT, it reminds the user that an empty condition will select all rows. That is not the case when additional conditions are being collected; then, an empty condition merely leaves the query unchanged. The prompt in query_cust3b() reflects this difference.

The answer() Function

This example introduces another general-purpose subroutine for warning or prompting the user. The answer() function (see page 477) takes a message string and three answer strings (which may be null). The user is shown the message and prompted for a choice from among the answers. The MATCHES operator is used in an unusual way to detect valid responses.

Function Overview

Function Name	Purpose
scroller_2()	Runs the browsing menu, fetching rows on request.
query_cust3a()	Executes a CONSTRUCT statement and returns the resulting conditional expression.
query_cust3b()	Like query_cust3a(), but with different prompt message and a different treatment of the null query.
clear_lines()	Clears any number of lines starting at any line. *See description in Example 6.*
answer()	A user-alert subroutine that takes one to three possible user responses and returns the one the user chooses.
msg()	Displays a brief, informative message. *See description in Example 5.*

The f_answer Form

1➤ The f_answer form displays an alert message and takes a one-character response from a short list of possible responses.

2➤ The msg field is a multi-line field which displays the alert message.

f_answer form file

1➤
```
DATABASE formonly

SCREEN
{

  [msg                                              ]
  [msg                                              ]
  [msg                                              ]
  [msg                                              ]


}

ATTRIBUTES
```
2➤
```
 msg = formonly.msgtext, WORDWRAP;

INSTRUCTIONS
  DELIMITERS "  "
```

The MAIN Function

1➤ Any version of the example database may be used with this example.

2➤ DEFER INTERRUPT prevents the Interrupt key from terminating the program. Instead, it sets the global variable int_flag, which is tested following CONSTRUCT to see if the user cancelled the statement. The Interrupt key also is used with the Exit option of the browsing menu.

The program will still work if this statement is removed, but pressing Interrupt will terminate the program immediately.

3➤ The query_cust3a() function appears on page 475. It uses CONSTRUCT to generate a conditional expression. If the user cancels the operation, query_cust3a() returns a null string, which terminates the WHILE loop and ends the program.

The scroller_2() Function

4➤ The second variable stores the current query condition. It is initialized from cond, the function argument. When conditions are added by the Revise operation, they are appended to recond. The full SELECT statement is stored in selstmt.

5➤ The read-ahead scroll logic uses three records to cache customer rows. This is discussed in the section "Fetching Ahead" on page 451 and on page 456.

4GL source file

```
1➤ DATABASE stores2t

###############################################
MAIN
###############################################
  DEFINE        cond CHAR(250), -- conditional clause from CONSTRUCT
                more SMALLINT   -- continue flag

2➤ DEFER INTERRUPT

  OPTIONS
    HELP FILE "hlpmsgs",
    FORM LINE 5,
    COMMENT LINE 5,
    MESSAGE LINE 19

  OPEN FORM f_customer FROM "f_customer"
  DISPLAY FORM f_customer

  LET more = TRUE
  WHILE more

3➤  CALL query_cust3a() RETURNING cond
    IF cond IS NOT NULL THEN
        LET more = scroller_2(cond)      -- Query = TRUE, Exit = FALSE
    ELSE                                    -- query was cancelled
        LET more = FALSE
    END IF

  END WHILE

  CLOSE FORM f_customer
  CLEAR SCREEN
END MAIN

###############################################
FUNCTION scroller_2(cond)
###############################################
  DEFINE    cond        CHAR(250),   -- initial query condition
4➤          recond,                  -- query as extended/contrained
            selstmt     CHAR(500),   -- full SELECT statement
5➤          curr_cust,               -- curr_cust: the row now being displayed
            next_cust,               -- the row to display when Next is chosen
            prior_cust               -- the row to display when Prior is chosen
                        RECORD LIKE customer.*,
            retval,                  -- value to RETURN from function
            fetch_dir,               -- flag showing direction of travel in list
            using_next,              -- flag values: going fwd using fetch next,
            using_prior,                -- ...going bwd using fetch prior, or
            at_end         SMALLINT     -- ...at either end of the list
```

6➤ The Exit menu option sets retval to FALSE; the Query option sets it to TRUE. The WHILE loop, will remain in control until one of them is chosen.

7➤ Note that the SELECT statement contains an ORDER BY clause. This contrasts with Example 19, in which the ordering was physical.

8➤ The View Customer menu is similar to the menu present in Example 19. The Revise and Show_cond options are new.

9➤ A discussion of this BEFORE MENU logic appears on page 456.

```
    LET using_next = +1
    LET using_prior = -1
    LET at_end = 0
    LET recond = cond-- initialize query condition

    LET retval = 99-- neither TRUE nor FALSE

6➤  WHILE retval <> TRUE AND retval <> FALSE  -- ie while not Query or Exit

7➤      LET selstmt = "SELECT * FROM customer WHERE ",
            recond CLIPPED, " ORDER BY customer_num"
        PREPARE prep_stmt FROM selstmt
        DECLARE cust_row SCROLL CURSOR FOR prep_stmt
        OPEN cust_row

        DISPLAY
"--------------------------------------------Press CTRL-W for Help----------"
          AT 3, 1
8➤      MENU "View Customers"

9➤          BEFORE MENU   -- Set up as for First, but with chance of zero rows
                SHOW OPTION ALL
                FETCH FIRST cust_row INTO curr_cust.*
                IF SQLCA.SQLCODE = NOTFOUND THEN
                    ERROR "There are no rows that satisfy this query."
                    HIDE OPTION ALL
                    SHOW OPTION "Query"
                    SHOW OPTION "Exit"
                    NEXT OPTION "Query"
                ELSE -- found at least one row
                    DISPLAY BY NAME curr_cust.*
                    HIDE OPTION "Prior"
                    LET fetch_dir = using_next
                    FETCH NEXT cust_row INTO next_cust.*
                    IF SQLCA.SQLCODE = 0 THEN-- at least 2 rows
                        NEXT OPTION "Next"
                    ELSE                        -- only 1 row in set
                        HIDE OPTION "Next"
                        NEXT OPTION "Query"
                    END IF
                END IF

            COMMAND KEY(ESC,Q) "Query"
                    "Query for a different set of customers." HELP 130
                LET retval = TRUE
                EXIT MENU

            COMMAND "Revise" "Apply more conditions to current query."
                    HELP 131
```

10➤ The query_cust3b() function allows the user to specify additional selection criteria. If the user interrupts the CONSTRUCT or enters no criteria it returns a null string. This function is very similar to the query_cust3a() function that appears later in this example.

11➤ The LET statement is executed when the user entered some criteria. The new criteria are appended (along with the AND operator) to the previous conditional expression. The EXIT MENU statement ends the menu.

Since retval has not been changed, the loop continues. The SELECT is recreated, the cursor reopened, and the menu starts up again.

12➤ The answer() function uses the WORDWRAP option to display a string (the CLIPPED recond variable) in a sub-window. The three null strings tell answer() to display no choices and wait for the user to press the RETURN key.

The query_cust3a() Function

13➤ This function collects the initial criteria at the start of the program and when the user chooses the Query menu option.

The query_cust3b() function is not displayed. It is identical except for the text of the messages it displays, for example where this function asks "Did you really want to accept all rows?" the other asks "Did you mean to add no new conditions?"

14➤ The answer() function is called with two nonempty responses. The function returns the response the user selects.

```
10➤            CALL query_cust3b() RETURNING cond
               IF cond IS NOT NULL THEN    -- some condition entered
11➤               LET recond = recond CLIPPED, " AND ", cond CLIPPED
                  EXIT MENU                  -- close and re-open the cursor
               ELSE           -- construct clears form, refresh the display
                  DISPLAY BY NAME curr_cust.*
               END IF

            COMMAND "Show-cond" "Display the current query conditions."
                  HELP 132
12➤            CALL answer(recond CLIPPED,"","","")
```

See Example 19.

```
    ##############################################
13➤ FUNCTION query_cust3a() -- used for initial query
    ##############################################
      DEFINE        q_cust    CHAR(120),
                    msgtxt    CHAR(150)

      CALL clear_lines(1,4)
      DISPLAY "CUSTOMER QUERY-BY-EXAMPLE 2"
        AT 4, 24
      CALL clear_lines(2, 16)
      DISPLAY
        " Enter search criteria and press Accept. Press CTRL-W for Help."
        AT 16,1 ATTRIBUTE (REVERSE, YELLOW)
      DISPLAY " Press Cancel to exit w/out searching."
        AT 17,1 ATTRIBUTE (REVERSE, YELLOW)

      LET int_flag = FALSE
      CONSTRUCT BY NAME q_cust ON customer.customer_num, customer.company,
                          customer.address1, customer.address2,
                          customer.city, customer.state,
                          customer.zipcode, customer.fname,
                          customer.lname, customer.phone
            HELP 30
        AFTER CONSTRUCT
          IF (NOT int_flag) THEN
            IF (NOT FIELD_TOUCHED(customer.*)) THEN
              LET msgtxt = "You did not enter any search criteria. ",
                           "Do you really want to select all rows?"
14➤           IF "No-revise" = answer(msgtxt,"Yes-all","No-revise","") THEN
                CONTINUE CONSTRUCT
              END IF
            END IF
          END IF
      END CONSTRUCT

      IF int_flag THEN
        LET int_flag = FALSE
```

The answer() Function

15➤ The answer() function is a general-purpose routine for displaying a message to the user and getting a simple answer. Example 20 calls answer() at three points in the program:

- The Show_cond menu option (to display the current query criteria).
- The query_cust3a() function (to determine whether the user wants to select all rows).
- The query_cust3b() function (to determine whether the user wants to add criteria to the query).

16➤ The f_answer form has a four-line character field with the WORDWRAP option. It displays the message text.

17➤ The initial letters of the one, two or three valid responses are converted to uppercase and combined into a character class list in the form supported by the MATCHES predicate (that is, three elements enclosed in brackets).

18➤ When the caller supplies no valid responses, the function simply displays the message and waits for RETURN. In this case it returns no value to the caller.

19➤ When the caller supplies a response, the function sets up a prompt string that reads either "Choose *A* or *B*" or else "Choose *A*, *B* or *C*."

```
      CALL clear_lines(2,16)
      CALL msg("Customer query terminated.")
      LET q_cust = NULL
    END IF

    CALL clear_lines(1,4)
    CALL clear_lines(2,16)

    RETURN (q_cust)
  END FUNCTION  {query_cust3a}

  ###############################################
15➤ FUNCTION answer(msg,ans1,ans2,ans3)
  ###############################################
    DEFINE    msg               CHAR(255),  -- input text for display
              ans1,ans2,ans3    CHAR(10),   -- possible user responses or nulls
              inp               CHAR(1),    -- user's one-character reply
              j                 SMALLINT,   -- misc index
              codes             CHAR(5),    -- match string [abc]
              choose            CHAR(50)    -- prompt string

16➤ OPEN WINDOW ans_win AT 10,10
      WITH FORM "f_answer"
      ATTRIBUTE(BORDER,PROMPT LINE LAST,FORM LINE FIRST)
    DISPLAY msg TO msgtext

17➤ LET codes = "[",UPSHIFT(ans1[1]),
                    UPSHIFT(ans2[1]),
                    UPSHIFT(ans3[1]), "]" -- make a class

18➤ IF LENGTH(ans1) = 0 THEN -- all-blank or null
      PROMPT "Press RETURN to continue: " FOR inp
    ELSE
19➤   LET choose = "Choose ",ans1 CLIPPED
      IF (LENGTH(ans2) * LENGTH(ans3)) <> 0 THEN -- both given
        LET choose = choose CLIPPED, ", ", ans2 CLIPPED,
                    " or ", ans3 CLIPPED
      ELSE -- not both ans2 and ans3, possibly neither
        IF LENGTH(ans2) <> 0 THEN
          LET choose = choose CLIPPED, " or ", ans2 CLIPPED
        END IF
      END IF
      LET inp = "\n" -- one thing a user cannot enter at a prompt
```

20➤ The character class expression (see Note 17) is used to test the user's response. Many people overlook the fact that MATCHES can be used in **4GL** statements, and that its comparison pattern need not be a literal string, but can be a variable.

```
20➤     WHILE NOT UPSHIFT(inp) MATCHES codes
          PROMPT choose CLIPPED, " ",codes,": " FOR inp
        END WHILE
      END IF
      CLOSE WINDOW ans_win
      IF LENGTH(ans1) <> 0 THEN
        CASE
          WHEN UPSHIFT(inp) = UPSHIFT(ans1[1])
            LET choose = ans1
          WHEN UPSHIFT(inp) = UPSHIFT(ans2[1])
            LET choose = ans2
          WHEN UPSHIFT(inp) = UPSHIFT(ans3[1])
            LET choose = ans3
        END CASE
        RETURN choose
      END IF
    END FUNCTION
```

To locate any function definition see the Function Index on page 728.

21

Using an Update Cursor

This example demonstrates the use of an update cursor. An update cursor allows you to lock rows as the cursor selects them from the database. You can then use the WHERE CURRENT clause of the UPDATE or DELETE statement to update or delete the row. This example uses an UPDATE WHERE CURRENT statement to allow the user to specify which orders to update with a paid date.

Displaying Multiple Forms

Suppose that the stores2t database only tracked which orders have been paid; a different database contained the actual accounting tables. The user of stores2t receives a Paid Orders report from the Accounting department after orders are paid in the accounting database. This report lists the orders to be paid sorted by date of payment and, within a single date by customer number. The user goes through this report and updates the orders.

To update an order, the user enters information in three steps:

1. The date the orders were paid is entered on the f_date form.
2. The customer number or company name of the customer whose orders have been paid is entered on the f_custkey form.
3. Confirmation of the update of the order (currently displaying on the f_payord form) is entered in a confirmation window.

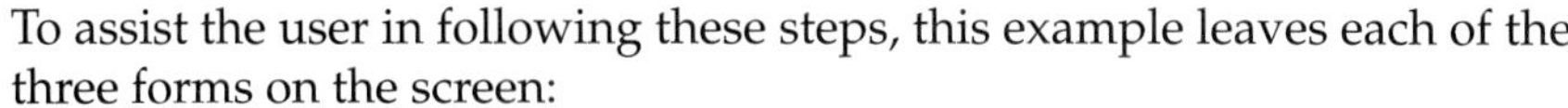

To assist the user in following these steps, this example leaves each of the three forms on the screen:

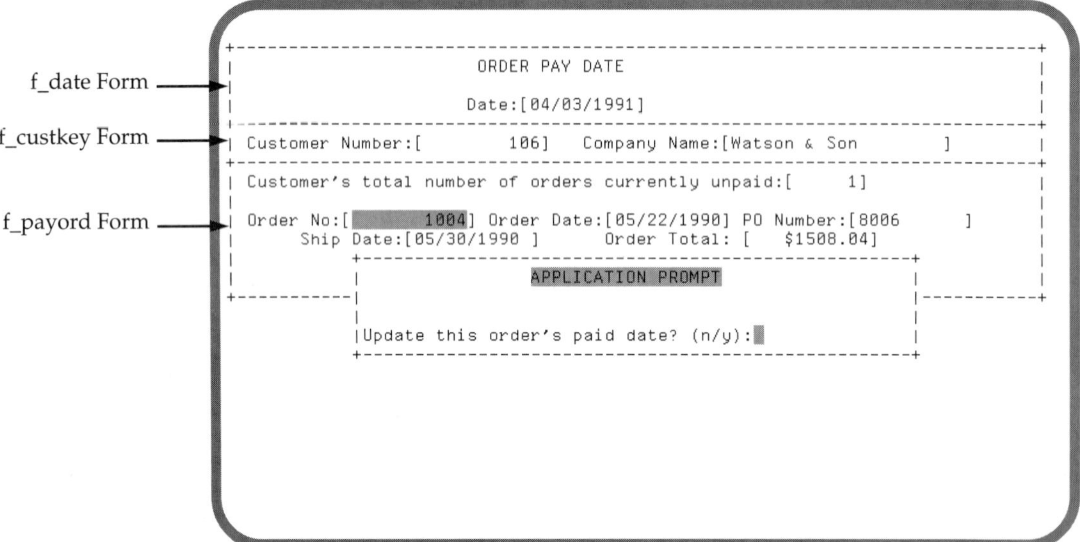

Because none of these forms is closed until data entry is complete, the user is able to see all entered information at once.

Updating Rows

4GL provides two methods of updating or deleting rows:

- Using a WHERE clause in an UPDATE or DELETE statement to specify which row or rows to affect *as a group*.
- Using a WHERE CURRENT OF clause in an UPDATE or DELETE in conjunction with an update cursor to affect rows *one at a time*.

Using the WHERE clause in an UPDATE and DELETE is demonstrated in Example 9. You specify the WHERE clause condition and the statement updates or deletes all matching rows. If the UPDATE (or DELETE) fails on one of the rows, the entire UPDATE (or DELETE) fails. Any successful updates performed on rows before the failure are cancelled and any rows after the failure are not processed. The update cursor provides a way to control an update on a row-by-row basis.

Using an Update Cursor

With an update cursor, the SELECT requests an exclusive lock on the row as it is fetched. The program can then update this row by using the WHERE CURRENT OF clause of the UPDATE statement.

The update cursor offers the following advantages:

- The UPDATE or DELETE with the WHERE CURRENT OF clause will not fail due to a locking conflict because the program has already obtained a lock on each selected row.
- The user can page through the selected set of rows without being concerned that the data within these rows will change (the exclusive lock prevents other users from modifying or deleting the row).
- The program can test whether to update or delete each of the selected rows specified. For example, the program can allow the user to choose whether to reject or accept the update of a row.
- The program can test the success of the update or delete operation for each selected row. If the operation fails, the program can choose to continue on to the next selected row, to exit the cursor, or to skip over the row.

The disadvantages of the update cursor are:

- The application loses some concurrency because an exclusive lock is obtained on each selected row when it is fetched. No other user can modify the selected rows until the locks are released.
- When this exclusive lock is released depends upon whether or not the database supports transactions:
  - If the database supports transactions: the row lock is released when the transaction ends (with COMMIT WORK or ROLLBACK WORK) if the row has been updated, or when the next row is fetched if the row has not been updated.
  - If the database does not support transactions: the row lock is released when the update cursor is closed (with CLOSE) or when the next row is fetched (whichever occurs first), regardless of whether the row has been updated.
- The SELECT statement of the cursor cannot include the ORDER BY clause and is limited to a single table.
- An update cursor cannot be a scrolling cursor.

For these reasons, you should not usually use an update cursor to just select and view data. In such cases, use a normal cursor or a scrolling cursor because they do not obtain locks as they fetch rows.

Handling Locked Rows

This example does not check the locking status of rows found by the update cursor. If this update cursor encounters a lock on one of the selected rows, this program exits with a runtime error (**ISAM** = -107). To perform this checking, the program should either:

- Replace the FOREACH statement with the FETCH statement within a loop and check the status variable after the FETCH for a possible locking error.
- Execute the SET LOCK MODE TO WAIT statement.

For more information on checking for locking errors, see Example 23.

Function Overview

Function Name	Purpose
input_date()	Accepts user input for the date to mark the orders as paid.
open_ckey()	Opens the f_custkey form.
close_ckey()	Closes the f_custkey form.
find_cust()	Accepts user input of a customer number or company name and then finds a customer based on either of these values.
cust_popup2()	Retrieves all customers and displays them in an array form so the user can choose the appropriate customer. *See description in Example 12.*
find_unpaid()	Determines the number of unpaid orders for the specified customer.
pay_orders()	Finds, displays, and updates the unpaid orders for the current customer with the specified paid date. This function uses an update cursor.
calc_order()	Selects information from multiple tables to summarize an order. *See description in Example 12.*
tax_rates()	Supplies the appropriate tax schedule for a customer. *See description in Example 4.*
init_msgs()	Initializes the members of the ga_dsplymsg array to null. *See description in Example 2.*
message_window()	Opens a window and displays the contents of the ga_dsplymsg global array. *See description in Example 2.*
prompt_window()	Displays a message and prompts the user for affirmation or negation. This function is a variation on the message_window() function that appears in Example 2. *See description in Example 4.*
msg()	Displays a brief, informative message. *See description in Example 5.*
clear_lines()	Clears any number of lines starting at any line. *See description in Example 6.*

The f_date Form

1➤ Since this form does not contain a field based on columns of the database, no database is specified. Therefore, the DATABASE statement specifies formonly. Note that no TABLE section has been defined.

2➤ The SCREEN section of the form file contains the image displayed on the screen when the f_date form is open and displaying.

3➤ This form contains a single field: a date. Since the field is not connected to a column of the database table, it needs to have its field type defined. By not connecting the field to a column, this form can accept input for any date value.

The f_payord Form

1➤ This form contains fields connected to a database column; it must specify the database that contains the column definition. This form will work with any version of the stores2 database.

2➤ The SCREEN section of the form file contains the image displayed on the screen when the f_payord form is open and displaying.

3➤ This form uses columns from a single table: orders.

4➤ All fields on this form are defined as NOENTRY. This attribute prevents the cursor from stopping in these fields during data entry. The effect of this attribute is to create a "display-only" form: one that can display information but that does not allow the user to enter input.

Because program execution will not stop on this form, the program must have a way to pause to allow the user to see the data. In this example, the pay_orders() function displays a confirmation window to allow the user to see the order data and then decide whether or not to update this order with a paid date.

5➤ Because the order amount is not stored in the database, the f005 field must be defined as FORMONLY. The program calculates the order amount (with the calc_order() function) and displays it in this field.

f_date form file

```
1➤ DATABASE formonly

2➤ SCREEN
   {


                         Date:[f000       ]


   }

   ATTRIBUTES
3➤ f000 = formonly.a_date TYPE DATE;
```

f_payord form file

```
1➤ DATABASE stores2t

2➤ SCREEN
   {
    Customer's total number of orders currently unpaid:[f000   ]

    Order No:[f001       ] Order Date:[f002       ] PO Number:[f003       ]
         Ship Date:[f004       ]          Order Total: [f005       ]

   }

3➤ TABLES
   orders

   ATTRIBUTES
4➤ f000 = FORMONLY.total_unpaid, NOENTRY;

   f001 = orders.order_num, NOENTRY;
   f002 = orders.order_date, NOENTRY;
   f003 = orders.po_num, NOENTRY;
   f004 = orders.ship_date, NOENTRY;
5➤ f005 = FORMONLY.order_total, NOENTRY;
```

The DATABASE and GLOBALS Statements

1➤ This program must use the stores2t database or any version of the stores2 database that uses transactions.

2➤ The global record gr_customer holds the column values for a row in the customer table.

3➤ The global record gr_payord holds the columns values from the orders table that are displayed on the f_payord form.

4➤ The global record, gr_charges, holds the values needed to calculate the order total for a single order. This record is used by the calc_order() function.

5➤ The ga_dsplymsg array is used as input to the message_window() function, described in Example 2, and prompt_window() function, described in Example 3.

The MAIN Function

6➤ The input_date() function accepts user input of a date from the f_date form. It returns TRUE if the user enters a date and FALSE if the user terminates the input with the Cancel key. This date is the date of payment for the orders and defaults to the current date.

7➤ The open_ckey() function opens a bordered window called w_custkey and displays the f_custkey form in this window.

8➤ The WHILE loop enables the user to update order dates for several customers. As long as the keep_going flag is TRUE, the program calls the find_cust() function to allow the user to enter a new customer number.

9➤ The find_cust() function accepts user input for the customer number or company name of the customer whose orders are to be marked as paid. It returns TRUE if the user enters the customer information and FALSE if the user terminates the INPUT with the Cancel key.

10➤ Since the find_cust() function stores the user input in the gr_customer record, these LET statements copy this information into gr_payord global record, which stores the order paid data.

11➤ The find_unpaid() function determines the number of unpaid orders for the specified customer.

4GL source file

```
1➤ DATABASE stores2t

   GLOBALS
2➤   DEFINE        gr_customer        RECORD LIKE customer.*,
3➤                 gr_payord          RECORD
                                        paid_date      LIKE orders.paid_date,
                                        customer_num   LIKE orders.customer_num,
                                        company        LIKE customer.company,
                                        order_num      LIKE orders.order_num,
                                        order_date     LIKE orders.order_date,
                                        po_num         LIKE orders.po_num,
                                        ship_date      LIKE orders.ship_date
                                      END RECORD,
4➤                 gr_charges         RECORD
                                        tax_rate       DECIMAL(5,3),
                                        ship_charge    LIKE orders.ship_charge,
                                        sales_tax      MONEY(9),
                                        order_total    MONEY(11)
                                      END RECORD

5➤   DEFINE        ga_dsplymsg ARRAY[5] OF CHAR(48)

   END GLOBALS

   ########################################
   MAIN
   ########################################
     DEFINE        keep_going     SMALLINT,
                   num_unpaid     SMALLINT

     OPTIONS
       FORM LINE FIRST,
       MESSAGE LINE LAST

     DEFER INTERRUPT

6➤   IF input_date() THEN
       LET keep_going = TRUE
7➤     CALL open_ckey()
8➤     WHILE keep_going
9➤       IF find_cust() THEN
10➤        LET gr_payord.customer_num = gr_customer.customer_num
           LET gr_payord.company = gr_customer.company
11➤        LET num_unpaid = find_unpaid()
```

12➤ If the specified customer has unpaid orders, then the pay_orders() function is called to control the selection and update of these orders. The total number of unpaid orders is passed to pay_orders() as an argument to be displayed on the f_payord form.

13➤ If the user has terminated customer input with the Cancel key, then keep_going is FALSE, terminating the WHILE loop (see Note 8).

14➤ The close_ckey() function deallocates the memory used by the f_custkey form and its window.

The input_date() Function

15➤ The f_date form displays in a bordered window called w_paydate. At the top of this window, the program displays instructions for the user on how to enter data on the form.

16➤ The INPUT statement accepts the date from the screen field a_date and stores it in the program variable gr_payord.paid_date. This date is the date of payment for the orders.

17➤ Before the user can enter data, the program initializes the date with today's date if the field is currently empty.

18➤ If the user has cleared the field, the program moves the cursor back to the paid_date field. This test ensures that a value exists in the gr_payord.paid_date field.

19➤ The clear_lines() function clears the form instructions from the screen. These instructions no longer apply once execution has left the f_date form.

20➤ If the user presses Cancel, the function resets the int_flag variable, closes the form and window, and returns FALSE.

21➤ If execution reaches this point, the user has entered a paid date so the function returns TRUE. Note that the f_date form is left on the screen so the user can see the specified paid date as the data entry continues.

```
12➤         IF (num_unpaid > 0) THEN
              CALL pay_orders(num_unpaid)
            END IF
          ELSE
13➤         LET keep_going = FALSE
          END IF
        END WHILE
      END IF

14➤   CALL close_ckey()
      CLEAR SCREEN
    END MAIN

    ########################################
    FUNCTION input_date()
    ########################################

15➤   OPEN WINDOW w_paydate AT 2,3
        WITH 6 ROWS, 76 COLUMNS
        ATTRIBUTE (BORDER, COMMENT LINE 2)

      OPEN FORM f_date FROM "f_date"
      DISPLAY FORM f_date

      DISPLAY "ORDER PAY DATE" AT 1,24
      CALL clear_lines(1, 6)
      DISPLAY " Enter order paid date and press Accept. Press Cancel to exit."
        AT 6, 1 ATTRIBUTE (REVERSE, YELLOW)

16➤   INPUT gr_payord.paid_date FROM a_date
17➤     BEFORE FIELD a_date
          IF gr_payord.paid_date IS NULL THEN
            LET gr_payord.paid_date = TODAY
          END IF

18➤     AFTER FIELD a_date
          IF gr_payord.paid_date IS NULL THEN
            ERROR "You must enter a Paid Date for the orders."
            NEXT FIELD paid_date
          END IF

      END INPUT

19➤   CALL clear_lines(1, 6)
20➤   IF int_flag THEN
        LET int_flag = FALSE
        CLOSE FORM f_date
        CLOSE WINDOW w_paydate
        RETURN (FALSE)
      END IF

21➤   RETURN (TRUE)
    END FUNCTION -- input_date --
```

The open_ckey() Function

22➤ The f_custkey form displays in a bordered window called w_custkey. This window redefines the COMMENT LINE and the FORM LINE so that the f_custkey form displays at the top of the w_custkey window. By default, FORM LINE is 3 and the f_custkey form would display on the third line of w_custkey.

The close_ckey() Function

23➤ The close_ckey() function closes the f_custkey form and its window w_custkey. These statements deallocate memory resources used by these two screen structures.

The find_cust() Function

24➤ The program displays the user instructions for the f_custkey form at the top of the w_custkey window. The call to clear_lines() clears out the instruction lines so any previous text will be removed before the new instructions display.

25➤ The INPUT statement accepts input for the customer number and company name. The user can select a customer by entering either of these values.

26➤ Before the user can enter the customer number, the program displays a message indicating the presence of a popup window. If desired, the user can press either F5 or CONTROL-F to see the numbers and names of all customers defined in the database.

27➤ If the gr_customer.customer_num variable has a non-null value, then the user has entered the customer number in the customer_num field. The program checks that a customer with this number exists in the database.

Note that if gr_customer.customer_num is NULL, execution is allowed to continue to the company field. This feature allows the user to select a customer by entering either the customer number or the company name. See Note 32 for more information.

28➤ If the SELECT statement (in Note 27) does not find a customer row for the specified customer number, then the user entered an invalid number. The program notifies the user of the error, clears out the customer number field, and returns the cursor to this field so the user can enter another number.

```
########################################
FUNCTION open_ckey()
########################################

22➤  OPEN WINDOW w_custkey AT 6,3
       WITH 5 ROWS, 76 COLUMNS
       ATTRIBUTE (BORDER, COMMENT LINE 2, FORM LINE FIRST)

     OPEN FORM f_custkey FROM "f_custkey"
     DISPLAY FORM f_custkey

END FUNCTION -- open_ckey --

########################################
FUNCTION close_ckey()
########################################

23➤  CLOSE FORM f_custkey
     CLOSE WINDOW w_custkey

END FUNCTION -- close_ckey --

########################################
FUNCTION find_cust()
########################################
  DEFINE        cust_cnt     SMALLINT

24➤  CALL clear_lines(2, 3)
     DISPLAY " Enter customer number or company name."
       AT 3, 1 ATTRIBUTE (REVERSE, YELLOW)
     DISPLAY " Press Accept to continue or Cancel to exit."
       AT 4, 1 ATTRIBUTE (REVERSE, YELLOW)

25➤  LET int_flag = FALSE
     INPUT BY NAME gr_customer.customer_num, gr_customer.company

26➤    BEFORE FIELD customer_num
         MESSAGE "Enter a customer number or press F5 (CTRL-F) for a list."

27➤    AFTER FIELD customer_num
         IF gr_customer.customer_num IS NOT NULL THEN
           SELECT company
           INTO gr_customer.company
           FROM customer
           WHERE customer_num = gr_customer.customer_num

28➤        IF (status = NOTFOUND) THEN
             ERROR
           "Unknown Customer number. Use F5 (CTRL-F) to see valid customers."
             LET gr_customer.customer_num = NULL
             NEXT FIELD customer_num
           END IF
```

29➤ If the SELECT statement (in Note 27) finds a customer row for the specified customer number, it selects the company name into the gr_customer.company variable. The program displays this variable on the f_custkey form.

30➤ If the user has entered a valid customer number, execution need not continue to the company field (because the program has already selected this name from the database and displayed it on the form). The EXIT INPUT statement exits this INPUT statement and execution resumes after the END INPUT.

31➤ If execution continues to the company field, the user has not entered a customer number. Before the user can enter this value, the program displays a message indicating the presence of a popup window. If desired, the user can press either F5 or CONTROL-F to see the numbers and names of all customers defined in the database.

32➤ This test ensures that the user enters a company name. Unlike the customer_-num field, the company field cannot be left empty. The program must have either the customer number or the company name to select a customer from the database. If the user omits the customer number, execution can continue to the company field (see Note 27). However, if the user omits the company name as well, the program cannot locate the customer.

33➤ The program checks that a customer with the specified name exists in the database. When it verified the existence of a customer based on a customer number, the program was able to assume that, if this customer existed, one and only one customer row would have this number. This assumption is valid because the customer number is the primary key of the customer table.

The SELECT statement in Note 27 is able to select the company name at the same time it determines whether a matching customer row exists, because this SELECT is guaranteed to return at most only one row. If the row exists, then gr_customer.company is initialized with the company name, and if it does not exist, gr_customer.company is null.

However, when the program verifies the existence of a customer based on a company name, it cannot make this assumption about uniqueness. Several customers in the database could have the same company name because this column does not have to be unique. For this reason, the program cannot select the customer number while it checks for the existence of the row. Such a SELECT could possibly return more than one row, generating a runtime error. To prevent such an error, the program breaks the verification into two steps:

1. Count how many customer rows have a matching company name.
2. Select the customer number when the program can guarantee the uniqueness of the company name.

```
29➤      DISPLAY BY NAME gr_customer.company

30➤      MESSAGE ""
         EXIT INPUT
       END IF

31➤  BEFORE FIELD company
       MESSAGE "Enter a company name or press F5 (CTRL-F) for a list."

     AFTER FIELD company
32➤    IF gr_customer.company IS NULL THEN
         ERROR "You must enter either a customer number or company name."
         NEXT FIELD customer_num
       END IF

33➤    SELECT COUNT(*)
       INTO cust_cnt
       FROM customer
       WHERE company = gr_customer.company
```

To perform this first step, this SELECT statement uses the COUNT(*) aggregate. The code in Note 34 guarantees that a company name is unique so the code in Note 36 can select the customer number.

34➤ If the SELECT statement (in Note 33) finds more than one customer row with this company name, the program must notify the user that the company name is not unique. It suggests choosing the customer from the popup list because this form cannot handle a non-unique company name.

A possible enhancement to this function would be to display the customer numbers of all customer rows with this company name and allow the user to select which one was desired.

35➤ If the SELECT statement (in Note 33) does not find any customers with the specified company name, then this name is invalid. The program notifies the user of the error, clears the company name field, and returns the cursor to this field so the user can enter another name.

36➤ If execution reaches this point, the SELECT statement (in Note 33) has found only one customer row with the specified company name. It is now possible to select the customer number without using a cursor because the SELECT is guaranteed to return only one row (See Note 33 for more information).

37➤ The user can display the customer popup window from either the customer_-num or the company field. The built-in function INFIELD() returns a TRUE or FALSE value indicating whether the cursor is currently in the specified field. If the cursor is in either of these fields, then the CONTROL-F and F5 sequences initiate a popup window. If the cursor is in any other field, these sequences have no effect.

38➤ The cust_popup2() function displays the customer popup window on the f_custsel form. It returns the customer number and company name of the customer that the user selected. This function is described in detail in Example 12.

39➤ If gr_customer.customer_num is NULL, then the user terminated the customer popup with the Cancel key and no customer has been selected. This LET statement initializes the gr_customer.company variable to NULL so that the company field on f_custkey is empty when the cursor enters it.

40➤ If the user selects a customer from the popup window, the program displays the customer number and company name appear on the f_custkey form. Note that it is not necessary to verify the customer number in the ON KEY clause because the values have come from the popup window which only displays valid customers.

```
34➤      IF (cust_cnt > 1) THEN
           ERROR "Company name is not unique. Press F5 (CTRL-F) for a list."
           NEXT FIELD company
         END IF

35➤      IF (cust_cnt = 0) THEN
           ERROR "Unknown company name. Press F5 (CTRL-F) for a list."
           NEXT FIELD company
         END IF

36➤      SELECT customer_num
         INTO gr_customer.customer_num
         FROM customer
         WHERE company = gr_customer.company

         DISPLAY BY NAME gr_customer.customer_num
         MESSAGE ""

       ON KEY (F5, CONTROL-F)
37➤      IF INFIELD(customer_num) OR INFIELD(company) THEN
38➤        CALL cust_popup2()
             RETURNING gr_customer.customer_num, gr_customer.company

39➤        IF gr_customer.customer_num IS NULL THEN
             LET gr_customer.company = NULL
40➤        ELSE
             DISPLAY BY NAME gr_customer.customer_num, gr_customer.company
             EXIT INPUT
           END IF
         END IF
```

41➤ This AFTER INPUT clause ensures that the user does not press the Accept key before selecting a customer:

- If gr_customer.customer_num is NULL, then no customer has been selected when the INPUT statement exits.
- If int_flag is FALSE, then the AFTER INPUT is being executed because the user has pressed the Accept key to exit the INPUT. The int_flag variable would be TRUE if the user had pressed the Cancel key.

Execution cannot continue to the next form until the user selects a customer.

42➤ If the user has terminated the INPUT with Cancel, then the program resets the int_flag variable, erases the form's instructions, and returns FALSE.

43➤ If the user has exited the INPUT with Accept (or RETURN from the last field), this function returns TRUE. Note that the f_custkey form is left on the screen so the user can see the selected customer as the data entry continues. The f_date form also remains open so that the paid date displays.

The find_unpaid() Function

44➤ This SELECT statement uses the COUNT(*) aggregate to determine the number of unpaid orders for the current customer. An unpaid order is one which has a NULL value in the paid_date field of the orders table.

45➤ If the current customer has no unpaid orders, then the function notifies the user. It then returns zero (0) to indicate that no orders can be paid for the specified customer.

46➤ If the current customer has unpaid orders, then the function prompts the user to confirm whether to begin marking orders as paid.

47➤ If the user confirms the update, then the function returns the number of unpaid orders. Otherwise, the function returns zero (0) to indicate that no orders should be paid for the specified customer.

```
41➤     AFTER INPUT
          IF (gr_customer.customer_num IS NULL) AND (NOT int_flag) THEN
            ERROR
       "Cannot display the summary yet. Enter the customer or press Cancel to exit."
            NEXT FIELD customer_num
          END IF

      END INPUT

42➤   IF int_flag THEN
        LET int_flag = FALSE
        CALL clear_lines(1, 4)
        RETURN (FALSE)
      END IF

43➤   RETURN (TRUE)

    END FUNCTION -- find_cust --

    ########################################
    FUNCTION find_unpaid()
    ########################################
      DEFINE        unpaid_cnt    SMALLINT

44➤   SELECT COUNT(*)
      INTO unpaid_cnt
      FROM orders
      WHERE customer_num = gr_payord.customer_num
        AND paid_date IS NULL

45➤   IF (unpaid_cnt = 0) THEN
        LET ga_dsplymsg[1] = "Customer: ",
            gr_payord.customer_num USING "<<<<<<<<<<<",
            " (", gr_payord.company CLIPPED, ")"
        LET ga_dsplymsg[2] = " has no unpaid orders."
        CALL message_window(8,14)
        RETURN (0)
      END IF

46➤   LET ga_dsplymsg[1] = "This customer has ", unpaid_cnt USING "<<<<<<",
                           " unpaid order(s)."
47➤   IF prompt_window("Are you ready to begin paying these orders? ", 8,14)
      THEN
        RETURN (unpaid_cnt)
      ELSE
        RETURN (0)
      END IF

    END FUNCTION -- find_unpaid --
```

The pay_orders() Function

48➤ The f_payord form displays in a bordered window called w_payord. The total_unpaid field of this form is initialized with the total number of unpaid orders, as determined by the find_unpaid() function (see Note 47) and passed in as an argument to this function.

49➤ This DECLARE statement declares an update cursor for the update of order paid dates. It finds all unpaid orders for the current customer and selects only those columns whose values display on the f_payord form.

Note that the FOR UPDATE clause is what makes this cursor an update cursor. The update cursor uses the FOR UPDATE OF clause to restrict update of the orders table to only the paid_date column.

50➤ Because the stores2t database uses transactions (and is not MODE ANSI), the entire update cursor must be within a transaction. This BEGIN WORK statement precedes the opening of the update cursor.

51➤ The FOREACH opens the c_payord update cursor (in the first iteration), obtains an exclusive lock on the first matching row, and then places the values into the corresponding variables in the gr_payord record. In subsequent iterations, FOREACH obtains the exclusive lock, then places the values into the program variables. Note that these locks are not released until the transaction is either committed or rolled back (see Note 60).

52➤ The calc_order() function calculates the total amount of the order. This amount is displayed on the f_payord form so the user can check the paid amount in the database against the paid amount on the hardcopy report.

This function does not include code to handle what happens if the selected row is already locked by another user. The program exits with a runtime error if it encounters such a locked row. See the section titled "Handling Locked Rows" in the overview of this example for more information about this limitation.

53➤ The CLEAR statement clears out the specified fields on the f_payord form. The program does not use the CLEAR FORM statement because the field containing the number of unpaid orders does not need to be cleared. These DISPLAY statements display the new order information on the f_payord form.

54➤ The prompt_window() function prompts for confirmation before updating the displayed order with the paid date.

55➤ As each row is selected by the cursor, upd_cnt is incremented by one. This variable keeps the running total of the number of orders that have been updated.

```
    ########################################
    FUNCTION pay_orders(total_unpaid)
    ########################################
      DEFINE        total_unpaid    SMALLINT,

                    upd_cnt         SMALLINT,
                    msg_txt         CHAR(10),
                    success         SMALLINT

48➤   OPEN WINDOW w_payord AT 8, 3
        WITH 6 ROWS, 76 COLUMNS
        ATTRIBUTE (BORDER)

      OPEN FORM f_payord FROM "f_payord"
      DISPLAY FORM f_payord

      DISPLAY BY NAME total_unpaid

      LET success = TRUE

49➤   DECLARE c_payord CURSOR FOR
        SELECT order_num, order_date, po_num, ship_date
        FROM orders
        WHERE customer_num = gr_payord.customer_num
          AND paid_date IS NULL
      FOR UPDATE OF paid_date

50➤   BEGIN WORK

      LET upd_cnt = 0
51➤   FOREACH c_payord INTO gr_payord.order_num,
                            gr_payord.order_date,
                            gr_payord.po_num,
                            gr_payord.ship_date

52➤     CALL calc_order(gr_payord.order_num)

53➤     CLEAR order_num, order_date, po_num, ship_date, order_total
        DISPLAY BY NAME gr_payord.order_num
          ATTRIBUTE (REVERSE, YELLOW)
        DISPLAY BY NAME gr_payord.order_date, gr_payord.po_num,
                        gr_payord.ship_date, gr_charges.order_total

54➤     IF prompt_window("Update this order's paid date?", 13, 14) THEN
55➤         LET upd_cnt = upd_cnt + 1
```

56➤ The UPDATE is surrounded by the WHENEVER ERROR statement to turn off automatic error checking before the UPDATE and to turn it back on after the UPDATE has been performed. Because the automatic checking is off when the UPDATE is executed, the program must perform its own error checking to determine the success of the statement (see Note 58).

57➤ If the user confirms the update, the program updates the current order with the paid date. The UPDATE statement uses the WHERE CURRENT OF clause to access the update cursor's current row. This row has already been locked by the cursor. Note that the UPDATE can only change the paid_date column because the update cursor has restricted update access to this column with the FOR UPDATE OF paid_date clause (see Note 49).

58➤ If the UPDATE statement is successful, **4GL** sets the global variable status to zero. If an error occurs, the status variable has a negative value. In the case of an error, the function notifies the user and sets the success flag to FALSE. This flag is checked after the FOREACH loop closes to determine whether to commit or rollback the current transaction (see Note 60).

Note that this program chose to exit completely when it encountered an error. However, because you can handle the success of the update on a row-by-row basis, your program could instead perform a retry or skip to the next row without generating an error.

59➤ This CLOSE statement closes the cursor. Even though open cursors are closed by ROLLBACK WORK and COMMIT WORK, you should explicitly close an update cursor when it is no longer needed so that resources allocated to the cursor can be released. Since the stores2t database has transactions (but is not MODE ANSI), this CLOSE statement must be issued from within a transaction (before the COMMIT WORK or ROLLBACK WORK).

60➤ Because the stores2t database uses transactions (and is not MODE ANSI), the program must end the transaction started by the BEGIN WORK statement (see Note 50). The value of the success variable determines how to handle the current transaction. If success is TRUE, then the COMMIT WORK statement saves the changes in the database. Otherwise, the ROLLBACK WORK statement terminates the transaction, without saving the changes. Both the COMMIT WORK and the ROLLBACK WORK statements release all row and table locks obtained by the update cursor. Either of these statements would also close any open cursors (except WITH HOLD cursors), so neither can exist within the FOREACH loop.

61➤ These statements deallocate the memory used by the f_payord form by closing the form and its window.

```
56➤ WHENEVER ERROR CONTINUE
57➤       UPDATE orders SET paid_date = gr_payord.paid_date
          WHERE CURRENT OF c_payord
    WHENEVER ERROR STOP

58➤       IF (status < 0) THEN
            ERROR status USING "-<<<<<<<<<<<",
      ": Unable to update order with paid date. No changes saved."
            LET success = FALSE
            LET upd_cnt = 0
            EXIT FOREACH
          END IF
        END IF
      END FOREACH

59➤   CLOSE c_payord

60➤   IF success THEN
        COMMIT WORK
      ELSE
        ROLLBACK WORK
      END IF

61➤   CLOSE FORM f_payord
      CLOSE WINDOW w_payord
```

62➤ Once the Order update is complete, the program notifies the user of the number of orders updated. If no orders have been updated (upd_cnt is zero), then a message string called msg_txt is assigned the string "0". For non-zero numbers, the msg_txt string is formatted with a USING clause to left justify the numeric string. An upd_cnt of zero requires special formatting because the "<<<<<<" notation displays a blank for a zero value.

The msg_txt string is then concatenated with text and stored in the ga_dsplymsg global array for use with the message_window() function.

```
62➤   IF upd_cnt = 0 THEN
        LET msg_txt = "0"
      ELSE
        LET msg_txt = upd_cnt USING "<<<<<<"
      END IF
      LET ga_dsplymsg[1] = "Paid date updated for ", msg_txt CLIPPED,
                           " order(s)."
      CALL message_window(10,12)

    END FUNCTION -- pay_orders --
```

To locate any function definition see the Function Index on page 728.

22

Determining Database Features

This example demonstrates how the features of a database are made available in the SQLCA.SQLAWARN array immediately after the database is opened, and how a program can save and use this information.

The SQLAWARN Array

The SQL Communications Area, or SQLCA, is updated by the database engine after any SQL operation. One component of the SQLCA is an array of eight characters, the SQLAWARN array. In **4GL**, the array is indexed starting from 1. (In an **ESQL/C** program, it is indexed starting from zero; this sometimes causes confusion.) Full details on the settings of SQLCA fields are in your SQL reference material.

Whenever the engine opens a new database—that is, whenever it executes the DATABASE or CREATE DATABASE statement—it sets the SQLAWARN characters to reflect the features of the database and the engine. The values set at this time are:

SQLAWARN[2] Contains *W* only if the database has a transaction log. If so, use of the COMMIT WORK statement is necessary; if not, COMMIT WORK will cause an error.

SQLAWARN[3] Contains *W* if the database is ANSI-compliant. When this is the case, the use of some Informix extensions to SQL cause a warning (a *W* in SQLAWARN[6]) and some will cause an error.

SQLAWARN[4] Contains *W* if the database engine is **INFORMIX-OnLine**. Otherwise the standard database engine is in use. The engines use different syntax for a few statements.

SQLAWARN[5] Contains *W* if the database engine stores FLOAT values in DECIMAL format. This only affects a few desktop systems that lack FLOAT support.

The SQLAWARN values can be saved and used to guide the operations of the program. They must be captured immediately after the DATABASE statement because the next SQL statement will overwrite them.

Opening the Database

The heart of this example is a function named open_db(). It opens a database dynamically and stores the facts about it into a global record. It captures the values from SQLAWARN as well as whether the engine supports the SET LOCK MODE statement.

The open_db() function takes a database name as its argument. The name string may include the word EXCLUSIVE, so that the function may be used to get exclusive access to a database as well as normal access. The name string may also include a sitename as allowed by **INFORMIX-STAR** and **INFORMIX-NET**.

When it succeeds in opening the database, open_db() returns TRUE, otherwise FALSE. When it fails to open the database, it uses the ERROR statement to display information about the reason.

Conditional Transactions

Once the SQLAWARN values have been captured, the program can modify its operations based on them. One area where knowledge of the database is helpful is transaction processing.

A database can be switched from logging to not logging, and ANSI compliance can be added after the database has been created and is in use. This leaves your program open to the following kinds of problems:

- Every program that modifies data should specify explicit transactions. They help to organize the application design and to ensure data integrity. But if the program executes COMMIT WORK in a database without a log, an SQL error results.
- If the database has a transaction log and the program does not use explicit transactions, performance problems can occur. For example, **INFORMIX-OnLine** can run out of locks, or a logical log can fill up, if a transaction goes on too long without an explicit COMMIT WORK.

- In most databases the program should mark the start of each transaction with BEGIN WORK, but in an ANSI-compliant database the use of BEGIN WORK is not allowed; only COMMIT WORK and ROLLBACK WORK are used.

These problems can be resolved with relative ease by writing short functions that conditionally perform transaction statements based on the database information left behind by open_db(). This example contains three such functions:

begin_wk()
: Performs a BEGIN WORK statement if the current database has a transaction log and is not ANSI-compliant.

commit_wk()
: Performs a COMMIT WORK statement if the current database has a transaction log.

rollback_wk()
: Performs a ROLLBACK WORK statement if the current database has a transaction log.

Calls to these functions can be written where transactions should logically begin or end. If transactions are supported by the database, the correct statements are executed.

Function Overview

Function Name	Purpose
open_db()	Opens a database using dynamic SQL and saves information about it for later use. Returns TRUE or FALSE.
begin_wk()	Executes a BEGIN WORK statement provided that open_db() says the database uses Informix-style transactions.
commit_wk()	Executes a COMMIT WORK statement provided that open_db() says the database uses transactions.
rollback_wk()	Executes a ROLLBACK WORK statement provided that open_db() says the database uses transactions.

The GLOBALS Statement and MAIN Function

1➤ The open_db() function fills in the fields of the gr_database record. The transaction functions such as begin_wk() test the fields, especially has_log. The fields are declared as SMALLINT rather than CHARACTER so that they can be used directly in conditional expressions: "IF gr_database.has_log THEN" instead of "IF gr_database.has_log = "W" THEN."

2➤ If it encounters an error, open_db() documents it with an ERROR statement. ERROR is a screen-oriented statement, and does not mix well with simple DISPLAY statements. This use of DISPLAY...AT puts the program into full-screen mode so that ERROR will display properly. (Run the program without the AT clause, naming a nonexistent database, to see what happens.) A real program would ordinarily be in full-screen mode as a result of displaying a form.

3➤ The return value from open_db() is Boolean; it returns TRUE when the database is open. The remaining statements in the function display in words the implications of the information that has been captured in the gr_database record.

4GL source file

```
   GLOBALS
1➤   DEFINE gr_database RECORD
                              db_known    SMALLINT,    -- following fields are usable
                              has_log     SMALLINT,    -- based on SQLAWARN[2]
                              is_ansi     SMALLINT,    -- based on SQLAWARN[3]
                              is_online   SMALLINT,    -- based on SQLAWARN[4]
                              can_wait    SMALLINT     -- supports "set lock mode to wait"
                           END RECORD
   END GLOBALS

   ########################################
   MAIN
   ########################################
     DEFINE   db       CHAR(50),
              ret      INTEGER

2➤   DISPLAY "Example 22, testing open_db function." AT 1,1
     OPTIONS PROMPT LINE 3

     PROMPT "Enter name of database to try: " FOR db
3➤   IF open_db(db) THEN
       DISPLAY "Database is open."
       IF gr_database.is_online THEN
         DISPLAY "The engine is Informix-OnLine."
         DISPLAY "It supports SET LOCK MODE TO WAIT [n]"
       ELSE
         DISPLAY "The engine is Informix-SE."
         IF gr_database.can_wait THEN
           DISPLAY "It supports SET LOCK MODE TO WAIT."
         ELSE
           DISPLAY "It does not support SET LOCK MODE."
         END IF
       END IF
       IF gr_database.is_ansi THEN
         DISPLAY "The database is ANSI-compliant, that is,"
         IF gr_database.is_online THEN
           DISPLAY " it was created with LOG MODE ANSI."
         ELSE
           DISPLAY " START DATABASE...MODE ANSI was used on it."
         END IF
         DISPLAY "A transaction is always in effect; COMMIT WORK ends."
       ELSE
         DISPLAY "The database uses Informix extensions to ANSI SQL."
         IF gr_database.has_log THEN
           DISPLAY "It has a transaction log; BEGIN/COMMIT WORK used."
         ELSE
           DISPLAY "The database does not have a transaction log."
         END IF
       END IF
```

4➤ In a real application, if the database failed to open, this would probably be the best action: to pause for a few seconds to allow reading the error message and then to end the program.

The open_db() Function

5➤ The variable dbname is sized to accommodate a sitename and, optionally, the word EXCLUSIVE. Possible arguments range from "stores2" up to "uk_dossier@london exclusive".

6➤ It is not usually necessary to close the current database before executing DATABASE, and if there is no database open at present, this statement will return error -349. However, when the current database is in another server accessed via **INFORMIX-NET**, you must close the current database before opening another one. So here the database is closed and the program tests for the expected error code.

7➤ Since **4GL** allows you to supply the database name in a program variable when you execute the DATABASE statement, it would have been possible to write simply

```
DATABASE dbname
```

A more elaborate method using PREPARE and EXECUTE is employed for two reasons:

- It allows the word EXCLUSIVE to be passed as part of the database name string. (The alternative would have been to have two DATABASE statements, one with and one without EXCLUSIVE, and a second function argument to choose between them.)
- The PREPARE statement checks the syntax of the contents of dbname. This makes it possible to diagnose and report bad name syntax apart from other errors.

8➤ A database has been opened successfully. When a prepared DATABASE statement is successfully executed, the statement is automatically freed. An attempt to FREE it will return an error. This passage of code can proceed to record the information in SQLAWARN.

```
4➤    ELSE -- error opening db?
        DISPLAY "Database did not open correctly." AT 4,1
        SLEEP 10 -- leave error message visible before program end
      END IF
    END MAIN

    #######################################
    FUNCTION open_db(dbname)
    #######################################
5➤    DEFINE  dbname  CHAR(50),

              dbstmt  CHAR(60), -- "DATABASE " plus the above
              sqlr    SMALLINT

      LET gr_database.db_known = FALSE -- initialize with safe values
      LET gr_database.has_log = FALSE
      LET gr_database.is_ansi = FALSE
      LET gr_database.is_online = FALSE
      LET gr_database.can_wait = FALSE

    WHENEVER ERROR CONTINUE
6➤    CLOSE DATABASE
      IF SQLCA.SQLCODE <> 0 AND SQLCA.SQLCODE <> -349 THEN
        ERROR "Error ",SQLCA.SQLCODE," closing current database."
        RETURN FALSE
      END IF -- either 0 or -349 is OK here
      LET dbstmt = "DATABASE ",dbname
7➤    PREPARE prepdbst FROM dbstmt
      IF SQLCA.SQLCODE <> 0 THEN -- big syntax trouble in "dbname"
        ERROR "Not an acceptable database name: ",dbname
        RETURN FALSE
      END IF
      EXECUTE prepdbst
      LET sqlr = SQLCA.SQLCODE
    WHENEVER ERROR STOP

      IF sqlr = 0 THEN-- we have opened the database
8➤      LET gr_database.db_known = TRUE
        IF SQLCA.SQLAWARN[2] = "W" THEN
          LET gr_database.has_log = TRUE
        END IF
        IF SQLCA.SQLAWARN[3] = "W" THEN
          LET gr_database.is_ansi = TRUE
        END IF
        IF SQLCA.SQLAWARN[4] = "W" THEN
          LET gr_database.is_online = TRUE
        ELSE -- not online, check lock support
          SET LOCK MODE TO WAIT
          IF SQLCA.SQLCODE = 0 THEN -- didn't get -527 or -513
            LET gr_database.can_wait = TRUE
          END IF
          SET LOCK MODE TO NOT WAIT -- restore default, ignore return code
        END IF
```

9➤ If the prepared DATABASE statement was *not* successful, it was *not* automatically freed, and the program should do it. An analysis of the most likely errors that can follow a DATABASE statement then takes place.

The begin_wk() Function

10➤ The begin_wk() function issues a BEGIN WORK if the database uses transactions and is not ANSI-compliant. In an ANSI-compliant database a transaction is always in effect and the program only marks the ends of transactions, not their beginnings.

```
    ELSE -- the database did not open; display a message
9➤    FREE prepdbst -- since not freed automatically when stmt fails
      CASE
        WHEN (sqlr = -329 OR sqlr = -827)
          ERROR dbname CLIPPED,
            ": Database not found or no system permission."
        WHEN (sqlr = -349)
          ERROR dbname CLIPPED,
            " not opened, you do not have Connect privilege."
        WHEN (sqlr = -354)
          ERROR dbname CLIPPED,
            ": Incorrect database name format."
        WHEN (sqlr = -377)
          ERROR "open_db() called with a transaction still incomplete."
        WHEN (sqlr = -512)
          ERROR "Unable to open in exclusive mode, db probably in use."
        OTHERWISE
          ERROR dbname CLIPPED,
            ": error ",sqlr," on DATABASE statement."
      END CASE
    END IF
    RETURN gr_database.db_known
  END FUNCTION  -- open_db --

  #######################################
10➤ FUNCTION begin_wk()
  #######################################

    IF gr_database.db_known
        AND NOT gr_database.is_ansi
        AND gr_database.has_log
    THEN

  WHENEVER ERROR CONTINUE
      BEGIN WORK
      IF SQLCA.SQLCODE <> 0 THEN
        ERROR "Error ", SQLCA.SQLCODE,
          " on BEGIN WORK (isam #", SQLCA.SQLERRD[2], ")"
      END IF
  WHENEVER ERROR STOP

    END IF
  END FUNCTION  -- begin_wk --
```

The commit_wk() Function

11➤ The commit_wk() function makes COMMIT WORK conditional on whether the database uses transactions.

The rollback_wk() Function

12➤ The rollback_wk() function makes ROLLBACK WORK conditional on whether the database uses transactions.

```
    #######################################
11➤ FUNCTION commit_wk()
    #######################################

      IF  gr_database.db_known
          AND gr_database.has_log
      THEN

    WHENEVER ERROR CONTINUE
        COMMIT WORK
        IF SQLCA.SQLCODE <> 0 THEN
          ERROR "Error ", SQLCA.SQLCODE,
            " on COMMIT WORK (isam #", SQLCA.SQLERRD[2], ")"
        END IF
    WHENEVER ERROR STOP

      END IF
    END FUNCTION  -- commit_wk --

    #######################################
12➤ FUNCTION rollback_wk()
    #######################################

      IF  gr_database.db_known
          AND gr_database.has_log
      THEN
    WHENEVER ERROR CONTINUE
        ROLLBACK WORK
        IF SQLCA.SQLCODE <> 0 THEN
          ERROR "Error ", SQLCA.SQLCODE,
            " on ROLLBACK WORK (isam #", SQLCA.SQLERRD[2], ")"
        END IF
    WHENEVER ERROR STOP

      END IF
    END FUNCTION  -- rollback_wk --
```

To locate any function definition see the Function Index on page 728.

23

Handling Locked Rows

This example demonstrates how to handle a failed row fetch when the row is locked by another process. If a fetch fails due to a locked row, the program can repeat the fetch a specified number of times. If the lock is released during these fetch attempts, the program can access the row. By distinguishing between a locked row and other fetch errors, the program is able to retry the fetch instead of exiting with an error:

```
+------------------------------------------------------------------------------+
|LOCK DEMO:   Lock Table  Try Update  Release Lock  Exit                       |
|Find and try updating a customer row.                                         |
|                                                                              |
|                                                                              |
|                                                                              |
|  Customer Number: [        107] Company Name: [Athletic Supplies   ]         |
|   Address: [42 Jordan Avenue     ]                                           |
|            [                    ]                                           |
|      City: [Palo Alto      ]   State: [CA]  Zip Code: [94304         ]      |
|                                                                              |
|   Contact Name: [Charles        ][Ream            ]                         |
|      Telephone: [415-356-9876      ]                                        |
|                                                                              |
|                                                                              |
|                                                                              |
| Press Accept to save new customer data. Press CTRL-W for Help.               |
| Press Cancel to exit w/out saving.                                           |
|Customer row is locked. Retry #8                                              |
+------------------------------------------------------------------------------+
```

Locks and Transactions

A transaction is the unit the database uses to group modifications made to data. The database makes sure that all modifications made within a transaction are either saved (committed to disk) or are rejected (the changes are rolled back) as a group. To provide this capability, the database locks all rows altered during a transaction and holds all locks until the transaction ends. Locks prevent other processes from modifying the data.

The following **4GL** statements acquire locks:

- UPDATE
- DELETE
- INSERT
- FETCH or FOREACH (if the cursor is declared as FOR UPDATE)
- LOCK TABLE

The stores2t database uses transactions, so programs which access this database must execute these statements within a transaction. For more information on starting and ending transactions, see Example 11.

One of the benefits of transactions is that database changes can be grouped. The disadvantage is that other programs are likely to encounter a locked row (because other programs are retaining locks until the transaction ends). For this reason, it is important to test for locked rows.

If your database is not MODE ANSI or does not use transactions, locks are released as soon as an operation completes:

- For an INSERT, UPDATE or DELETE operation, locks are released when the statement completes.
- For a FETCH (or FOREACH) of an update cursor, the lock is released when the next row is fetched.
- For a LOCK TABLE, the lock is released with an UNLOCK TABLE statement.

Even though locks are released more quickly in a database without transactions, a program should still test for lock conflicts as they can occur.

Testing for Locked Rows

If another transaction holds a lock on a row when your program tries to access it, **4GL** returns an error. A program can anticipate locked rows in a couple of ways:

- Use the SET LOCK MODE statement so **4GL** waits on any locked row until the competing process releases the lock.
- Perform a "retry" for the locked row.

This example demonstrates the second solution. Although the SET LOCK MODE statement requires much less programming, it has the disadvantage that a program may appear to "hang" if it must wait for a long time before the desired row is unlocked. The **OnLine** engine supports a SET LOCK MODE option that allows you to specify the number of seconds to wait for a lock to be released. However, this option is not supported by the **SE** engine.

Performing a retry for a locked row has the following advantages:

- It works with both an **OnLine** and an **SE** engine.
- It notifies the user that the program is attempting the lock retries.

This solution waits for the lock to be released but then "gives up" if it fails to obtain the lock after a specified number of tries.

Running the Lock Test

To see how the program repeatedly attempts to fetch a locked row, you must run this program at the same time on two different terminals. On one terminal, you lock the customer table in shared mode. Shared mode allows other transactions to read the table but prevents them from modifying the table (with updates or deletes). On the second terminal, you attempt to update a row in this table. Because the customer table is locked by another transaction, you can see the program trying to repeatedly fetch the row. If the lock is not released before the specified number of retries, the update fails.

Run this program at two terminals as follows:

1. On Terminal 1, run the example and choose the "Lock Table" option.

   This option places a shared lock on the customer table.

2. On Terminal 2, run the example and choose the "Lock Table" option.

   The response to this option depends on the type of database engine you are using:

   - If you are using an **SE** engine, this second "Lock Table" request fails because only one process can have a shared lock on a single table. The option notifies you that another user has already locked the table.
   - If you are using an **OnLine** engine, this second "Lock Table" request is successful. Both Terminal 1 and Terminal 2 can hold a shared lock on the customer table. The option notifies you that the lock is successful. However, even though Terminal 2 is able to obtain a shared lock on the table, it will still encounter a lock conflict when attempting to update a row (See Step 5 below). Recall that a shared lock allows a process to read rows in a table but prevents it from updating or deleting these rows.

3. On Terminal 2, choose the "Try Update" option and specify the number of times to retry a failed fetch. A good value to start with is around five (5).
4. On Terminal 2, enter the customer number or company name of the customer to update and press Accept.

   The customer information displays on the screen (because terminal 1 has locked the table in SHARE MODE).
5. On Terminal 2, make a change to a field on the customer form and then press Accept.

   Because the table is locked by another user, the program cannot update the customer row. It performs the specified number of retrys to acquire the lock, waiting for the lock to be released. Because the lock is not released from Terminal 1 within the time taken by these retries, the update fails.
6. On Terminal 2, choose the "Try Update" option a second time. At the prompt, specify a large number of retries (ten or more), and then enter the desired customer number or name. Modify the data in one of the customer fields but *do not press Accept yet.*
7. On Terminal 2, press Accept; then immediately return to Terminal 1.
8. On Terminal 1, choose the "Release Lock" option and immediately look at the screen of Terminal 2.
9. On Terminal 2 you will see the Retry messages stop once the lock is released at Terminal 1.

   With the lock released, the program is able to update the customer row with the new information.

Function Overview

Function Name	Purpose
lock_menu()	Displays the LOCK DEMO menu to allow the user to choose whether to lock the customer table, try to update a customer row, or release the lock on the customer table.
bang()	Prompts the user for a command and executes the command. *See description in Example 3.*
lock_cust()	Tries to obtain a lock on the customer table (SHARE MODE).
try_update()	Finds a specified customer and then tries to update this customer row.
get_repeat()	Accepts user input for the number of repeats to perform in getting the lock before giving up.
open_ckey()	Opens the f_custkey form. *See description in Example 21.*
close_ckey()	Closes the f_custkey form. *See description in Example 21.*
find_cust()	Accepts user input of a customer number or company name and then finds a customer based on either of these values. *See description in Example 21.*
cust_popup2()	Retrieves all customers and displays them in an array form so the user can choose the appropriate customer. *See description in Example 12.*
change_cust()	Collects changes to current row. *See description in Example 6.*
row_locked()	Checks the value of SQLCA.SQLERRD[2] to see of the status value is negative due to a locking conflict. ISAM errors: -107, -113, -134, -143, -144, and -154 are treated as locking conflicts.
update_cust2()	Checks for a locked row before updating a customer row. If locked row found, the function performs "number_of_trys" retries to acquire lock before giving up and returning an error.
test_success()	Tests the "status" value and returns 1 (if the update was successful, 0 (if the update failed with a non-locking error, or -1 (if the update failed with a locking error).
clear_lines()	Clears any number of lines starting at any line. *See description in Example 6.*
msg()	Displays a brief, informative message. *See description in Example 5.*

The DATABASE Statement and MAIN Function

1➤ This example requires the stores2t database.

2➤ The lock_menu() function displays the menu that allows the user to run the locking tests. Notes about this menu begin with Note 6.

The lock_menu() Function

3➤ The another_user variable indicates whether the customer table is locked by another user. This variable is initialized to "U" (Unknown) because the state of the table lock is unknown until the user chooses the "Lock Table" option. Once this option executes, another_user is set to either "Y" or "N" (See Notes 8 and 12).

4➤ The BEGIN WORK statement appears before the MENU statement because each menu option performs a task that must be performed within a transaction.

5➤ The curr_tx flag indicates whether an active transaction exists. It is initialized to TRUE because the preceding BEGIN WORK statement started a new transaction. Since the program has no way of knowing which option the user had previously chosen, each option must check the setting of curr_tx to determine whether or not to begin or end the transaction.

6➤ The LOCK DEMO menu allows the user to choose a locking task to: lock ("Lock Table") the customer table, unlock this table ("Release Lock"), or attempt an update on this table ("Try Update"). Each option checks the setting of curr_tx to determine whether or not a transaction is active.

7➤ The "Lock Table" option requests a lock on the customer table. A lock request needs to have a transaction active before it can lock the customer table so this option tests the curr_tx variable (for more information about curr_tx, see Note 5). If curr_tx is TRUE, a transaction is current. However, if curr_tx is FALSE (no transaction is current), the option issues the BEGIN WORK statement to begin a new transaction. Once this new transaction begins, the curr_tx flag is set to TRUE.

4GL source file

```
1➤ DATABASE stores2t

   GLOBALS
     DEFINE        gr_customer RECORD LIKE customer.*,
                   gr_workcust RECORD LIKE customer.*
   END GLOBALS

   ########################################
   MAIN
   ########################################

     OPTIONS
       HELP FILE "hlpmsgs",
       COMMENT LINE LAST-3,
       MESSAGE LINE LAST,
       FORM LINE 5

     DEFER INTERRUPT

     OPEN WINDOW w_locktst AT 2,3
       WITH 18 ROWS, 76 COLUMNS
       ATTRIBUTE (BORDER)

2➤   CALL lock_menu()

     CLOSE WINDOW w_locktst
     CLEAR SCREEN

   END MAIN

   ########################################
   FUNCTION lock_menu()
   ########################################
     DEFINE  curr_tx          SMALLINT,
             another_user     CHAR(1)

3➤   LET another_user = "U"

4➤   BEGIN WORK
5➤   LET curr_tx = TRUE

     DISPLAY
     "--------------------------------------------Press CTRL-W for Help----------"
       AT 3, 1
6➤   MENU "LOCK DEMO"
         COMMAND "Lock Table" "Lock the customer table." HELP 140
7➤         IF NOT curr_tx THEN
             BEGIN WORK
             LET curr_tx = TRUE
           END IF
```

8➤ The lock_cust() function attempts to lock the customer table. This function returns a single character status code in the another_user variable to indicate the success of the lock request. If the lock request fails because another user has already locked the table, lock_cust() returns a "Y". If the lock request is successful, lock_cust() returns "N". See Note 3 for more information about the another_user variable.

9➤ The "Try Update" option attempts to update a row of the customer table. Because the row is selected with an update cursor, the update must occur within an active transaction. If curr_tx is FALSE, the option begins a new transaction with BEGIN WORK and resets curr_tx to TRUE.

10➤ The try_update() function actually attempts the customer row update. If the function returns TRUE, the update was successful so the current transaction's work is saved in the database with COMMIT WORK. If the function returns FALSE, the update was not successful so the transaction's work is not saved.

11➤ Once the current transaction is ended (with either COMMIT WORK or ROLLBACK WORK), the curr_tx flag is set to FALSE.

12➤ The "Release Lock" option attempts to unlock the customer table. To determine the state of the customer table lock, the "Release Lock" option needs to be preceded by the "Lock Table" option, so the lock_cust() function is called. If the another_user variable is still "U", lock_cust() has not been called (See Note 8).

13➤ If the lock_cust() function has been called, then the "Release Lock" option checks whether the current table is locked by another user or locked by the current user. If the table is locked by another user, this user cannot release the lock.

14➤ If this user has locked the table, then the lock can be released. However, an unlock request must occur within an active transaction so this option tests the curr_tx variable (for more information about curr_tx, see Note 5). If curr_tx is TRUE, then the program executes a COMMIT WORK statement to release all locks and then sets the curr_tx flag to FALSE. If curr_tx is FALSE, then no tables are locked (because a lock can only be granted within a transaction).

15➤ The "Exit" option ends an active transaction with a COMMIT WORK. The call to COMMIT WORK explicitly ends the transaction even though active transactions are ended when the program exits.

```
8➤        CALL lock_cust() RETURNING another_user

          NEXT OPTION "Try Update"

        COMMAND "Try Update" "Find and try updating a customer row."
              HELP 141
9➤        IF NOT curr_tx THEN
            BEGIN WORK
            LET curr_tx = TRUE
          END IF
10➤       IF try_update() THEN
            COMMIT WORK
            CALL msg("Customer has been updated.")
          ELSE
            ROLLBACK WORK
            CALL msg("Customer has not been updated.")
          END IF
11➤       LET curr_tx = FALSE
          CLEAR WINDOW w_locktst

        COMMAND "Release Lock" "Release lock on customer table."
              HELP 142
12➤       IF another_user = "U" THEN
            CALL msg("Status of table lock is unknown. Run 'Lock' option.")
            NEXT OPTION "Lock Table"
          ELSE
13➤         IF another_user = "Y" THEN
              CALL msg("Cannot release another user's lock.")
            ELSE
14➤           IF curr_tx THEN
                COMMIT WORK
                LET curr_tx = FALSE
                CALL msg("Lock on customer table has been released.")
              END IF
            END IF
          END IF

        COMMAND KEY ("!")
          CALL bang()

        COMMAND KEY ("E", "e", "X", "x") "Exit" "Exit program."
            HELP 100
15➤       IF curr_tx THEN
            COMMIT WORK
          END IF
          EXIT MENU

    END MENU

  END FUNCTION  -- lock_menu --
```

The lock_cust() Function

16➤ The another_user variable indicates whether or not the customer table is locked. The state of the table lock is determined by the status variable after the LOCK TABLE executes (See Note 18).

17➤ The LOCK TABLE statement requests a shared lock on the customer table. A shared lock allows other users to read rows in this table but prevents them from updating or deleting these rows. This statement is surrounded by WHENEVER ERROR statements to turn off automatic error checking before the LOCK TABLE and to turn it back on afterward. Because the automatic checking is off when the LOCK TABLE executes, the program must perform its own error checking to determine the success of the statement.

18➤ If the LOCK TABLE is not successful, the function checks the cause of the failure. If another user has already locked the table (status=-289, it sets the another_user variable to "Y". Otherwise, it displays an error message to notify the user of the cause of the failure.

19➤ If the LOCK TABLE was successful, the function notifies the user that the customer table is now locked.

20➤ The lock_cust() function returns the setting of the another_user variable so that the calling program can determine whether another user has a lock on the customer table (See Note 13).

The try_update() Function

21➤ The get_repeat() function prompts the user for the number of retries (the number of times that the program tries to obtain the lock before giving up). If a desired row is locked, it cannot be fetched by the cursor. This function returns the specified number of retries or zero (0).

22➤ If the user presses presses Cancel at the prompt, get_repeat() returns zero (0). The program exits the "Try Update" option and returns to the LOCK DEMO menu.

23➤ The open_ckey() function displays the f_custkey form in the w_custkey window. This function is described in Example 21.

```
     ########################################
     FUNCTION lock_cust()
     ########################################
       DEFINE another_user     CHAR(1)

16➤    LET another_user = "N"
17➤  WHENEVER ERROR CONTINUE
       LOCK TABLE customer IN SHARE MODE
     WHENEVER ERROR STOP

18➤    IF (status < 0) THEN
         IF status = -289 THEN
           CALL msg("Table is currently locked by another user.")
           LET another_user = "Y"
         ELSE
           ERROR status USING "-<<<<<<<<<<<",
             ": Unable to lock customer table."
         END IF
19➤    ELSE
         CALL msg("Customer table is now locked.")
       END IF

20➤    RETURN another_user

     END FUNCTION  -- lock_cust --

     ########################################
     FUNCTION try_update()
     ########################################
       DEFINE  success         SMALLINT,
               number_of_trys  SMALLINT

21➤    LET number_of_trys = get_repeat()
22➤    IF number_of_trys = 0 THEN
         RETURN FALSE
       END IF

23➤    CALL open_ckey()

       LET success = FALSE
```

24➤ The find_cust() function allows the user to select a customer by entering either a customer number or company name. This function is described in Example 21. If find_cust() returns TRUE, the user has specified a valid customer.

25➤ The close_ckey() function closes the f_custkey form. This function is described in Example 21.

26➤ The program displays the customer information for the specified customer on the f_customer form. A copy of the selected customer row is saved in the gr_workcust global record so that the program can restore the original row values to the screen if the user cancels the update (See Note 28).

27➤ If the user exits the f_customer form with the Accept key, the program calls the update_cust2() function. The update_cust2() function uses an update cursor to lock the desired row. If the row is already locked, update_cust2() tries to get the row for the specified number of retries. The change_cust() function is described in Example 6.

28➤ If the update_cust2() function returns TRUE, the specified row has been updated and the program clears the form. If update_cust2() returns FALSE, the row has not been updated; either the row was locked or the UPDATE failed. In either case, the program restores the original values of the row to the form.

29➤ The try_update() function returns TRUE if the row was updated and FALSE otherwise.

The get_repeat() Function

30➤ The trys variable is defined as type CHAR so that the user can enter any character (numbers, letters, or symbols) without incurring a data type error.

```
24➤   IF find_cust() THEN
25➤     CALL close_ckey()

26➤     OPEN FORM f_customer FROM "f_customer"
        DISPLAY FORM f_customer

        SELECT *
        INTO gr_customer.*
        FROM customer
        WHERE customer_num = gr_customer.customer_num

        LET gr_workcust.* = gr_customer.*
        DISPLAY BY NAME gr_customer.*

27➤     IF change_cust() THEN
          CALL update_cust2(number_of_trys) RETURNING success
28➤       IF success THEN
            CLEAR FORM
          ELSE
            LET gr_customer.* = gr_workcust.*
            DISPLAY BY NAME gr_customer.*
          END IF
        END IF

        CLOSE FORM f_customer
      ELSE
        CALL close_ckey()
      END IF

29➤   RETURN success

    END FUNCTION  -- try_update --

    ########################################
    FUNCTION get_repeat()
    ########################################
      DEFINE  invalid_resp    SMALLINT,
              trys            CHAR(2),
              numtrys         SMALLINT

      OPEN WINDOW w_repeat AT 6,7
        WITH 3 ROWS, 65 COLUMNS
        ATTRIBUTE (BORDER, PROMPT LINE 3)

      DISPLAY
      " Enter number of retries and press Accept. Press CTRL-W for Help."
        AT 1, 1 ATTRIBUTE (REVERSE, YELLOW)
      LET invalid_resp = TRUE
      WHILE invalid_resp
        LET int_flag = FALSE
30➤     PROMPT "How many times should I try getting a locked row? "
          FOR trys HELP 143
```

31➤ These WHENEVER statements use the ANY clause keyword to ensure that the status variable is set (and execution does not stop) after each **4GL** statement. Without this keyword, status is only set after SQL and screen statements (in **i4gl**) or after most statements (in **r4gl**).

32➤ The LET statement attempts to assign the input received from the PROMPT to an integer variable. This assignment should execute without error because **4GL** can convert the character representation of a number to an integer value and the user should have entered an integer value. However, if the user entered letters or symbols, this conversion fails because **4GL** cannot convert these characters to an integer. The WHENEVER ANY ERROR statement prevents the program from encountering a runtime error if such a conversion is attempted.

33➤ If the data conversion in the LET statement fails, **4GL** sets the status variable to a negative value. The program tells the user the desired type of data and reprompts for input.

34➤ If the user pressed Cancel at the prompt, the program interprets the key as a signal to exit the "Try Update" menu option. It resets the int_flag, sets the number of retries to zero (0) to indicate that the user does not want to continue and exits the WHILE loop.

35➤ Since a negative value or zero is not valid, the program tells the user the desired type of data and reprompts for input.

36➤ If execution reaches this point, the data entered is valid. The program sets the invalid_resp flag to FALSE to exit the WHILE loop.

37➤ This function returns the specified number of lock retries. If the user has cancelled the PROMPT, the function returns zero (See Note 34).

The update_cust2() Function

38➤ This function declares an update cursor to select the specified customer row. This update cursor locks the selected row as it is fetched. If the fetch is successful, the UPDATE (see Note 43) should succeed (a locking error was not encountered).

```
31➤ WHENEVER ANY ERROR CONTINUE      --* convert character answer to
32➤     LET numtrys = trys           --*   an integer and check for
    WHENEVER ANY ERROR STOP          --*   conversion errors

33➤     IF (status < 0) THEN         --* encountered conversion error
          ERROR "Please enter a positive integer number"
          CONTINUE WHILE
        END IF

34➤     IF int_flag THEN
            LET int_flag = FALSE
            LET numtrys = 0
            EXIT WHILE
        END IF

35➤     IF (numtrys <= 0) THEN        --* integer < 0
          ERROR "Please enter a positive integer number"
          CONTINUE WHILE
        END IF

36➤     LET invalid_resp = FALSE

      END WHILE

      CLOSE WINDOW w_repeat
37➤   RETURN numtrys

    END FUNCTION  -- get_repeat --

    ########################################
    FUNCTION update_cust2(number_of_trys)
    ########################################
      DEFINE  number_of_trys  SMALLINT,

              try_again       SMALLINT,
              try             SMALLINT,
              cust_num        LIKE customer.customer_num,
              success         SMALLINT,
              msg_txt         CHAR(78)

38➤   DECLARE c_custlck CURSOR FOR
        SELECT customer_num
        FROM customer
        WHERE customer_num = gr_customer.customer_num
      FOR UPDATE

      LET success = FALSE
      LET try_again = TRUE
      LET try = 0
```

39➤ A WHILE loop controls the fetch of the customer row. If the fetch fails due to a locking error, try_again is set to TRUE and the WHILE loops to retry the fetch.

40➤ The example uses the OPEN, FETCH, and CLOSE statements instead of the FOREACH, so it can test the status of each row as it is fetched. The FOREACH statement executes the statements within the FOREACH block if status is zero. If the status is not zero, FOREACH exits the loop and closes the cursor. By using a FETCH, the program can distinguish between a fetch which failed due to a locked row and one which failed for some other reason, and perform the appropriate actions.

41➤ The FETCH statement is surrounded by the WHENEVER ERROR statement so the program can perform its own checking of the status variable.

42➤ The test_success() function examines the status variable and returns:

- 1 if status is zero (the fetch was successful)
- 0 if status indicates that the fetch failed due to some non-locking error
- -1 if status indicates that the fetch failed due to a locked row

43➤ If the fetch was successful, the desired customer row is fetched and locked. The program updates the row with the new customer information. The success variable is set to TRUE to indicate that the customer update was successful.

44➤ If the fetch failed because the program encountered some non-locking error, the program notifies the user of the cause of the error and sets the success variable to FALSE.

45➤ If the fetch failed because the desired row is locked, the program increments its count of the number of retries performed and checks to see if this count exceeds the number of retries specified by the user. If not, the program notifies the user that it is going to try again to obtain the lock. It sets the try_again flag to TRUE so the WHILE loop reiterates. If it has already attempted the specified number of retries, the program sets the success variable to FALSE to indicate that the update failed.

46➤ The program closes the update cursor so that cursor resources can be reallocated. Notice that any lock held on the customer row is not released because the current transaction has not yet ended (See Note 10).

47➤ The function returns a TRUE or FALSE value indicating whether or not the update was successful.

```
39➤    WHILE try_again

40➤      OPEN c_custlck

         LET try_again = FALSE

41➤  WHENEVER ERROR CONTINUE
         FETCH c_custlck INTO cust_num
     WHENEVER ERROR STOP

42➤      CALL test_success(status) RETURNING success

         CASE success
43➤        WHEN 1  --* FETCH was successful

     WHENEVER ERROR CONTINUE
             UPDATE customer SET customer.* = gr_customer.*
             WHERE CURRENT OF c_custlck
     WHENEVER ERROR STOP

             IF (status < 0) THEN
               ERROR status USING "-<<<<<<<<<<<",
                 ": Unable to update current customer."
             ELSE
               LET success = TRUE
             END IF

44➤        WHEN 0  --* FETCH encountered non-locking error
             ERROR status USING "-<<<<<<<<<<<",
               ": Unable to open customer cursor for update."
             SLEEP 3
             LET success = FALSE

45➤        WHEN -1  --* FETCH encountered locked row
             LET try = try + 1
             IF (try <= number_of_trys) THEN
               LET msg_txt = "Customer row is locked. Retry #", try USING "<<<"
               CALL msg(msg_txt CLIPPED)
               CLOSE c_custlck
               LET try_again = TRUE
             ELSE
               LET success = FALSE
             END IF
         END CASE

       END WHILE

46➤    CLOSE c_custlck

47➤    RETURN success

     END FUNCTION  -- update_cust2 --
```

The test_success() Function

48➤ The test_success() function expects to receive the status variable as an argument. A negative value indicates an error.

49➤ The row_locked() function examines the **ISAM** error code to determine whether a locked row caused the fetch to fail. If so, it returns TRUE; and otherwise it returns FALSE.

50➤ The function sets the return code so that it returns 1 if the status variable is zero, 0 if the status variable indicates a non-locking error, and -1 if the status variable indicates a locking error.

The row_locked() Function

51➤ The CASE statement tests the value of the SQLCA.SQLERRD[2] variable. If the fetch (see Note 41) fails, the status variable indicates a failure and the **ISAM** error code indicates the cause of the failure.

ISAM error code values of -107, -113, -134, -143, -144, and -154 indicate that a lock request cannot be granted. In this case, the function returns TRUE. Otherwise, it returns FALSE.

```
########################################
FUNCTION test_success(db_status)
########################################
  DEFINE  db_status       SMALLINT,

          success         SMALLINT

48➤  IF (db_status < 0) THEN
49➤    IF row_locked() THEN          --* encountered locked row
      LET success = -1
    ELSE                          --* encountered non-locking error
      LET success = 0
    END IF
  ELSE                            --* didn't encounter error
    LET success = 1
  END IF

50➤  RETURN success

END FUNCTION  -- test_success --

########################################
FUNCTION row_locked()
########################################
  DEFINE  locked  SMALLINT

51➤  CASE SQLCA.SQLERRD[2]
    WHEN -107
      LET locked = TRUE
    WHEN -113
      LET locked = TRUE
    WHEN -134
      LET locked = TRUE
    WHEN -143
      LET locked = TRUE
    WHEN -144
      LET locked = TRUE
    WHEN -154
      LET locked = TRUE
    OTHERWISE
      LET locked = FALSE
  END CASE

  RETURN locked

END FUNCTION  -- row_locked --
```

To locate any function definition see the Function Index on page 728.

24

Using a Hold Cursor

This example demonstrates how to:

- Use **4GL** to write a batch-oriented program, as opposed to the interactive, screen-oriented programs in the other examples.
- Use an update journal to shift database updates to off-peak hours.
- Use a cursor WITH HOLD to maintain a table scan position across transaction boundaries.

To demonstrate the processing of a journal of updates, a table of update requests (referred to as the journal) must exist. A file of simulated updates against the orders table accompanies this example. A driver program loads this into a table before running the example code.

This example completes the following actions:

1. Opens the database dynamically to check for the use of transactions (as in Example 22).
2. Makes a temporary copy of the orders table so that the updates will not have a permanent effect.
3. Creates an update journal table and loads it from a source file.
4. Performs the updates in the journal, generating a report as it goes.
5. Saves the contents of the update journal table in the ex24.out file.
6. Restores the original contents of the orders table.

The Update Journal

You can use an update journal to defer updates of a heavily-used table to off-peak hours so that the updates will have less impact on the performance of interactive queries.

A table update is a disk-intensive operation. Not only must the row of data be replaced on disk, but at least one page of each index on the table must be rewritten. While these operations take place, rows of data and index pages are locked. This can cause delays in the execution of interactive queries.

One way to avoid these effects is to write the updated information into a table of updates rather than the original table. Each row of such an update journal reflects one pending update. After peak hours, when interactive queries are few and the hardware is no longer operating at full capacity, the deferred updates can be applied in a single batch process.

One problem with this scheme is that updates are not recorded in the updated table at the time they are entered. In many applications this does not matter; it is acceptable for the appearance of new data to be delayed by a day. It is also possible to write the query applications so that they test the update journal, and either display the latest information from it, or display an indication that there are updates pending against a displayed record.

Contents of an Update Journal

An update journal is a table. Each row describes one deferred update, containing all the information needed to validate the update, apply it, and trace the source of the problem if the update cannot be applied.

In this example, the orders table in the demonstration database is the subject of the updates. The update journal contains the following columns.

journal_id — A SERIAL field that gives each update request a unique id.

upd_status — A field containing letter code *N* (for a new update) or *D* (for one that has been applied).

order_num — A foreign key to the orders table, giving the order to which the update applies.

entered_by — The USER value of the user who entered the update. Essential for follow-up in the event the order is erroneous.

enter_date — A timestamp showing the time the update was logged in the journal, giving the time to the second.

org_*xx* Copies of the updatable columns of the original row of orders as they were when the update was entered. For example, org_si contains the original of the ship_instruct column.

upd_*xx* New values for updatable columns, or null if a column is not to be updated. For example, a new value for ship_instruct would appear in upd_si.

The upd_status column is used to separate updates that have been applied from those that have not. The cursor that selects each journal row uses a WHERE clause that tests for *N* in this column. The last step in applying an update is to change this column of the journal row to *D* for done. Then, if the updating program is interrupted for some reason, it can be run again without fear that it will apply an update twice.

Transaction processing is essential to make this update-status check work reliably. That is, the update of a row of the orders table and the change of upd_status in the corresponding row of the journal must be part of the same transaction. That ensures that both will take place or that neither will. Without this assurance the program could update the orders table but be interrupted before setting upd_status to *D*. Then an update might be applied twice.

The journal record contains two copies of any changed column: one as the row should be prior to the update, the other as the it should be after the update. The program tests the existing row against the original values before applying the update. This is an essential safeguard to ensure that the update is applied to the same data that the human operator saw. This check guards against a variety of unlikely but still plausible errors. For example, if someone uses interactive SQL or some other means to enter a change to the orders table manually, this test will prevent a journalled update from overriding that change.

Using a Cursor WITH HOLD

Normally the end of a transaction forces all cursors to close and releases all locks. These requirements make it easier to implement the database and log operations that are necessary to ensure all updates are committed to disk safely.

While you cannot avoid releasing all locks, it is not essential to close all cursors. You can declare a non-scrolling cursor WITH HOLD, which will remain open and retain its position across a transaction boundary.

A hold cursor is especially convenient for processing an update journal. Each update should be handled as a single transaction in these steps:

1. Read the next unapplied row in the journal.
2. Read and lock the target row of the table.
3. Verify the update against the current contents of the table row.
4. Update the table row.
5. Change the status in the row of the journal table.
6. Commit the transaction.

If the last step closed the cursor on the journal table, it would have to be opened again prior to each update. These frequent reopenings would be inefficient and time consuming.

Comparisons in the Presence of Nulls

Null values present an interesting case when completing the steps outlined above. By definition, null values are not equal to anything; this includes other null values. The reason is that a null value is an unknown value. The only reasonable result of a comparison between an unknown and anything else, is unknown. Neither TRUE nor FALSE is a reasonable answer.

The **4GL** language treats a Boolean expression that involves an unknown value as being equivalent to FALSE. For example, an IF statement that compares a null will *always* execute its ELSE part.

```
IF A = B THEN -- if A and/or B is null, result is always false
    DISPLAY "true"
ELSE
    DISPLAY "false"
END IF
```

The preceding statement will display `false` when A is null, when B is null, *and when both are null.* This does not accord with most people's expectations.

This example needs to compare values that may be null, and recognize when they are alike, meaning that either both are null or else they are equal. The like() subroutine performs this comparison. It returns TRUE if the two values are "like" each other in this sense.

Function Overview

Function Name	Purpose
update_driver()	A model of the central logic of a batch update program: reads rows from the update journal, validates and applies them.
upd_rep()	A report function used to document the operations of upd_driver(), printing a line for each update transaction.
like()	Function returning TRUE when two values are either equal or both null, FALSE otherwise.
check_db_priv()	Function returning TRUE if the current user has a specified level of database privilege, FALSE otherwise.
open_db()	Opens a database using dynamic SQL and saves information about it for later use. Returns TRUE or FALSE. *See description in Example 22.*
begin_wk()	Executes a BEGIN WORK statement provided that open_db() says the database uses Informix-style transactions. *See description in Example 22.*
commit_wk()	Executes a COMMIT WORK statement provided that open_db() says the database uses transactions. *See description in Example 22.*
rollback_wk()	Executes a ROLLBACK WORK statement provided that open_db() says the database uses transactions. *See description in Example 22.*
save_orders()	Makes a copy of the orders table in a temporary table.
restore_orders()	Restores the rows of the orders table that appear in the update journal.
save_journal()	Saves the contents of the update journal table (upd_journal) in the file ex24.out before dropping this table.
build_journal()	Creates the simulated update journal table and loads it from an ASCII file.

The GLOBALS Statement

1➤ The fields in the gr_database record are set by the open_db() function. They are used by the begin_wk() and related functions introduced in Example 22. These functions deal with transaction management.

2➤ The jrn record matches the initial five columns of the upd_journal table. Since that table is not part of the stores2t database when this program is compiled, the record cannot be defined using LIKE.

3➤ The ver (verify) and set records receive the two copies of updatable columns from a journal row. The original values are held in ver and the new values in set. The current contents of a row of orders is read into cur. An update can only be performed when the fields of cur are like those of ver.

The MAIN Function

4➤ The program uses a DISPLAY and a PROMPT statement to ask the user for the database name. Since PROMPT is a user interface statement, the program also initializes the int_flag built-in variable to FALSE.

5➤ If the user pressed Cancel, the program resets the int_flag variable and performs no further action. The program sets the default database name to "stores2t" if the user does not enter a name.

Resetting the int_flag is not required in this case, since the program ends when the user presses Cancel. However, it is good programming practice to always reset the int_flag in case you change the program at some future point.

6➤ Since the program opens the database dynamically (open_db() analyzes it while performing this function) it provides the user with the opportunity to name a different database. In case of error, the program ends, leaving the error message from open_db() on the screen.

7➤ The check_db_priv() function (see page 558) returns TRUE if the current user has at least the indicated level of privilege in the current database. This example needs Resource privilege in order to rename the orders table and create the upd_journal table.

4GL source file

```
    DATABASE stores2t

    GLOBALS
1➤    DEFINE        gr_database RECORD
                        db_known    SMALLINT,  -- following fields are usable
                        has_log     SMALLINT,  -- based on SQLAWARN[2]
                        is_ansi     SMALLINT,  -- based on SQLAWARN[3]
                        is_online   SMALLINT,  -- based on SQLAWARN[4]
                        can_wait    SMALLINT   -- supports "set lock mode to wait"
                    END RECORD
    END GLOBALS

2➤  DEFINE          jrn RECORD
                        journal_id   INTEGER,
                        upd_status   CHAR(1),
                        order_num    INTEGER,
                        entered_by   CHAR(8),
                        enter_date   DATETIME YEAR TO SECOND
                    END RECORD,
3➤                  ver,      -- table values BEFORE update
                    set,      -- new updated table values
                    cur RECORD LIKE orders.* -- table values currently in db

    #########################################
    MAIN
    #########################################
      DEFINE          reppath    CHAR(80),
                      dbname     CHAR(10),
                      valid_db   SMALLINT

      DEFER INTERRUPT

      LET valid_db = FALSE

4➤    DISPLAY "Enter the name of the example database, or simply press"
      LET int_flag = FALSE
      PROMPT  "RETURN to use 'stores2t': " FOR dbname

5➤    IF int_flag THEN
        LET int_flag = FALSE
      ELSE
        IF LENGTH(dbname) = 0 THEN
          LET dbname = "stores2t"
        END IF
6➤      IF  open_db(dbname) THEN
7➤        IF NOT check_db_priv("R") THEN
            DISPLAY "Sorry, you must have at least Resource privilege"
            DISPLAY "in that database for this example to work."
            DISPLAY "Run the program again with a different database."
```

8➤ If both open_db() and check_db_priv() complete successfully, the program sets the valid_db variable to TRUE so that the body of the program will be executed (See Note 9).

9➤ If valid_db is TRUE, the user has entered a valid database which has been opened. The program can now perform the journal updates. The save_orders() function saves the current contents of the orders table in a temporary table. The build_journal() function then creates and loads the upd_journal table used to hold the journal update information.

10➤ At this point the preliminary work is complete and the update_driver() function (the main routine) is called. The update_driver() function checks the upd_journal table and performs the appropriate updates to the orders table.

Following completion of the routine, the program calls the restore_orders() function to drop the updated orders, restoring the example database to its prior state.

11➤ The save_journal() function saves the contents of the upd_journal table in the ex24.out file. The program drops the upd_journal table when it finishes; you can inspect the ex24.out file after the program finishes to view the contents of the upd_journal table.

12➤ The program drops the copy of the orders table (qsave_orders) so the database is returned to its state before the program executed.

The update_driver() Function

13➤ The function uses the length of its argument to determine where to send the report output. If no argument exists, the length is zero and the function directs report output to the screen. If an argument does exist, the function directs report output to the file named by this argument.

14➤ The keywords WITH HOLD establish jrnlupd as a hold cursor, one that will not close automatically when a transaction ends. The use of FOR UPDATE makes this an update cursor as well as a hold cursor. When a row of the update journal is fetched, it is locked. The lock is released at the end of a transaction, however. Note that the many columns of an update journal row are read into three different variables.

```
          ELSE
8➤          LET valid_db = TRUE
          END IF
        END IF
      END IF

9➤    IF valid_db THEN
        CALL save_orders()           -- save contents of orders table
        IF  build_journal() THEN     -- create the upd_journal

          DISPLAY ""
          DISPLAY "Enter a pathname to receive the update report output."
          DISPLAY "For output to the screen, just press RETURN."
          LET int_flag = FALSE
          PROMPT "Report pathname or null: " FOR reppath

          IF int_flag THEN
              LET int_flag = FALSE
          ELSE
10➤           CALL update_driver(reppath)-- run the real example
              CALL restore_orders() -- fix updated orders table
          END IF

11➤       CALL save_journal()

        END IF
12➤     DROP TABLE qsave_orders
      END IF

    END MAIN

    ##########################################
    FUNCTION update_driver(rep)
    ##########################################
      DEFINE        rep          CHAR(80),

                    oops, num    SMALLINT

13➤   IF LENGTH(rep) = 0 THEN
        START REPORT upd_rep
      ELSE
        START REPORT upd_rep TO rep
      END IF

14➤   DECLARE jrnlupd CURSOR WITH HOLD FOR
        SELECT * INTO jrn.*,
                      ver.ship_instruct THRU ver.paid_date,
                      set.ship_instruct THRU set.paid_date
        FROM upd_journal
        WHERE upd_status = "N"
      FOR UPDATE
```

15➤ The ordupd cursor fetches and locks each row of the orders table as needed.

Since it is not a hold cursor, it is automatically closed when a transaction ends, and has to be reopened for the next transaction.

16➤ The BEGIN WORK statement must be executed outside the FOREACH loop to ensure that a transaction exists before the jrnlupd update cursor performs the first fetch.

17➤ The FOREACH loop (which ends on page 549) controls the batch update process. It requests a lock on an upd_journal row and, if the request is successful, reads the contents of this row into the jrn, ver, and set module records.

18➤ The ordupd cursor fetches the row in the orders table. This row will be updated with the entries in the current upd_journal row.

The oops variable accumulates errors throughout a single update. If oops contains zero at the bottom of the loop, the transaction is committed; if not, it is rolled back.

19➤ The arguments to the upd_rep() function are four strings which the function prints in four columns across the page. In most cases the columns, from left to right, contain the following information:

- the name of a column in orders
- a verify (original) value
- a set (update) value
- a diagnostic message when required.

The report prints "(null)" for a null value, so the statement passes a string consisting of one blank to display a blank column.

20➤ The logic in this IF is repeated for each updatable field. The logic can be paraphrased as follows:

```
IF there have been no errors so far,
AND an update value was given for this column THEN
     IF the table has not changed since the update was journalled THEN
          save the updating value, count it, and log it in the report
     ELSE
          log an error
```

21➤ When all the fields have been validated, the cur record contains a mix of existing column values and updated values. When it is known that at least one update field existed and there were no errors, all the columns are updated and the journal record is stamped "done." Since errors are not being trapped, any error will end the program, automatically rolling back the transaction.

```
15➤  DECLARE ordupd CURSOR FOR
       SELECT * INTO cur.* FROM orders
       WHERE order_num = jrn.order_num
     FOR UPDATE

16➤  CALL begin_wk()

17➤  FOREACH jrnlupd
18➤    OPEN ordupd
       FETCH ordupd
       LET oops = SQLCA.SQLCODE
       IF oops = 0 THEN
         LET num = 0
       ELSE
19➤      OUTPUT TO REPORT upd_rep(" "," "," ","order_num not found")
       END IF
20➤    IF oops = 0 AND NOT like(ver.ship_instruct,set.ship_instruct) THEN
         IF like(ver.ship_instruct,cur.ship_instruct) THEN
           LET cur.ship_instruct = set.ship_instruct
           LET num = num+1
           OUTPUT TO REPORT upd_rep("ship_instruct",
                                    ver.ship_instruct,
                                    set.ship_instruct,
                                    " ")
         ELSE
           LET oops = 1
           OUTPUT TO REPORT upd_rep("ship_instruct",
                                    ver.ship_instruct,
                                    cur.ship_instruct,
                                    "no match: orig & current")
         END IF
       END IF
       IF oops = 0 AND NOT like(ver.backlog,set.backlog) THEN
```

See Note 20.

```
       END IF
       IF oops = 0 THEN
         IF num > 0 THEN
   WHENEVER ERROR CONTINUE
21➤        UPDATE orders SET (ship_instruct,backlog,
             po_num,ship_date,ship_weight,ship_charge,paid_date)
             = (cur.ship_instruct THRU cur.paid_date)
           WHERE CURRENT OF ordupd
   WHENEVER ERROR STOP
           IF status < 0 THEN
             OUTPUT TO REPORT upd_rep("orders table not updated",
                                      " "," ",status)
             LET oops = 1
           ELSE
   WHENEVER ERROR CONTINUE
             UPDATE upd_journal SET upd_status = "D"
             WHERE CURRENT OF jrnlupd
   WHENEVER ERROR STOP
```

22➤ If the two UPDATE statements are successful, commit the current transaction. Otherwise, roll back this transaction. Ending the transaction in either way closes the ordupd cursor, releases the lock on the orders row, and releases the lock on the upd_journal row. Because the jrnlupd cursor is a WITH HOLD cursor, this cursor is not closed.

23➤ The call to begin_wk() starts a new transaction for the next iteration of the FOREACH loop. A transaction must be current before the FOREACH attempts to lock the upd_journal now.

24➤ When the FOREACH loop exits, the program must end the current transaction. If rows have been updated, the oops variable is zero and the current transaction is committed. If the program encountered errors during the updates or if the FOREACH loop did not find upd_journal rows, oops is non-zero and the transaction is rolled back.

The upd_rep() Report Function

25➤ The upd_rep() report function documents the action of the update loop.

A more comprehensive approach to documenting a batch of updates would capitalize on the upd_status column, setting it to a code letter for each type of error, or to *D* for done. A separate program could then print a report of the results. Such a program would select completed updates (those with upd_status not equal to *N*). It could sort and group on the entered_by column.

Yet another variation would be to supply the user an interactive screen form with which he or she could check the status of their own updates for errors.

```
          IF status < 0 THEN
            OUTPUT TO REPORT upd_rep("upd_journal not updated",
                                     " "," ",status)
            LET oops = 1
          ELSE
            OUTPUT TO REPORT upd_rep(" ",
                                     " "," ","orders table updated")
          END IF
        END IF
      ELSE
        OUTPUT TO REPORT upd_rep(" "," "," ","no changed fields")
        LET oops = 1
      END IF
    END IF
22➤ IF oops = 0 THEN
      CALL commit_wk()
    ELSE
      CALL rollback_wk()
    END IF

23➤ CALL begin_wk()

  END FOREACH

24➤ IF oops = 0 THEN
    CALL commit_wk()
  ELSE
    CALL rollback_wk()
  END IF

  FINISH REPORT upd_rep

END FUNCTION  -- update_driver --

#########################################
25➤ REPORT upd_rep(f,v1,v2,x)
#########################################
  DEFINE       f,v1,v2,x    CHAR(25),

               prev_upd     INTEGER

  OUTPUT
    LEFT MARGIN 0

  FORMAT
    FIRST PAGE HEADER
      PRINT 20 SPACES, "UPDATE JOURNAL REPORT"
      PRINT 20 SPACES, "Run on: ", TODAY
      LET prev_upd = 0
```

26➤ At the start of each journal row, the report prints the update header information. Then for each requested column, it is called to print the column name and old and new values (or an error message).

27➤ If the second argument is blank, the report prints out a blank line. Otherwise, the argument contains the old value (before the update) for a column. The report prints out this value following the "BEFORE:" header.

```
26➤     ON EVERY ROW
          IF jrn.journal_id <> prev_upd THEN
            LET prev_upd = jrn.journal_id
            PRINT
            PRINT 2 SPACES, "UPDATE ",
                jrn.journal_id USING "####",
                " against Order ",
                jrn.order_num USING "#####"
            PRINT 4 SPACES, "Entered by ",
                jrn.entered_by,
                " on ", jrn.enter_date
          END IF

          PRINT 6 SPACES, f;

27➤       IF v1[1] = " " THEN
            PRINT " ";
          ELSE
            PRINT 1 SPACE, "BEFORE: ";
            IF v1 IS NULL THEN
              PRINT "(null)"
            ELSE
              PRINT v1
            END IF
          END IF

          PRINT 32 SPACES;
          IF v2[1] = " " THEN
            PRINT " "
          ELSE
            PRINT "AFTER: ";
            IF v2 IS NULL THEN
              PRINT "(null)"
            ELSE
              PRINT v2
            END IF
          END IF

          PRINT 6 SPACES;
          IF x[1] = " " THEN
            PRINT " "
          ELSE
            PRINT "STATUS: ", x CLIPPED
          END IF
          SKIP 1 LINE

    END REPORT  -- upd_rep --
```

The save_orders() Function

28➤ This function preserves the original contents of the orders table by storing the current contents of this table in a temporary table. The point is to preserve the original contents of the demonstration database. This is not part of the demonstration of an update journal, only an example of using data definition statements.

The restore orders() Function

29➤ Rather than restore the orders table wholesale, this function restores only the rows whose numbers appear in the update journal.

The build_journal() Function

30➤ The build_journal() function prepares the upd_journal table that is used in this example.

31➤ If the upd_journal table exists in the database, the program uses the DROP TABLE statement to remove it.

```
     ##########################################
28➤  FUNCTION save_orders()
     ##########################################
       DEFINE      j     SMALLINT

       SELECT COUNT(*)
       INTO j
       FROM informix.systables
       WHERE tabname = "qsave_orders"

       IF j = 0 THEN    -- the table has not yet been saved
         CREATE TABLE qsave_orders (order_num INTEGER, order_date DATE,
                                    customer_num INTEGER, ship_instruct CHAR(40),
                                    backlog CHAR(1), po_num CHAR(10),
                                    ship_date DATE, ship_weight DECIMAL(8,2),
                                    ship_charge MONEY(6), paid_date DATE)
         INSERT INTO qsave_orders SELECT * FROM orders
         DISPLAY "Contents of orders table saved in temp table: qsave_orders."
       ELSE
         DISPLAY "Copy of orders table ('qsave_orders') exists."
       END IF

     END FUNCTION  -- save_orders --

     ##########################################
29➤  FUNCTION restore_orders()
     ##########################################

       DELETE FROM orders
       WHERE order_num IN
         (SELECT DISTINCT order_num FROM upd_journal)

       INSERT INTO orders
         SELECT * FROM qsave_orders
         WHERE order_num IN
            (SELECT DISTINCT order_num FROM upd_journal)

     END FUNCTION -- restore_orders --

     ##########################################
30➤  FUNCTION build_journal()
     ##########################################
       DEFINE         fpath, afile    CHAR(80),
                      j               SMALLINT

31➤    SELECT COUNT(*)
       INTO j
       FROM systables
       WHERE tabname = "upd_journal"
```

32➤ The CREATE TABLE statement adds the upd_journal table to the database.

To execute this CREATE TABLE statement and the one in save_orders(), you must have Resource privilege in the database. The columns with the prefix "org_" contain the values of the row before the update. The columns with the "upd_" prefix contain the row values after the update. These columns are grouped so that they can be read into a record defined as "LIKE orders".

33➤ After creating the table, the function uses the LOAD command to fill it with a few example update requests. You can add or change lines in that text file to test the program operation.

```
    IF j <> 0 THEN -- one exists, may be updated, drop it
      DROP TABLE upd_journal
    END IF
32➤ CREATE TABLE upd_journal (
        journal_id SERIAL,          -- unique id of update item
        upd_status CHAR(1),         -- N=new, X=error, A=applied
        order_num  INTEGER,         -- foreign key to orders
        entered_by CHAR(8),         -- user who entered update
        enter_date DATETIME YEAR TO SECOND, -- ...and when
        org_si     CHAR(40),        -- org_si = original_ship_instruct
        org_bl     CHAR(1),         -- backlog
        org_po     CHAR(10),        -- po_num
        org_sd     DATE,            -- ship_date
        org_sw     DECIMAL(8,2),    -- ship_weight
        org_sc     MONEY(6),        -- ship_charge
        org_pd     DATE,            -- paid_date
        upd_si     CHAR(40),        -- upd_si = update_ship_instruct
        upd_bl     CHAR(1),         -- backlog
        upd_po     CHAR(10),        -- po_num
        upd_sd     DATE,            -- ship_date
        upd_sw     DECIMAL(8,2),    -- ship_weight
        upd_sc     MONEY(6),        -- ship_charge
        upd_pd     DATE             -- paid_date
        )

33➤ DISPLAY "Simulated update journal table upd_journal created."
    DISPLAY ""
    DISPLAY "To load the simulated update journal we need a file pathname"
    DISPLAY "for the file ex24.unl ."
    DISPLAY "It came in the same directory as the source file of this program."
    DISPLAY ""
    DISPLAY "Enter a pathname, including the final slash (or backslash)."
    DISPLAY "For the current working directory just press RETURN."
    DISPLAY ""

    LET int_flag = FALSE
    PROMPT  "Path to ex24.unl file: " FOR fpath
    IF int_flag THEN
      RETURN (FALSE)
    END IF

    LET afile = fpath CLIPPED, "ex24.unl"
    DISPLAY "Loading from ",afile CLIPPED
    LOAD FROM afile INSERT INTO upd_journal
    DISPLAY "Update journal table loaded."
    DISPLAY ""

    RETURN (TRUE)

  END FUNCTION  -- build_journal --
```

The save_journal() Function

34➤ The save_journal() function saves the contents of the upd_journal table in the ex24.out file. By saving the image of this table after the updates complete, you can examine the updates performed on the table. You cannot query the database for the upd_journal table because the program drops the table.

The like() Function

35➤ The like() function compares two character strings. If the two strings match, the function returns TRUE. Otherwise, it returns FALSE. It treats two NULL values as equal.

The check_db_priv() Function

36➤ The check_db_priv() function returns TRUE if the current user has at least a certain level of privilege in the current database. The privilege level (in this case, "R" for Resource) is passed into the function as an argument by the MAIN function.

```
    #########################################
34➤ FUNCTION save_journal()
    #########################################

        UNLOAD TO "ex24.out" SELECT * FROM upd_journal
        IF status < 0 THEN
            DISPLAY "Unable to store contents of journal table in ex24.out file."
        ELSE
            DISPLAY "New contents of journal table stored in ex24.out file."
            DROP TABLE upd_journal
            IF status < 0 THEN
                DISPLAY "Unable to drop journal table."
            END IF
        END IF

        DISPLAY "Dropped journal table: upd_journal."

    END FUNCTION  -- save_journal --

    #########################################
35➤ FUNCTION like(a,b)
    #########################################
      DEFINE     a,b     CHAR(255)

      IF (a IS NULL) AND (b IS NULL) THEN
        RETURN TRUE
      ELSE
        IF a = b THEN
          RETURN TRUE
        ELSE
          RETURN FALSE
        END IF
      END IF

    END FUNCTION  -- like --

    #########################################
36➤ FUNCTION check_db_priv(wanted)
    #########################################
      DEFINE        wanted        CHAR(1),

                    actual        CHAR(1),
                    retcode       SMALLINT

      LET retcode = FALSE -- assume failure
    WHENEVER ERROR CONTINUE -- no need to crash program on error here
      LET actual = "?" -- ..just make sure we have usable data

      DECLARE dbgrant CURSOR FOR
        SELECT usertype INTO actual
        FROM informix.sysusers
        WHERE username = USER
           OR username = "public" -- alway lowercase
```

37➤ Since a user may have been granted privileges by more than one other user, and since grants to "public" apply, the function needs a cursor to loop over an unknown number of rows from the sysusers catalog table. However, it abandons the search as soon as it finds the desired level of privilege.

38➤ The program frees its cursor since cursors are sometimes in short supply and this one will probably not be used more than once in a program.

```
37➤   FOREACH dbgrant
        CASE wanted
          WHEN "C"
            IF actual <> "?" THEN
              LET retcode = TRUE-- any privilege includes "C"
            END IF
          WHEN "R"
            IF actual <> "C" AND actual <> "?" THEN
              LET retcode = TRUE -- "D" or "R" is ok for "R"
            END IF
          WHEN "D"
            IF actual = "D" THEN
              LET retcode = TRUE -- the only real "D" is "D"
            END IF
        END CASE

        IF retcode THEN
          EXIT FOREACH
        END IF
      END FOREACH

38➤   FREE dbgrant
      RETURN retcode
    WHENEVER ERROR STOP

    END FUNCTION  -- check_db_priv --
```

To locate any function definition see the Function Index on page 728.

25

Logging Application Errors

This program demonstrates how to create and operate an error log file using three **4GL** library functions:

STARTLOG()	Creates the log file.
ERR_GET()	Gets the error message text associated with a particular SQL or **4GL** error number.
ERRORLOG()	Writes a line to an error log file.

The actual operations of the program are a reprise of the customer-table maintenance operations documented in Example 17 (which in turn is built on Example 9). The program allows the user to query for a display of customer rows. While one row is visible, the user may choose to update or delete the row, or add a new row.

This example differs from Example 9 (see "Accessing a Table with a Single Row Form" on page 165) in three ways.

First, the MAIN block installs a unique index on the company column of the customer table. The demonstration database does not normally have such an index. (The reason is that a single customer company might have multiple divisions or multiple retail outlets, each with its own address and person to contact. The company name would be the same in these rows, but the value in customer_num would make them unique.)

The unique index on the company column affords a simple, repeatable method for causing an SQL error, thus testing the operation of the error log.

The MAIN block drops the index at the end of the program, restoring the database to its normal condition.

Second, the functions that contain the SQL statements have been changed in two ways:

- They use the WHENEVER ERROR CONTINUE statement so that the program continues when an SQL error is returned.
- They report such errors by calling an error-logging function.

Finally, functions have been added to initialize the error log and write to it.

The 4GL Error Log

Every **4GL** program writes to an error log file, but by default it is the screen. **4GL** itself writes only one kind of message to the error log: the message that describes an error that terminates a program.

A program can call the STARTLOG() function to initialize a permanent error log file. The argument to STARTLOG() is a filename or a complete file pathname of the error log. If the program ends due to an error, **4GL** will write the terminating error display into the log. In addition, you can use the ERRORLOG() function to write lines into the error log.

If the error log file exists when a program calls STARTLOG(), output is appended to the file. Thus one file could contain the logged output of multiple program runs. (However the error log cannot be shared; it may be open to only one program at a time.)

There are a number of possible uses for the error log file. This example demonstrates a common one: logging all SQL errors in detail, as they occur.

Another possible use is debugging, especially debugging of errors that occur unpredictably or at long intervals. You can seed a program with calls to ERRORLOG() so that it leaves a trail of its operations in the error log. Instruct the users that, when the error occurs, they are to terminate the program and copy the error log file for later analysis.

Debug logging is one instance of *instrumenting* a program: adding code to record the operations of a program so they can be analyzed. You can instrument a program in order to analyze its performance. You can instrument a program in order to analyze patterns of usage: which program features are heavily used, and which are little used or perhaps not used at all? You can instrument a program so as to record work habits or to detect attempts to breach security.

For all these uses the key function is ERRORLOG(), which writes one line to the log file. A simple debugging call might resemble the following.

```
CALL ERRORLOG("now entering update routine")
```

However, ERRORLOG() typically needs assistance in at least two ways:

- A typical log entry for any purpose will contain several pieces of information; for example the name of a function and one or two of its argument values, or an error code and a statement type. But ERRORLOG() accepts only a single character string as its argument.
- Logging takes time and may impair the speed of the program. Before you build instrumentation into a program you need a way to turn it on and off, preferably without recompiling the program.

The solution to all three problems lies in creating your own logging function. This example does just that (see the log_entry() function on page 578). The purpose of a logging function is to receive one or more arguments that are specific to a situation, to format them into one or more lines of text, and to write these with the built-in ERRORLOG() function. When all log output is centralized in your logging function you can add features to it.

The logging function can do such things as:

- Insert the program name in each entry, if more than one program appends data to the same error log file.
- Format different types of entries in different ways, based on a type-of-entry argument. For example, debugging log entries might be code "D" while SQL errors might be code "S"; these could be formatted differently.
- Check a global variable to see if log entries are enabled, and do nothing when they are not.

The last point answers the performance problem mentioned above. A global variable that controls logging can be initialized when the program starts up, possibly from a table in the database. Alternatively, you could put logging under user control through a menu choice. The global variable that controls logging need not be a simple on/off choice.

You could classify log entries on a numerical scale of urgency; then the global could be an integer showing the urgency level an entry must have before it can be logged. Or the global variable could be a character string specifying a class of entry codes; then the logging function could use the MATCHES operator to test the type of an entry against the global variable to see if it should be logged. For example, if the global contained [S], only SQL errors might be logged, but [SD] would enable debugging entries also.

In general, the simple facility of the error log can be put to many uses if the other features of **4GL** are used with imagination to supplement it.

SQLCODE Versus Status

Immediately after a program executes an SQL statement, the status variable contains the SQL error code associated with the execution of the statement. However, the status variable is also used to report the success or failure of other **4GL** statements, including common ones such as DISPLAY and OPEN WINDOW. It is not safe to assume that an SQL error code will still remain in status even one statement following the SQL statement.

Except immediately following an SQL statement, it is best to refer to the SQL error code in its actual location, SQLCA.SQLCODE. This field is changed only by SQL statements. In this example, all calls to log_entry() pass it SQLCA.SQLCODE and not status.

Function Overview

Function Name	Purpose
create_index()	Installs a unique index on the customer table. This creates a reliable means of causing an SQL error that can be logged.
drop_index()	Drops the unique index on the customer table, restoring the database to normal.
init_log()	Initializes an error log of the specified name.
cust_menu3()	Displays the customer menu and allows the user to choose whether to add a new customer or query for an existing customer. Differs from cust_menu2() in example 17 only in calling browse_custs3() instead of browse_custs2().
browse_custs3()	Displays results of a query on the screen one row at a time, calling next_action4() to allow user to choose an action. Differs from browse_custs2() in Example 17 only in calling next_action4() instead of next_action3().
next_action4()	Displays a menu that allows the user to choose the action to take: see the next row, update the current row, or delete the current row. Calls addupd_cust() both for an insert and an update and uses error logging in the insert, update, delete functions.

insert_cust2()	Inserts a customer row. Uses error logging to record database errors occurring during INSERT.
update_cust3()	Updates a customer row. Uses error logging to record database errors occurring during UPDATE.
delete_cust2()	Deletes a customer row. Uses error logging to list database errors occurring during DELETE.
log_entry()	Creates an error log entry noting that an error has occurred in a specified function.
get_user()	Returns the user-id of the current user.
addupd_cust()	Combines insertion and update functions in a single routine to eliminate duplication of code. *See description in Example 9.*
bang()	Prompts the user for a command and executes the command. *See description in Example 3.*
clear_lines()	Clears any number of lines starting at any line. *See description in Example 6.*
init_msgs()	Initializes the members of the ga_dsplymsg array to null. *See description in Example 2.*
message_window()	Opens a window and displays the contents of the ga_dsplymsg global array. *See description in Example 2.*
msg()	Displays a brief, informative message. *See description in Example 5.*
message_window()	Opens a window and displays the contents of the ga_dsplymsg global array. *See description in Example 2.*
query_cust2()	Lets the user create a query by example. *See description in Example 6.*
state_popup()	Displays a lookup list of the states from the state table so the user can choose the appropriate state. *See description in Example 9.*
verify_delete()	Checks for dependent rows in other tables. *See description in Example 6.*

The DATABASE Statement and MAIN Function

1➤ This program can be used with any version of the demonstration database. It uses only the customer table.

2➤ See the discussion of this and the next statement in Example 17 ("The MAIN Function" on page 382).

3➤ When an error log is used, it should be initialized as early as possible in the program, so it is available to record errors in other initialization steps.

For example, in an early version of this program, init_log() was not called until create_index() had finished; but then create_index() had no way to report an error that it encountered.

4➤ The program adds a unique index on the customer.company column. This gives you a simple way to cause an SQL error that can be logged: by adding a customer that has a duplicate company name.

5➤ For discussion of this and the following statement see Example 17.

6➤ When the program ends, it drops the unique index on customer.company and restores the demonstration database to its normal condition.

The create_index() Function

7➤ The create_index() function creates the index mentioned in Note 4. If the CREATE INDEX statement ends with an error, the function checks for one common case: that the index already exists. This could occur, for example, if you run the program under the **Debugger** and exit without completing all the statements. If another error occurs, the function documents it on the error log and returns FALSE, signalling that the program cannot continue.

4GL source file

```
1➤ DATABASE stores2t

   GLOBALS
     DEFINE       gr_customer     RECORD LIKE customer.*,
                  gr_workcust     RECORD LIKE customer.*,
                  g_username      CHAR(8)

     DEFINE       ga_dsplymsg ARRAY[5] OF CHAR(48)
   END GLOBALS

   ########################################
   MAIN
   ########################################

2➤   OPTIONS
       HELP FILE "hlpmsgs",
       FORM LINE 5,
       COMMENT LINE 5,
       MESSAGE LINE LAST

     DEFER INTERRUPT

3➤   CALL init_log("errlog")

4➤   IF create_index() THEN
5➤     OPEN WINDOW w_main AT 2,3
        WITH 18 ROWS, 75 COLUMNS
        ATTRIBUTE (BORDER)

       OPEN FORM f_customer FROM "f_customer"
       DISPLAY FORM f_customer
       CALL cust_menu3()
       CLEAR SCREEN
6➤     CALL drop_index()
     ELSE
       LET ga_dsplymsg[1] = "Unable to create a unique index on the"
       LET ga_dsplymsg[2] = "  company column. Please check the 'errlog'"
       LET ga_dsplymsg[3] = "  file for more detailed information."
       CALL message_window(9, 15)
     END IF

   END MAIN

   ########################################
7➤ FUNCTION create_index()
   ########################################

   WHENEVER ERROR CONTINUE
     CREATE UNIQUE INDEX comp_ix ON customer (company)
   WHENEVER ERROR STOP
```

The drop_index() Function

8➤ At the conclusion of the program it calls the drop_index() function to drop the unique index on the company column. Errors are reported to the error log.

9➤ At this point the status variable contains the result of the DROP INDEX statement.

10➤ At this point the status variable contains the result of executing the ERROR statement. The error code returned by DROP INDEX has been replaced. However, the SQL error code is still present in SQLCA.SQLCODE where it will remain until the program executes the next SQL statement.

The init_log() Function

11➤ The init_log() function uses the built-in STARTLOG() function to initialize the **4GL** log file. The filename is passed as an argument. In this program, it is a simple character constant in the MAIN block. Other options include taking it from the command line, or from the database.

The cust_menu3() Function

12➤ The cust_menu3() function is identical to the cust_menu2() function in Example 17, except that it calls browse_cust3() instead of browse_cust2(). For more information see "The cust_menu2() Function" on page 382.

```
     IF (status < 0) THEN
       IF (status <> -316) THEN   --* if index already exists: OK
           CALL log_entry(SQLCA.SQLCODE, "create_index()")
           RETURN (FALSE)
       END IF
     END IF

     RETURN (TRUE)

   END FUNCTION  -- create_index --

   ########################################
8➤ FUNCTION drop_index()
   ########################################

   WHENEVER ERROR CONTINUE
     DROP INDEX comp_ix
   WHENEVER ERROR STOP

9➤   IF (status < 0) THEN
       ERROR status USING "-<<<<<<<<<<<",
         ": Unable to drop company column index."
10➤    CALL log_entry(SQLCA.SQLCODE, "drop_index()")
     END IF

   END FUNCTION  -- drop_index --

   ########################################
11➤ FUNCTION init_log(logname)
   ########################################
     DEFINE        logname    CHAR(10)

     CALL STARTLOG(logname)

     CALL get_user() RETURNING g_username

   END FUNCTION  -- init_log --

   ########################################
12➤ FUNCTION cust_menu3()
   ########################################
     DEFINE        st_custs    CHAR(150)

     DISPLAY
     "--------------------------------------------Press CTRL-W for Help----------"
       AT 3, 1
     MENU "CUSTOMER"
```

See cust_menu1() in Example 9.

The browse_custs3() Function

13➤ After customer rows are selected, the browse_custs3() function manages the user's access to them. It is identical to browse_custs2() in Example 17, except that it calls next_action4() instead of next_action3(). See "The browse_custs2() Function" on page 384 for more information.

14➤ This version of the browse function displays the number of customer rows selected. It gets this number from an element in the SQLERRD array of global SQLCA record. The database fills SQLERRD[3] with the number of rows processed. After a SELECT statement, this value is the number of rows selected.

```
    COMMAND "Query" "Look up customer(s) in the database." HELP 11
      CALL query_cust2() RETURNING st_custs
      IF st_custs IS NOT NULL THEN
        CALL browse_custs3(st_custs)
      END IF
      CALL clear_lines(1,4)
```

See cust_menu1() in Example 9.

```
  END MENU
END FUNCTION  -- cust_menu3 --

########################################
13➤ FUNCTION browse_custs3(selstmt)
########################################
  DEFINE        selstmt         CHAR(150),

                fnd_custs       SMALLINT,
                end_list        SMALLINT,
                num_found       SMALLINT
```

See browse_custs() in Example 6.

```
  FOREACH c_cust INTO gr_customer.*

14➤ LET num_found = SQLCA.SQLERRD[3]
    IF num_found IS NULL THEN
      LET num_found = 0
    END IF
    DISPLAY " Number of Customers Selected: ", num_found USING "<<<<<<"
      AT 14,1 ATTRIBUTE (REVERSE, YELLOW)

    LET fnd_custs = TRUE
    DISPLAY BY NAME gr_customer.*

    IF NOT next_action4() THEN
      LET end_list = FALSE
      EXIT FOREACH
    ELSE
      LET end_list = TRUE
    END IF
    LET gr_workcust.* = gr_customer.*
  END FOREACH

  CALL clear_lines(4, 14)
```

See browse_custs() in Example 6.

```
 IF end_list THEN
    CALL msg("No more customer rows.")
  END IF
```

The next_action4() Function

15➤ After a customer record is located and displayed, the next_action4() function presents a menu of possible next actions. It is quite similar to the next_action() function in Example 6 (see "The next_action() Function" on page 126). It differs from Example 6 and from other similar functions in Examples 9 and 17 only in the names of the subfunctions it calls to perform the user's actions.

```
  CLEAR FORM

END FUNCTION  -- browse_custs3 --

########################################
15➤ FUNCTION next_action4()
########################################
  DEFINE nxt_action SMALLINT

  LET nxt_action = TRUE

  MENU "CUSTOMER MODIFICATION"
    COMMAND "Next" "View next selected customer." HELP 20
      EXIT MENU

    COMMAND "Update" "Update current customer on screen."
        HELP 21
      CALL clear_lines(1,14)  -- clear out "Number Selected" message
      IF addupd_cust("U") THEN
        CALL update_cust3()
      END IF
      CALL clear_lines(2,16)
      NEXT OPTION "Next"

    COMMAND "Delete" "Delete current customer on screen."
        HELP 22
      CALL clear_lines(1,14)  -- clear out "Number Selected" message
      CALL delete_cust2()
      IF gr_workcust.customer_num IS NOT NULL THEN

-- * there was a previous customer in the list: restore it to the screen
        LET gr_customer.* = gr_workcust.*
        DISPLAY BY NAME gr_customer.*
      END IF
      NEXT OPTION "Next"

    COMMAND KEY ("E","e","X","x") "Exit" "Return to CUSTOMER Menu"
        HELP 24
      LET nxt_action = FALSE
      EXIT MENU
  END MENU

  RETURN nxt_action

END FUNCTION  -- next_action4 --
```

The insert_cust2() Function

16➤ The insert_cust2() function is called from add_upd_cust() to insert a new customer record. It differs from very similar functions in Examples 9 and 17 (see "The insert_cust() Function" on page 182) in that it reports errors by calling log_entry(). The earlier versions of this function report an SQL error with the ERROR statement, which appears on the screen only.

17➤ As before, this statement (and any other that involves screen or disk activity) will reset the contents of the status variable. This explains why in the following statement, the SQL error code is passed by naming SQLCA.SQLCODE, not status.

The update_cust3() Function

18➤ The update_cust3() function is called from add_upd_cust() to update a customer record. It differs from very similar functions in Examples 6 and others in that it reports errors by calling log_entry() (see "The update_cust() Function" on page 130). The earlier versions of this function report an SQL error with the ERROR statement, which appears on the screen only.

```
    ########################################
16➤ FUNCTION insert_cust2()
    ########################################

    WHENEVER ERROR CONTINUE
      INSERT INTO CUSTOMER
      VALUES (0, gr_customer.fname, gr_customer.lname,
              gr_customer.company, gr_customer.address1,
              gr_customer.address2, gr_customer.city,
              gr_customer.state, gr_customer.zipcode,
              gr_customer.phone)
    WHENEVER ERROR STOP

      IF (status < 0) THEN
17➤     ERROR status USING "-<<<<<<<<<<<", ": Unable to complete customer insert."
        CALL log_entry(SQLCA.SQLCODE, "insert_cust2()")

      ELSE
        LET gr_customer.customer_num = SQLCA.SQLERRD[2]
        DISPLAY BY NAME gr_customer.customer_num

        LET ga_dsplymsg[1] = "Customer has been entered in the database."
        LET ga_dsplymsg[2] = "  Number: ",
              gr_customer.customer_num USING "<<<<<<<<<<<",
              "  Name: ", gr_customer.company
        CALL message_window(9, 15)
      END IF

    END FUNCTION  -- insert_cust2 --

    ########################################
18➤ FUNCTION update_cust3()
    ########################################

    WHENEVER ERROR CONTINUE
      UPDATE customer SET customer.* = gr_customer.*
      WHERE customer_num = gr_customer.customer_num
    WHENEVER ERROR STOP

      IF (status < 0) THEN
        ERROR status USING "-<<<<<<<<<<<",
          ": Unable to complete customer update."
        CALL log_entry(SQLCA.SQLCODE, "update_cust3()")
      END IF

    END FUNCTION  -- update_cust3 --
```

The delete_cust2() Function

19➤ This function is called to delete a customer record. It differs from very similar functions in Examples 6 and others in that it reports errors by calling log_entry() (see "The delete_cust() Function" on page 130). The earlier versions of this function report an SQL error with the ERROR statement, which appears on the screen only.

The log_entry() Function

20➤ The log_entry() function reports an SQL error by writing several lines into the error log file. This error log file was initialized with the **4GL** STARTLOG() function (see Notes 3 and 11). Here is a sample of its output:

```
Date: 06/28/1991     Time: 09:45:20
User: nerfball       Function: insert_cust2()
Error Number: -239  ISAM Error: -100
Error: Could not insert new row - duplicate value in a UNIQUE INDEX column.
```

```
    #######################################
19➤ FUNCTION delete_cust2()
    #######################################

      IF (prompt_window("Are you sure you want to delete this?", 10, 15)) THEN

        IF verify_delete() THEN

    WHENEVER ERROR CONTINUE
          DELETE FROM customer
          WHERE customer_num = gr_customer.customer_num
    WHENEVER ERROR STOP

          IF (status < 0) THEN
            ERROR status USING "-<<<<<<<<<<<",
              ": Unable to complete customer delete."
            CALL log_entry(SQLCA.SQLCODE, "delete_cust2()")
          ELSE
            CALL msg("Customer has been deleted.")
            CLEAR FORM
          END IF
        ELSE
          LET ga_dsplymsg[1] = "Customer ",
                  gr_customer.customer_num USING "<<<<<<<<<<<",
                  " has placed orders and cannot be"
          LET ga_dsplymsg[2] = "                  deleted."
          CALL message_window(7, 8)
        END IF
      END IF

    END FUNCTION  -- delete_cust2 --

    #######################################
20➤ FUNCTION log_entry(errstat, fname)
    #######################################
      DEFINE        errstat     INTEGER,
                    fname       CHAR(20),

                    isam_err    INTEGER,
                    errtxt      CHAR(70),
                    errline     CHAR(225),
                    uname       CHAR(8)
```

21➤ The parts of the log entry come from the following sources:

- The date and time are supplied by **4GL**.
- The user name is acquired by calling the get_user() function.
- The function name and the error number are passed as arguments.
- The **ISAM** error number is retrieved from the SQL Communications area (the function assumes that no other SQL statement has been executed since the error occurred).
- The error message text is retrieved from the **4GL** ERR_GET() library function.

These elements are formatting into a single character variable with newlines (indicated by "\n") to divide the three lines.

The get_user() function performs a SELECT statement to retrieve the user name, thus updating the error codes in the SQL Communications area. The function must save the **ISAM** error code before calling get_user().

22➤ The built-in ERRORLOG() function makes the actual entry to the **4GL** error log. It sends the entry to the error log initialized by the STARTLOG() function (See Note 11). In this example, the error log is the "errlog" file.

The get_user() Function

23➤ The get_user() function returns the user id of the current user. Since the USER function is not available in **4GL**, a SELECT statement is used to retrieve the user id of the current user. The FROM and WHERE clauses in the SELECT statement reference a row in a table that always exists.

In order not to have to use a cursor, the SELECT must be written so that it returns only one row. This function selects the row of systables that names itself (systables); it is sure to exist and sure to be unique. The owner name "informix" is required only in an ANSI-compliant database.

```
21➤   LET isam_err = SQLCA.SQLERRD[2]    -- save it before it vanishes

      CALL ERR_GET(errstat) RETURNING errtxt

      LET errline = "User: ", g_username, "      Function: ",
            fname CLIPPED, "\n", "Error Number: ",
            errstat USING "-<<<<<<<<<<<", "  ISAM Error: ",
            isam_err USING "-<<<<<<<<<<<", "\n", "Error: ",
            errtxt CLIPPED, "\n",
            "--------------------------------------------------"

22➤   CALL ERRORLOG(errline CLIPPED)

    END FUNCTION  -- log_entry --

    ########################################
23➤ FUNCTION get_user()
    ########################################
        DEFINE uid LIKE informix.sysusers.username

        SELECT USER INTO uid
        FROM informix.systables -- table guaranteed to exist
        WHERE tabname = "systables" -- row sure to exist and be singular

        RETURN uid
    END FUNCTION  -- get_user --
```

To locate any function definition see the Function Index on page 728.

26

Managing Multiple Windows

This example shows how you can put more than one window on the screen. The program uses the windows to "tile" the screen instead of overlapping them. When it starts, the screen looks like this:

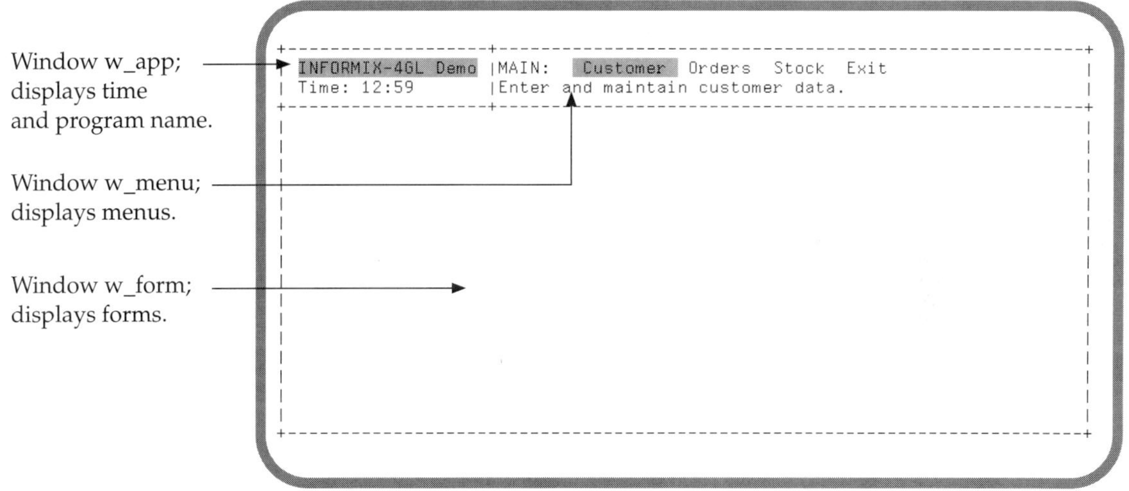

Managing Windows

Tiling windows gives you more control over the layout of the display. The MENU command creates a menu that fills the window from left to right. This program displays both a logo and the time to the left of the menu because the logo and the menu appear in separate windows.

Windows can overlap to any extent. The CURRENT WINDOW statement brings one window to the front and makes it the focus of keyboard input. Although these windows appear to abut neatly, their borders overlap by one character, so that the vertical line between "Demo" and "MAIN" is composed of the right border of window w_app and the left border of w_menu.

When a MENU statement or a DISPLAY FORM statement is executed, its output goes to the current window. The current window is the one named in the most recent CURRENT WINDOW or OPEN WINDOW statement. This example program is careful to make the menu window current before entering a MENU statement, and to make the form window current before displaying a form.

The forms displayed by this program are the same forms used in the other example programs. A form is not tied to any particular window or program; it can be displayed in any window so long as the window has enough rows and columns to hold it.

4GL does not offer multitasking, so it is not possible to operate the time display asynchronously from the other windows. The clock will not advance while the user is thinking, or away from the keyboard. A function named new_time() updates the time display. Calls to new_time() are inserted following each point at which user input is requested.

Using Dummy Functions

While this program offers a two-level hierarchy of menus, neither menu actually does anything. All functions that would add, update, query or report have been left undefined. Instead, each menu command calls a *dummy function* to display the string "Function not implemented yet."

This is a valid and useful design technique: it permits you to design the interface to an application, including forms, and to test it and get feedback from the user population, early in the development process. Then you can add functions one at a time, concentrating on each function in isolation. Many of the functions from other examples could be slotted into the framework of this program. For instance, the query-by-example from Example 5 could be dropped in with little change.

Function Overview

Function Name	Purpose
dsply_screen()	Opens the 3 application windows.
close_screen()	Closes the 3 application windows.
menu_main()	Makes the menu window (w_menu) current and displays the MAIN menu in it.
curr_wndw()	Makes a new application window current.
sub_menu()	Displays the requested sub_menu (CUSTOMER, ORDERS, or STOCK) and opens the appropriate form in the form window (w_form).
new_time()	Makes the application window (w_app) current and displays the updated system time in it.
dummymsg()	Development routine that displays message "Function not implemented yet."
bang()	Prompts the user for a command and executes the command. *See description in Example 3.*
dsply_logo()	Displays the logo form with the current date. *See description in Example 1.*
msg()	Displays a brief, informative message. *See description in Example 5.*

The MAIN Function

1➤ The dsply_logo() function, which appears in Example 1, fills the screen with a decorative application logo for the specified number of seconds.

2➤ The dsply_screen() function opens all windows. The call to menu_main() starts the real business of the program.

The dsply_screen() Function

3➤ The OPEN WINDOW statement creates the small decorative window in the upper left corner. Two fixed strings, the program name and the legend "Time:", are displayed into it.

An alternate way to initialize the contents of a static window is to display a small form into it. This would put the text of the window outside the program and in a form where it could be maintained separately.

4➤ Each call to new_time() updates the time display in the w_app window. These calls are scattered through the program in an attempt to keep the time display reasonably current.

5➤ The left border of the w_menu window overlaps the right border of w_app. On some terminals, the upper-left and upper-right corners of window borders are drawn with distinct symbols. On such a terminal the corner symbol at row 2, column 22 will switch between left and right orientations as the windows are alternately made current.

6➤ Window w_form is sized to hold most of the forms used in other examples. Its upper border overlaps the lower borders of the other windows. It is not essential to overlap borders in this way, but every row and column is precious on most terminals.

The close_screen() Function

7➤ This function cleans up all windows at the termination of the program.

4Gl menu file

```
########################################
MAIN
########################################

  DEFER INTERRUPT

1➤  CALL dsply_logo(3)
  CLEAR SCREEN

2➤  CALL dsply_screen()
  CALL menu_main()

  CALL close_screen()
  CLEAR SCREEN
END MAIN

########################################
FUNCTION dsply_screen()
########################################

3➤  OPEN WINDOW w_app AT 2,3
    WITH 2 ROWS, 19 COLUMNS
    ATTRIBUTE(BORDER, MESSAGE LINE LAST)

  DISPLAY " INFORMIX-4GL Demo " -- blank before "I" allows for SG#1
    AT 1, 1 ATTRIBUTE(REVERSE, RED) -- terminals
  DISPLAY "Time:" AT 2, 2
4➤  CALL new_time()

5➤  OPEN WINDOW w_menu AT 2,23
    WITH 2 ROWS, 56 COLUMNS
    ATTRIBUTE(BORDER)

6➤  OPEN WINDOW w_form AT 5,3
    WITH 16 ROWS, 76 COLUMNS
    ATTRIBUTE(BORDER, FORM LINE 1,
              MESSAGE LINE LAST, PROMPT LINE LAST)

END FUNCTION  -- dsply_screen --

########################################
7➤ FUNCTION close_screen()
########################################

  CLOSE WINDOW w_form
  CLOSE WINDOW w_menu
  CLOSE WINDOW w_app

END FUNCTION  -- close_screen --
```

The curr_wndw() Function

8➤ This function encapsulates the process of switching windows, so that the names of the windows do not have to be propagated throughout the application. Window names are not known outside the source module containing the OPEN WINDOW statement, so a function in a different module could not execute the CURRENT WINDOW statement in any event. This function is also a convenient place for a breakpoint when debugging.

The new_time() Function

9➤ The new_time() function updates the time display. It is called from everywhere that a delay completes. No practical way is available to update the time concurrently with other activities.

10➤ The time is displayed using row and column coordinates. This approach has the disadvantage that knowledge of the window layout is incorporated into the program. Another approach would be to initialize w_app with a (very small) form containing a form-only field for the time, and to use DISPLAY TO *field name* for the time. Then the function would not be dependent on the layout of the window; they could be changed independently.

The dummymsg() Function

11➤ The dummymsg() function is called wherever a feature has not yet been coded (in this example, almost everywhere). It makes the form window current before displaying its message. If it did not, the message might appear on top of the menu or (truncated) within the time window.

The menu_main() Function

12➤ The menu_main() function displays and executes the main menu. It first makes the menu window current; otherwise the menu would appear in whichever window was current at the time.

When a menu command is selected, it calls the sub_menu() function and passes a parameter indicating the selected menu command. When control returns from sub_menu(), **4GL** makes current the menu window.

```
   #########################################
8➤ FUNCTION curr_wndw(wndw)
   #########################################
     DEFINE wndw CHAR(1)

     CASE wndw
       WHEN "M"
         CURRENT WINDOW IS w_menu
       WHEN "F"
         CURRENT WINDOW IS w_form
       WHEN "A"
         CURRENT WINDOW IS w_app
     END CASE

   END FUNCTION  -- curr_wndw --

   #########################################
9➤ FUNCTION new_time()
   #########################################
     DEFINE the_time DATETIME HOUR TO MINUTE

     CALL curr_wndw("A")
     LET the_time = CURRENT
10➤  DISPLAY the_time AT 2,8

   END FUNCTION  -- new_time --

   #########################################
11➤ FUNCTION dummymsg()
   #########################################

     CALL curr_wndw("F")
     CALL msg("Function Not Implemented Yet")

   END FUNCTION  -- dummymsg --

   #########################################
12➤ FUNCTION menu_main()
   #########################################

     CALL curr_wndw("M")

     MENU "MAIN"
       COMMAND "Customer" "Enter and maintain customer data."
         CALL sub_menu("C")
         CALL curr_wndw("M")

       COMMAND "Orders" "Enter and maintain orders."
         CALL sub_menu("O")
         CALL curr_wndw("M")
```

13➤ The KEY clause in the MENU statement allows you to associate a maximum of four keys with a menu option.

The sub_menu() Function

14➤ The sub_menu() function is called from the main menu. It displays the appropriate menu and form for each menu choice.

The function takes advantage of the fact that the MENU statement accepts variables for the menu title, command names, and command option descriptions. It also uses a variable to specify the name of the form which appears in the w_form window.

15➤ The menu_opt variable receives the parameter passed to the function. It acts as a flag to set the appropriate form and sets the index into the s_menu array.

The s_menu array holds the information about each submenu. The appropriate record in the array is then passed to a MENU statement.

The idx variable serves as the index into the array.

16➤ The series of LET statements loads the menu information into the array.

```
      COMMAND "Stock" "Enter and maintain stock list."
        CALL sub_menu("S")
        CALL curr_wndw("M")

13➤   COMMAND KEY("!")
        CALL bang()
        CALL curr_wndw("M")

      COMMAND KEY ("E", "e", "X", "x") "Exit"
          "Exit program and return to operating system."
        EXIT MENU
    END MENU

  END FUNCTION  -- menu_main --

  ########################################
14➤ FUNCTION sub_menu(menuopt)
  ########################################
15➤ DEFINE menuopt         CHAR(1),

           s_menu ARRAY[3] OF RECORD
                  menuname        CHAR(10),
                  option1         CHAR(15),
                  optdesc1        CHAR(50),
                  option2         CHAR(15),
                  optdesc2        CHAR(50),
                  option3         CHAR(15),
                  optdesc3        CHAR(50)
           END RECORD,

           idx            SMALLINT,
           form_name      CHAR(10)

16➤ LET s_menu[1].menuname = "CUSTOMERS"
    LET s_menu[1].option1 = "Add"
    LET s_menu[1].optdesc1 = "Add new customer(s) to the database."
    LET s_menu[1].option2 = "Query"
    LET s_menu[1].optdesc2 = "Look up customers information."
    LET s_menu[1].option3 = "Report"
    LET s_menu[1].optdesc3 = "Create customer reports."

    LET s_menu[2].menuname = "ORDERS"
    LET s_menu[2].option1 = "Place"
    LET s_menu[2].optdesc1 = "Add new order to database and print invoice."
    LET s_menu[2].option2 = "Query"
    LET s_menu[2].optdesc2 = "Look up and display order information."
    LET s_menu[2].option3 = "Report"
    LET s_menu[2].optdesc3 = "Create order reports."

    LET s_menu[3].menuname = "STOCK"
    LET s_menu[3].option1 = "Add"
    LET s_menu[3].optdesc1 = "Add new stock item(s) to the database."
    LET s_menu[3].option2 = "Query"
```

17➤ The current window is set to w_form.

18➤ The value of menuopt determines the setting of the form_name variable (which is used in the following OPEN FORM statement) and the idx index into the s_menu array (which loads the submenu).

19➤ Once the function displays the appropriate form in the w_form window, the call to curr_wndw() resets the current window. The following MENU statement will display in the w_menu window.

20➤ The menu title, list of options, and list of option descriptions are contained in one row in the s_menu array. The idx index into the array was set in the previous CASE statement.

Some menu commands are set using variables, while others use literal strings. Since all submenus include an Exit option and a "bang" option, they are hardcoded into the statement and are not passed to the statement as variables.

The **4GL** MENU statement allows you to use variables for the name of the menu, for command names, and for command descriptions. However, you cannot use a variable for the help number associated with a command.

21➤ After each menu choice, the time display is updated.

```
     LET s_menu[3].optdesc2 = "Look up and display stock information."
     LET s_menu[3].option3 = "Report"
     LET s_menu[3].optdesc3 = "Create stock reports."

17➤  CALL curr_wndw("F")

18➤  CASE menuopt
       WHEN "C"
         LET form_name = "f_customer"
         LET idx = 1
       WHEN "O"
         LET form_name = "f_orders"
         LET idx = 2
       WHEN "S"
         LET form_name = "f_stock"
         LET idx = 3
     END CASE

     OPEN FORM the_option FROM form_name
     DISPLAY FORM the_option

19➤  CALL curr_wndw("M")

20➤  MENU s_menu[idx].menuname
       COMMAND s_menu[idx].option1 s_menu[idx].optdesc1
          CALL dummymsg()
       COMMAND s_menu[idx].option2 s_menu[idx].optdesc2
          CALL dummymsg()
       COMMAND s_menu[idx].option3 s_menu[idx].optdesc3
          CALL dummymsg()
       COMMAND KEY ("!")
          CALL bang()
       COMMAND KEY ("E", "e", "X", "x") "Exit" "Return to MAIN Menu."
         CLEAR WINDOW w_form
         EXIT MENU
     END MENU

21➤  CALL new_time()

   END FUNCTION  -- sub_menu --
```

To locate any function definition see the Function Index on page 728.

27

Displaying Menu Options Dynamically

This example shows how to use a scroll cursor to modify the database (insert, update and/or delete rows) while allowing concurrent updates. It is based on Example 20. You should understand the read-ahead scrolling and query revision features of Example 20 before reading this program.

The Scroll Cursor and Volatile Data

The benefit of a scroll cursor is that it can fetch any row in a selected (active) set of rows. In a static database, the contents of the selected set will remain constant. However, when multiple programs can modify the database concurrently, the set of selected rows may change from one moment to the next. At any instant, another program might:

- Add a row that should be part of the selected set.
- Delete a row that was part of the selected set.
- Update a row that was part of the selected set in such a way that it should no longer be selected.
- Update a row that was not selected in such a way that it now should be included in the set of rows returned by the query.

The scroll cursor commands such as FETCH PRIOR, FETCH ABSOLUTE *n*, or FETCH LAST require that the selected set remains constant until the cursor is closed. If the set of rows can change from moment to moment, the very concept of the next, the last or the *n*th row becomes confused, particularly when the rows being fetched are the result of a join.

To make FETCH work predictably and repeatably, the database engine creates a stable selection set by saving the rows in a temporary table as it first finds them. This saved set of rows — a *snapshot* of the original data as it was when first fetched — is retained until the cursor is closed.

You can use the program in Example 20 to test this aspect of a scroll cursor:

1. Start the program and view several rows.
2. From a different user session, open the same database and delete one of the rows you viewed.
3. Return to the ex20 program. You will still be able to see the row that was deleted. It has been cached in the temporary table.
4. Now use the Query option and enter the same criteria. When the cursor is closed and reopened, the deleted row will be absent from the set.

This illustrates two things about a scroll cursor:

- It can display *stale data*, that is, rows that no longer accurately reflect the database contents.
- It can be *resynchronized* by closing it and opening it again with the same selection criteria. The set of rows found on reopening may be somewhat different than they were before and will reflect the current state of the database.

Resynchronizing a Scroll Cursor

The scroll cursor should be resynchronized whenever the program finds that the database no longer matches the cached rows. This can happen whenever the program displays a row, and will happen whenever a user modifies a row.

In this example, the loop that supports scrolling starts by opening the scroll cursor. Next comes a MENU statement, followed by a close of the cursor. When a menu option finds that the cursor is showing stale data, it forces resynchronization by exiting the MENU statement. The cursor is closed at the bottom of the loop, then reopened at the top.

One problem exists with this plan: it may frustrate the user. If the set of selected rows is large, the user may spend a lot of time finding a particular row. It would be confusing for the program to suddenly reset the cursor to the first row of the set. After closing and reopening the cursor, the program must try to position the cursor on, or at least near to, its previous position.

This is done by maintaining a count of the current scroll position in the selected set. This scroll position is not the same as the row id; the row id is relative to the whole table, while the scroll position is relative to the particular set of rows that match the current query.

The scroll position can be precisely maintained across most menu choices. It is set to 1 at the start and whenever First is chosen. Each use of Next increments it; each use of Prior decrements it. When the cursor is reopened, a FETCH ABSOLUTE command can set the cursor to the desired row in the set. Or nearly to it. The *n*th now in the current set may not be the same *n*th row as before the cursor was closed. Rows might have been inserted or deleted, but at least the cursor will be close to its former row.

There is one operation under which the scroll position cannot be maintained exactly. When the user chooses Last, the program uses FETCH LAST to display the last record in the set. But since the program does not know how many rows are in the set, it cannot tell what scroll position it has reached.

However, the program does know its position relative to the last row. So the program assigns the scroll position zero to the last row. The Prior choice decrements this; the row prior to the last is row -1 relative to the last row. The Next choice increments it, still maintaining the correct relative position with respect to the last row.

Thus when the program reopens the cursor and finds that the scroll position is a negative number, it can reestablish that position by performing a FETCH LAST command followed by a FETCH RELATIVE of the desired row.

Updating Rows Fetched Through a Scroll Cursor

Since a scroll cursor does not necessarily show the database as it really is, you cannot declare a scroll cursor for update. A cursor used to modify rows (that is, either update or delete them) must be an ordinary cursor.

Then how can you modify a row that was fetched through a scroll cursor? The answer is that you must use a regular cursor to fetch the row and modify it through that cursor. However, you should keep in mind that when a row is subsequently fetched through the update cursor, time has elapsed since it was originally fetched through the scroll cursor. Various changes may take place during this interim period such as:

- The row might have been modified by another program.
- The row might no longer exist.

Obviously, if the row is deleted, it cannot be modified. But if a row has been changed, it should not be modified, since it is possible that the modification is no longer applicable to the changed row.

At a high level, the method of modifying a row fetched with a scroll cursor is as follows:

1. Fetch the row with the scroll cursor.
2. Declare a second cursor for an update and associate it with a SELECT statement that returns only the desired row.

3. Open the cursor and fetch the row, locking it for exclusive use.

   If the row is not found, it has been deleted or changed so that it no longer fits the selection criteria.

4. Compare the column values to those returned through the scroll cursor.

   If there is any difference, the modification might no longer be applicable and the row should not be modified.

5. Perform the UPDATE or DELETE using WHERE CURRENT OF the update cursor.

In every case, the scroll cursor is now stale; at least for this one row, it no longer reflects the actual table. Hence it should be resynchronized by closing and reopening it.

Using the Row ID

This example relies on the *row id*, a unique integer that is associated with every row of a table. The row id may be thought of as another column in each table, a column that is initialized with random integer values when the table is created. A row retains its row id as long as it exists. You can select ROWID as if it were a column in the table, and you can use a comparison to ROWID in a WHERE clause in order to retrieve a specific row.

Here are some cautions related to the use of the row id. First, row id values are reassigned when rows are deleted and other rows inserted. Second, row id values change when a table is unloaded and reloaded. Thus you can never assume that a row will retain its row id permanently. In particular, you should never store row id values in a table as foreign keys to other tables. However, the row id is extremely useful for keeping track of specific rows during the life of a single cursor.

In this example, the scroll cursor selects *only* the row id value (and nothing else). The scroll cursor is used to generate a list of the row ids of the rows that meet the query criteria.

When it is time to display a row to the user, the row is fetched using an ordinary cursor. ROWID is appended to the other query conditions when building the WHERE clause. This prevents the unlikely case in which the original row has been deleted and another, unrelated row inserted at the same row id. Including both the ROWID value and the user-specified query conditions ensures that the query returns the intended row— or no row at all. If the row is no longer found, it has been deleted and the scroll cursor needs to be resynchronized. If it is found, the column values fetched are the very latest ones; they reflect any update up to the present time.

When the user asks to update a row, the row is re-fetched using an update cursor, thus locking it for exclusive use. All fields of the returned row are checked against the row as it first was displayed to make sure it has not changed.

Similarly, when the user asks to delete a row, the test of ROWID and the other query conditions are used in a DELETE statement. This is a less stringent test than is applied prior to UPDATE (when all the columns are tested to make sure none has changed). It is possible to delete a row which had recently been updated by a different user.

A fetch using the row id is very fast; the row id encodes the physical address of the row on the disk, so not even an index lookup is needed. The fetches and re-fetches take little time.

Checking User Authorization

This example permits the user to insert, update or delete new rows. However, not all users are authorized to do these things.

The program looks up the user's privileges in the systabauth system catalog when it starts up. Then it only displays menu choices for the actions permitted the user.

The get_tab_auth() function performs this task. It returns a character string in the format used in systabauth, which contains one character for each table-level privilege. The program checks the second character to see if the user has Update privilege, and the fifth character to see if Delete privilege has been granted. It hides the menu choices that are not allowed.

Function Overview

Function Name	Purpose
scroller_3()	Runs the browsing menu, fetching and modifying rows on request. Uses row ids to track rows.
query_cust3a()	Executes a CONSTRUCT statement and returns the resulting conditional expression. *See description in Example 20.*
query_cust3b()	Like query_cust3a(), but with different prompt message and a different treatment of the null query. *See description in Example 20.*
get_user()	Returns the user-id of the current user. *See description in Example 25.*
get_tab_auth()	Returns the current user's privileges on a specified table.
sel_merged_auth()	Selects all privileges and returns the superset of privileges. Since the key to systabauth is grantor+grantee+tabid, a given grantee may have multiple grants for a given table.
merge_auth()	Returns the superset of two tabauth strings, retaining any letter in preference to a hyphen, and uppercase letters in preference to lower.
disp_row()	Displays a row given its row id, checking that it still exists and matches the query constraints.
del_row()	Deletes a row given its row id, checking that it still exists and matches the query constraints.
upd_row()	Updates a row given its row id, checking that it exists and is unchanged from when it first displays.
like()	Function returning TRUE when two values are either equal or both null, FALSE otherwise. *See description in Example 24.*
open_db()	Opens a database using dynamic SQL and saves information about it for later use. Returns TRUE or FALSE. *See description in Example 22.*
begin_wk()	Executes a BEGIN WORK statement provided that open_db() says the database uses Informix-style transactions. *See description in Example 22.*
commit_wk()	Executes a COMMIT WORK statement provided that open_db() says the database uses transactions. *See description in Example 22.*
rollback_wk()	Executes a ROLLBACK WORK statement provided that open_db() says the database uses transactions. *See description in Example 22.*
clear_lines()	Clears any number of lines starting at any line. *See description in Example 6.*

answer()	A user-alert subroutine that takes one to three possible user responses and returns the one the user chooses. *See description in Example 20.*
msg()	Displays a brief, informative message. *See description in Example 5.*

The GLOBALS Statement and MAIN Function

1➤ Any version of the example database may be used here.

2➤ The gr_database record is set by the open_db() function to reflect the features of the database.

3➤ The program prompts the user for the name of the database to use. Since the database will be opened dynamically, the example gives the user the opportunity to name a different database.

4GL source file

```
1➤ DATABASE stores2t

   GLOBALS
2➤     DEFINE      gr_database RECORD
                       db_known   SMALLINT,     -- following fields are usable
                       has_log    SMALLINT,     -- based on sqlawarn[2]
                       is_ansi    SMALLINT,     -- based on sqlawarn[3]
                       is_online  SMALLINT,     -- based on sqlawarn[4]
                       can_wait   SMALLINT      -- supports "set lock mode to wait"
                   END RECORD
   END GLOBALS

   # Module variables shared by scroller_3() and disp_row()
   DEFINE          m_querycond  CHAR(500),        -- current query condition text
                   mr_currcust RECORD LIKE customer.*    -- current row contents

   ########################################
   MAIN
   ########################################
     DEFINE        cond      CHAR(150),  -- conditional clause from CONSTRUCT
                   more      SMALLINT,   -- continue flag
                   dbname    CHAR(10)

     DEFER INTERRUPT

     OPTIONS
       HELP FILE "hlpmsgs",
       FORM LINE 5,
       COMMENT LINE 5,
       MESSAGE LINE 19

     OPEN WINDOW w_db AT 2, 3
       WITH 4 ROWS, 65 COLUMNS
       ATTRIBUTE (BORDER, PROMPT LINE 3)

3➤   DISPLAY "Enter name of standard demo database, or press RETURN to"
       AT 2,2
     LET int_flag = FALSE
     PROMPT "  use 'stores2t' database: " FOR dbname
     IF int_flag THEN
       LET int_flag = FALSE
       CLOSE WINDOW w_db
       EXIT PROGRAM
     END IF

     CLOSE WINDOW w_db
     IF LENGTH(dbname)=0 THEN
       LET dbname = "stores2t"
     END IF
```

4➤ The open_db() function attempts to open the specified database. It returns FALSE only if it fails to open the database requested. This function is discussed in Example 24.

The scroller_3() Function

5➤ cust_priv will receive the output of the get_tab_auth() function (see page 622). It is unconventional but valid to define a variable LIKE a column of a system catalog. The name of the system catalog table systabauth is qualified with the owner name informix. This is allowed anywhere, but would only be required in an ANSI-compliant database.

6➤ The variables curr_rid, next_rid, and prior_rid are used in this program the same way the variables curr_cust, next_cust and prior_cust were used in Examples 19 and 20: to hold the row currently being displayed and the adjacent ones. However, in this program only a row id is kept for each row.

7➤ The get_tab_auth() function is on page 622. It returns a string of characters that encodes the current user's privileges with respect to the given table.

8➤ The scroll_pos variable contains the scroll position, here initialized to 1 because the first time this routine is entered, the first row of the selected set should be displayed to the user.

9➤ As in Examples 19 and 20, the program remains in this loop (which ends on page 615) until the user selects the Query or Exit menu choices. Each time through the loop, the scroll cursor c_custrid is opened and then closed. Thus the code for any other menu choice can force resynchronization of the cursor simply by exiting the menu and thus iterating the loop.

```
4➤  IF open_db(dbname)=FALSE THEN     -- open db, find out about logging
      DISPLAY "Unable to open that database, sorry." AT 20,1
      EXIT PROGRAM
    END IF
```

Remainder of function is identical to that in Example 20 except it calls scroller_3() instead of scroller_2().

```
END MAIN

########################################
FUNCTION scroller_3(start_cond)
########################################
5➤  DEFINE    start_cond CHAR(150),-- initial query condition

              cust_priv   LIKE informix.systabauth.tabauth, -- privilege in table
              scroll_sel  CHAR(500), -- SELECT statement for scroll cursor
6➤            curr_rid,              -- row id of row now being displayed,
              next_rid,              -- ..of row to display when Next is chosen,
              prior_rid   INTEGER,   -- ..of row to display when Prior is chosen
                                     -- (row-ids are integers)
              fetch_dir,             -- flag showing direction of travel in list
              using_next,            -- flag values: going fwd using fetch next,
              using_prior,           -- ...going bwd using fetch prior, or
              at_end,                -- ...at either end of the list
              retval,                -- value to RETURN from function
              misc        SMALLINT,  -- scratch number
              scroll_pos  SMALLINT   -- abs or rel position in selection set
                                     -- no one can manually scroll > 32K records

    LET using_next = +1
    LET using_prior = -1
    LET at_end = 0

    LET m_querycond = start_cond  -- initialize query condition
7➤  LET cust_priv = get_tab_auth("customer") -- our user's privileges

8➤  LET scroll_pos = 1           -- initial position is First
    LET retval = 99              -- neither TRUE nor FALSE
9➤  WHILE retval <> TRUE AND retval <> FALSE -- ie while not Query or Exit

      LET scroll_sel = "SELECT ROWID FROM customer WHERE ",m_querycond CLIPPED
      PREPARE scroll_prep FROM scroll_sel
      DECLARE c_custrid SCROLL CURSOR FOR scroll_prep
      OPEN c_custrid

      DISPLAY
    "-------------------------------------------Press CTRL-W for Help----------"
        AT 3, 1
```

10➤ The MENU statement ends on page 615.

11➤ The set of selected rows could turn out to be empty for the following reasons:

- The initial query selected no rows
- The conditions added following a Revise menu choice qualified no rows
- The selected rows have all been deleted or updated so they no longer meet the conditions following a resynchronization.

12➤ The time needed to resynchronize depends on the previous scroll position. If it is 1 or a small absolute number, only a few rows will have to be read. But if it was Last, or relative to Last, the program will have to use a FETCH LAST, causing the engine to read all rows and save them. Since some time may pass, a message is displayed to warn the user.

13➤ Since at least one row exists, it is time to display or hide the Update and Delete menu choices, based on the user's privileges in this table.

14➤ A scroll position greater than 1 indicates that the absolute position is known and is not First. The following code tries to establish the prior, current and next rows as they would have been. However, any of these rows may no longer be part of the selected set. These lines try to read the "prior" and "current" rows; if they are found, the SQLCODE will be zero.

15➤ If the program gets this far, prior and current rows are known. The Next menu choice is enabled depending on whether a "next" row can also be found. (If not, the current row is also the last in the set.)

16➤ If the "prior" or "current" row is no longer in the set, the set has become smaller. The program sets a scroll position of Last (handled below).

17➤ A negative scroll position is relative to the last row in the set. The following lines try to establish the "current" and "next" rows. Success in fetching both will be reflected in SQLCODE. The FETCH LAST operation forces the database engine to find and cache all selected rows, and could take a long time to perform.

18➤ The current row (or some row at the same position) has been restored. Now the Prior menu choice is enabled or disabled depending on the existence of a row in the prior position.

```
10➤ MENU "View Customers"

      BEFORE MENU -- Set up as for First, but with chance of zero rows
        SHOW OPTION ALL -- should *not* be needed, see problem 8734
        FETCH FIRST c_custrid INTO curr_rid -- test for empty set
        IF SQLCA.SQLCODE = NOTFOUND THEN
11➤       ERROR "There are no rows that satisfy this query."
          HIDE OPTION ALL
          SHOW OPTION "Query"
          SHOW OPTION "Exit"
          NEXT OPTION "Query"
        ELSE   -- set contains at least one row
12➤       MESSAGE "Setting cursor position, be patient"
13➤       IF cust_priv[2] = "-" THEN
            HIDE OPTION "Update"
          END IF
          IF cust_priv[5] = "-" THEN
            HIDE OPTION "Delete"
          END IF
          IF scroll_pos > 1 THEN  -- try for former absolute position
14➤         LET misc = scroll_pos - 1  -- start with "prior" row
            FETCH ABSOLUTE misc c_custrid INTO prior_rid
            IF SQLCA.SQLCODE = 0 THEN  -- that worked, get current
              FETCH NEXT c_custrid INTO curr_rid
            END IF
            IF SQLCA.SQLCODE = 0 THEN  -- got current row, set up "Next"
15➤           LET fetch_dir = using_next
              FETCH NEXT c_custrid INTO next_rid
              IF SQLCA.SQLCODE = 0 THEN
                NEXT OPTION "Next"
              ELSE
                HIDE OPTION "Next"
                NEXT OPTION "First"
              END IF
            ELSE        -- current row unavailable, go for "Last"
16➤           LET scroll_pos = 0
            END IF
          END IF        -- scroll_pos > 1
          IF scroll_pos < 0 THEN  -- try for former relative position
17➤         FETCH LAST c_custrid INTO curr_rid -- establish position
            LET misc = scroll_pos + 1 -- start with "next" row
            FETCH RELATIVE misc c_custrid INTO next_rid
            IF SQLCA.SQLCODE = 0 THEN -- ok, try for current
              FETCH PRIOR c_custrid INTO curr_rid
            END IF
            IF SQLCA.SQLCODE = 0 THEN -- got current, set up "Prior"
18➤           LET fetch_dir = using_prior
              FETCH PRIOR c_custrid INTO prior_rid
              IF SQLCA.SQLCODE = 0 THEN
                NEXT OPTION "Prior"
```

19➤ If the "current" or "next" row is no longer in the set, the set has become smaller. The program sets a scroll position of First (handled below).

20➤ The scroll position was, or has been forced to, Last. Fetch the last row (which must exist since the set has been shown to contain at least one row) and make it current. Display the Prior choice if more than one row exists.

21➤ The scroll position was, or has been forced to, First. Fetch the first row (it may already have been fetched, but if that is the case, this fetch will take little time). Display the Next choice if more than one row exists.

22➤ The disp_row() function (on page 612) fetches the column values for a given row id and displays them in the form. If the row is no longer part of the selected set, the function returns FALSE.

This IF statement appears in several menu commands. Whenever disp_row() returns FALSE, the program exits the menu, thus forcing the cursor to resynchronize.

```
          ELSE
            HIDE OPTION "Prior"
            NEXT OPTION "Last"
          END IF
        ELSE      -- current row unavailable, go for "First"
19➤       LET scroll_pos = 1
        END IF
      END IF         -- scroll_pos < 0
20➤   IF scroll_pos = 0 THEN -- do just as for "Last" choice
        FETCH LAST c_custrid INTO curr_rid
        HIDE OPTION "Next" -- can't go onward from here
        LET fetch_dir = using_prior
        FETCH PRIOR c_custrid INTO prior_rid
        IF SQLCA.SQLCODE = 0 THEN-- at least 2 rows in set
          NEXT OPTION "Prior"
        ELSE         -- only 1 row in set
          HIDE OPTION "Prior"
          NEXT OPTION "Query"
        END IF
      END IF -- scroll_pos = 0 = last
21➤   IF scroll_pos = 1 THEN        -- do just as for "First" choice
        FETCH FIRST c_custrid INTO curr_rid
        HIDE OPTION "Prior"         -- can't back up from #1
        LET fetch_dir = using_next
        FETCH NEXT c_custrid INTO next_rid
        IF SQLCA.SQLCODE = 0 THEN   -- at least 2 rows
          NEXT OPTION "Next"
        ELSE                        -- only 1 row in set
          HIDE OPTION "Next"
          NEXT OPTION "Query"
        END IF
      END IF -- scroll_pos = 1 = First
      MESSAGE ""                    -- clear "please wait" message
22➤   IF disp_row(curr_rid) = FALSE THEN
        EXIT MENU
      END IF
    END IF

  COMMAND KEY(ESC,Q) "Query" "Query for a different set of customers."
      HELP 130
    LET retval = TRUE
    EXIT MENU

  COMMAND "Revise" "Restrict the current query by adding conditions."
       HELP 131
    CALL query_cust3b() RETURNING start_cond
    IF start_cond IS NOT NULL THEN   -- some condition entered
      LET m_querycond = m_querycond CLIPPED, " AND ", start_cond CLIPPED
      EXIT MENU                      -- close and re-open the cursor
```

23➤ When the First choice is made, an absolute scroll position is established. The remainder of the code in this section is essentially the same as that in the scroller_1() function in Example 19, with row ids replacing entire customer rows.

24➤ When the Next choice is made, the scroll position can be incremented. This is true regardless of whether it is an absolute position counting from First or a relative position counting from Last. The remainder of this section is essentially the same as that in the scroller_1() function in Example 19.

```
  ELSE            -- construct clears form, refresh the display
    IF disp_row(curr_rid) = FALSE THEN
      EXIT MENU
    END IF
  END IF

COMMAND "First" "Display first customer in selected set."
    HELP 133
  FETCH FIRST c_custrid INTO curr_rid  -- this cannot return NOTFOUND
  IF disp_row(curr_rid) = FALSE THEN
    EXIT MENU
  END IF
23➤  LET scroll_pos = 1   -- know an absolute position
  HIDE OPTION "Prior"  -- can't back up from #1
  LET fetch_dir = using_next
  FETCH NEXT c_custrid INTO next_rid
  IF SQLCA.SQLCODE = 0 THEN  -- at least 2 rows
    SHOW OPTION "Next"-- it might be hidden
    NEXT OPTION "Next"
  ELSE    -- only 1 row in set
    HIDE OPTION "Next"
    NEXT OPTION "Query"
  END IF

COMMAND "Next" "Display next customer in selected set."
    HELP 134
  LET prior_rid = curr_rid
  LET curr_rid = next_rid
  IF disp_row(curr_rid) = FALSE THEN
    EXIT MENU
  END IF
24➤  LET scroll_pos = scroll_pos+1
  SHOW OPTION "Prior"
  CASE (fetch_dir)
    WHEN using_next
      FETCH NEXT c_custrid INTO next_rid
    WHEN at_end
      FETCH RELATIVE +2 c_custrid INTO next_rid
    WHEN using_prior
      FETCH RELATIVE +3 c_custrid INTO next_rid
  END CASE
  IF SQLCA.SQLCODE = NOTFOUND THEN
    LET fetch_dir = at_end
    HIDE OPTION "Next"
    NEXT OPTION "First"
  ELSE
    LET fetch_dir = using_next
  END IF
```

25➤ When the Prior choice is made, the scroll position can be decremented. This is true regardless of whether it is an absolute position counting from First or a relative position counting from Last. The remainder of this section is essentially the same as that in the scroller_1() function in Example 19.

26➤ When the Last choice is made, the program no longer knows an absolute position (because it never knows exactly how many rows are selected). This statement establishes a relative position with respect to the last row. The remainder of this section is essentially the same as that in the scroller_1() function in Example 19.

```
COMMAND "Prior" "Display previous customer in selected set."
    HELP 135
  LET next_rid = curr_rid
  LET curr_rid = prior_rid
  IF disp_row(curr_rid) = FALSE THEN
    EXIT MENU
  END IF
25➤  LET scroll_pos = scroll_pos-1
  SHOW OPTION "Next"
  CASE (fetch_dir)
    WHEN using_prior
      FETCH PRIOR c_custrid INTO prior_rid
    WHEN at_end
      FETCH RELATIVE -2 c_custrid INTO prior_rid
    WHEN using_next
      FETCH RELATIVE -3 c_custrid INTO prior_rid
  END CASE
  IF SQLCA.SQLCODE = NOTFOUND THEN
    LET fetch_dir = at_end
    HIDE OPTION "Prior"
    NEXT OPTION "Last"
  ELSE
    LET fetch_dir = using_prior
  END IF

COMMAND "Last" "Display final customer in selected set."
    HELP 136
  FETCH LAST c_custrid INTO curr_rid
  IF disp_row(curr_rid) = FALSE THEN
    EXIT MENU
  END IF
26➤  LET scroll_pos = 0    -- position now relative to last row
  HIDE OPTION "Next"    -- can't go onward from here
  FETCH PRIOR c_custrid INTO prior_rid
  LET fetch_dir = using_prior
  IF SQLCA.SQLCODE = 0 THEN   -- at least 2 rows in set
    SHOW OPTION "Prior"       -- it might have been hidden
    NEXT OPTION "Prior"
  ELSE                        -- only 1 row in set
    HIDE OPTION "Prior"
    NEXT OPTION "Query"
  END IF

COMMAND "Update" "Modify contents of current row."
    HELP 137
  CALL upd_row(curr_rid)
  EXIT MENU                   -- force cursor to reopen
```

The disp_row() Function

27➤ The disp_row() function takes a row id, fetches the column values for that row, and displays them in the screen form. The function checks for stale data and, if it is found, displays nothing and returns FALSE. The caller function then knows that the scroll cursor should be resynchronized.

28➤ The SELECT statement combines the query condition with a request for a specific row id. The row id was produced using the same initial query conditions. If the row no longer matches this condition, it must have been updated by another user.

29➤ This is the expected and usual result: a return code of zero from the FETCH indicates that the row was found.

30➤ An SQL code of NOTFOUND means that one of the WHERE clauses failed. Either there is no row with this row id (it must have been deleted) or else it does not match the criteria it matched previously, when the scroll cursor was opened.

```
        COMMAND "Delete" "Delete the current row."
            HELP 138
          IF "Yes" = answer("Are you sure you want to delete this?",
                                                  "Yes","No","")

          THEN
            CALL del_row(curr_rid)
            CLEAR FORM
          END IF
          CLOSE c_custrid
          NEXT OPTION "Query"

        COMMAND KEY(INTERRUPT,"E") "Exit" "Exit program."
            HELP 100
          LET retval = FALSE
          EXIT MENU
      END MENU

      CLOSE c_custrid
    END WHILE    -- while retval neither FALSE nor TRUE
    RETURN retval

  END FUNCTION  -- scroller_3 --

  ########################################
27➤ FUNCTION disp_row(rid)
  ########################################
     DEFINE       rid          INTEGER,

                  err, ret     SMALLINT,
                  get_sel      CHAR(500)

28➤   LET get_sel = "SELECT * FROM customer",
                  " WHERE ROWID = ", rid,
                  " AND ", m_querycond CLIPPED
    PREPARE prep_get FROM get_sel
    DECLARE c_getrow CURSOR FOR prep_get
    OPEN c_getrow

  WHENEVER ERROR CONTINUE
    FETCH c_getrow INTO mr_currcust.*
    LET err = SQLCA.SQLCODE
  WHENEVER ERROR STOP

    CLOSE c_getrow
    FREE c_getrow
    LET ret = TRUE -- assume it will work
    CASE err
29➤     WHEN 0              -- good, got the data
        DISPLAY BY NAME mr_currcust.*
30➤     WHEN NOTFOUND -- row deleted or changed beyond recognition
        ERROR "Selected row no longer exists -- resynchronizing"
        SLEEP 2
        LET ret = FALSE
```

31➤ Negative return codes are unlikely. However, if one occurs, this function should not return FALSE. To do so would cause the cursor to be closed and reopened, after which this function would be called again with the same row id, possibly resulting in an endless loop.

The del_row() Function

32➤ The del_row() function accepts a row id and deletes it, provided that it still matches the original query criteria. It does not impose a stringent test (the original criteria might be no more than "customer_num > 1"). Furthermore, it takes no account of the dependencies in other tables on rows of this table. (Before a customer row is deleted, any orders with the same customer number should be deleted, and before an order is deleted, its items should be deleted.)

33➤ As in the preceding function, the prior query condition is appended to the row id value to create the WHERE clause.

34➤ Because of the use of the row id, the DELETE will affect either one row or none. Testing this number for 1 is equivalent to testing SQLCODE for zero.

35➤ Use of either COMMIT WORK or ROLLBACK WORK will close all cursors, including the scroll cursor.

The upd_row() Function

36➤ The upd_row() function lets the user update a row. It performs the following actions:

1. Input is accepted in all fields except the primary key.
2. The user is asked for confirmation.
3. The row is fetched again and verified as unchanged.
4. The update is performed.

```
31➤    OTHERWISE            -- locked row? hardware error?
         ERROR "SQL error ",err," fetching row."
         SLEEP 2  -- leave screen unchanged, return TRUE, avoiding a loop
       END CASE
       RETURN ret

   END FUNCTION  -- disp_row --

   ########################################
32➤ FUNCTION del_row(rid)
   ########################################
     DEFINE        rid       INTEGER,

                   ret       SMALLINT,
                   del_stm   CHAR(500)

33➤  LET del_stm = "DELETE FROM customer",
                   " WHERE ROWID = ", rid,
                   " AND ", m_querycond CLIPPED
     PREPARE prep_del FROM del_stm
     CALL begin_wk()       -- do BEGIN WORK if supported

   WHENEVER ERROR CONTINUE
     EXECUTE prep_del
34➤  LET ret = SQLCA.SQLERRD[3] -- count of rows deleted, should be 1
   WHENEVER ERROR STOP

     IF ret = 1 THEN       -- good, deleted that row
35➤    CALL commit_wk()    -- make it official
     ELSE                 -- bad, no row deleted
       ERROR "SQL problem, delete not done -- resynchronizing"
       CALL rollback_wk() -- end failed transaction
       SLEEP 3
     END IF
     FREE prep_del
   END FUNCTION  -- del_row --

   ########################################
36➤ FUNCTION upd_row(rid)
   ########################################
     DEFINE        rid               INTEGER,

                   reject, touched   SMALLINT,
                   rejmsg            CHAR(80),
                   pr_updcust        RECORD LIKE customer.*,
                   pr_testcust       RECORD LIKE customer.*,
                   cust_cnt          SMALLINT

     LET pr_updcust.* = mr_currcust.*
     LET int_flag = 0
     CALL clear_lines(2, 16)
     DISPLAY  " Enter new data and press Accept to update."
       AT 16, 1 ATTRIBUTE (REVERSE, YELLOW)
```

37➤ The user is explicitly not allowed to enter a new customer number.

38➤ This AFTER FIELD clause performs a very simple validation for the state code. A more complete verification might provide a popup window with a list of valid codes from the state table. See the AFTER FIELD clause for the state field in the addupd_cust() function (in Example 9) for this more complete verification.

39➤ The built-in FIELD_TOUCHED() function takes a list of screen fields and returns TRUE if any were modified.

40➤ A series of tests within an IF statement ensures that the update is valid and sets reject to TRUE if it is not. The first test is to see if the user ended the INPUT operation with the Accept key rather than Interrupt. The second is to make sure at least one field was modified. If these are so, then the user is asked for confirmation.

41➤ Those tests succeeding, a transaction is begun and the row is fetched once more. This SELECT tests only the row id (the column values will be checked later using program code). The cursor specifies FOR UPDATE, so the engine locks the row that is fetched.

```
     DISPLAY " Press Cancel to exit without changing database."
       AT 17, 1 ATTRIBUTE (REVERSE, YELLOW)
37➤  INPUT BY NAME pr_updcust.company, pr_updcust.address1, pr_updcust.address2,
                   pr_updcust.city, pr_updcust.state, pr_updcust.zipcode,
                   pr_updcust.fname, pr_updcust.lname, pr_updcust.phone
     WITHOUT DEFAULTS

38➤    AFTER FIELD state
         IF pr_updcust.state IS NULL THEN
           ERROR "You must enter a state code. Please try again."
           NEXT FIELD state
         END IF

         SELECT COUNT(*)
         INTO cust_cnt
         FROM state
         WHERE code = pr_updcust.state

         IF (cust_cnt = 0) THEN
           ERROR
             "Unknown state code. Please try again."
           LET pr_updcust.state = NULL
           NEXT FIELD state
         END IF

       AFTER INPUT
39➤      LET touched =  FIELD_TOUCHED(fname,lname,company,
                                      address1,address2,
                                      city,state,
                                      zipcode,phone)
     END INPUT

40➤  IF int_flag THEN
       LET rejmsg = "Update cancelled at your request - resynchronizing."
       LET reject = TRUE
     ELSE
       IF NOT touched THEN
         LET rejmsg =
           "No data entered so database unchanged - resynchronizing."
         LET reject = TRUE
       ELSE
         IF "No" = answer("OK to go ahead and update the database?",
                          "Yes","No","")
         THEN
           LET rejmsg = "Database not changed - resynchronizing."
           LET reject = TRUE
         END IF
       END IF
     END IF
     IF NOT reject THEN
41➤    CALL begin_wk()
```

42➤ This IF statement applies two tests:

- The first part tests whether the row was successfully fetched for update.
- The second part tests whether the fetched row is identical in every field to the row that previously was displayed.

The second test requires a verbose expression. **4GL** does not allow comparison between whole record variables. Neither pr_testcust=mr_currcust nor pr_testcust.*=mr_currcust.* is permitted, so the fields must be compared individually. In this case, some of the fields may contain null values, and nulls do not compare as equal. Therefore the like() function from Example 24 is used to find out if the fields are both null or else equal in non-null contents.

43➤ The UPDATE statement assigns the values in the pr_updcust record to the current customer row. When you use the * notation in an update statement, the program knows not to update the serial column.

44➤ An error at this point is very unlikely since the row was successfully fetched and locked previously, and the user is known to have Update privilege. The UPDATE statement is not covered by WHENEVER ERROR CONTINUE, so if it should fail, the program would terminate and the transaction would be rolled back automatically. Hence the unconditional call to commit_wk() is valid.

```
WHENEVER ERROR CONTINUE
    DECLARE c_updrow CURSOR FOR
      SELECT * INTO pr_testcust.* FROM customer
      WHERE ROWID = rid
    FOR UPDATE

    OPEN c_updrow
    FETCH c_updrow
WHENEVER ERROR STOP
42➤ IF SQLCA.SQLCODE = 0
        AND pr_testcust.customer_num = mr_currcust.customer_num
        AND like(pr_testcust.fname,mr_currcust.fname)
        AND like(pr_testcust.lname,mr_currcust.lname)
        AND like(pr_testcust.company,mr_currcust.company)
        AND like(pr_testcust.address1,mr_currcust.address1)
        AND like(pr_testcust.address2,mr_currcust.address2)
        AND like(pr_testcust.city,mr_currcust.city)
        AND like(pr_testcust.state,mr_currcust.state)
        AND like(pr_testcust.zipcode,mr_currcust.zipcode)
        AND like(pr_testcust.phone,mr_currcust.phone)
    THEN
      UPDATE customer SET fname = pr_updcust.fname,
                          lname  = pr_updcust.lname,
                          company  = pr_updcust.company,
                          address1  = pr_updcust.address1,
                          address2  = pr_updcust.address2,
                          city  = pr_updcust.city,
                          state  = pr_updcust.state,
                          zipcode  = pr_updcust.zipcode,
                          phone  = pr_updcust.phone
43➤     WHERE CURRENT OF c_updrow
44➤   CALL commit_wk()
      MESSAGE "Database updated - resynchronizing."
    ELSE
      LET rejmsg = "SQL problem updating row - not done - resynchronizing"
      LET reject = TRUE
      CALL rollback_wk()
    END IF
  END IF
  CALL clear_lines(2, 16)
  IF reject THEN
    ERROR rejmsg
  END IF
END FUNCTION --  upd_row --
```

The get_tab_auth() Function

45➤ The get_tab_auth() function returns the table-level privileges of the current user for a specified table (or view). Privileges are encoded in the table systabauth. See *The Informix Guide to SQL: Reference* for details on the system catalogs and the schema of the systables and systabauth tables.

Briefly, the privileges are encoded as a string of seven letters. Each letter stands for one privilege; if the user lacks the privilege, the letter is a hyphen. A user might have more than one grant of privileges, and also inherits any privileges granted to the public. This function produces the logical superset of all grants that apply to the current user on the specified table.

46➤ In an ANSI-compliant database, table names may be qualified with owner names. The following passage checks the function argument for an owner name and pulls it out to a separate variable.

47➤ The systables table maps owner names and table names to table id numbers. The following lines try to retrieve the tabid for the table name in the argument.

48➤ No owner name was given, and if the database is not ANSI-compliant, none is needed; tablenames will be unique. But in an ANSI-compliant database there could be two or more tables with the same name and different owners. In this case the SELECT would cause an error by producing more than one row. To prevent this, we select the MIN of what we expect to be a set of 1.

49➤ The name tabname is both a variable and a column in systables. The prefix @ specifies that the column is intended here.

50➤ The combination of owner name and tablename is unique in any database, so no MIN is needed here.

51➤ Table id numbers for user-defined tables start at 100. If theTabid is less, either the caller passed the name of a system table or, more likely, the tablename was not found so the initial value of -1 in theTabid has not been changed. Definitions of the two functions called in this statement follow.

```
     ########################################
45➤  FUNCTION get_tab_auth(tabname)
     ########################################
       DEFINE tabname  CHAR(32),   -- allow "owner.tabname"

              theTable LIKE informix.systables.tabname, -- tablename part of above
              theOwner LIKE informix.systables.owner,   -- ownerid part, if any
              theTabid LIKE informix.systables.tabid,   -- tabid from systables
              auth LIKE informix.systabauth.tabauth,    -- final authorization string
              j,k      SMALLINT

46➤    LET theOwner = NULL      -- assume owner not included
       FOR j = 1 to LENGTH(tabname) - 1
         IF tabname[j] = "." THEN
           EXIT FOR
         END IF
       END FOR
       IF tabname[j] = "." THEN          -- is an "owner." part, extract
         LET theOwner = tabname[1,j-1]   -- save "owner" omitting "."
         LET k = LENGTH(tabname)         -- not allowed in subscript!
         LET tabname = tabname[j+1,k]    -- drop "owner."
       END IF
       LET theTable = tabname CLIPPED

       LET auth = "-------"              -- assume no privileges at all
       LET theTabid = -1                 -- sentinel value in case no such table
47➤    IF theOwner IS NULL THEN
48➤      SELECT MIN(tabid) INTO theTabid
         FROM informix.systables
49➤      WHERE @tabname = theTable
       ELSE
50➤      SELECT tabid INTO theTabid
         FROM informix.systables
         WHERE @tabname = theTable
           AND owner = theOwner
       END IF

51➤    IF theTabid >= 100 THEN -- table exists & is user-defined
         LET auth = merge_auth( sel_merged_auths(get_user(), theTabid),
                                sel_merged_auths("public", theTabid) )
       END IF

       RETURN auth
     END FUNCTION  -- get_tab_auth --
```

The sel_merged_auths() Function

52➤ The primary key of systabauth is composed of grantor, grantee, and tablename. That is, a given grantee may have more than one grant of privilege with respect to a given table (one from the table's owner an d one from a database administrator, for example). This function finds all grants for one user and one table and returns their superset. It uses a FOREACH loop to retrieve the rows of systabauth.

The merge_auth() Function

53➤ The merge_auth() function merges two privilege strings. In its output it preserves letters in preference to hyphens (privileges over lack of privilege) and uppercase letters in preference to lowercase (privileges WITH GRANT OPTION over those without).

```
########################################
52➤ FUNCTION sel_merged_auths(userid,theTabid)
########################################
  DEFINE      userid            LIKE informix.sysusers.username,
              theTabid          LIKE informix.systables.tabid,
              allAuth, oneAuth LIKE informix.systabauth.tabauth

  LET allAuth = "-------"
  DECLARE c_authval CURSOR FOR
    SELECT tabauth INTO oneAuth
    FROM informix.systabauth
    WHERE grantee = userid
      AND tabid = theTabid

  FOREACH c_authval
    LET allAuth = merge_auth(allAuth,oneAuth)
  END FOREACH

  CLOSE c_authval
  RETURN allAuth
END FUNCTION  -- sel_merged_auths --

########################################
53➤ FUNCTION merge_auth(oldauth,newauth)
########################################
  DEFINE        oldauth, newauth LIKE informix.systabauth.tabauth,

                k                SMALLINT

  FOR k = 1 to LENGTH(oldauth)
    IF (oldauth[k] = "-")          -- no privilege in this position
        OR (UPSHIFT(oldauth[k]) = newauth[k]) -- new is "with grant option"
    THEN
      LET oldauth[k] = newauth[k]
    END IF
  END FOR
  RETURN oldauth
END FUNCTION  -- merge_auth --
```

To locate any function definition see the Function Index on page 728.

28

Writing Recursive Functions

4GL supports recursion, although with some restrictions. The program in this example demonstrates recursion with two different algorithms related to "bill of materials processing", that is, processing items that have a parent-child relationship.

Representing Hierarchical Data

Many kinds of data have a naturally hierarchical structure: family bloodlines, business and military organizations, computer subroutine libraries, and assemblies of manufactured parts. Such data is often displayed as a tree, as in the following example.

The component parts of a product appear in the diagram. The product is a *Large red wagon*, which is composed of a *Wagon handle assembly, an 18-in fixed axle*, and so on. The boxes represent objects; the vertical lines represent the relationship "is contained in" or "contains," depending on the direction of travel. Some of the parts are themselves assemblies, although not all parts are shown here.

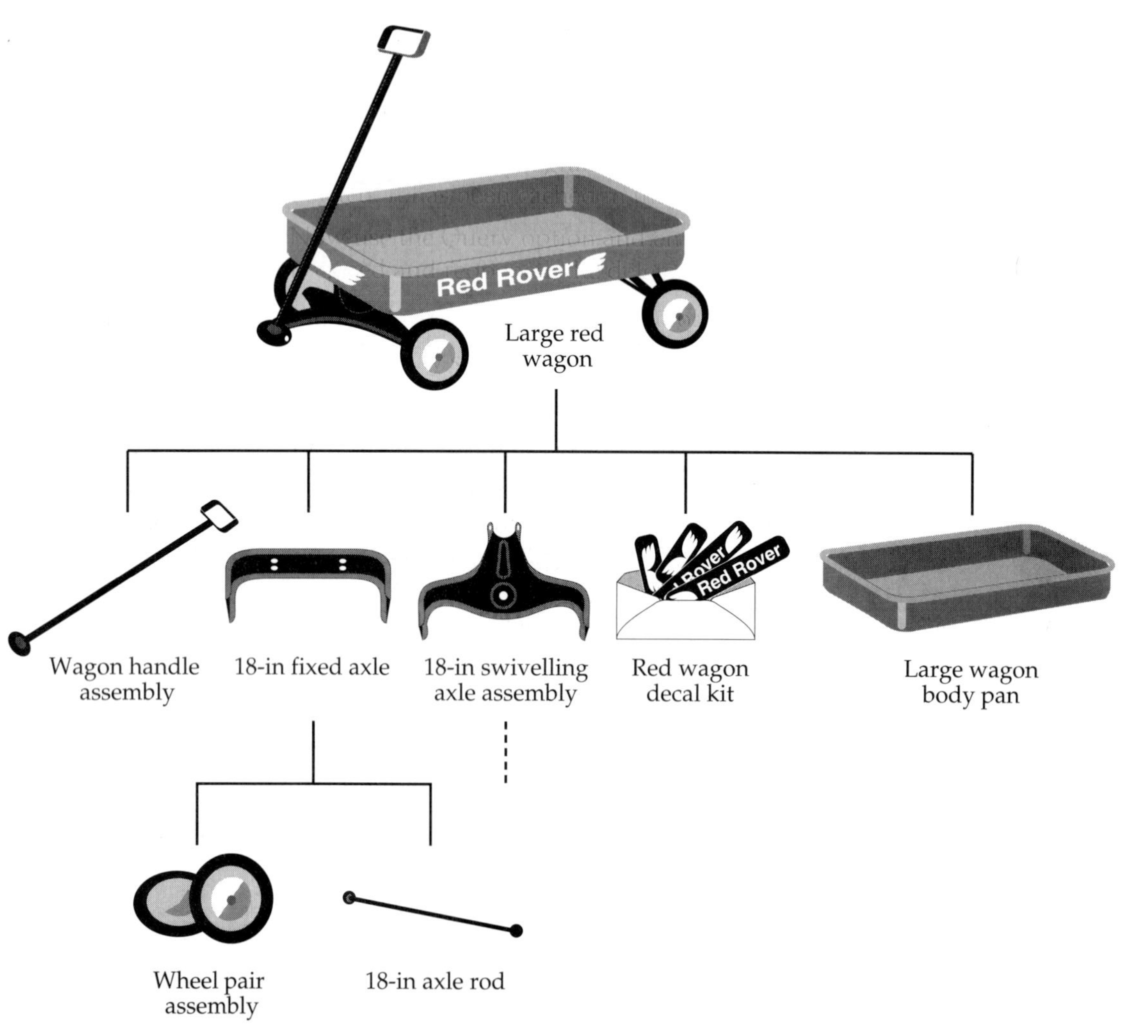

With a few changes, the same figure could represent the table of organization of the personnel of a bank. Then the vertical lines would represent "supervises" or "reports to."

The same data can be represented in a table that specifies parent-child relationships.

Parent	Child	Count
Large red wagon	Wagon handle assembly	1
Large red wagon	18-in fixed axle	1
18-in fixed axle	wheel pair assembly	1
wheel pair assembly	9-in rubber wheel	2
wheel pair assembly	plastic end cap	2
18-in fixed axle	18-in axle rod	1
Large red wagon	18-in swivelling axle assembly	1
Large red wagon	Large wagon body pan	1
Large red wagon	Red wagon decal kit	1

This table contains more information than the preceding diagram; it contains a count of the number of children of each type. A *Large red wagon* contains one *18-in fixed axle*, which contains one *Wheel pair assembly*, which in turn contains two *9-in rubber wheel* parts.

In a relational database, a table such as this is the natural way to represent hierarchical data. As a practical matter, it would be a waste of space to store so many redundant copies of a title such as "Large red wagon." But that problem is easily handled by giving each unique part a numeric key, and storing the descriptive titles just once in a table with other descriptive data.

(table PARTREE)

Parent	Child	Count
76566	76549	1
76566	76561	1
76561	76559	1
76559	76547	2
...		

(table PARTS)

Part	Description
76566	Large red wagon
76569	Wagon handle assembly
...	

It is easy to formulate some queries against this type of table. For example, what are the top-level assemblies? They are the ones that are not part of any other assembly; that is, they never appear in the Child column.

```
SELECT part, description FROM PARTS
WHERE 0 = (
        SELECT COUNT(*) FROM PARTREE
        WHERE PARTS.part = PARTREE.child )
```

The unit parts (the ones that have no components) are the parts that never appear in the Parent column. A similar query could list them.

The Parts Explosion Problem

It is also simple to ask a question such as, what are the components of a *Large red wagon*? They are the parts that have *Large red wagon* as their Parent.

```
SELECT part, description FROM PARTS main, PARTREE
WHERE   main.part = PARTREE.child
AND     PARTREE.parent = (
                SELECT part FROM PARTS sub
                WHERE sub.description = "Large red wagon" )
```

But this only lists the parts that are the immediate children of 76566, "Large red wagon." The immediate children are the ones that are directly connected to *Large Red Wagon* in the tree, the five that appear on the second row of the tree diagram. In order to list *all* the parts of a *Large red wagon* you must list not only its immediate children, but also their immediate children, and the children of those parts, and so on through the generations until only unit parts remain. Here is a portion of such a list, as generated by this example program.

```
076566 (  1) large red wagon
     076549 (  1) wagon handle assembly
         076540 (  1) speed nut #8
         076542 (  1) plastic end cap
         076550 (  1) wagon handle
         076551 (  1) handle clevis pin
     076561 (  1) 18-in fixed axle
         076559 (  1) wheel pair assembly
             076541 (  2) speed nut #2
             076542 (  2) plastic end cap
             076546 (  2) bracket mount kit
                 076543 (  2) stove bolt
                 076544 (  2) flat washer
                 076545 (  2) nut
             076547 (  2) 9-in rubber wheel
             076557 (  1) axle bracket left
             076558 (  1) axle bracket right
         076560 (  1) 18-in axle rod
     076563 (  1) 18-in swivelling axle assembly
         076556 (  1) swivel mount kit
            076546 (  2) bracket mount kit
                076543 (  2) stove bolt
```

The Parts Explosion in 4GL

A listing of this sort is called a *parts explosion*. Producing a parts explosion is a recursive task. Its logic could be sketched as follows.

```
Function explode(part,level)
    List the details of part, indented by level
    For each child of part
        call explode(child,level+1)
    End for
End function
```

A call to explode(76566,0) would produce an explosion of the parts in a *Large Red Wagon*. It remains only to implement the two lines "List the details of *part*..." and "For each child of *part*..." The first can be done most simply with a report function.

Given the tables shown on page 629, the natural way to implement "For each child of *part*..." would seem to be with a cursor and a FOREACH loop, something like this fragment (which will *not* work).

```
    DECLARE c_kid CURSOR FOR
        SELECT child FROM PARTREE WHERE parent = part
    FOREACH c_kid
        CALL explode(kid,level+1)
```

This is *not* a workable solution. The reason is that the data structures used to implement a cursor are static objects. Even though the cursor is declared within the body of a function, it is not local to that function; it is a module variable.

If this function were actually implemented, it would fail in the following way: on the first call, the FOREACH statement would open the cursor and produce the first child of the top-level part. The function would then call itself. The FOREACH statement would again OPEN the cursor. Opening a cursor that is open causes it to be closed (losing the position of the top-level function) and reopened.

The second level function would read its first child number and call itself at a third level, where the cursor would be closed and reopened, and so on until a level was reached at which there were no child parts. Here the FOREACH loop would find no data on the first fetch, and would end, closing the cursor.

Each calling function would then get an error when its copy of the FOREACH loop tried to fetch the next row from a closed cursor.

To summarize this explanation: When using a cursor within a recursive function, you cannot keep the cursor open across the recursive function call. It must be used in one of two ways:

1. Opened before the first recursive call and not closed until the recursion has ended.
2. Opened, used completely, and closed again at each level of the recursion.

In this example program, the second method is used for the parts explosion. At each level, before the recursive call takes place, the cursor is opened, all relevant rows are fetched and saved in an array, and the cursor is closed.

The Parts Inventory

The parts explosion answers the question, what are the component parts of a Large Red Wagon? As an assembly list, it shows all the parts in the order they would be assembled, and it shows sub-assemblies. A related question is, what is the *inventory* of parts that compose a Large Red Wagon? The inventory is a summary of the parts explosion. It shows only the unit parts required, along with a total of the number of times each is used. For example, the parts explosion shows the use of a fixed axle and a swivelling axle assembly, each containing two *9-in rubber wheel* parts. The parts inventory would show only that a total of four of the wheels are needed somewhere in the product. Here is part of an inventory report as generated by the example program:

```
Unit parts used in large red wagon                (076566)
   1 of speed nut #8                              (076540)
   4 of speed nut #2                              (076541)
   5 of plastic end cap                           (076542)
  12 of stove bolt                                (076543)
  12 of flat washer                               (076544)
  12 of nut                                       (076545)
   4 of 9-in rubber wheel                         (076547)
   1 of wagon handle                              (076550)
```

One way to produce an inventory is to "walk" the tree recursively using logic that can be sketched as follows:

```
FUNCTION inventory(part,count)
    IF part has children THEN
        FOR each child of part which is used child-count times,
            CALL inventory(child,count * child-count)
        END FOR
    ELSE it is a unit part,
        Tally the use of count units of part.
    END IF
END FUNCTION
```

The Inventory Report in 4GL

The method of implementing the loop over all children is the same as in the parts explosion. In this problem, the interesting question is, how best to keep a tally of parts? The units will be found in the order they appear in the parts explosion. It will be as if you were keeping a tally on a pad while an assistant called out numbers to you: "A speed nut...two wheels...four bolts...another speed nut."

The parts will not be encountered in any particular order. Neither the number of total entries, nor the number of unique parts, can be known in advance. (Indeed, in some applications there might be hundreds of each.) After all the unit parts have been tallied, it will be necessary to sort them by part and accumulate the totals.

The usual programming solution to a problem of this kind is to list all the unit parts in an array as they were found, and then to sort the array. However, sorting and summing are particular skills of the SQL database engine. Why not call upon them? So this example stores each unit part in a temporary table in the database. When the entire tree has been scanned, a final phase of the program opens a cursor on the temporary table. It uses a SELECT statement with the GROUP BY and ORDER BY clauses so that it can simply read the summary lines from the table in the order they should be printed.

This approach clearly takes more time to execute than would a program with an in-memory table. The clause WITH NO LOG is used when creating the temporary table to ensure the minimum amount of disk activity. Even so, there will be a call to the database engine for each item to be tallied, and this is many times as lengthy as an assignment to an array. The compensating benefits are program simplicity and the speed with which the example was implemented. Nevertheless, a production program to be used repeatedly would probably implement an in-memory array and sort.

Function Overview

Function Name	Purpose
explode_all()	Starts the report for the parts explosion listing, then calls the recursive function explode() once for each top-level part.
explode()	Recursive function that writes a parts explosion for one part.
kaboom()	Report function that produces the parts explosion listing.
inventory_all()	Starts the report for the inventory listing, then calls the recursive function inventory() once for each top-level part.
inventory()	Recursive function that writes an inventory for one part.
inven_rep()	Report function that produces the inventory listing.
pushkids()	Finds all children of a given part and pushes their numbers and use counts onto a stack in memory. It returns the number of child parts stacked for use as a loop count.
pop_a_kid()	Pops one child part number and count from stack.
set_up_tables()	Creates and loads the PARTS and PARTREE tables used by the example code.
tear_down_tables()	Removes PARTS and PARTREE tables so as to restore the database to its original condition.

The MAIN Function

1➤ The ma_kidstack array is a stack that holds the unprocessed child parts for all recursive levels. The index m_nextkid points to top-of-stack. The function pushkids() (page 645) adds parts to the stack, and pop_a_kid() (page 647) removes one. These are module variables (defined outside any function but not in a GLOBALS section). If the functions were in a separate source module (this would probably be the case if they were used in more than one program), the variables would be global.

2➤ The set_up_tables() function prompts the user for the name of a database, creates the PARTS and PARTREE tables, and loads them from a text file distributed with the source.

3➤ The c_parent cursor is used to drive both example functions. The method of identifying top-level parts (using a subquery to count the number of rows in which each candidate part appears as a child) is not as slow as might be supposed. An index should be placed on the child column in a production database. The database engine will read only the index while executing the subquery. Since index pages are often found in page buffers in memory, many (if not most) of the subqueries will require no disk I/O.

The explode_all() Function

4➤ The first part of the explode_all() function starts the explosion report to a user-specified destination. If the user does not enter a filename, the program sends the report output to the screen.

4GL source file

```
   --*Module variables
1➤ DEFINE  ma_kidstack        ARRAY[200] OF INTEGER, -- two items per pushed kid
           m_nextkid          SMALLINT,    -- MUST BE INITIALIZED TO ZERO
           m_theDb, m_fpath   CHARACTER(80)

   ########################################
   MAIN
   ########################################

2➤   CALL set_up_tables()   -- exits program unless tables are ok

     LET m_nextkid = 0

3➤   DECLARE c_parent CURSOR FOR
       SELECT DISTINCT mainq.parent
       FROM PARTREE mainq
       WHERE 0 = ( SELECT COUNT(*)
                   FROM PARTREE subq
                   WHERE subq.child=mainq.parent )

     CALL explode_all()      -- parts explosion for all parents
     CALL inventory_all() -- parts inventory for all parents
     CALL tear_down_tables() -- offers to remove tables & does

   END MAIN

   ########################################
4➤ FUNCTION explode_all()
   ########################################
     DEFINE   dada INTEGER

     DISPLAY ""
     DISPLAY ""
     DISPLAY "DEMONSTRATING PARTS EXPLOSION"
     DISPLAY ""
     DISPLAY "Specify a filename to receive the parts explosion report"
     DISPLAY "  file or just press RETURN for report to the screen."
     DISPLAY ""
     PROMPT "File: " FOR m_fpath
     DISPLAY ""
     DISPLAY ″Generating the file ″, m_fpath CLIPPED, ″. Please wait...″
     DISPLAY ""

     IF LENGTH(m_fpath) = 0 THEN
       START REPORT kaboom
     ELSE
       START REPORT kaboom TO m_fpath
     END IF
```

5➤ The function opens the c_parent cursor (declared in the MAIN program) and then calls the explode() recursive function for each top-level part.

The explode() Function

6➤ The explode() function works with the kaboom() report function to implement the recursive display of the parts explosion.

7➤ The function finds the description for the current part than sends the part information to the kaboom() report function to be printed out.

6➤ The pushkids() function finds all the child parts of the current part. It "pushes" these parts onto the stack, implemented by the ma_kidstack array. This function returns the number of child parts.

The pushkids() function uses a cursor over the PARTREE table to find all child parts of part pn. If a cursor was an object with local scope, it could be defined here and the following loop would use a FOREACH. Since this is not the case (as discussed in "The Parts Explosion in 4GL" on page 631), it is necessary to open the cursor, read all the rows it finds (child parts), save them on a stack, and close the cursor before beginning the recursion.

9➤ For each of the child parts, the explode() function:

1. Calls the pop_a_kid() function to take a single part off the top of the ma_kidstack array and return the part number and the number times this part is used.
2. Decrements the number of child parts remaining on the stack.
3. Calls itself (the recursive call) to perform the same procedure on the child part.

The recursion on a top-level part stops when there are no more child parts left for this part.

```
5➤   FOREACH c_parent INTO dada
       CALL explode(dada,1,0) -- used once at level 0
     END FOREACH

     FINISH REPORT kaboom

   END FUNCTION  -- explode_all --

   ########################################
6➤ FUNCTION explode(pn,pu,ln)
   ########################################
     DEFINE        pn      INTEGER,   -- this part number
                   pu      INTEGER,   -- number of times used at this level
                   ln      INTEGER,   -- level in the tree

                   nkids   SMALLINT,  -- number of children pn has
                   kn      INTEGER,   -- part number of one kid
                   ku      INTEGER,   -- its usage count
                   pdesc   CHAR(40)   -- description of pn

7➤   SELECT descr INTO pdesc
     FROM PARTS
     WHERE partnum = pn

     OUTPUT TO REPORT kaboom(pn,pdesc,pu,ln) -- list current part

8➤   CALL pushkids(pn) RETURNING nkids -- get, save all its children
9➤   WHILE nkids > 0
       CALL pop_a_kid() RETURNING kn, ku
       LET nkids = nkids - 1
       CALL explode(kn,ku,ln+1) -- here's the recursion!
     END WHILE

   END FUNCTION  -- explode --
```

The kaboom() Report Function

10➤ The report function uses the recursive level two ways. In this statement, it prints an extra line of space before a top-level part. In the next, it prints indenting spaces to match the level number.

The inventory_all() Function

11➤ Like the explode_all() function, the inventory _all() function starts the report to a user-specified destination and then applies the recursive function, in turn, to each top-level part.

12➤ The function opens the c_parent cursor (declared in the MAIN program) a second time and then calls the inventory() recursive function for each top-level part.

```
#########################################
REPORT kaboom(part,desc,use,level)
#########################################
  DEFINE        part       INTEGER,
                desc       CHAR(40),
                use        INTEGER,
                level      INTEGER,

                j          SMALLINT

  FORMAT
    PAGE HEADER
      PRINT COLUMN 20, "PARTS EXPLOSION REPORT - PAGE",
          PAGENO USING "###"
      PRINT COLUMN 30, TODAY
      SKIP 3 LINES

    ON EVERY ROW
10>   IF level = 0 THEN
        PRINT -- blank line before each parent
      END IF
      FOR j = 1 TO level
        PRINT 4 SPACES; -- indent to show recursive levels
      END FOR
      PRINT part USING "&&&&&&"," 
        (",use USING "---",") ",desc CLIPPED
END REPORT

#########################################
11> FUNCTION inventory_all()
#########################################
  DEFINE        papa     INTEGER

  DISPLAY "DEMONSTRATING PARTS USAGE INVENTORY"
  DISPLAY ""
  DISPLAY "Specify a filename to receive the inventory report"
  DISPLAY "  file or just press RETURN for report to the screen."
  DISPLAY ""
  PROMPT  "File: " FOR m_fpath
  DISPLAY "Generating the file ", m_fpath CLIPPED, ". Please wait..."
  DISPLAY ""

  IF LENGTH(m_fpath) = 0 THEN
    START REPORT inven_rep
  ELSE
    START REPORT inven_rep TO m_fpath
  END IF

12> FOREACH c_parent INTO papa-- for each top-level part
    CALL inventory(papa,0)-- this assembly used 0 times
  END FOREACH
```

The inventory() Function

13➤ The input to the inventory() function is a part number and the count of that part that is needed. (Imagine your assistant calling out "two wheels...a bolt...".) If the part proves to be a unit part, it must be tallied in the temp table. If not, this function should be applied to each of its component parts.

14➤ The tally must be initialized for each top level part. A part-count of zero is passed as a flag, alerting the function that this is a top-level part and it should initialize the temporary table at the start, and produce the report at the end. Such special cases are not aesthetically pleasing. You might prefer to rewrite this function, moving the set-up and reporting passages out to the inventory_all() function where they arguably belong.

15➤ This is the point at which a unit part is tallied by inserting a row in the table.

16➤ The recursion for a composite part takes place at this point in the code.

17➤ After processing a top-level part (so all recursions have been unwound), lines are generated for the inventory report. First a heading for the top-level part and then the summarized rows of the table.

18➤ All of the work in this report is being done in the SELECT statement. Note that the temporary table is being joined to the PARTS table to pick up descriptions.

Suppose that the PARTS table also contained a cost field. It would be simple to select a total cost for each unique unit part.

```
     FINISH REPORT inven_rep

   END FUNCTION  -- inventory_all --

   ########################################
13➤ FUNCTION inventory(pn,un)
   ########################################
     DEFINE        pn INTEGER,     -- major assembly to inventory
                   un INTEGER,     -- quantity needed (0 means top level)

                   nkids SMALLINT, -- number of progeny of pn
                   mulfac SMALLINT,-- quantity of part pn needed
                   kn INTEGER,      -- one child
                   ku INTEGER,      -- number of parts kn in one part pn
                   desc CHAR(40)    -- one descriptor

14➤  LET mulfac = un       -- usually true except for kludge:
     IF un = 0 THEN        -- this is top-level call, initialize temp table
       CREATE TEMP TABLE invenTemp (partnum INTEGER, used INTEGER )
         WITH NO LOG
       LET mulfac = 1      -- even parent is used once
     END IF

     CALL pushkids(pn) RETURNING nkids-- stack all children
     IF nkids = 0 THEN     -- part pn is noncomposite: count it
15➤    INSERT INTO invenTemp VALUES(pn,mulfac)
      ELSE                 -- part pn is an assembly, inventory it
       WHILE nkids > 0     -- by inventorying each of its kids
         CALL pop_a_kid() RETURNING kn, ku
         LET nkids = nkids - 1
16➤      CALL inventory(kn,ku*mulfac)     -- recurse!
       END WHILE
     END IF

     IF un = 0 THEN -- this is a top level call, now do the report
17➤    SELECT descr INTO desc
       FROM PARTS
       WHERE partnum = pn

       OUTPUT TO REPORT inven_rep(pn,0,desc)

18➤    DECLARE c_unitpart CURSOR FOR -- scanning the temp table
         SELECT t.partnum, SUM(t.used), p.descr
         INTO kn,ku,desc
         FROM invenTemp t, PARTS p
         WHERE t.partnum = p.partnum
         GROUP BY t.partnum, p.descr
         ORDER BY t.partnum

       FOREACH c_unitpart
         OUTPUT TO REPORT inven_rep(kn,ku,desc)
       END FOREACH
```

The inven_rep() Report Function

19➤ The inven_rep() function receives rows passed by the inventory() function and prints a line of the Inventory report.

The pushkids() Function

20➤ The pushkids() function pushes the component parts of a given part on a stack. It would benefit from some additional code:

- You could add safeguards against running off the end of the stack.
- You could add code to measure and report the stack high-water mark so that you could tune the size of the global array over time.

21➤ The c_kid cursor obtains the child parts for a specified parent part. In a production system there should be an index on at least the parent column. In that case, the set of rows with parent=pn could be found very quickly. The ORDER BY clause is not strictly necessary at this point. It ensures that child parts are pushed from largest to smallest number, and hence that they are popped by the calling function in numeric sequence. This makes the reports come out sorted. However, it would be better to remove the sort from such a heavily-used SQL operation if possible. The sorting could be done at other stages of processing.

The simplest solution might be to sort the numbers on the stack in this very function. The number of child parts pushed at any level is not likely to be large, so a simple insertion sort would be satisfactory, and probably much faster than invoking the database engine's sort module on a small set of data.

```
    DROP TABLE invenTemp
  END IF
END FUNCTION  -- inventory --

########################################
19➤ REPORT inven_rep(part,use,desc)
########################################
  DEFINE         part, use    INTEGER,
                 desc         CHAR(40)

  FORMAT
    PAGE HEADER
      PRINT COLUMN 26, "INVENTORY REPORT - PAGE ",
            PAGENO USING "###"
      PRINT COLUMN 36, TODAY
      SKIP 3 LINES

    ON EVERY ROW
      IF use > 0 THEN-- not the top level part
        PRINT use USING "####", " of ",desc,"
           (", part USING "&&&&&&",")"
      ELSE -- top level, do a control break
        PRINT
          PRINT "Base parts used in ",desc,
                " (",part USING "&&&&&&",")"
          PRINT
    END IF
END REPORT  -- inven_rep --

########################################
20➤ FUNCTION pushkids(pn)
########################################
  DEFINE         pn,                -- parent number

                 kn,                -- kid number
                 ku      INTEGER,   -- kid usage
                 oldtop  SMALLINT   -- save old stack top for counting number pushed

21➤ DECLARE c_kid CURSOR FOR -- all children of part pn
    SELECT child, used INTO kn, ku
    FROM PARTREE
    WHERE parent = pn
    ORDER BY child DESC

  LET oldtop = m_nextkid
```

22➤ The c_kid cursor is opened, used and closed again at each recursive level.

The pop_a_kid() Function

23➤ The pop_a_kid() function pops a single part from the stack implemented by the ma_kidstack array. These parts are pushed onto this stack by the pushkids() function.

This function would benefit from additional code which checked for popping from an empty stack.

The set_up_tables() Function

24➤ The function prompts for the name of the database containing the PARTS and PARTREE tables. These tables contain the part information used by this example. If the user does not enter a database name, the program assumes it will need to create these tables, so it prompts the user for the name of the database in which to create them. By default, the program uses the stores2t database.

22➤
```
  FOREACH c_kid
    LET m_nextkid = m_nextkid + 1
    LET ma_kidstack[m_nextkid] = kn
    LET m_nextkid = m_nextkid + 1
    LET ma_kidstack[m_nextkid] = ku
  END FOREACH

  RETURN (m_nextkid - oldtop)/2
END FUNCTION  -- pushkids --

########################################
```
23➤
```
FUNCTION pop_a_kid()
########################################
  DEFINE        kn,                   -- kid number from stack
                ku      INTEGER       -- kid usage from stack

  LET ku = ma_kidstack[m_nextkid]
  LET m_nextkid = m_nextkid - 1
  LET kn = ma_kidstack[m_nextkid]
  LET m_nextkid = m_nextkid - 1

  RETURN kn, ku
END FUNCTION  -- pop_a_kid --


########################################
FUNCTION set_up_tables()
########################################
 DEFINE        j, k    SMALLINT,
                afile   CHAR(80)

WHENEVER ERROR CONTINUE -- don't crash if things don't exist
```
24➤
```
  DISPLAY "DEMONSTRATING A RECURSIVE FUNCTION"
  DISPLAY ""
  DISPLAY "This program uses two tables named PARTS and PARTREE."
  DISPLAY ""
  DISPLAY "Please enter the name of a database where these tables"
  DISPLAY "  now exist. If they do not exist now, just press RETURN."
  DISPLAY ""
  PROMPT  "Database name: " FOR m_theDb
  DISPLAY ""

  IF LENGTH(m_theDb CLIPPED) = 0 THEN
    DISPLAY "Please enter the name of a database where we can create"
    DISPLAY "  those two tables. Press RETURN to use the stores2t"
    DISPLAY "  database."
    DISPLAY ""
    PROMPT  "Database name: " FOR m_theDb
    DISPLAY ""
    IF LENGTH(m_theDb) = 0 THEN
         LET m_theDb = "stores2t"
    END IF
```

25➤ The DATABASE statement attempts to open the specified database. If this open fails because the database does not exist (status = -329), the function asks the user whether to create this database. If the user wants a new database, the CREATE DATABASE statement creates it.

If the specified database exists but the DATABASE statement cannot open it, the program notifies the user and exits.

26➤ Once the database is open, the program checks for the existence of the PARTS and PARTREE tables. If these tables exist, the program prompts for the pathname of the directory where the example's load files can be found. These load files are called ex28pa.unl (for the PARTS table) and ex28pt.unl (for the PARTREE table). By default these files exist in the same directory as the other application files.

```
25➤     DATABASE m_theDb
        IF SQLCA.SQLCODE = -329 THEN
            DISPLAY "Database ", m_theDb CLIPPED,
                    " does not exist (or if it does, you"
            DISPLAY "  do not have Connect privilege in it).  We will try to"
            DISPLAY "  create the database."
            DISPLAY ""
            LET SQLCA.SQLCODE = 0 -- does create db not set this?
            CREATE DATABASE m_theDb
            IF SQLCA.SQLCODE = 0 THEN
                    DISPLAY "Database has been created."
                    DISPLAY ""
            END IF

        END IF
      ELSE
        DATABASE m_theDb
      END IF
      IF SQLCA.SQLCODE <> 0 THEN
        DISPLAY "Sorry, error ",SQLCA.SQLCODE,
                " opening or creating the database ",m_theDb CLIPPED
        EXIT PROGRAM
      END IF

26➤   LET j = 0      -- in case no table is there
      LET k = 0
      SELECT COUNT(*)
      INTO j
      FROM PARTS

      SELECT COUNT(*)
      INTO k
      FROM PARTREE

      IF 0 < (j*k) THEN -- both tables exist, have rows
        DISPLAY "The needed tables do exist in this database. Thank you."
        RETURN
      END IF
    -- at least one table does not exist or is empty

      DISPLAY "To load the tables we need the file pathname for two files:"
      DISPLAY "          ex28pa.unl  and  ex28pt.unl"
      DISPLAY "  They came in the same directory as this program file."
      DISPLAY ""
      DISPLAY "  Enter a pathname, including the final slash or backslash."
      DISPLAY "  If it is the current working directory just press RETURN."
      DISPLAY ""
      PROMPT  "Path to those files: " FOR m_fpath
```

27➤ If the PARTS and PARTREE tables do not exist, the program uses the CREATE TABLE statement to create them. Because the WHENEVER ERROR STOP statement precedes these CREATE TABLE statements, any error encountered creates a runtime error.

This function could be enhanced to check for possible causes of failure for each CREATE TABLE statement and to recover from them. This enhancement would require moving the WHENEVER statement after the CREATE TABLE statements and adding the appropriate error checking code to the program.

28➤ The LOAD statements load the data in the ex28pa.unl and ex28pt.unl files into the PARTS and PARTREE tables.

The tear_down_tables() Function

29➤ The function asks the user whether to drop the PARTS and PARTREE tables from the database. By dropping these tables, the program restores the database to its state before this example was run.

30➤ If the database is empty once these two tables are dropped, the program asks the user whether to drop the entire database. It determines whether the database is empty by counting the number of tables defined in the system catalog systables with table id's greater than 99. User-defined tables have table id's which start with 100.

```
      WHENEVER ERROR STOP

27➤     CREATE TABLE PARTS(partnum INTEGER, descr CHAR(40))
        DISPLAY "Table PARTS has been created."

        CREATE TABLE PARTREE(parent INTEGER, child INTEGER, used INTEGER)
        DISPLAY "Table PARTREE has been created."
        DISPLAY ""

        LET afile = m_fpath CLIPPED, "ex28pa.unl"
        DISPLAY "Loading PARTS from ",afile CLIPPED
28➤     LOAD FROM afile INSERT INTO PARTS
        DISPLAY "Table PARTS has been loaded."
        DISPLAY ""
        LET afile = m_fpath CLIPPED, "ex28pt.unl"
        DISPLAY "Loading PARTREE from ",afile CLIPPED
        LOAD FROM afile INSERT INTO PARTREE
        DISPLAY "Table PARTREE has been loaded."
        DISPLAY ""

      END FUNCTION  -- set_up_tables --

      ########################################
      FUNCTION tear_down_tables()
      ########################################
        DEFINE       ans     CHAR(1),
                     j       SMALLINT

        DISPLAY "We can leave the PARTS and PARTREE tables for use again"
        DISPLAY "  (or for you to modify and experiment with), or we can"
        DISPLAY "  drop them from the database."
        DISPLAY ""
29➤     PROMPT  "Do you want to drop the two tables? (y/n): " FOR ans
        IF ans MATCHES "[yY]" THEN
          DROP TABLE PARTS
          DROP TABLE PARTREE
          DISPLAY "Tables dropped."

30➤       SELECT COUNT(*) INTO j
          FROM informix.systables
          WHERE tabid > 99

          IF j = 0 THEN -- no more tables left
            DISPLAY "Database ",m_theDb CLIPPED," is empty now."
            PROMPT  "Do you want to drop the database also? (y/n): " FOR ans
```

31➤ If the user chooses to drop the database, the program provides a confirmation prompt. Dropping a database destroys all data and cannot be undone.

32➤ If the user does not want to drop the PARTS and PARTREE tables, the program just exits.

```
         IF ans MATCHES "[yY]" THEN
           DISPLAY ""
31➤        DISPLAY "You have chosen to REMOVE the ", m_theDb CLIPPED,
                   " database. This step cannot be undone."
           PROMPT "Are you sure you want to drop this database? (y/n): "
             FOR ans
           IF ans MATCHES "[yY]" THEN
                   CLOSE DATABASE

   WHENEVER ERROR CONTINUE
                   DROP DATABASE m_theDb
   WHENEVER ERROR STOP
                   IF (status < 0) THEN
                     DISPLAY "Sorry, error ", SQLCA.SQLCODE,
                       " while trying to drop the database ", m_theDb CLIPPED
                     EXIT PROGRAM
                   END IF

                   DISPLAY ""
                   DISPLAY "The ", m_theDb CLIPPED, " database has been dropped."
               ELSE
                   DISPLAY "The ", m_theDb CLIPPED, " database has not been dropped."
               END IF
           END IF
       END IF
32➤  ELSE
       DISPLAY "Tables PARTS and PARTREE remain in database ",
                   m_theDb CLIPPED, "."
     END IF
   END FUNCTION  -- tear_down_tables --
```

To locate any function definition see the Function Index on page 728.

29

Generating Mailing Labels

This example demonstrates the use of several report functions. The report in this example prints "three-up" address labels; that is, labels in three columns across the page. (For a general discussion on reports in **4GL** see Example 14.)

The row producer portion of the program simply scans the customer table in the demonstration database; it has no idea of what format will be used for the report. Any changes to the format (for example from three-up format to single column) are confined to the report generator; no changes are necessary to the row producer.

Label Stationery

In the United States, multicolumn label stock is printed on sheets 8.5 by 11 inches (21.5 by 29 cm). Printers usually print at ten characters per inch, making an 85-character line. (**4GL** only supports fixed-pitch printers; it does not yet make provision for proportionally-spaced fonts.)

These numbers may require adjustment to suit other paper sizes and other printers. Such adjustments should be confined strictly to the report generator. They should not be allowed to affect the logic of the row producing parts of the program.

The code in this example produces three uniform columns on an 85-character line. Since three does not divide 85 evenly, each column consists of a three-character "gutter" (blank space) and a 24-column label width, leaving a four-character margin on the right.

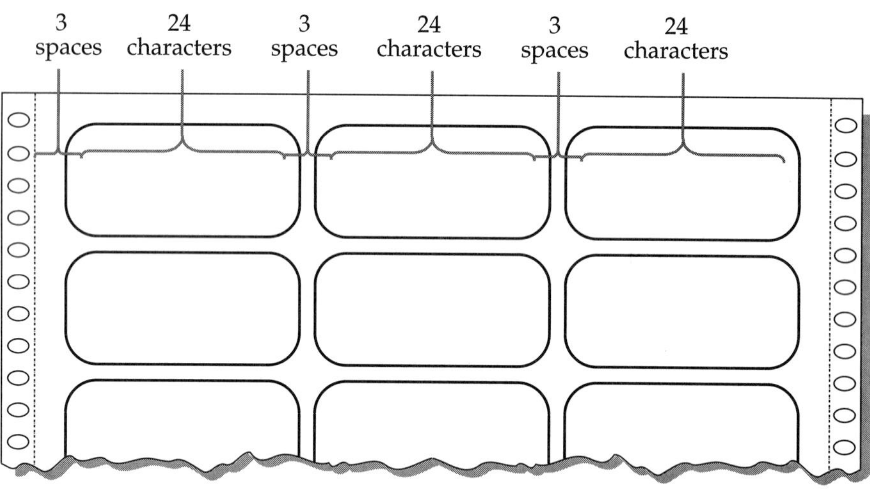

The code of the report function explicitly sets these parameters. They can be adapted easily to new formats.

Printing a Multi-Column Report

4GL includes no built-in support for multi-column reports. You must design the logic for creating one into the report generator function. While the basic idea is simple, the implementation can be tricky.

A report function contains a section headed ON EVERY ROW which is executed for each new row of data that comes out of the row producer. To produce a three-column report, the report function must include a variable containing the current column number (colno in this example). Then the ON EVERY ROW section can proceed as shown in the following pseudo-code:

```
ON EVERY ROW
    Increment colno
    Save the current row's data in an array based on colno
    IF colno = 3 THEN
        print the accumulated data
        set colno to 0
    END IF
```

This approach requires that you resolve two additional complications:

- First, the variable colno must be initialized.

  That can be done in the FIRST PAGE HEADER section of the report function.

- Second, one or two rows may remain to be printed at the end of the program.

  4GL provides an ON LAST ROW section in which these residual rows can be displayed.

You can save the rows as they arrive in two ways. They can be saved as data in program variables of the same types (INTEGER, MONEY, and so on), or they can be formatted and saved as characters.

Under the first scheme, the report function might contain code like the following fragment:

```
DEFINE troika ARRAY[3] OF RECORD LIKE …
ON EVERY ROW
    LET colno = colno + 1
    LET troika[colno] = a global record variable
    IF colno = 3 THEN
        statements to print data from troika[1 to 3]
        LET colno = 0
    END IF
```

While this method is conceptually simple, it turns out that the PRINT statements needed to print fields from three records across multiple lines become quite convoluted. Therefore, this example presents a different approach.

In the second method, each data row is formatted for printing as it is received. However, instead of using the PRINT statement, the data is converted to character strings and assigned to columns within page-wide character strings. When the third row has been formatted, the wide strings contain an image of the print lines of the report. They can then be written with very simple PRINT statements. For the full details, see the code listing. The essence can be seen in this fragment.

```
DEFINE  margins ARRAY[3] OF SMALLINT,
        lines ARRAY[6] OF CHAR(85)
ON EVERY ROW
    LET colno = colno + 1
    LET j = margins[colno]
    LET k = j + 27
    LET lines[1][j,k] = first data field
    LET lines[2][j,k] = second data field
    ...
```

These statements rely on two **4GL** features. First, **4GL** supports assignment to a substring, even to a substring of an array element. In the example, the variables j and k define a substring in the page-width character strings. The expression on the right of the LET statement will be padded to the necessary width. Second, functions such as USING, which are normally thought of in connection with the PRINT statement, can actually be used in any expression. Hence the formatting of the lines can be done in assignment statements.

Function Overview

Function Name	Purpose
three_up()	The report function to print mailing labels.

The MAIN Function

1➤ The report generator is initialized with the START REPORT statement. One of two forms of the statement is used, depending on whether output is to the screen or to a file.

2➤ Each execution of an OUTPUT TO REPORT statement sends the data, a row at a time, to the three_up() report function.

3➤ The FINISH REPORT statement ends the report, including any LAST ROW processing, and closes the output file.

The three_up() Report Function

4➤ The current_column variable stores the current column (from zero to three). The columnar format of the report is encoded in the column_width, gutter_width, and margins variables.

5➤ As an extra feature, the report function keeps track of the lowest (lo_zip) and highest (hi_zip) zip codes displayed on each page and prints them in the page footer.

4GL source file

```
DATABASE stores2t

GLOBALS
  DEFINE        gr_customer    RECORD LIKE customer.*
END GLOBALS

########################################
MAIN
########################################
  DEFINE        repfile CHAR(80) -- report pathname

  DISPLAY "Enter a filename to receive the labels, or for"
  DISPLAY "output to the screen (stdout) just press RETURN."
  DISPLAY ""
  PROMPT "Filename: " FOR repfile
  DISPLAY ""
1➤  IF LENGTH(repfile)=0 THEN -- null response
    START REPORT three_up
    DISPLAY "Preparing labels for screen display..."
  ELSE -- filename
    START REPORT three_up TO repfile
    DISPLAY "Writing labels to file ", repfile CLIPPED,"..."
  END IF

  DECLARE c_cust CURSOR FOR
    SELECT * INTO gr_customer.*
    FROM customer
    ORDER BY zipcode,company

  FOREACH c_cust
2➤    OUTPUT TO REPORT three_up()
  END FOREACH

3➤  FINISH REPORT three_up

  CLEAR SCREEN
END MAIN

########################################
REPORT three_up() -- the report function
########################################
4➤  DEFINE    current_column,       -- current column, from 0 to 3
            column_width,         -- width of any label column
            gutter_width  SMALLINT,-- gap between columns
            margins       ARRAY[3] OF SMALLINT, -- starting margin of each column
            pageno        SMALLINT, -- current page number
5➤            lo_zip,             -- lowest zipcode on current page
            hi_zip        LIKE customer.zipcode, -- highest ditto
```

6➤ The lines array of strings holds the image of a row of address labels. The variables are made wide enough to allow for 12-character-per-inch printing.

The j and k variables are used as subscripts into each string. The city_fld variable holds the size of the city in the address and is used to determine the position of the state and zip code values on the same line. The line_num variable is the current line of the lines array and is used to keep track of whether the address has one line (address2 is null) or two.

7➤ The OUTPUT section specifies the page dimensions along with the margins.

The left margin is set to zero. In this report it proved simpler to divide the page into three uniform columns, each with its own left margin.

8➤ The FIRST PAGE HEADER allows you to print special material on the first report page. While no page header appears on the first or any other page in this report, this is the most convenient place to initialize the following variables:

pageno	A report must count pages explicitly; there is no system count of pages.
current_column	This starts the column-counter off before the first row arrives.
lo_zip, hi_zip	These are initialized the same way in the PAGE TRAILER section which follows.
column_width	
gutter_width	Here is encoded the columnar format, a repetition of gutter_width spaces followed by column_width data across the page.
margins	The decision encoded in the previous variables is implemented as the starting point for each column.

9➤ At this point, j and k are the starting and ending points for a substring that spans the data portion of the current column. In the following assignments, the company name and the first two lines of the address (address1 and address2) of the current row are assigned (if they are not null) to various lines of the lines array. **4GL** will automatically convert values of other types to character, and pad short strings to length. The USING function can also be employed to format the values.

```
6➤        lines         ARRAY[6] of CHARACTER(127), -- one row of labels
          j, k          SMALLINT,        -- misc indexes
          city_fld      SMALLINT,        -- size of city field
          line_num      SMALLINT         -- current line in lines array

   OUTPUT
     PAGE LENGTH 66
7➤   LEFT MARGIN 0               -- these must be tuned to match the
     TOP MARGIN 4                -- label stock in use
     BOTTOM MARGIN 4

   FORMAT
8➤   FIRST PAGE HEADER           -- initialize some variables
       LET pageno = 0
       LET current_column = 0
       LET lo_zip = NULL
       LET hi_zip = "00000"
       LET column_width = 25
       LET gutter_width = 3
       LET margins[1] = gutter_width
       LET margins[2] = margins[1]+column_width+gutter_width
       LET margins[3] = margins[2]+column_width+gutter_width
       FOR j = 1 TO 6
         LET lines[j] = " "
       END FOR

    ON EVERY ROW
      IF (lo_zip IS NULL) THEN -- starting new page
        LET lo_zip = gr_customer.zipcode
      END IF
      IF (hi_zip < gr_customer.zipcode) THEN
        LET hi_zip = gr_customer.zipcode
      END IF

      LET current_column = current_column + 1
      LET j = margins[current_column]
9➤    LET k = j + column_width - 1

      IF gr_customer.company IS NOT NULL THEN
        LET lines[2][j,k] = gr_customer.company
      END IF
      IF gr_customer.address1 IS NOT NULL THEN
        LET lines[3][j,k] = gr_customer.address1
      END IF
```

10➤ If the second line of the address is null, the program sets the line_num variable to 4 so that the next line (city, state, and zipcode) will print in line 4. There is no need to assign a value to the lines array because this array is already initialized with blanks (see Note 14). If the second address line is not null, the program assigns the address to the fourth line of the lines array and then sets line_num to 5 so that the city, state, and zipcode will not overwrite this line.

11➤ If the city column is null, skip past the space reserved for the city in the lines array (15 characters as defined in the database). Otherwise, print out the city name in the lines array at the line specified by line_num (see Note 10). The city_fld variable keeps the length of the current city name plus the trailing ", " string (a comma and a blank). If this name is null, the variable stores the maximum length of 15 plus the two additional characters.

12➤ If the state column is null, skip past the space reserved for the state code by incrementing the j index variable. This index now indicates the starting position of the zipcode. If the state column has a non-null value, assign this value at the end of the city name and then increment the j index to the beginning of the zipcode field.

13➤ The program assigns the zipcode value to the lines array only if it is non-null. If this value is null, the blanks already in the array can be printed out.

14➤ If the program has completed the third and final column of the line, it clears out the lines array to prepare this array for the next iteration.

15➤ The code in the ON LAST ROW section is called after the ON EVERY ROW code for the final row.

You might simply dump the lines array, but one time in three it will be empty and one time in 25 (or so) this will cause the program to print an extra, blank report page. Testing for column_number greater than zero averts printing a blank page.

```
10➤ IF gr_customer.address2 IS NULL THEN
      LET line_num = 4        -- move city, state up one line
    ELSE
      LET lines[4][j,k] = gr_customer.address2
      LET line_num = 5
    END IF

11➤ IF gr_customer.city IS NULL THEN
      LET city_fld = j + 15    -- move to 1st position past city
      LET k = city_fld + 1     -- make room for 2 chars (", ")
      LET lines[line_num][city_fld,k] = ", "
      LET city_fld = 17        -- 15 for city, 2 for ", "
    ELSE
      LET city_fld = LENGTH(gr_customer.city) + 2
      LET k = j + city_fld   -- make room for city name and ", "
      LET lines[line_num][j,k] = gr_customer.city CLIPPED, ", "
    END IF

12➤ IF gr_customer.state IS NULL THEN
      LET j = j + city_fld + 3    -- increment past state field
    ELSE
      LET j = j + city_fld + 1    -- move to 1st position past ", "
      LET k = j + 2               -- make room for 2 chars (state)
                                     --... plus 1 char (blank)
      LET lines[line_num][j,k] = gr_customer.state, " "
      LET j = k + 1               -- increment past state field
    END IF
13➤ IF gr_customer.zipcode IS NOT NULL THEN
      LET k = j + 4               -- make room for 5 chars (zip)
      LET lines[line_num][j,k] = gr_customer.zipcode
    END IF

14➤  IF current_column = 3 THEN  -- time to print lines and clear
       FOR j = 1 to 6
         PRINT lines[j]
         LET lines[j] = " "
       END FOR
       LET current_column = 0     -- ready for next set
     END IF

   ON LAST ROW
15➤  IF current_column > 0 THEN  -- print short last line
       FOR j = 1 TO 6
         PRINT lines[j]
       END FOR
     END IF
```

16➤ The code in the Page Trailer section is called each time the page fills up. In this case, the program prints a footer containing the low and high zipcodes.

```
      PAGE TRAILER
16➤     LET pageno = pageno + 1
        PRINT
        PRINT
        PRINT
        PRINT "page",pageno USING "-----",
            COLUMN 50,
            "Customers in zipcode ",lo_zip," to ",hi_zip
        LET lo_zip = NULL
        LET hi_zip = "00000"

END REPORT  -- three_up --
```

To locate any function definition see the Function Index on page 728.

30

Generating a Schema Listing

This example demonstrates how to decode some of the contents of the system catalog tables. Using these techniques, a program can discover at execution time the names of the tables and columns in a database, as well as the data types of the columns. This information is then prepared as a report.

The System Catalogs

The system catalogs are a group of tables that exist in every database and describe the contents of the database. The database engine creates the tables when it creates a new database. It updates the tables each time it executes data definition statements such as CREATE TABLE or ALTER INDEX. It uses the tables to process queries.

The system catalogs are not hidden from applications, and a program is free to query them to learn about the contents of the database. This program takes the catalog information and produces a schema listing.

The organization of the system catalogs is covered in depth in your SQL or **4GL** reference manual. Briefly, the following tables are the most important:

systables — Contains a basic definition of all permanent tables. The primary key consists of owner name and table name. The most important column is tabid, a serial number that represents each table in all other tables. All user-defined tables have tabid values >100.

syscolumns — Contains the data type of each column. The primary key consists of tabid and column number. Much of the code in this example is devoted to decoding the data type information.

sysindexes — Defines each index. The primary key consists of owner and index names.

sysusers — Lists the names of users who have been granted database privileges. The primary key is user name.

systabauth — Lists table-level privileges that have been granted. The primary key consists of the user names of grantor and grantee.

This example retrieves information from the systables and syscolumns tables. For an example of how to decode systabauth, see the section "The get_tab_auth() Function" on page 622.

Program Overview

The heart of this program is a very ordinary FOREACH loop. The program declares a cursor joining systables with syscolumns as follows:

```
DECLARE c_schema CURSOR FOR
SELECT tabname, nindexes, colname, colno, coltype, collength
    FROM informix.systables st, informix.syscolumns sc
    WHERE st.tabtype = "T" -- tables, not views
    AND st.tabid > 99 -- user tables, not system tables
    AND st.tabid = sc.tabid -- join condition
    ORDER BY st.tabname, sc.colno
```

Note that the names of system catalog tables are qualified with the owner name "informix." This is only necessary in ANSI-compliant databases, where an owner-name is required whenever you query a table you do not own. The owner name can be omitted in noncompliant databases (the usual case).

This cursor produces all the necessary information about each table, one row per column. In the central FOREACH loop the program decodes the data type information from the coltype and collength columns to produce a character string such as "INTERVAL YEAR TO MONTH" or "DECIMAL(3,8)." The code needed to do this occupies more than half the module. Then it displays the information about a column with an OUTPUT TO REPORT statement.

Decoding Data Type Information

When you define the data type of a column you use keywords, as in this example:

```
CREATE TABLE examp(
    uneek SERIAL,
    dough MONEY(9,2) NOT NULL )
```

The keywords are encoded for the engine's reference in the coltype and collength columns of the syscolumns table. Each is a SMALLINT. The value of coltype is a number between 0 and 16, giving the basic data type. 256 (hexadecimal 100) is added to this encoding when the NOT NULL clause is used. The value in collength specifies the length or precision of the column. The following table shows how these columns are used for each datatype. "MSB" means "most significant byte"; LSB means "least significant byte.

Data type	Coltype value	Collength value
CHARACTER	0	length
SMALLINT	1	n.a.
INTEGER	2	n.a.
FLOAT	3	n.a.
SMALLFLOAT	4	n.a
DECIMAL	5	precision in MSB, scale in LSB
SERIAL	6	n.a.
DATE	7	n.a.
MONEY	8	precision in MSB, scale in LSB
(not used)	9	n.a.
DATETIME	10	qualifier, see text
BYTE	11	n.a.
TEXT	12	n.a.
VARCHAR	13	reserve size in MSB, max in LSB
INTERVAL	14	qualifier, see text

The qualifiers for DATETIME and INTERVAL types are encoded in hexadecimal digits in the collength column. The four digits of the 16-bit column can be labelled 0*pls*, where

digit 0 — is the leading digit and is always zero.

digit *p* — is the precision of the first field of an INTERVAL, from 1 to 5 (recall that an INTERVAL, but not a DATETIME, has a specified precision for its first field, as in DAY(4) TO HOUR).

digit *l* — stands for the left, or larger, qualifier word (the YEAR in YEAR TO DAY).

digit *s* — stands for the second or smaller qualifier word, treating FRACTION(1) through FRACTION(5) as separate keywords.

4GL is not particularly well suited to dissecting a bit field like this into hexadecimal digits, so the example code includes functions to do it.

Displaying Indexes

This example only reports the number of indexes on each table, a fact recorded in systables. The sysindexes table contains the names of indexes and their characteristics, but this information is not selected or displayed in the program. It would not be difficult to write a program to report on all indexes. The following cursor would select the important items for display.

```
DECLARE c_index CURSOR FOR
SELECT   idxname     -- char(18)
        ,owner       -- char(8)
        ,tabname     -- char(18)
        ,idxtype     -- char(1), "U"=unique, "D"=dups
        ,clustered   -- char(1), "C"=clustered, else " "
FROM informix.sysindexes si, informix.systables st
WHERE   si.tabid > 99    -- user tables, not sys catalog
AND     si.tabid = st.tabid -- join to get tabname
ORDER BY tabname, idxname
```

After reading the program in this example, you should be able to use this cursor definition to compose a program that prints a report listing all indexes.

The sysindexes table also contains a series of columns named part*n*, one for each possible column that may be used in a composite index. These columns specify which columns are covered by the index. (If you understand the design of relational databases you may be surprised to see that this table is not normalized. A normalized table has no groups of repeated columns. However, the system catalog was designed to meet specific needs of the database engine, not to support general queries.)

Each part*n* column specifies one column from the indexed table. It contains the colno value from syscolumns, as a positive number if the column has an ascending index, and as a negative number if the column has a descending index.

For example, if the following statement is executed in the usual demonstration database it will create a test index on two columns of the customer table:

```
CREATE test_ix ON customer (fname,lname DESC)
```

If you then display all columns of sysindexes for the row where idxname is test_ix, you will find that:

- the part1 column contains 2, the column number of fname in the customer table.
- the part2 column contains -3, the negative of the column number lname in the customer table.
- the remaining part*n* columns contain zero.

The **OnLine** database engine allows up to 16 columns in a composite index, so it builds a sysindexes entry with columns part1 through part16. Other Informix engines support only eight columns, and in a database managed by one of those engines the columns part9 through part16 do not exist. If you need to select these columns you can detect which database engine you are using at the time of opening a database: see Example 22, “Determining Database Features” on page 507.

Function Overview

Function Name	Purpose
get_dbname()	Accepts user input of the name of a database whose schema is to be printed, using the f_name form.
schema()	Gathers the schema information from the system tables and sends it to the report for formatting.
convert_type()	Converts the integer column type and length information stored in syscolumns into a string representation of the column’s data type.
cnvrt_dt()	Converts the integer column length of a DATETIME field (“clngth”) into qualifier keywords (YEAR, MONTH, ...).

cnvrt_varch()	Converts the integer column length of a VARCHAR field ("clngth") into the maximum and minimum column lengths.
cnvrt_intvl()	Converts the integer column length of an INTERVAL field ("clngth") into qualifier keywords (YEAR, MONTH, ...).
qual_fld()	Converts a hex digit "fvalue" into the corresponding field qualifier (YEAR, MONTH, ...).
intvl_lngth()	Converts the field qualifier range values ("large_lngth" and "small_lngth") into qualifiers (YEAR, MONTH, ...).
to_hex()	Converts a decimal number into a string representation of a hex number.
hex_digit()	Converts a decimal digit into a hex character 0-9, A-F.
dec_digit()	Converts a hex character (0-9, A-F) into a decimal value 0-15.
schema_rpt()	Report to create the schema listing.
report_output()	Displays the Report Destination menu and returns a flag indicating the user's choice. *See description in Example 15.*
init_msgs()	Initializes the members of the ga_dsplymsg array to null. *See description in Example 2.*
open_db()	Opens a database using dynamic SQL and saves information about it for later use. Returns TRUE or FALSE. *See description in Example 22.*
prompt_window()	Displays a message and prompts the user for affirmation or negation. This function is a variation on the message_window() function that appears in Example 2. *See description in Example 4.*
msg()	Displays a brief, informative message. *See description in Example 5.*
clear_lines()	Clears any number of lines starting at any line. *See description in Example 6.*

The GLOBALS Statement

1➤ This program contains no DEFINE LIKE statements and does not depend on a database schema, so it does not begin with a DATABASE statement.

2➤ The gr_database record is filled by the open_db() function when it opens the database. The is_online field is copied and displayed in the first report line.

3➤ This variable is used when communicating with the init_msgs() function.

The MAIN Function

4➤ The get_dbname() function asks the user to supply the name of a database. If the user does not cancel with the Interrupt key, a name is returned.

5➤ If the open_db() function succeeds in opening the database, it returns TRUE.

6➤ Once the database is open, the program calls a function to generate the report.

7➤ If the open_db() function encounters an error it displays a message. If the program ended immediately at that point, the screen would clear before the user could read the error message, so the SLEEP statement leaves the message visible for three seconds.

The get_dbname() Function

8➤ The f_name form is described in Example 13.

4GL source file

```
1➤ GLOBALS
2➤   DEFINE gr_database RECORD
                            db_known   SMALLINT,    -- following fields are usable
                            has_log    SMALLINT,    -- based on SQLAWARN[2]
                            is_ansi    SMALLINT,    -- based on SQLAWARN[3]
                            is_online  SMALLINT,    -- based on SQLAWARN[4]
                            can_wait   SMALLINT     -- supports "set lock mode to wait"
                          END RECORD

3➤   DEFINE ga_dsplymsg ARRAY[5] OF CHAR(48)
   END GLOBALS

   #######################################
   MAIN
   #######################################
     DEFINE         dbname     CHAR(50),
                    msg_txt    CHAR(110),
                    answer     CHAR(1)

     OPTIONS
       FORM LINE 2,
       COMMENT LINE 3,
       MESSAGE LINE 6,
       ERROR LINE LAST - 1

     OPEN WINDOW w_schema AT 2,3
       WITH 9 ROWS, 76 COLUMNS
       ATTRIBUTE (BORDER, COMMENT LINE 3)

4➤   CALL get_dbname() RETURNING dbname
     IF dbname IS NOT NULL THEN
       CALL clear_lines(5, 4)
5➤     IF open_db(dbname) THEN
6➤       CALL schema(dbname)
7➤     ELSE -- unable to open specified db,
         SLEEP 3 -- give user time to read open_db()'s error msg
       END IF
     END IF

     CLOSE WINDOW w_schema
     CLEAR SCREEN

   END MAIN

   #######################################
   FUNCTION get_dbname()
   #######################################
     DEFINE     dbname     CHAR(50)

8➤   OPEN FORM f_name FROM "f_name"
     DISPLAY FORM f_name
```

9➤ The purpose of this function is to get a database name from the user. Here it reads input from the one field of the f_name form.

10➤ The user is not allowed to exit the field without providing a database name. This AFTER FIELD block is also executed when the user presses the Accept key.

The schema() Function

11➤ The pr_schema record receives the items fetched from the systables and syscolumns tables. This record is passed as an argument to the report function.

12➤ The report_output() function is discussed in Example 15. It offers the user three choices for the destination of a report: the screen, the printer, or a file. It returns a single letter "S" or "P" or "F" respectively.

```
    DISPLAY "DATABASE SCHEMA LISTING"
      AT 2, 20
    DISPLAY " Press Accept to print schema or Cancel to exit w/out printing."
      AT 8, 1  ATTRIBUTE (REVERSE, YELLOW)

    LET int_flag = FALSE
9➤  INPUT dbname FROM a_char
      BEFORE FIELD a_char
        MESSAGE " Enter the name of the database."

10➤   AFTER FIELD a_char
        IF dbname IS NULL THEN
          ERROR "You must enter a database name."
          NEXT FIELD a_char
        END IF
    END INPUT
    IF int_flag THEN
      LET int_flag = FALSE
      LET dbname = NULL -- input ended with ^C, take the hint
    END IF

    CLOSE FORM f_name
    RETURN (dbname)

  END FUNCTION  -- get_dbname --

  #######################################
  FUNCTION schema(dbname)
  #######################################
    DEFINE    dbname           CHAR(50),
11➤           pr_schema  RECORD
                           dbname        CHAR(50),
                           is_online     SMALLINT,
                           tabname       CHAR(18),
                           nindexes      SMALLINT,
                           colname       CHAR(18),
                           colno         SMALLINT,
                           coltype       SMALLINT,
                           collength     SMALLINT
              END RECORD,

              coltypename      CHAR(50),
              print_option     CHAR(1),
              file_name        CHAR(20)

12➤ LET print_option = report_output("SCHEMA LISTING", 5, 10)
```

13➤ The CASE statement constructs a filename that should be unique for the database name, so that you can display the schema of several databases, each to its file. You would need to modify the form of the filename for PC/DOS.

14➤ The dbname and is_online elements of the pr_schema record are constant for all rows of the report. They are included in the record only for convenience in passing them to the report function.

15➤ This cursor definition drives the report. As discussed in the overview, it returns one row for each column of each non-catalog table.

16➤ The FOREACH loop processes the rows selected by the cursor.

17➤ All information about a column of a table is returned by the cursor, but the data type is encoded. The convert_type() function converts it to a string of keywords and numbers (just as would be used in a CREATE TABLE statement.)

18➤ The report destination is passed as an argument to the report function for one reason: so that if output is to the screen, it can stop after each 22 lines of output and wait for the user to press the RETURN key.

```
    CASE (print_option)
13➤   WHEN "F" -- build filename "DBxxx.lst" where "xxx" is the name
               -- of the database whose schema is being listed
        LET file_name = "DB"
        IF LENGTH(dbname) > 10 THEN -- limit length of name
          LET file_name = file_name CLIPPED, dbname[1,10]
        ELSE
          LET file_name = file_name CLIPPED, dbname CLIPPED
        END IF
        LET file_name = file_name CLIPPED, ".lst"

        START REPORT schema_rpt TO file_name
        MESSAGE " Writing schema report to ", file_name CLIPPED,
                " -- please wait."
        SLEEP 2

      WHEN "P"
        START REPORT schema_rpt TO PRINTER
        MESSAGE "Sending schema report to printer -- please wait."
        SLEEP 2

      WHEN "S"
        START REPORT schema_rpt
        MESSAGE "Preparing report for screen -- please wait."

    END CASE

14➤ LET pr_schema.dbname = dbname
    LET pr_schema.is_online = gr_database.is_online
15➤ DECLARE c_schema CURSOR FOR
      SELECT tabname, nindexes, colname, colno, coltype, collength
      FROM informix.systables st, informix.syscolumns sc
      WHERE st.tabtype = "T"     -- tables, not views
        AND st.tabid > 99        -- user tables, not system tables
        AND st.tabid = sc.tabid -- join condition
      ORDER BY st.tabname, sc.colno

16➤ FOREACH c_schema INTO pr_schema.tabname THRU pr_schema.collength

17➤   CALL convert_type(pr_schema.coltype, pr_schema.collength)
        RETURNING coltypename
18➤   OUTPUT TO REPORT schema_rpt (pr_schema.*, coltypename, print_option)

    END FOREACH

    FINISH REPORT schema_rpt

  END FUNCTION  -- schema --
```

The convert_type() Function

19➤ This function controls the translation into words of the values from the coltype and collength columns.

See the section "Decoding Data Type Information" on page 671 for a description of how these columns store information.

20➤ The string not_null will be appended to each data type display in the report. It contains "NOT NULL" when a column was defined as such.

The IF statement initializes the variable to null, then sets it to the string only if the NOT NULL clause was used.

21➤ The CASE statement decodes all the coltype values once the NOT NULL flag is stripped. WHEN clauses handle the easier cases internally and relegate others to subroutines.

22➤ CHAR is a relatively easy case. The length from collength needs only to be formatted for display inside parentheses.

23➤ The next few cases are easier still.

24➤ For DECIMAL, the precision and scale values must be extracted from the individual bytes of collength. The LET statement divides by 256 to accomplish this. That is a safe procedure so long as the value in the most significant byte is certain to be less than 128. **4GL** always does signed division, and if the MSB contained is in excess of 128, the result of the division would be negative. However, the precision of DECIMAL never exceeds 32, so the value is always positive.

25➤ The column is SERIAL when coltype_name is 6.

26➤ MONEY values are recorded much like DECIMAL values. However, MONEY has a default scale value of 2, which DECIMAL does not (when the scale is omitted from a DECIMAL declaration, floating decimal is assumed). Here the display of scale is suppressed unless it is other than the default.

```
    ########################################
19➤ FUNCTION convert_type(coltype_num, col_length)
    ########################################
      DEFINE    coltype_num    SMALLINT,
                col_length     SMALLINT,

                msize          SMALLINT,
                nsize          SMALLINT,
                coltype_name   CHAR(50),
                dt_length      CHAR(35),
                intv_length    CHAR(35),
                not_null       CHAR(9),
                max_length     SMALLINT,
                min_length     SMALLINT

20➤   LET not_null = NULL
      IF coltype_num >= 256 THEN
        LET coltype_num = coltype_num - 256
        LET not_null = " NOT NULL"
      END IF

21➤   CASE coltype_num
        WHEN 0
22➤       LET coltype_name = "CHAR(",
               col_length USING "<<<<<<<<<<<", ")"
23➤     WHEN 1
          LET coltype_name = "SMALLINT"
        WHEN 2
          LET coltype_name = "INTEGER"
        WHEN 3
          LET coltype_name = "FLOAT"
        WHEN 4
          LET coltype_name = "SMALLFLOAT"
24➤     WHEN 5
          LET msize = col_length / 256
          LET nsize = col_length mod 256
          LET coltype_name = "DECIMAL(", msize USING "<<<<<",
                             ",", nsize USING "<<<<<", ")"
25➤     WHEN 6  -- in the SERIAL field: no account has been made of serials
                --   with starting values
          LET coltype_name = "SERIAL"
        WHEN 7
          LET coltype_name = "DATE"
26➤     WHEN 8
          LET msize = col_length / 256
          LET nsize = col_length mod 256
          LET coltype_name = "MONEY(", msize USING "<<<<<"
          IF nsize <> 2 THEN -- scale not default 2, show it
            LET coltype_name = coltype_name CLIPPED,
                               ",", nsize USING "<<<<<"
          END IF
          LET coltype_name = coltype_name CLIPPED, ")"
```

27➤ The extraction of the qualifier of DATETIME is too complicated to fit in a WHEN block. The cnvt_dt() function performs this operation.

28➤ The extraction of the maximum and reserved sizes of VARCHAR is also consigned to a subroutine. The reserved-size number is only included in the output when it is different from the default of zero.

The cnvrt_varch() Function

29➤ The cnvrt_varch() function extracts the sizes of a VARCHAR column. The two sizes are in the most and least significant bytes of collength. Since they can exceed 127, it is not safe to extract them by division.

30➤ The to_hex() function converts a SMALLINT value to four hexadecimal digits and returns them as a character string.

31➤ The dec_digit() function returns the decimal value of a single hexadecimal digit. Here the decimal values of the two digits of each byte are used to reconstruct the byte value. This is one way to avoid the problems posed by signed division.

```
      WHEN 9 -- should not occur
        LET coltype_name = "PLAN 9"
27➤   WHEN 10 -- datetime, handle in subroutine
        CALL cnvrt_dt(col_length) RETURNING dt_length
        LET coltype_name = "DATETIME ", dt_length CLIPPED
      WHEN 11
        LET coltype_name = "BYTE"
      WHEN 12
        LET coltype_name = "TEXT"
28➤   WHEN 13 -- varchar, handle in subroutine
        CALL cnvrt_varch(col_length) RETURNING max_length, min_length
        LET coltype_name = "VARCHAR(", max_length CLIPPED
        IF min_length > 0 THEN -- min not default of zero, show it
            LET coltype_name = coltype_name CLIPPED, ",", min_length CLIPPED
        END IF
        LET coltype_name = coltype_name CLIPPED, ")"
      WHEN 14 -- interval, handle in subroutine
        CALL cnvrt_intvl(col_length) RETURNING intv_length
        LET coltype_name = "INTERVAL ", intv_length CLIPPED
      OTHERWISE -- ???
        LET coltype_name = "UNDEFINED: ", coltype_num
      END CASE
      LET coltype_name = coltype_name CLIPPED, not_null

      RETURN (coltype_name)
  END FUNCTION  -- convert_type --

  #######################################
29➤ FUNCTION cnvrt_varch(clngth)
  #######################################
    DEFINE    clngth         SMALLINT,

              hex_length     CHAR(4),
              min_length     SMALLINT,
              max_length     SMALLINT

30➤ LET hex_length = to_hex(clngth, 4)

31➤ LET min_length = dec_digit(hex_length[1]) * 16
                   + dec_digit(hex_length[2])
    LET max_length = dec_digit(hex_length[3]) * 16
                   + dec_digit(hex_length[4])

    RETURN max_length, min_length
  END FUNCTION  -- cnvrt_varch --
```

The cnvrt_dt() Function

32➤ The cnvrt_dt() function decodes the qualifier of a DATETIME column. Some typical qualifiers include: YEAR TO DAY, HOUR TO FRACTION, and FRACTION TO FRACTION(4).

33➤ The qualifier of a DATETIME column is encoded in the hexadecimal digits *0pls* of the collength value. The to_hex() function returns the digits.

34➤ The qual_fld() function converts one digit to its corresponding keyword, returning the word as a character string, saved here in large_fld. The function also returns a default precision, which is not used here. It is needed only when decoding an INTERVAL.

35➤ The keyword for the smaller or second field is saved. The first argument to qual_fld() tells it which field it is decoding, as there are a few differences in representation between the larger and smaller keywords.

The cnvrt_intvl() Function

36➤ The cnvrt_intvl() function decodes an INTERVAL qualifier. The procedure is similar to that for DATETIME but with one additional step. When the precision of the larger field is different from the default precision, it has to be displayed. That is, INTERVAL HOUR TO SECOND uses the default precision of 2 for the larger field, HOUR. INTERVAL HOUR(4) TO SECOND uses a non-default precision and the string "(4)" has to be produced and inserted in the output.

37➤ The second value returned by qual_fld(), the default precision of the keyword, is saved. (It was not significant when decoding DATETIME columns (see Note 34).

38➤ The task of deciding the default and actual precisions of the INTERVAL is deferred to the function intvl_lngth(). It returns zero if the actual precision is the default precision, otherwise it returns the number to be displayed with the larger field.

```
    #######################################
32➤ FUNCTION cnvrt_dt(clngth)
    #######################################
      DEFINE    clngth          SMALLINT,

                large_fld       CHAR(11),
                small_fld       CHAR(11),
                dt_size         CHAR(35),
                hex_length      CHAR(3),
                null_size       SMALLINT

33➤   LET hex_length = to_hex(clngth, 3)

34➤   CALL qual_fld("l", hex_length[2])
        RETURNING large_fld, null_size

35➤   CALL qual_fld("s", hex_length[3])
        RETURNING small_fld, null_size

      LET dt_size = large_fld CLIPPED, " TO ", small_fld CLIPPED
      RETURN (dt_size CLIPPED)
    END FUNCTION  -- cnvrt_dt --
    #######################################
36➤ FUNCTION cnvrt_intvl(clngth)
    #######################################
      DEFINE    clngth          SMALLINT,
                large_fld       CHAR(11),
                large_size      SMALLINT,
                small_fld       CHAR(11),
                small_size      SMALLINT,
                intv_size       CHAR(35),
                hex_length      CHAR(3),
                fld_lngth       SMALLINT,
                i               SMALLINT

      LET hex_length = to_hex(clngth,3)

37➤   CALL qual_fld("l", hex_length[2])
        RETURNING large_fld, large_size

      CALL qual_fld("s", hex_length[3])
        RETURNING small_fld, small_size

38➤   LET fld_lngth = intvl_lngth(hex_length, large_size, small_size)
      IF fld_lngth > 0 THEN
        LET i = LENGTH(large_fld) + 1
        LET large_fld[i, i + 2] = "(", fld_lngth USING "<", ")"
      END IF

      LET intv_size = large_fld CLIPPED, " TO ", small_fld CLIPPED
      RETURN (intv_size)
    END FUNCTION  -- cnvrt_intvl --
```

The qual_fld() Function

39➤ The qual_fld() function uses a CASE statement to decode one hexadecimal digit from collength as a DATETIME or INTERVAL qualifier keyword. Note two things about the encoding:

- Separate codes are devoted to each of the possible precisions of FRACTION(1) through FRACTION(5).
- The encodings are so designed that *p*=*s*-*l*+2 (that is, subtracting the code of the larger keyword from the code for the smaller) yields the number of digits in the total qualifier. For example, a qualifier YEAR TO DAY has 6=4-0 digits.

40➤ The MATCHES operator is used just in case the hexadecimal translation function is changed to generate lowercase instead of uppercase letters.

41➤ If the hexadecimal digit is a "C" (decimal 12), the data type contains a FRACTION(2) field qualifier. The way this FRACTION field is printed depends on whether it is the first or the second qualifier. If it is the first qualifier, then fvalue is "1" and the qualifier is printed without the precision because an INTERVAL value cannot specify precision on the first qualifier. If FRACTION is the second qualifier, then the precision of 2 is specified (the default precision for the second qualifier is 3).

42➤ If the hexadecimal digit is a "C" (decimal 12), the data type contains a FRACTION(3) field qualifier. Since the default precision for the second qualifier is 3, this qualifier does not specify the precision in the schema listing.

```
    #######################################
39➤ FUNCTION qual_fld(ftype, fvalue)
    #######################################
      DEFINE    ftype, fvalue    CHAR(1),

                fld_name         CHAR(11),
                fld_size         SMALLINT

      CASE
        WHEN (fvalue = "0")           --* YEAR qualifier
          LET fld_name = "YEAR"
          LET fld_size = 4

        WHEN (fvalue = "2")           --* MONTH qualifier
          LET fld_name = "MONTH"
          LET fld_size = 2

        WHEN (fvalue = "4")           --* DAY qualifier
          LET fld_name = "DAY"
          LET fld_size = 2

        WHEN (fvalue = "6")           --* HOUR qualifier
          LET fld_name = "HOUR"
          LET fld_size = 2

        WHEN (fvalue = "8")           --* MINUTE qualifier
          LET fld_name = "MINUTE"
          LET fld_size = 2

40➤     WHEN (fvalue MATCHES "[Aa]") --* SECOND qualifier
          LET fld_name = "SECOND"
          LET fld_size = 2

        WHEN (fvalue MATCHES "[Bb]") --* FRACTION(1) qualifier
          LET fld_name = "FRACTION(1)"
          LET fld_size = 1

        WHEN (fvalue MATCHES "[Cc]") --* FRACTION(2) qualifier
41➤       LET fld_size = 2            --*  (default for 1st qualifier)
          IF ftype = "1" THEN
            LET fld_name = "FRACTION"
          ELSE
            LET fld_name = "FRACTION(2)"
          END IF

        WHEN (fvalue MATCHES "[Dd]") --* FRACTION(3) qualifier
42➤       LET fld_name = "FRACTION"   --*  (default for 2nd qualifier)
          LET fld_size = 3

        WHEN (fvalue MATCHES "[Ee]") --* FRACTION(4) qualifier
          LET fld_name = "FRACTION(4)"
          LET fld_size = 4
```

43➤ The returned fld_name string contains the keyword for the qualifier. The fld_size number is used only for calculating the precision of the larger field of an INTERVAL.

The intvl_lngth() Function

44➤ The intvl_lngth() function examines the two qualifier keywords and the total precision of an INTERVAL to decide whether the first field of the INTERVAL uses a non-default precision. If it does, the function returns that precision so it can be included in the output.

45➤ Since the hexadecimal values for field qualifiers are sequential, the difference between the first and second qualifiers indicates the number of fields being tracked by the INTERVAL.

46➤ If num_flds is zero (0), the same qualifier keyword is in both the first and second qualifiers. If the internal length (hex_lngth[1]) matches the default length (large_lngth), the function returns zero to indicate that the field uses the default precision. Otherwise, it returns the non-default precision.

47➤ The only combination for which the hexadecimal values of the two qualifiers differ by one is FRACTION(2) TO FRACTION(3). Since these are the default precisions for each qualifier, the function returns zero.

48➤ The hexadecimal values for the qualifiers FRACTION(2) to FRACTION(1) differ by a value of -1. Since FRACTION(2) is the default precision for the first qualifier, the function returns zero.

49➤ For all other INTERVAL qualifiers, the function calculates the default length required for the field. If this default length does not match the internal length (hex_lngth[1]), then the function returns the non-default precision used by the first qualifier.

```
      WHEN (fvalue MATCHES "[Ff]") --* FRACTION(5) qualifier
        LET fld_name = "FRACTION(5)"
        LET fld_size = 5

      OTHERWISE
        LET fld_name = "uh oh: ", fvalue
        LET fld_size = 0
    END CASE

43➤ RETURN fld_name, fld_size

  END FUNCTION  -- qual_fld --

  #######################################
44➤ FUNCTION intvl_lngth(hex_lngth, large_lngth, small_lngth)
  #######################################
    DEFINE    hex_lngth         CHAR(3),
              large_lngth       SMALLINT,
              small_lngth       SMALLINT,

              dec_lngth         SMALLINT,
              default_lngth     SMALLINT,
              num_flds          SMALLINT,
              ret_lngth         SMALLINT

    LET dec_lngth = dec_digit(hex_lngth[1])
45➤ LET num_flds = dec_digit(hex_lngth[3]) - dec_digit(hex_lngth[2])
    CASE num_flds
46➤   WHEN 0      -- intvl has only 1 field
        IF dec_lngth = large_lngth THEN
          LET ret_lngth = 0
        ELSE
          LET ret_lngth = dec_lngth
        END IF

47➤   WHEN 1      -- intvl is FRACTION(2) to FRACTION(3) (default)
        LET ret_lngth = 0

48➤   WHEN -1     -- intvl is FRACTION(2) to FRACTION(1)
        LET ret_lngth = 0

      OTHERWISE   -- intvl has 2,3,4, or 5 fields
49➤     LET default_lngth = (large_lngth + small_lngth) + (num_flds - 2)
        IF default_lngth = dec_lngth THEN
          LET ret_lngth = 0
        ELSE
          LET ret_lngth = large_lngth + ( dec_lngth - default_lngth )
        END IF
    END CASE

    RETURN ret_lngth

  END FUNCTION  -- intvl_lngth --
```

The to_hex() Function

50➤ The to_hex() function converts a binary value to hexadecimal characters. The argument dec_number contains the binary value. It is assumed to be a 16-bit value. It is defined as an INTEGER because there are some 16-bit values that are not valid when stored in a SMALLINT variable (for example -32768). In this program it is always called to convert a value from systables.collength which is a SMALLINT column. The power argument specifies how many digits to convert. Its output is a string of power characters representing the least significant power digits of the input.

51➤ **4GL** does not support unsigned numbers. If this number appears to be negative, the function assumes that it started out as a 16-bit value with the most significant bit = 1. This sign bit would be propagated when the SMALLINT was assigned to the INTEGER, dec_number. Subtracting 216 cancels the sign bits, leaving an unsigned 16-bit value.

52➤ By initializing the output to zero characters, the function is made free to stop converting as soon as only zero is left in the_number.

53➤ The digits are produced, from most significant to least, in this loop. The method is similar to the hand method: divide by the largest power of 16 that will fit; take the quotient as the current digit and use the remainder for the next iteration. For example, convert dec_number=8194 for power=4:

1. Divide by 16^3=4096; quotient is 2, remainder is 2. Convert quotient into character and leave in hex_number[1].
2. the_num=2 is less than 162; leave hex_number[2] set to zero.
3. the_num=2 is less than 161; leave hex_number[3] set to zero.
4. the_num=2 is greater than 160; convert to character and leave in hex_number[4]. Result is "2002."

The hex_digit() Function

54➤ The hex_digit() function converts a number in the range of 0 to 15 into the corresponding hexadecimal digit character. It uses a CASE to select the letter-digits from 10 to 15. In the OTHERWISE clause, **4GL** automatic data conversion is used to convert values 0-9 into the corresponding character.

```
     ########################################
50➤  FUNCTION to_hex(dec_number, power)
     ########################################
       DEFINE     dec_number     INTEGER,
                  power          SMALLINT,

                  the_num        INTEGER,
                  i,j            SMALLINT,
                  hex_power      INTEGER,
                  hex_number     CHAR(4)

       LET the_num = dec_number
51➤    IF the_num < 0 THEN -- greater than 0x7fff, force to unsigned status
         LET the_num = 65536 + the_num
       END IF
       LET hex_power = 16 ** power
52➤    LET hex_number = "0000"

53➤    FOR i = 1 TO power
         IF the_num = 0 THEN
            EXIT FOR
         END IF
         LET hex_power = hex_power / 16
         IF the_num >= hex_power THEN
           LET hex_number[i] = hex_digit(the_num / hex_power)
           LET the_num = the_num MOD hex_power
         END IF
       END FOR
       RETURN (hex_number[1,power])
     END FUNCTION   -- to_hex --

     ########################################
54➤  FUNCTION hex_digit(dec_num)
     ########################################
       DEFINE     dec_num     SMALLINT,

                  hex_char    CHAR(1)

       CASE dec_num
         WHEN 10
           LET hex_char = "A"
         WHEN 11
           LET hex_char = "B"
         WHEN 12
           LET hex_char = "C"
         WHEN 13
           LET hex_char = "D"
         WHEN 14
           LET hex_char = "E"
         WHEN 15
           LET hex_char = "F"
```

The dec_digit() Function

55➤ The function converts a single hexadecimal digit character into its numeric value. A CASE is used for the digits A-F, while **4GL** automatic data conversion is used to convert characters 0-9 into the corresponding number.

The schema_rpt() Report Function

56➤ The report function is very ordinary. The program sends each row of data to the report function after the data type has been converted to a character string. Rows arrive ordered by tablename.

```
      OTHERWISE
        LET hex_char = dec_num
    END CASE
    RETURN hex_char
  END FUNCTION  -- hex_digit --

  #######################################
  FUNCTION dec_digit(hex_char)
  #######################################
    DEFINE    hex_char    CHAR(1),

              dec_num     SMALLINT

55➤ IF hex_char MATCHES "[ABCDEF]" THEN
      CASE hex_char
        WHEN "A"
          LET dec_num = 10
        WHEN "B"
          LET dec_num = 11
        WHEN "C"
          LET dec_num = 12
        WHEN "D"
          LET dec_num = 13
        WHEN "E"
          LET dec_num = 14
        WHEN "F"
          LET dec_num = 15
      END CASE
    ELSE
      LET dec_num = hex_char
    END IF
    RETURN dec_num

  END FUNCTION  -- dec_digit --

  #######################################
56➤ REPORT schema_rpt(r, coltypname, print_dest)
  #######################################
    DEFINE    r  RECORD
                    dbname          CHAR(50),
                    is_online       SMALLINT,
                    tabname         CHAR(18),
                    nindexes        SMALLINT,
                    colname         CHAR(18),
                    colno           SMALLINT,
                    coltype         SMALLINT,
                    collength       SMALLINT
              END RECORD,
              coltypname    CHAR(50),
              print_dest    CHAR(1)
```

57➤ The OUTPUT section does not include a PAGE LENGTH specification. The default page length (66) is used for all three kinds of output: to the printer, to a file, and to the screen, even though the screen at least needs a shorter page. The reason is that there is no way to specify page length dynamically; the PAGE LENGTH statement only accepts a constant which is evaluated at compile time. The special case of the screen is handled by EVERY ROW code.

58➤ Since the rows are passed to the report function in order by tablename, a change of tablename can be recognized as a group boundary. In the BEFORE GROUP section, the report prints lines describing the table as a whole.

59➤ After printing the data for one column, the EVERY ROW section checks the report destination, which is passed in as an argument. When output is to the screen, and when the line count exceeds a common screen size, the report pauses. After the pause it forces the start of a new page. No way exists to find out the actual screen size at run time.

The problem of a dynamic report page size could be generalized through the use of a global variable. The ON EVERY ROW code could compare the built-in LINENO function to the global variable, and force a new page whenever it was exceeded. That would permit the program to take a desired page size from the user at the same time the user selects the report destination.

```
57➤  OUTPUT
       LEFT MARGIN 0
       RIGHT MARGIN 80

     FORMAT
       FIRST PAGE HEADER
         PRINT COLUMN 40, "DATABASE SCHEMA LISTING FOR ",
                 r.dbname CLIPPED
         PRINT COLUMN 42, "INFORMIX-";
         IF r.is_online THEN
           PRINT COLUMN 51, "OnLine Database"
         ELSE
           PRINT COLUMN 51, "SE Database"
         END IF
         PRINT COLUMN 50, today
         SKIP 3 LINES

       PAGE HEADER
         PRINT COLUMN 60, "PAGE ", PAGENO USING "#&"
         SKIP 2 LINES


58➤    BEFORE GROUP OF r.tabname
         NEED 6 LINES
         PRINT "TABLE: ", r.tabname CLIPPED,
               COLUMN 30, "NUMBER OF INDEXES: ", r.nindexes USING "&<<<<"
         PRINT "----------------------------------------";
         PRINT "----------------------------------------"
         PRINT COLUMN 4, "Column", COLUMN 27, "Type"
         PRINT "----------------------------------------";
         PRINT "----------------------------------------"

       AFTER GROUP OF r.tabname
         SKIP 2 LINES

59➤    ON EVERY ROW
         PRINT COLUMN 4, r.colname, COLUMN 27, coltypname CLIPPED
         IF (print_dest = "S") AND (LINENO > 22) THEN
           PAUSE "Press RETURN to see next screen"
           SKIP TO TOP OF PAGE
         END IF
   END REPORT  -- schema_rpt --
```

To locate any function definition see the Function Index on page 728.

Appendix A

The Demonstration Database

The stores2 demonstration database contains a set of tables that describe an imaginary business. The examples in this book are based on this database.

This appendix contains four sections:

- The first section describes the structure of the tables in the stores2 database and lists the name and the data type of each column. The indexes on individual columns or on multiple columns are identified and classified as unique or as allowing duplicate values.
- The second section shows a graphic map of the tables in the stores2 database and indicates potential join columns.
- The third section describes the join columns that link some of the tables in the stores2 database, and illustrates how you can use these relationships to obtain information from multiple tables.
- The final section shows the data contained in each table of the stores2 database.

If you have modified or deleted some or all of the data in these tables, you can restore the stores2 database to its original form by running the sqldemo script supplied with **INFORMIX-4GL** release 4.1. See the section "The Demonstration Database and Application Files" on page 23 for information about how to create the database.

Structure of the Tables

The stores2 database contains information about a fictitious sporting goods distributor that services stores in the western United States. This database includes the following tables:

- customer
- orders
- items
- stock
- catalog
- cust_calls
- manufact
- state

The customer Table

The customer table contains information about the retail stores that place orders from the distributor. The columns of the customer table are as follows:

Column Name	Data Type	Description
customer_num	SERIAL(101)	system-generated customer number
fname	CHAR(15)	first name of store's representative
lname	CHAR(15)	last name of store's representative
company	CHAR(20)	name of store
address1	CHAR(20)	first line of store's address
address2	CHAR(20)	second line of store's address
city	CHAR(15)	city
state	CHAR(2)	state
zipcode	CHAR(5)	zip code
phone	CHAR(18)	phone number

The customer_num column is indexed and must contain unique values. The zipcode and state columns are indexed to allow duplicate values.

The orders Table

The orders table contains information about orders placed by the distributor's customers. The columns of the orders table are as follows:

Column Name	Data Type	Description
order_num	SERIAL(1001)	system-generated order number
order_date	DATE	date order entered
customer_num	INTEGER	customer number (from customer table)
ship_instruct	CHAR(40)	special shipping instructions
backlog	CHAR(1)	indicates order cannot be filled because the item is backlogged: y = yes n = no
po_num	CHAR(10)	customer purchase order number
ship_date	DATE	shipping date
ship_weight	DECIMAL(8,2)	shipping weight
ship_charge	MONEY(6)	shipping charge
paid_date	DATE	date order paid

The order_num column is indexed and must contain unique values. The customer_num column is indexed to allow duplicate values.

The items Table

An order can include one or more items. There is one row in the items table for each item in an order. The columns of the items table are as follows:

Column Name	Data Type	Description
item_num	SMALLINT	sequentially assigned item number for an order
order_num	INTEGER	order number (from orders table)
stock_num	SMALLINT	stock number for item (from stock table)
manu_code	CHAR(3)	manufacturer's code for item ordered (from manufact table)
quantity	SMALLINT	quantity ordered
total_price	MONEY(8,2)	quantity ordered × unit price = total price of item

The order_num column is indexed and allows duplicate values. A multiple-column index for the stock_num and manu_code columns also permits duplicate values.

The stock Table

The distributor carries 41 different types of sporting goods from various manufacturers. More than one manufacturer can supply a sporting good. For example, the distributor offers racer goggles from two manufacturers and running shoes from six manufacturers.

The stock table is a catalog of the items sold by the distributor. The columns of the stock table are as follows:

Column Name	Data Type	Description
stock_num	SMALLINT	stock number that identifies type of item
manu_code	CHAR(3)	manufacturer's code (from manufact table)
description	CHAR(15)	description of item
unit_price	MONEY(6,2)	unit price
unit	CHAR(4)	unit by which item is ordered: each pair case box
unit_descr	CHAR(15)	description of unit

The stock_num and manu_code columns are indexed and allow duplicate values. A multiple-column index for both the stock_num and manu_code columns allows only unique values.

The catalog Table

The catalog table describes each of the items in stock. Retail stores use this catalog when placing orders with the distributor. The columns of the catalog table are as follows:

Column Name	Data Type	Description
catalog_num	SERIAL(10001)	system-generated catalog number
stock_num	SMALLINT	distributor's stock number (from stock table)
manu_code	CHAR(3)	manufacturer's code (from manufact table)
cat_descr	TEXT	description of item
cat_picture	BYTE	picture of item (binary data)
cat_advert	VARCHAR(255, 65)	tag line underneath picture

The catalog_num column is indexed and must contain unique values. The stock_num and manu_code columns allow duplicate values. A multiple-column index for the stock_num and manu_code columns allows only unique values.

The catalog table appears only if you are using an **INFORMIX-OnLine** database engine.

The cust_calls Table

All customer calls for information on orders, shipments, or complaints are logged. The cust_calls table contains information about these types of customer calls. The columns of the cust_calls table are as follows:

Column Name	Data Type	Description
customer_num	INTEGER	customer number (from customer table)
call_dtime	DATETIME YEAR TO MINUTE	date and time call received
user_id	CHAR(18)	name of person logging call
call_code	CHAR(1)	type of call: B = billing error D = damaged goods I = incorrect merchandise sent L = late shipment O = other
call_descr	CHAR(240)	description of call
res_dtime	DATETIME YEAR TO MINUTE	date and time call resolved
res_descr	CHAR(240)	description of how call was resolved

A multiple-column index for both the customer_num and call_dtime columns allows only unique values. The customer_num column also has an index that allows duplicate values.

The manufact Table

Information about the nine manufacturers whose sporting goods are handled by the distributor is stored in the manufact table. The columns of the manufact table are as follows:

Column Name	Data Type	Description
manu_code	CHAR(3)	manufacturer's code
manu_name	CHAR(15)	name of manufacturer
lead_time	INTERVAL DAY(3) TO DAY	lead time for shipment of orders

The manu_code column has an index that requires unique values.

The state Table

The state table contains the names and postal abbreviations for the 50 states of the United States. It includes the following two columns:

Column Name	Data Type	Description
code	CHAR(2)	state code
sname	CHAR(15)	state name

The code column is indexed as unique.

The stores2 Database Map

Figure 1 displays the column names of the tables in the stores2 database. Shading connecting a column in one table to a column in another table indicates columns that contain the same information.

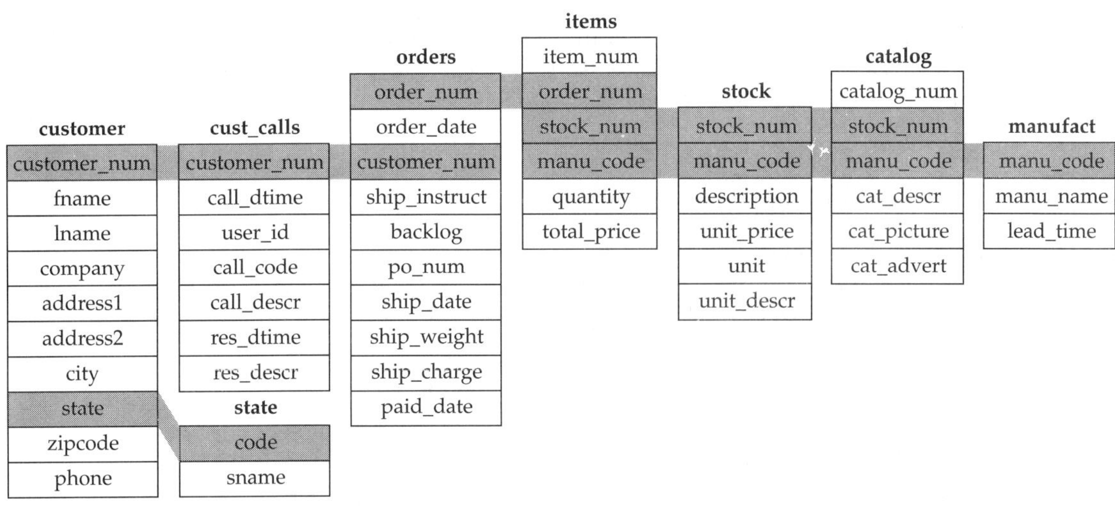

Figure 1 ***Tables in the stores2 database***

Join Columns That Link the Database

The tables of the stores2 database are linked together by the *join columns* shown in Figure 1 and identified in this section. You can use these columns to retrieve and display information from several tables at once, as if the information had been stored in a single table. Figures 1 through 8 show the join relationships among tables, and how information stored in one table supplements information stored in others.

Join Columns in the customer and orders Tables

The customer_num column joins the customer table and the orders table, as shown in Figure 2.

customer table (detail)

customer_num	fname	lname
101	Ludwig	Pauli
102	Carole	Sadler
103	Philip	Currie
104	Anthony	Higgins

orders table (detail)

order_num	order_date	customer_num
1001	05/20/1990	104
1002	05/21/1990	101
1003	05/22/1990	104
1004	05/22/1990	106

Figure 2 ***Tables joined by the customer_num column***

The customer table contains a customer_num column that holds a number identifying a customer, along with columns for the customer's name, company, address, and telephone number. For example, the row with information about Anthony Higgins contains the number 104 in the customer_num column. The orders table also contains a customer_num column that stores the number of the customer who placed a particular order.

According to Figure 2, customer 104 (Anthony Higgins) has placed two orders since his customer number appears in two rows of the orders table. Since the join relationship lets you select information from both tables, you can retrieve Anthony Higgins' name and address and information about his orders at the same time.

Join Columns in the orders and items Tables

The orders and items tables are linked by an order_num column that contains an identification number for each order. If an order includes several items, the same order number appears in several rows of the items table. Figure 3 shows this relationship.

***orders** table (detail)*

order_num	order_date	customer_num
1001	05/20/1990	104
1002	05/21/1990	101
1003	05/22/1990	104

***items** table (detail)*

item_num	order_num	stock_num	manu_code
1	1001	1	HRO
1	1002	4	HSK
2	1002	3	HSK
1	1003	9	ANZ
2	1003	8	ANZ
3	1003	5	ANZ

Figure 3 ***Tables joined by the order_num column***

Join Columns in the items and stock Tables

The items table and the stock table are joined by two columns: the stock_num column stores a stock number for an item, and the manu_code column stores a code that identifies the manufacturer. You need both the stock number and the manufacturer code to uniquely identify an item. For example, the item with the stock number 1 and the manufacturer code HRO is a Hero baseball glove, while the item with the stock number 1 and the manufacturer code HSK is a Husky baseball glove.

The same stock number and manufacturer code can appear in more than one row of the items table, if the same item belongs to separate orders, as illustrated in Figure 4.

items table (detail)

item_num	order_num	stock_num	manu_code
1	1001	1	HRO
1	1002	4	HSK
2	1002	3	HSK
1	1003	9	ANZ
2	1003	8	ANZ
3	1003	5	ANZ
1	1004	1	HRO

stock table (detail)

stock_num	manu_code	description
1	HRO	baseball gloves
1	HSK	baseball gloves
1	SMT	baseball gloves

Figure 4 *Tables joined by the stock_num and manu_code columns*

Join Columns in the stock and catalog Tables

The catalog table and the stock table are joined by two columns: the stock_num column stores a stock number for an item, and the manu_code column stores a code that identifies the manufacturer. You need both of these columns to uniquely identify an item. Figure 5 shows this relationship.

stock table (detail)

stock_num	manu_code	description
1	HRO	baseball gloves
1	HSK	baseball gloves
1	SMT	baseball gloves

catalog table (detail)

catalog_num	stock_num	manu_code
10001	1	HRO
10002	1	HSK
10003	1	SMT
10004	2	HRO

Figure 5 *Tables joined by the stock_num and manu_code columns*

Join Columns in the stock and manufact Tables

The stock table and the manufact table are joined by the manu_code column. The same manufacturer code can appear in more than one row of the stock table if the manufacturer produces more than one piece of equipment. This relationship is illustrated in Figure 6.

stock table (detail)

stock_num	manu_code	description
1	HRO	baseball gloves
1	HSK	baseball gloves
1	SMT	baseball gloves

manufact table (detail)

manu_code	manu_name
NRG	Norge
HSK	Husky
HRO	Hero

Figure 6 ***Tables joined by the manu_code column***

Join Columns in the cust_calls and customer Tables

The cust_calls table and the customer table are joined by the customer_num column. The same customer number can appear in more than one row of the cust_calls table if the customer calls the distributor more than once with a problem or question. This relationship is illustrated in Figure 7.

customer table (detail)

customer_num	fname	lname
101	Ludwig	Pauli
102	Carole	Sadler
103	Philip	Currie
104	Anthony	Higgins
105	Raymond	Vector
106	George	Watson

cust_calls table (detail)

customer_num	call_dtime	user_id
106	1990-06-12 08:20	maryj
127	1990-07-31 14:30	maryj
116	1990-11-28 13:34	mannyh
116	1989-12-21 11:24	mannyh

Figure 7 *Tables joined by the customer_num column*

Join Columns in the state and customer Tables

The state table and the customer table are joined by a column that contains the state code. This column is called code in the state table and state in the customer table. If several customers live in the same state, the same state code will appear in several rows of the table, as shown in Figure 8.

customer_num	fname	lname	...	state
101	Ludwig	Pauli	...	CA
102	Carole	Sadler	...	CA
103	Philip	Currie	...	CA

***customer** table (detail)*

code	sname
AK	Alaska
AL	Alabama
AR	Arkansas
AZ	Arizona
CA	California

***state** table (detail)*

Figure 8 *Tables joined by the state/code column*

Data in the stores2 Database

The tables that follow display the data in the stores2 database.

customer Table

customer_num	fname	lname	company	address1	address2	city	state	zipcode	phone
101	Ludwig	Pauli	All Sports Supplies	213 Erstwild Court		Sunnyvale	CA	94086	408-789-8075
102	Carole	Sadler	Sports Spot	785 Geary St		San Francisco	CA	94117	415-822-1289
103	Philip	Currie	Phil's Sports	654 Poplar	P. O. Box 3498	Palo Alto	CA	94303	415-328-4543
104	Anthony	Higgins	Play Ball!	East Shopping Cntr.	422 Bay Road	Redwood City	CA	94026	415-368-1100
105	Raymond	Vector	Los Altos Sports	1899 La Loma Drive		Los Altos	CA	94022	415-776-3249
106	George	Watson	Watson & Son	1143 Carver Place		Mountain View	CA	94063	415-389-8789
107	Charles	Ream	Athletic Supplies	41 Jordan Avenue		Palo Alto	CA	94304	415-356-9876
108	Donald	Quinn	Quinn's Sports	587 Alvarado		Redwood City	CA	94063	415-544-8729
109	Jane	Miller	Sport Stuff	Mayfair Mart	7345 Ross Blvd.	Sunnyvale	CA	94086	408-723-8789
110	Roy	Jaeger	AA Athletics	520 Topaz Way		Redwood City	CA	94062	415-743-3611
111	Frances	Keyes	Sports Center	3199 Sterling Court		Sunnyvale	CA	94085	408-277-7245
112	Margaret	Lawson	Runners & Others	234 Wyandotte Way		Los Altos	CA	94022	415-887-7235
113	Lana	Beatty	Sportstown	654 Oak Grove		Menlo Park	CA	94025	415-356-9982
114	Frank	Albertson	Sporting Place	947 Waverly Place		Redwood City	CA	94062	415-886-6677
115	Alfred	Grant	Gold Medal Sports	776 Gary Avenue		Menlo Park	CA	94025	415-356-1123
116	Jean	Parmelee	Olympic City	1104 Spinosa Drive		Mountain View	CA	94040	415-534-8822
117	Arnold	Sipes	Kids Korner	850 Lytton Court		Redwood City	CA	94063	415-245-4578
118	Dick	Baxter	Blue Ribbon Sports	5427 College		Oakland	CA	94609	415-655-0011
119	Bob	Shorter	The Triathletes Club	2405 Kings Highway		Cherry Hill	NJ	08002	609-663-6079
120	Fred	Jewell	Century Pro Shop	6627 N. 17th Way		Phoenix	AZ	85016	602-265-8754
121	Jason	Wallack	City Sports	Lake Biltmore Mall	350 W. 23rd Street	Wilmington	DE	19898	302-366-7511
122	Cathy	O'Brian	The Sporting Life	543 Nassau Street		Princeton	NJ	08540	609-342-0054
123	Marvin	Hanlon	Bay Sports	10100 Bay Meadows Rd	Suite 1020	Jacksonviille	FL	32256	904-823-4239
124	Chris	Putnum	Putnum's Putters	4715 S.E. Adams Blvd	Suite 909C	Bartlesville	OK	74006	918-355-2074
125	James	Henry	Total Fitness Sports	1450 Commonwealth Av		Brighton	MA	02135	617-232-4159
126	Eileen	Neelie	Neelie's Discount Sp	2539 South Utica Str		Denver	CO	80219	303-936-7731
127	Kim	Satifer	Big Blue Bike Shop	Blue Island Square	12222 Gregory Street	Blue Island	NY	60406	312-944-5691
128	Frank	Lessor	Phoenix University	Athletic Department	1817 N. Thomas Road	Phoenix	AZ	85008	602-533-1817

items Table (1 of 2)

item_num	order_num	stock_num	manu_code	quantity	total_price
1	1001	1	HRO	1	250.00
1	1002	4	HSK	1	960.00
2	1002	3	HSK	1	240.00
1	1003	9	ANZ	1	20.00
2	1003	8	ANZ	1	840.00
3	1003	5	ANZ	5	99.00
1	1004	1	HRO	1	250.00
2	1004	2	HRO	1	126.00
3	1004	3	HSK	1	240.00
4	1004	1	HSK	1	800.00
1	1005	5	NRG	10	280.00
2	1005	5	ANZ	10	198.00
3	1005	6	SMT	1	36.00
4	1005	6	ANZ	1	48.00
1	1006	5	SMT	5	125.00
2	1006	5	NRG	5	140.00
3	1006	5	ANZ	5	99.00
4	1006	6	SMT	1	36.00
5	1006	6	ANZ	1	48.00
1	1007	1	HRO	1	250.00
2	1007	2	HRO	1	126.00
3	1007	3	HSK	1	240.00
4	1007	4	HRO	1	480.00
5	1007	7	HRO	1	600.00
1	1008	8	ANZ	1	840.00
2	1008	9	ANZ	5	100.00
1	1009	1	SMT	1	450.00
1	1010	6	SMT	1	36.00
2	1010	6	ANZ	1	48.00
1	1011	5	ANZ	5	99.00
1	1012	8	ANZ	1	840.00
2	1012	9	ANZ	10	200.00
1	1013	5	ANZ	1	19.80
2	1013	6	SMT	1	36.00
3	1013	6	ANZ	1	48.00
4	1013	9	ANZ	2	40.00
1	1014	4	HSK	1	960.00
2	1014	4	HRO	1	480.00
1	1015	1	SMT	1	450.00
1	1016	101	SHM	2	136.00
2	1016	109	PRC	3	90.00
3	1016	110	HSK	1	308.00
4	1016	114	PRC	1	120.00
1	1017	201	NKL	4	150.00
2	1017	202	KAR	1	230.00
3	1017	301	SHM	2	204.00
1	1018	307	PRC	2	500.00

items Table (2 of 2)

item_num	order_num	stock_num	manu_code	quantity	total_price
2	1018	302	KAR	3	15.00
3	1018	110	PRC	1	236.00
4	1018	5	SMT	4	100.00
5	1018	304	HRO	1	280.00
1	1019	111	SHM	3	1499.97
1	1020	204	KAR	2	90.00
2	1020	301	KAR	4	348.00
1	1021	201	NKL	2	75.00
2	1021	201	ANZ	3	225.00
3	1021	202	KAR	3	690.00
4	1021	205	ANZ	2	624.00
1	1022	309	HRO	1	40.00
2	1022	303	PRC	2	96.00
3	1022	6	ANZ	2	96.00
1	1023	103	PRC	2	40.00
2	1023	104	PRC	2	116.00
3	1023	105	SHM	1	80.00
4	1023	110	SHM	1	228.00
5	1023	304	ANZ	1	170.00
6	1023	306	SHM	1	190.00

orders Table

order_num	order_date	customer_num	ship_instruct	backlog	po_num	ship_date	ship_weight	ship_charge	paid_date
1001	05/20/1990	104	express	n	B77836	06/01/1990	20.40	10.00	07/22/1990
1002	05/21/1990	101	PO on box; deliver back door only	n	9270	05/26/1990	50.60	15.30	06/03/1990
1003	05/22/1990	104	express	n	B77890	05/23/1990	35.60	10.80	06/14/1990
1004	05/22/1990	106	ring bell twice	y	8006	05/30/1990	95.80	19.20	
1005	05/24/1990	116	call before delivery	n	2865	06/09/1990	80.80	16.20	06/21/1990
1006	05/30/1990	112	after 10 am	y	Q13557		70.80	14.20	
1007	05/31/1990	117		n	278693	06/05/1990	125.90	25.20	
1008	06/07/1990	110	closed Monday	y	LZ230	07/06/1990	45.60	13.80	07/21/1990
1009	06/14/1990	111	next door to grocery	n	4745	06/21/1990	20.40	10.00	08/21/1990
1010	06/17/1990	115	deliver 776 King St. if no answer	n	429Q	06/29/1990	40.60	12.30	08/22/1990
1011	06/18/1990	104	express	n	B77897	07/03/1990	10.40	5.00	08/29/1990
1012	06/18/1990	117		n	278701	06/29/1990	70.80	14.20	
1013	06/22/1990	104	express	n	B77930	07/10/1990	60.80	12.20	07/31/1990
1014	06/25/1990	106	ring bell, kick door loudly	n	8052	07/03/1990	40.60	12.30	07/10/1990
1015	06/27/1990	110	closed Mondays	n	MA003	07/16/1990	20.60	6.30	08/31/1990
1016	06/29/1990	119	delivery entrance off Camp St.	n	PC6782	07/12/1990	35.00	11.80	
1017	07/09/1990	120	North side of clubhouse	n	DM354331	07/13/1990	60.00	18.00	
1018	07/10/1990	121	SW corner of Biltmore Mall	n	S22942	07/13/1990	70.50	20.00	08/06/1990
1019	07/11/1990	122	closed til noon Mondays	n	Z55709	07/16/1990	90.00	23.00	08/06/1990
1020	07/11/1990	123	express	n	W2286	07/16/1990	14.00	8.50	09/20/1990
1021	07/23/1990	124	ask for Elaine	n	C3288	07/25/1990	40.00	12.00	08/22/1990
1022	07/24/1990	126	express	n	W9925	07/30/1990	15.00	13.00	09/02/1990
1023	07/24/1990	127	no deliveries after 3 p.m.	n	KF2961	07/30/1990	60.00	18.00	08/22/1990

stock Table (1 of 2)

stock_num	manu_code	description	unit_price	unit	unit_descr
1	HRO	baseball gloves	250.00	case	10 gloves/case
1	HSK	baseball gloves	800.00	case	10 gloves/case
1	SMT	baseball gloves	450.00	case	10 gloves/case
2	HRO	baseball	126.00	case	24/case
3	HSK	baseball bat	240.00	case	12/case
4	HSK	football	960.00	case	24/case
4	HRO	football	480.00	case	24/case
5	NRG	tennis racquet	28.00	each	each
5	SMT	tennis racquet	25.00	each	each
5	ANZ	tennis racquet	19.80	each	each
6	SMT	tennis ball	36.00	case	24 cans/case
6	ANZ	tennis ball	48.00	case	24 cans/case
7	HRO	basketball	600.00	case	24/case
8	ANZ	volleyball	840.00	case	24/case
9	ANZ	volleyball net	20.00	each	each
101	PRC	bicycle tires	88.00	box	4/box
101	SHM	bicycle tires	68.00	box	4/box
102	SHM	bicycle brakes	220.00	case	4 sets/case
102	PRC	bicycle brakes	480.00	case	4 sets/case
103	PRC	front derailleur	20.00	each	each
104	PRC	rear derailleur	58.00	each	each
105	PRC	bicycle wheels	53.00	pair	pair
105	SHM	bicycle wheels	80.00	pair	pair
106	PRC	bicycle stem	23.00	each	each
107	PRC	bicycle saddle	70.00	pair	pair
108	SHM	crankset	45.00	each	each
109	PRC	pedal binding	30.00	case	6 pairs/case
109	SHM	pedal binding	200.00	case	4 pairs/case
110	PRC	helmet	236.00	case	4/case
110	ANZ	helmet	244.00	case	4/case
110	SHM	helmet	228.00	case	4/case
110	HRO	helmet	260.00	case	4/case
110	HSK	helmet	308.00	case	4/case
111	SHM	10-spd, assmbld	499.99	each	each
112	SHM	12-spd, assmbld	549.00	each	each
113	SHM	18-spd, assmbld	685.90	each	each
114	PRC	bicycle gloves	120.00	case	10 pairs/case

stock Table (2 of 2)

stock_num	manu_code	description	unit_price	unit	unit_descr
201	NKL	golf shoes	37.50	each	each
201	ANZ	golf shoes	75.00	each	each
201	KAR	golf shoes	90.00	each	each
202	NKL	metal woods	174.00	case	2 sets/case
202	KAR	std woods	230.00	case	2 sets/case
203	NKL	irons/wedges	670.00	case	2 sets/case
204	KAR	putter	45.00	each	each
205	NKL	3 golf balls	312.00	case	24/case
205	ANZ	3 golf balls	312.00	case	24/case
205	HRO	3 golf balls	312.00	case	24/case
301	NKL	running shoes	97.00	each	each
301	HRO	running shoes	42.50	each	each
301	SHM	running shoes	102.00	each	each
301	PRC	running shoes	75.00	each	each
301	KAR	running shoes	87.00	each	each
301	ANZ	running shoes	95.00	each	each
302	HRO	ice pack	4.50	each	each
302	KAR	ice pack	5.00	each	each
303	PRC	socks	48.00	box	24 pairs/box
303	KAR	socks	36.00	box	24 pair/box
304	ANZ	watch	170.00	box	10/box
304	HRO	watch	280.00	box	10/box
305	HRO	first-aid kit	48.00	case	4/case
306	PRC	tandem adapter	160.00	each	each
306	SHM	tandem adapter	190.00	each	each
307	PRC	infant jogger	250.00	each	each
308	PRC	twin jogger	280.00	each	each
309	HRO	ear drops	40.00	case	20/case
309	SHM	ear drops	40.00	case	20/case
310	SHM	kick board	80.00	case	10/case
310	ANZ	kick board	89.00	case	12/case
311	SHM	water gloves	48.00	box	4 pairs/box
312	SHM	racer goggles	96.00	box	12/box
312	HRO	racer goggles	72.00	box	12/box
313	SHM	swim cap	72.00	box	12/box
313	ANZ	swim cap	60.00	box	12/box

catalog Table (1 of 7)

catalog_num	stock_num	manu_code	cat_descr	cat_picture	cat_advert
10001	1	HRO8	Brown leather. Specify first baseman's or infield/outfield style. Specify right- or left-handed.	<BYTE value>	Your First Season's Baseball Glove
10002	1	HSK	Babe Ruth signature glove. Black leather. Infield/outfield style. Specify right- or left-handed	<BYTE value>	All-Leather, Hand-Stitched, Deep-Pockets, Sturdy Webbing that Won't Let Go
10003	1	SMT	Catcher's mitt. Brown leather. Specify right- or left-handed.	<BYTE value>	A Sturdy Catcher's Mitt With the Perfect Pocket
10004	2	HRO	Jackie Robinson signature glove. Highest Professional quality, used by National League.	<BYTE value>	Highest Quality Ball Available, from the Hand-Stitching to the Robinson Signature
10005	3	HSK	Pro-style wood. Available in sizes: 31, 32, 33, 34, 35.	<BYTE value>	High-Technology Design Expands the Sweet Spot
10006	3	SHM	Aluminum. Blue with black tape. 31", 20 oz or 22 oz; 32", 21 oz or 23 oz; 33", 22 oz or 24 oz;	<BYTE value>	Durable Aluminum for High School and Collegiate Athletes
10007	4	HSK	Norm Van Brocklin signature style.	<BYTE value>	Quality Pigskin with Norm Van Brocklin Signature
10008	4	HRO	NFL-Style pigskin.	<BYTE value>	Highest Quality Football for High School and Collegiate Competitions
10009	5	NRG	Graphite frame. Synthetic strings.	<BYTE value>	Wide Body Amplifies Your Natural Abilities by Providing More Power Through Aerodynamic Design
10010	5	SMT	Aluminum frame. Synthetic strings	<BYTE value>	Mid-Sized Racquet For the Improving Player
10011	5	ANZ	Wood frame, cat-gut strings.	<BYTE value>	Antique Replica of Classic Wooden Racquet Built with Cat-Gut Strings
10012	6	SMT	Soft yellow color for easy visibility in sunlight or artificial light	<BYTE value>	High-Visibility Tennis, Day or Night
10013	6	ANZ	Pro-core. Available in neon yellow, green, and pink.	<BYTE value>	Durable Construction Coupled with the Brightest Colors Available
10014	7	HRO	Indoor. Classic NBA style. Brown leather.	<BYTE value>	Long-Life Basketballs for Indoor Gymnasiums
10015	8	ANZ	Indoor. Finest leather. Professional quality.	<BYTE value>	Professional Volleyballs for Indoor Competitions
10016	9	ANZ	Steel eyelets. Nylon cording. Double-stitched. Sanctioned by the National Athletic Congress	<BYTE value>	Sanctioned Volleyball Netting for Indoor Professional and Collegiate Competition

catalog Table (2 of 7)

catalog_num	stock_num	manu_code	cat_descr	cat_picture	cat_advert
10017	101	PRC	Reinforced, hand-finished tubular. Polyurethane belted. Effective against punctures. Mixed tread for super wear and road grip.	<BYTE value>	Ultimate in Puncture Protection, Tires Designed for In-City Riding
10018	101	SHM	Durable nylon casing with butyl tube for superior air retention. Center-ribbed tread with herringbone side. Coated sidewalls resist abrasion.	<BYTE value>	The Perfect Tire for Club Rides or Training
10019	102	SHM	Thrust bearing and coated pivot washer/spring sleeve for smooth action. Slotted levers with soft gum hoods. Two-tone paint treatment. Set includes calipers, levers, and cables.	<BYTE value>	Thrust-Bearing and Spring-Sleeve Brake Set Guarantees Smooth Action
10020	102	PRC	Computer-aided design with low-profile pads. Cold-forged alloy calipers and beefy caliper bushing. Aero levers. Set includes calipers, levers, and cables	<BYTE value>	Computer Design Delivers Rigid Yet Vibration-Free Brakes
10021	103	PRC	Compact leading-action design enhances shifting. Deep cage for super-small granny gears. Extra strong construction to resist off-road abuse.	<BYTE value>	Climb Any Mountain: ProCycle's Front Derailleur Adds Finesse to Your ATB
10022	104	PRC	Floating trapezoid geometry with extra thick parallelogram arms. 100-tooth capacity. Optimum alignment with any freewheel.	<BYTE value>	Computer-Aided Design Engineers 100-Tooth Capacity Into ProCycle's Rear Derailleur
10023	105	PRC	Front wheels laced with 15g spokes in a 3-cross pattern. Rear wheels laced with 14g spikes in a 3-cross pattern.	<BYTE value>	Durable Training Wheels That Hold True Under Toughest Conditions
10024	105	SHM	Polished alloy. Sealed-bearing, quick-release hubs. Double-butted. Front wheels are laced 15g/2-cross. Rear wheels are laced 15g/3-cross.	<BYTE value>	Extra Lightweight Wheels for Training or High-Performance Touring
10025	106	PRC	Hard anodized alloy with pearl finish. 6mm hex bolt hardware. Available in lengths of 90-140mm in 10mm increments.	<BYTE value>	ProCycle Stem with Pearl Finish
10026	107	PRC	Available in three styles: Mens racing; Mens touring; and Womens. Anatomical gel construction with lycra cover. Black or black/hot pink.	<BYTE value>	The Ultimate In Riding Comfort, Lightweight With Anatomical Support

catalog Table (3 of 7)

catalog_num	stock_num	manu_code	cat_descr	cat_picture	cat_advert
10027	108	SHM	Double or triple crankset with choice of chainrings. For double crankset, chainrings from 38-54 teeth. For triple crankset, chainrings from 24-48 teeth.	<BYTE value>	Customize Your Mountain Bike With Extra-Durable Crankset
10028	109	PRC	Steel toe clips with nylon strap. Extra wide at buckle to reduce pressure.	<BYTE value>	Classic Toeclip Improved To Prevent Soreness At Clip Buckle
10029	109	SHM	Ingenious new design combines button on sole of shoe with slot on a pedal plate to give riders new options in riding efficiency. Choose full or partial locking. Four plates mean both top and bottom of pedals are slotted—no fishing around when you want to engage full power. Fast unlocking ensures safety when maneuverability is paramount.	<BYTE value>	Ingenious Pedal/Clip Design Delivers Maximum Power And Fast Unlocking
10030	110	PRC	Super-lightweight. Meets both ANZI and Snell standards for impact protection. 7.5 oz. Quick-release shadow buckle.	<BYTE value>	Feather-Light, Quick-Release, Maximum Protection Helmet
10031	110	ANZ	No buckle so no plastic touches your chin. Meets both ANZI and Snell standards for impact protection. 7.5 oz. Lycra cover.	<BYTE value>	Minimum Chin Contact, Feather-Light, Maximum Protection Helmet
10032	110	SHM	Dense outer layer combines with softer inner layer to eliminate the mesh cover, no snagging on brush. Meets both ANZI and Snell standards for impact protection. 8.0 oz.	<BYTE value>	Mountain Bike Helmet: Smooth Cover Eliminates the Worry of Brush Snags But Delivers Maximum Protection
10033	110	HRO	Newest ultralight helmet uses plastic shell. Largest ventilation channels of any helmet on the market. 8.5 oz.	<BYTE value>	Lightweight Plastic with Vents Assures Cool Comfort Without Sacrificing Protection
10034	110	HSK	Aerodynamic (teardrop) helmet covered with anti-drag fabric. Credited with shaving 2 seconds/mile from winner's time in Tour de France time-trial. 7.5 oz.	<BYTE value>	Teardrop Design Used by Yellow Jerseys, You Can Time the Difference
10035	111	SHM	Light-action shifting 10 speed. Designed for the city commuter with shock-absorbing front fork and drilled eyelets for carry-all racks or bicycle trailers. Internal wiring for generator lights. 33 lbs.	<BYTE value>	Fully Equipped Bicycle Designed for the Serious Commuter Who Mixes Business With Pleasure

catalog Table (4 of 7)

catalog_num	stock_num	manu_code	cat_descr	cat_picture	cat_advert
10036	112	SHM	Created for the beginner enthusiast. Ideal for club rides and light touring. Sophisticated triple-butted frame construction. Precise index shifting. 28 lbs.	<BYTE value>	We Selected the Ideal Combination of Touring Bike Equipment, Then Turned It Into This Package Deal: High-Performance on the Roads, Maximum Pleasure Everywhere
10037	113	SHM	Ultra-lightweight. Racing frame geometry built for aerodynamic handlebars. Cantilever brakes. Index shifting. High-performance gearing. Quick-release hubs. Disk wheels. Bladed spokes.	<BYTE value>	Designed for the Serious Competitor, The Complete Racing Machine
10038	114	PRC	Padded leather palm and stretch mesh merged with terry back; Available in tan, black, and cream. Sizes S, M, L, XL.	<BYTE value>	Riding Gloves For Comfort and Protection
10039	201	NKL	Designed for comfort and stability. Available in white & blue or white & brown. Specify size.	<BYTE value>	Full-Comfort, Long-Wearing Golf Shoes for Men and Women
10040	201	ANZ	Guaranteed waterproof. Full leather upper. Available in white, bone, brown, green, and blue. Specify size.	<BYTE value>	Waterproof Protection Ensures Maximum Comfort and Durability In All Climates
10041	201	KAR	Leather and leather mesh for maximum ventilation. Waterproof lining to keep feet dry. Available in white & gray or white & ivory. Specify size.	<BYTE value>	Karsten's Top Quality Shoe Combines Leather and Leather Mesh
10042	202	NKL	Complete starter set utilizes gold shafts. Balanced for power.	<BYTE value>	Starter Set of Woods, Ideal for High School and Collegiate Classes
10043	202	KAR	Full set of woods designed for precision control and power performance.	<BYTE value>	High-Quality Woods Appropriate for High School Competitions or Serious Amateurs
10044	203	NKL	Set of eight irons includes 3 through 9 irons and pitching wedge. Originally priced at $489.00.	<BYTE value>	Set of Irons Available From Factory at Tremendous Savings: Discontinued Line.
10045	204	KAR	Ideally balanced for optimum control. Nylon-covered shaft.	<BYTE value>	High-Quality Beginning Set of Irons Appropriate for High School Competitions
10046	205	NKL	Fluorescent yellow.	<BYTE value>	Long Drive Golf Balls: Fluorescent Yellow
10047	205	ANZ	White only.	<BYTE value>	Long Drive Golf Balls: White
10048	205	HRO	Combination fluorescent yellow and standard white.	<BYTE value>	HiFlier Golf Balls: Case Includes Fluorescent Yellow and Standard White

catalog Table (5 of 7)

catalog_num	stock_num	manu_code	cat_descr	cat_picture	cat_advert
10049	301	NKL	Super shock-absorbing gel pads disperse vertical energy into a horizontal plane for extraordinary cushioned comfort. Great motion control. Mens only. Specify size.	<BYTE value>	Maximum Protection For High-Mileage Runners
10050	301	HRO	Engineered for serious training with exceptional stability. Fabulous shock absorption. Great durability. Specify mens/womens, size.	<BYTE value>	Pronators and Supinators Take Heart: A Serious Training Shoe For Runners Who Need Motion Control
10051	301	SHM	For runners who log heavy miles and need a durable, supportive, stable platform. Mesh/synthetic upper gives excellent moisture dissipation. Stability system uses rear antipronation platform and forefoot control plate for extended protection during high-intensity training. Specify mens/womens, size.	<BYTE value>	The Training Shoe Engineered for Marathoners and Ultra-Distance Runners
10052	301	PRC	Supportive, stable racing flat. Plenty of forefoot cushioning with added motion control. Womens only. D widths available. Specify size.	<BYTE value>	A Woman's Racing Flat That Combines Extra Forefoot Protection With a Slender Heel
10053	301	KAR	Anatomical last holds your foot firmly in place. Feather-weight cushioning delivers the responsiveness of a racing flat. Specify mens/womens, size.	<BYTE value>	Durable Training Flat That Can Carry You Through Marathon Miles
10054	301	ANZ	Cantilever sole provides shock absorption and energy rebound. Positive traction shoe with ample toe box. Ideal for runners who need a wide shoe. Available in mens and womens. Specify size.	<BYTE value>	Motion Control, Protection, and Extra Toebox Room
10055	302	KAR	Re-usable ice pack with velcro strap. For general use. Velcro strap allows easy application to arms or legs.	<BYTE value>	Finally, An Ice Pack for Achilles Injuries and Shin Splints that You Can Take to the Office
10056	303	PRC	Neon nylon. Perfect for running or aerobics. Indicate color: Fluorescent pink, yellow, green, and orange.	<BYTE value>	Knock Their Socks Off With YOUR Socks!
10057	303	KAR	100% nylon blend for optimal wicking and comfort. We've taken out the cotton to eliminate the risk of blisters and reduce the opportunity for infection. Specify mens or womens.	<BYTE value>	100% Nylon Blend Socks - No Cotton!

catalog Table (6 of 7)

catalog_num	stock_num	manu_code	cat_descr	cat_picture	cat_advert
10058	304	ANZ	Provides time, date, dual display of lap/cumulative splits, 4-lap memory, 10hr count-down timer, event timer, alarm, hour chime, waterproof to 50m, velcro band.	<BYTE value>	Athletic Watch w/4-Lap Memory
10059	304	HRO	Split timer, waterproof to 50m. Indicate color: Hot pink, mint green, space black.	<BYTE value>	Waterproof Triathlete Watch In Competition Colors
10060	305	HRO	Contains ace bandage, anti-bacterial cream, alcohol cleansing pads, adhesive bandages of assorted sizes, and instant-cold pack.	<BYTE value>	Comprehensive First-Aid Kit Essential for Team Practices, Team Traveling
10061	306	PRC	Converts a standard tandem bike into an adult/child bike. User-tested Assembly Instructions	<BYTE value>	Enjoy Bicycling With Your Child On a Tandem; Make Your Family Outing Safer
10062	306	SHM	Converts a standard tandem bike into an adult/child bike. Lightweight model.	<BYTE value>	Consider a Touring Vacation For the Entire Family: A Lightweight, Touring Tandem for Parent and Child
10063	307	PRC	Allows mom or dad to take the baby out, too. Fits children up to 21 pounds. Navy blue with black trim.	<BYTE value>	Infant Jogger Keeps A Running Family Together
10064	308	PRC	Allows mom or dad to take both children! Rated for children up to 18 pounds.	<BYTE value>	As Your Family Grows, Infant Jogger Grows With You
10065	309	HRO	Prevents swimmer's ear.	<BYTE value>	Swimmers Can Prevent Ear Infection All Season Long
10066	309	SHM	Extra-gentle formula. Can be used every day for prevention or treatment of swimmer's ear.	<BYTE value>	Swimmer's Ear Drops Specially Formulated for Children
10067	310	SHM	Blue heavy-duty foam board with Shimara or team logo.	<BYTE value>	Exceptionally Durable, Compact Kickboard for Team Practice
10068	310	ANZ	White. Standard size.	<BYTE value>	High-Quality Kickboard
10069	311	SHM	Swim gloves. Webbing between fingers promotes strengthening of arms. Cannot be used in competition.	<BYTE value>	Hot Training Tool - Webbed Swim Gloves Build Arm Strength and Endurance
10070	312	SHM	Hydrodynamic egg-shaped lens. Ground-in anti-fog elements; Available in blue or smoke.	<BYTE value>	Anti-Fog Swimmer's Goggles: Quantity Discount.
10071	312	HRO	Durable competition-style goggles. Available in blue, grey, or white.	<BYTE value>	Swim Goggles: Traditional Rounded Lens For Greater Comfort.

catalog Table (7 of 7)

catalog_num	stock_num	manu_code	cat_descr	cat_picture	cat_advert
10072	313	SHM	Silicone swim cap. One size. Available in white, silver, or navy. Team Logo Imprinting Available	<BYTE value>	Team Logo Silicone Swim Cap
10073	313	ANZ	Silicone swim cap. Squared-off top. One size. White.	<BYTE value>	Durable Squared-off Silicone Swim Cap
10074	302	HRO	Re-usable ice pack. Store in the freezer for instant first-aid. Extra capacity to accommodate water and ice.	<BYTE value>	Water Compartment Combines With Ice to Provide Optimal Orthopedic Treatment

cust_calls Table

customer_num	call_dtime	user_id	call_code	call_descr	res_dtime	res_descr
106	1990-06-12 8:20	maryj	D	Order was received, but two of the cans of ANZ tennis balls within the case were empty	1990-06-12 8:25	Authorized credit for two cans to customer, issued apology. Called ANZ buyer to report the QA problem.
110	1990-07-07 10:24	richc	L	Order placed one month ago (6/7) not received.	1990-07-07 10:30	Checked with shipping (Ed Smith). Order sent yesterday- we were waiting for goods from ANZ. Next time will call with delay if necessary.
119	1990-07-01 15:00	richc	B	Bill does not reflect credit from previous order	1990-07-02 8:21	Spoke with Jane Akant in Finance. She found the error and is sending new bill to customer
121	1990-07-10 14:05	maryj	O	Customer likes our merchandise. Requests that we stock more types of infant joggers. Will call back to place order.	1990-07-10 14:06	Sent note to marketing group of interest in infant joggers
127	1990-07-31 14:30	maryj	I	Received Hero watches (item # 304) instead of ANZ watches		Sent memo to shipping to send ANZ item 304 to customer and pickup HRO watches. Should be done tomorrow, 8/1
116	1989-11-28 13:34	mannyn	I	Received plain white swim caps (313 ANZ) instead of navy with team logo (313 SHM)	1989-11-28 16:47	Shipping found correct case in warehouse and express mailed it in time for swim meet.
116	1989-12-21 11:24	mannyn	I	Second complaint from this customer! Received two cases right-handed outfielder gloves (1 HRO) instead of one case lefties.	1989-12-27 08:19	Memo to shipping (Ava Brown) to send case of left-handed gloves, pick up wrong case; memo to billing requesting 5% discount to placate customer due to second offense and lateness of resolution because of holiday

manufact Table

manu_code	manu_name	lead_time
ANZ	Anza	5
HSK	Husky	5
HRO	Hero	4
NRG	Norge	7
SMT	Smith	3
SHM	Shimara	30
KAR	Karsten	21
NKL	Nikolus	8
PRC	ProCycle	9

state Table

code	sname	code	sname
AK	Alaska	MT	Montana
AL	Alabama	NE	Nebraska
AR	Arkansas	NC	North Carolina
AZ	Arizona	ND	North Dakota
CA	California	NH	New Hampshire
CT	Connecticut	NJ	New Jersey
CO	Colorado	NM	New Mexico
D.C.	DC	NV	Nevada
DE	Delaware	NY	New York
FL	Florida	OH	Ohio
GA	Georgia	OK	Oklahoma
HI	Hawaii	OR	Oregon
IA	Iowa	PA	Pennsylvania
ID	Idaho	PR	Puerto Rico
IL	Illinois	RI	Rhode Island
IN	Indiana	SC	South Carolina
KS	Kansas	SD	South Dakota
KY	Kentucky	TN	Tennessee
LA	Louisiana	TX	Texas
MA	Massachusetts	UT	Utah
MD	Maryland	VA	Virginia
ME	Maine	VT	Vermont
MI	Michigan	WA	Washington
MN	Minnesota	WI	Wisconsin
MO	Missouri	WV	West Virginia
MS	Mississippi	WY	Wyoming

The Function Index lists all functions that appear in the example programs and specifies the pages in the book where the functions appear.

Page numbers identify the locations in the book where a function is called. Boldface numbers indicate the location where the text of the function is displayed and annotated.

Function names in uppercase are built-in **4GL** functions.

Function Index

A

B

C

Bold number indicates where function is defined

K

L

M

N

O

P

Q

R

Bold number indicates where function is defined

S

T

U

V

Bold number indicates where function is defined